GREEN LANTERNS

VOL.3 POLARITY

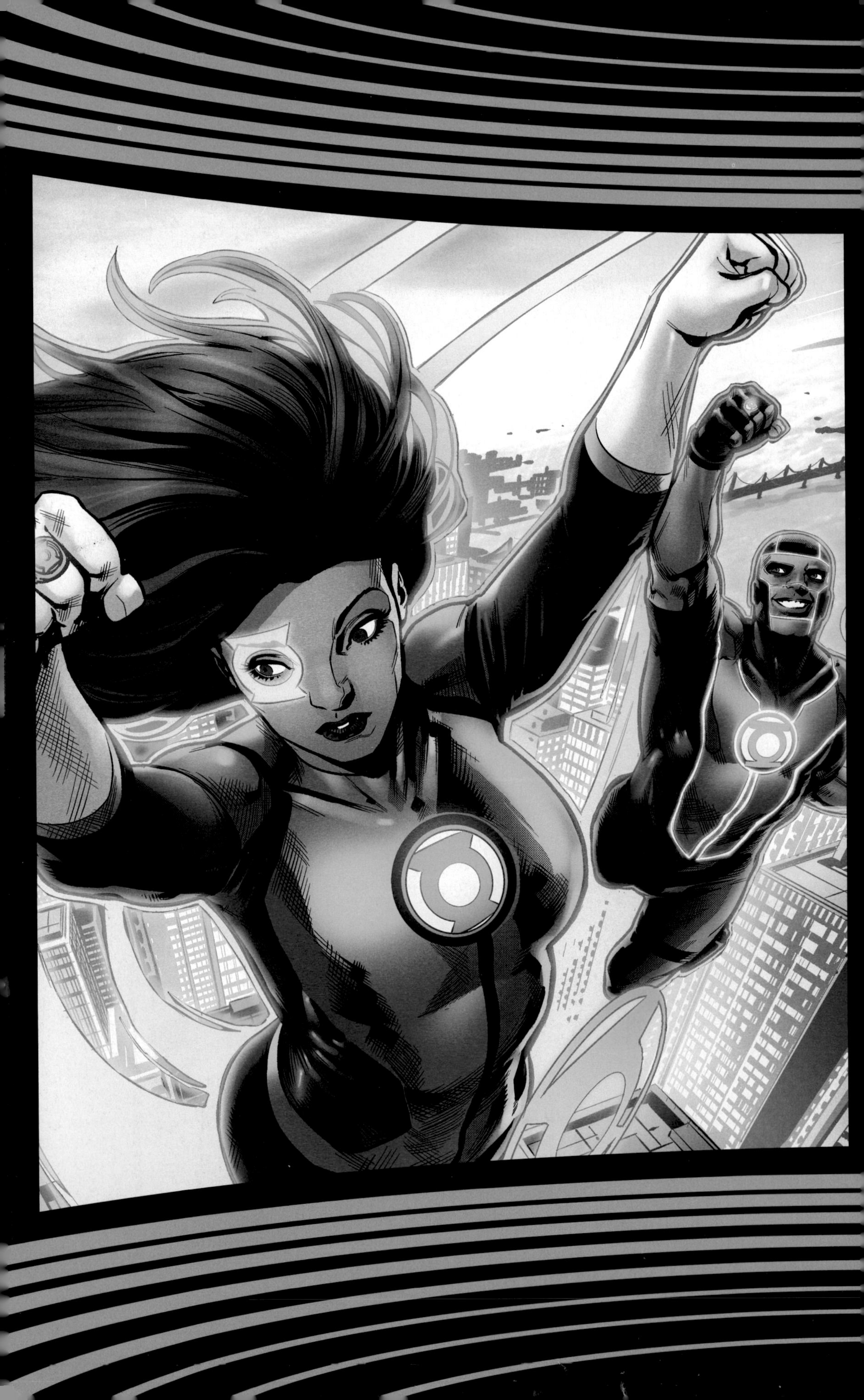

GREEN LANTERNS
VOL.3 POLARITY

SAM HUMPHRIES
writer

EDUARDO PANSICA * ROBSON ROCHA * RONAN CLIQUET
NEIL EDWARDS * JAY LEISTEN * KEITH CHAMPAGNE
JULIO FERREIRA * TOM DERENICK * MIGUEL MENDONCA
SCOTT HANNA * DANIEL HENRIQUES * JOE PRADO
artists

BLOND * ALEX SOLLAZZO
colorists

DAVE SHARPE * TRAVIS LANHAM
letterers

ROBSON ROCHA, DANIEL HENRIQUES and JASON WRIGHT
collection cover artists

BATMAN created by BOB KANE with BILL FINGER
SUPERMAN created by JERRY SIEGEL and JOE SHUSTER
By special arrangement with the Jerry Siegel family

MIKE COTTON Editor - Original Series * **ANDREW MARINO** Associate Editor - Original Series
JEB WOODARD Group Editor - Collected Editions * **PAUL SANTOS** Editor - Collected Edition
STEVE COOK Design Director - Books * **MONIQUE GRUSPE** Publication Design

BOB HARRAS Senior VP - Editor-in-Chief, DC Comics

DIANE NELSON President * **DAN DiDIO** Publisher * **JIM LEE** Publisher * **GEOFF JOHNS** President & Chief Creative Officer
AMIT DESAI Executive VP - Business & Marketing Strategy, Direct to Consumer & Global Franchise Management * **SAM ADES** Senior VP - Direct to Consumer
BOBBIE CHASE VP - Talent Development * **MARK CHIARELLO** Senior VP - Art, Design & Collected Editions
JOHN CUNNINGHAM Senior VP - Sales & Trade Marketing * **ANNE DePIES** Senior VP - Business Strategy, Finance & Administration
DON FALLETTI VP - Manufacturing Operations * **LAWRENCE GANEM** VP - Editorial Administration & Talent Relations
ALISON GILL Senior VP - Manufacturing & Operations * **HANK KANALZ** Senior VP - Editorial Strategy & Administration
JAY KOGAN VP - Legal Affairs * **THOMAS LOFTUS** VP - Business Affairs
JACK MAHAN VP - Business Affairs * **NICK J. NAPOLITANO** VP - Manufacturing Administration
EDDIE SCANNELL VP - Consumer Marketing * **COURTNEY SIMMONS** Senior VP - Publicity & Communications
JIM (SKI) SOKOLOWSKI VP - Comic Book Specialty Sales & Trade Marketing * **NANCY SPEARS** VP - Mass, Book, Digital Sales & Trade Marketing

GREEN LANTERNS VOL. 3: POLARITY

DC Comics, 2900 West Alameda Ave., Burbank, CA 91505
Printed by LSC Communications, Kendallville, IN, USA. 8/11/17. First Printing.
ISBN: 978-1-4012-7371-2

Library of Congress Cataloging-in-Publication Data is available.

PEFC Certified
Printed on paper from sustainably managed forests, controlled sources
PEFC
PEFC/29-31-337
www.pefc.org

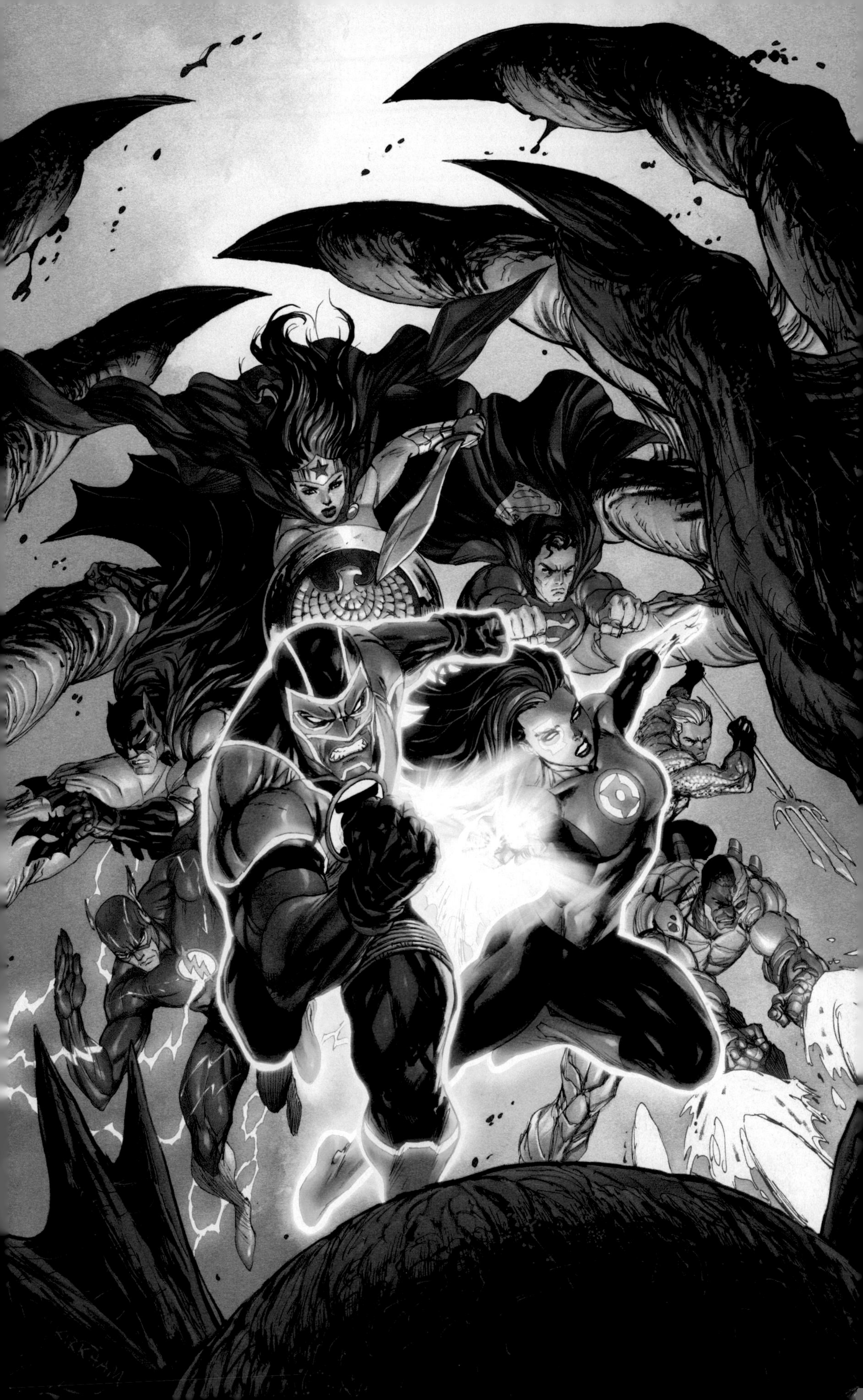

"A DAY IN THE LIFE"

TOM DERENICK thumbnails * MIGUEL MENDONCA penciller
SCOTT HANNA inker * Cover by TYLER KIRKHAM and TOMEU MOREY

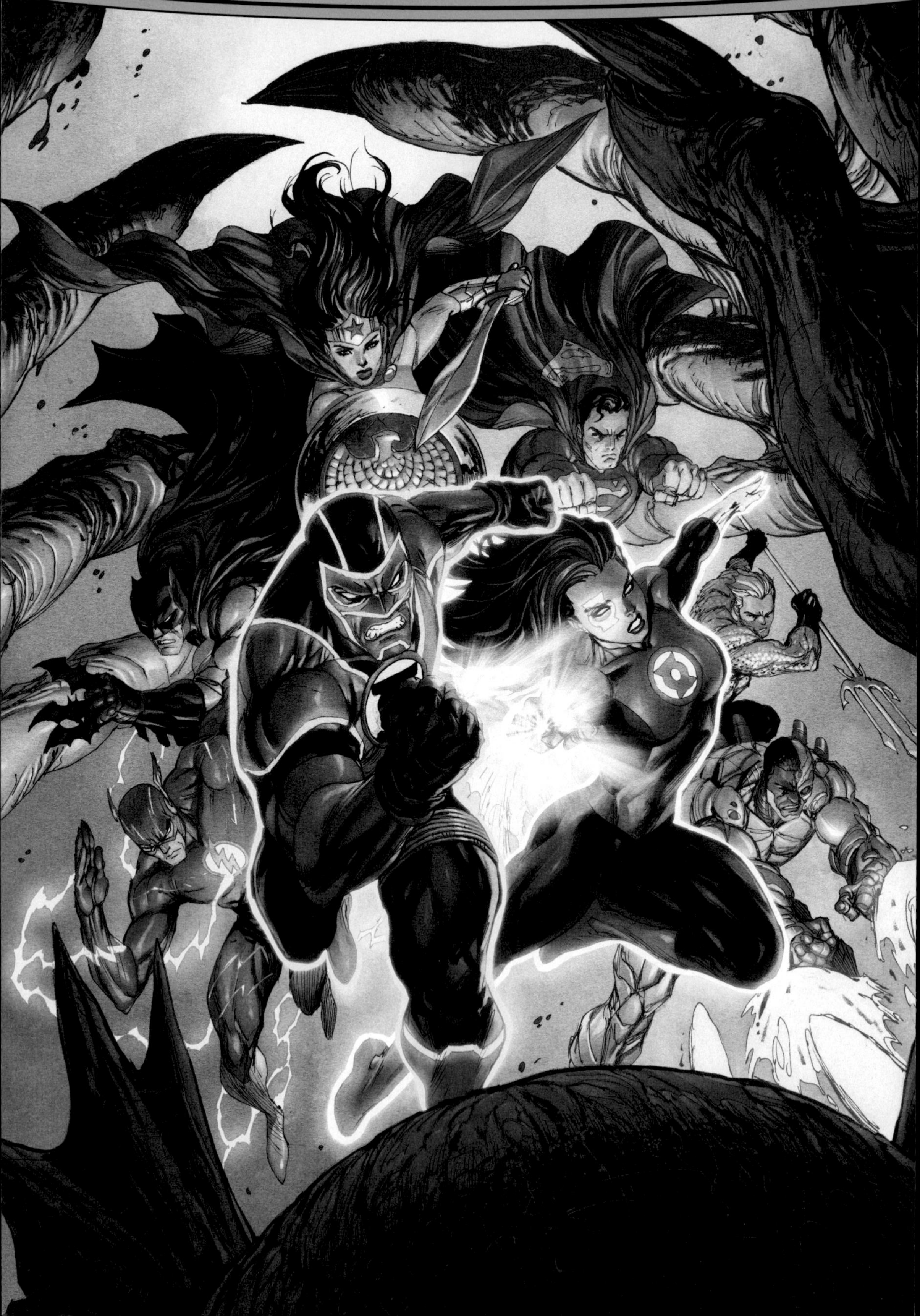

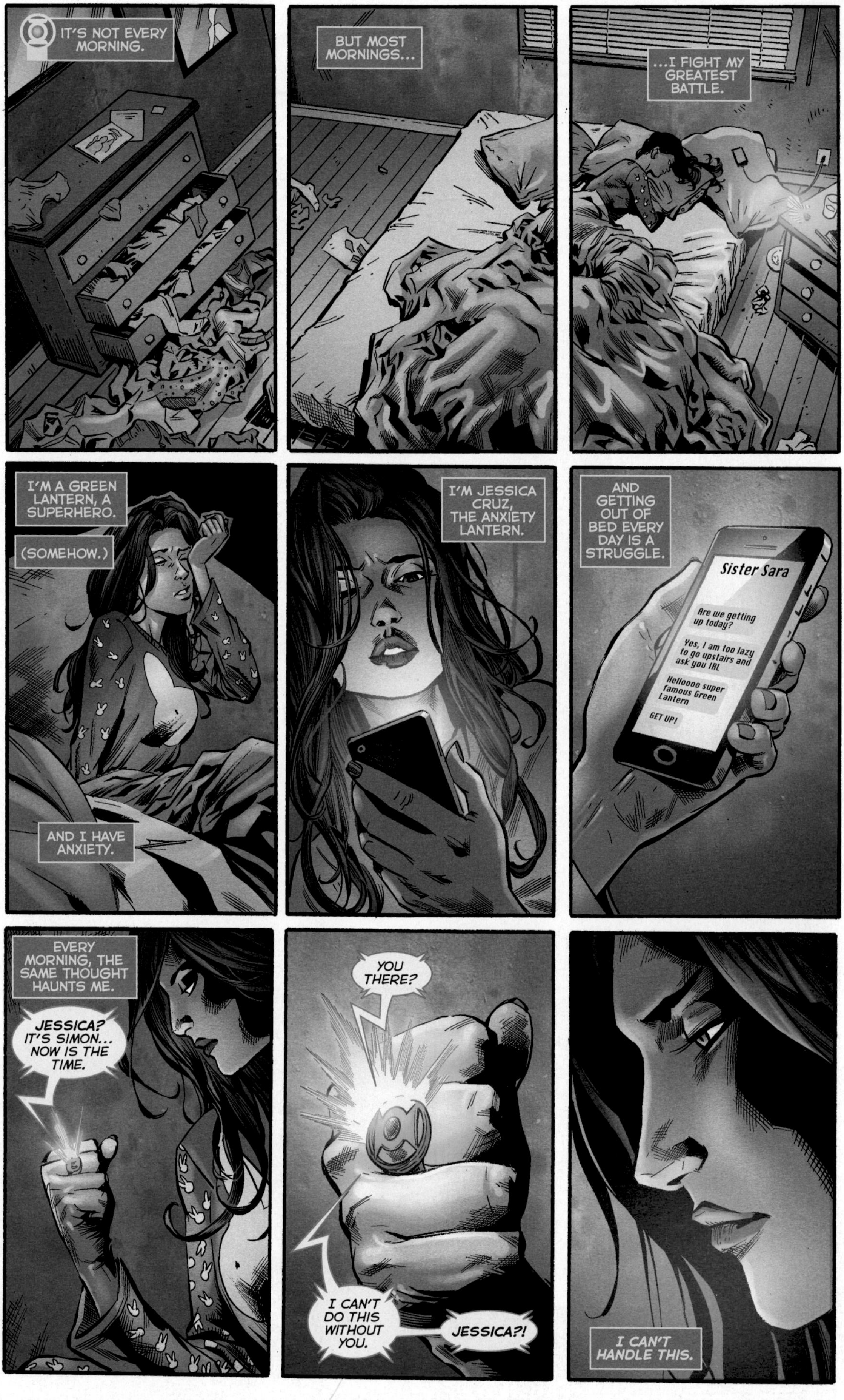
IT'S NOT EVERY MORNING.
BUT MOST MORNINGS...
...I FIGHT MY GREATEST BATTLE.
I'M A GREEN LANTERN, A SUPERHERO.
(SOMEHOW.)
AND I HAVE ANXIETY.
I'M JESSICA CRUZ, THE ANXIETY LANTERN.
AND GETTING OUT OF BED EVERY DAY IS A STRUGGLE.
Sister Sara
Are we getting up today?
Yes, I am too lazy to go upstairs and ask you IRL
Helloooo super famous Green Lantern
GET UP!
EVERY MORNING, THE SAME THOUGHT HAUNTS ME.
JESSICA? IT'S SIMON... NOW IS THE TIME.
YOU THERE?
I CAN'T DO THIS WITHOUT YOU.
JESSICA?!
I CAN'T HANDLE THIS.

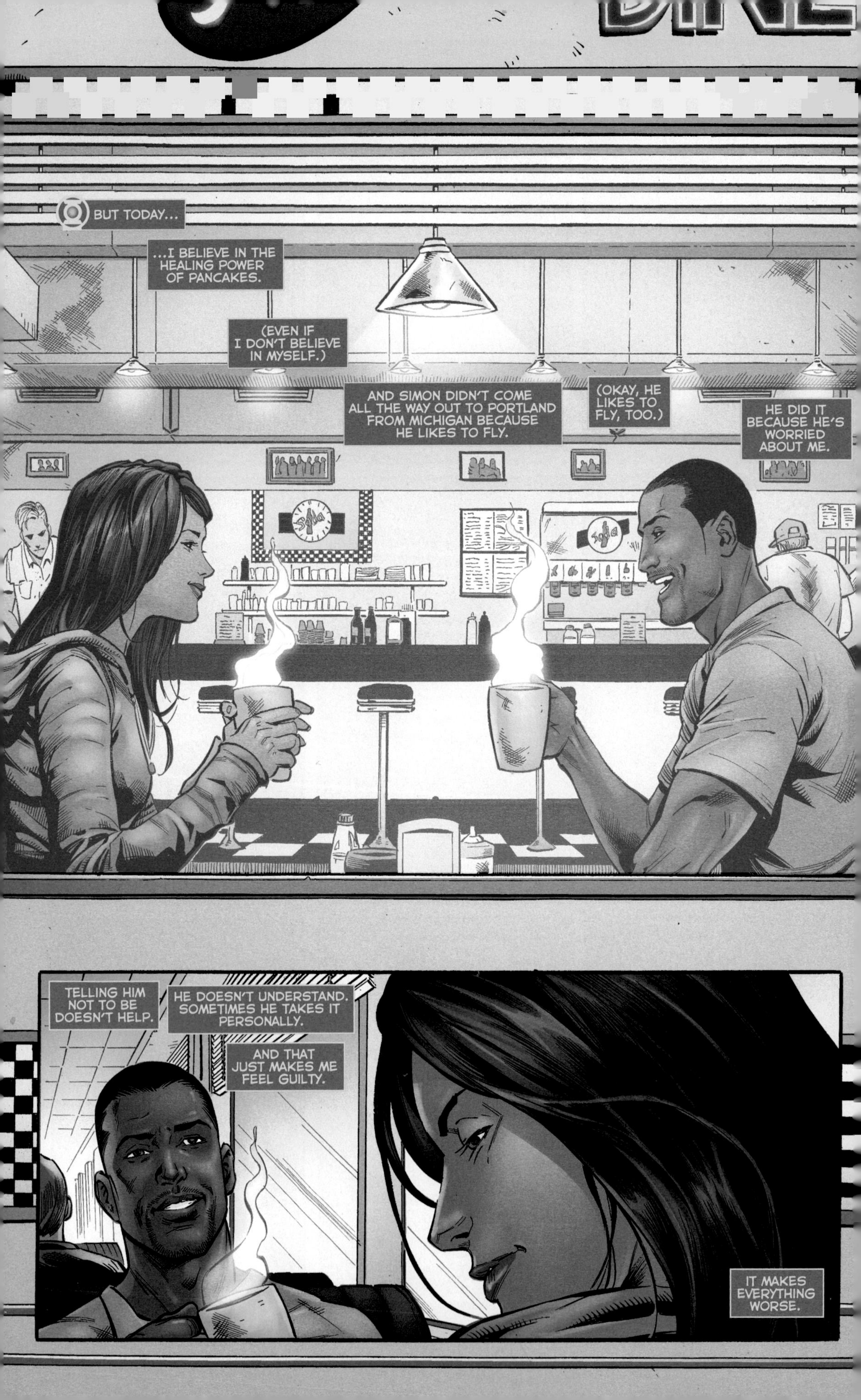

BUT TODAY...
...I BELIEVE IN THE HEALING POWER OF PANCAKES.
(EVEN IF I DON'T BELIEVE IN MYSELF.)
AND SIMON DIDN'T COME ALL THE WAY OUT TO PORTLAND FROM MICHIGAN BECAUSE HE LIKES TO FLY.
(OKAY, HE LIKES TO FLY, TOO.)
HE DID IT BECAUSE HE'S WORRIED ABOUT ME.
TELLING HIM NOT TO BE DOESN'T HELP.
HE DOESN'T UNDERSTAND. SOMETIMES HE TAKES IT PERSONALLY.
AND THAT JUST MAKES ME FEEL GUILTY.
IT MAKES EVERYTHING WORSE.

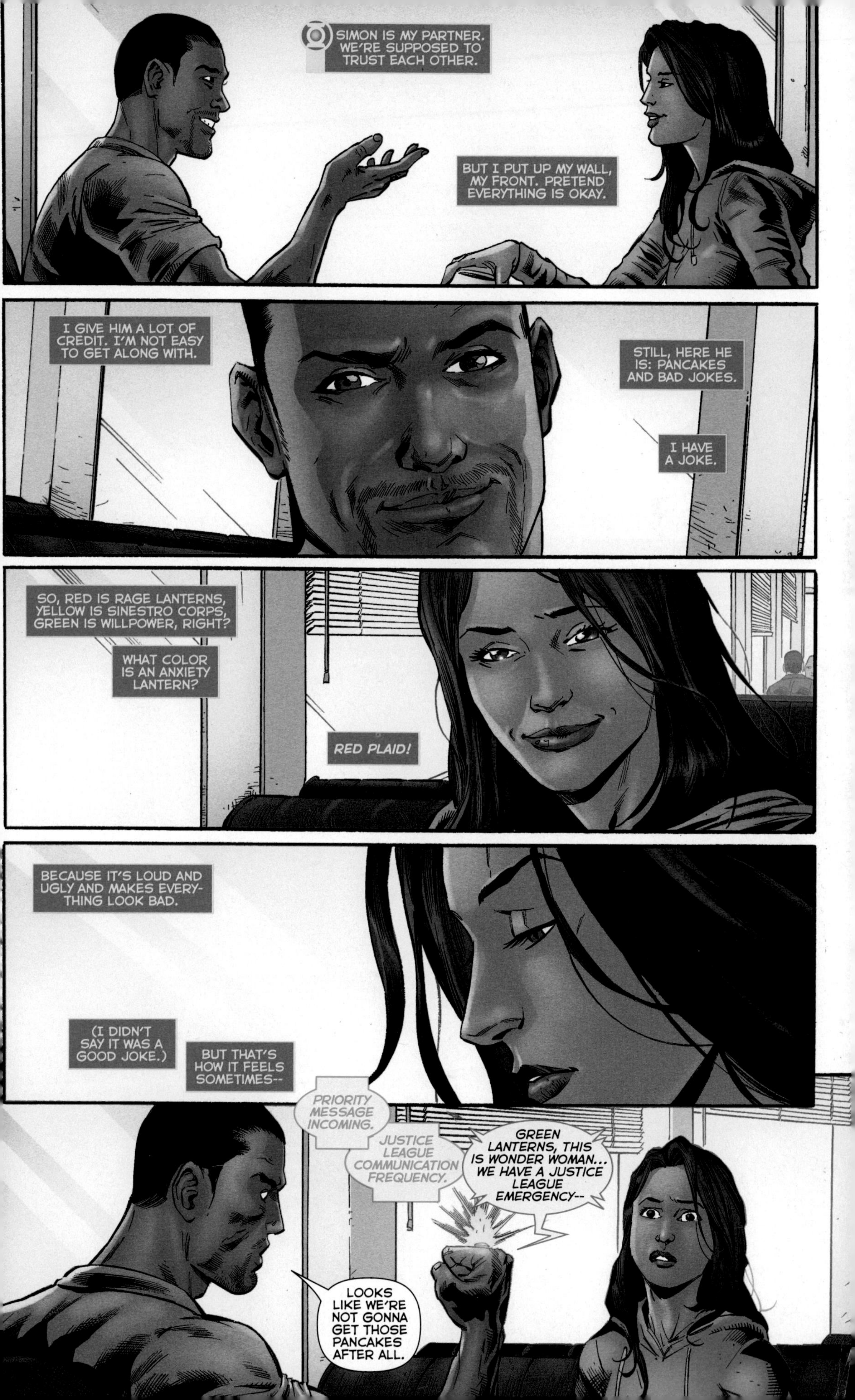
SIMON IS MY PARTNER. WE'RE SUPPOSED TO TRUST EACH OTHER.
BUT I PUT UP MY WALL, MY FRONT. PRETEND EVERYTHING IS OKAY.
I GIVE HIM A LOT OF CREDIT. I'M NOT EASY TO GET ALONG WITH.
STILL, HERE HE IS: PANCAKES AND BAD JOKES.
I HAVE A JOKE.
SO, RED IS RAGE LANTERNS, YELLOW IS SINESTRO CORPS, GREEN IS WILLPOWER, RIGHT?
WHAT COLOR IS AN ANXIETY LANTERN?
RED PLAID!
BECAUSE IT'S LOUD AND UGLY AND MAKES EVERY-THING LOOK BAD.
(I DIDN'T SAY IT WAS A GOOD JOKE.)
BUT THAT'S HOW IT FEELS SOMETIMES--
PRIORITY MESSAGE INCOMING.
JUSTICE LEAGUE COMMUNICATION FREQUENCY.
GREEN LANTERNS, THIS IS WONDER WOMAN... WE HAVE A JUSTICE LEAGUE EMERGENCY--
LOOKS LIKE WE'RE NOT GONNA GET THOSE PANCAKES AFTER ALL.

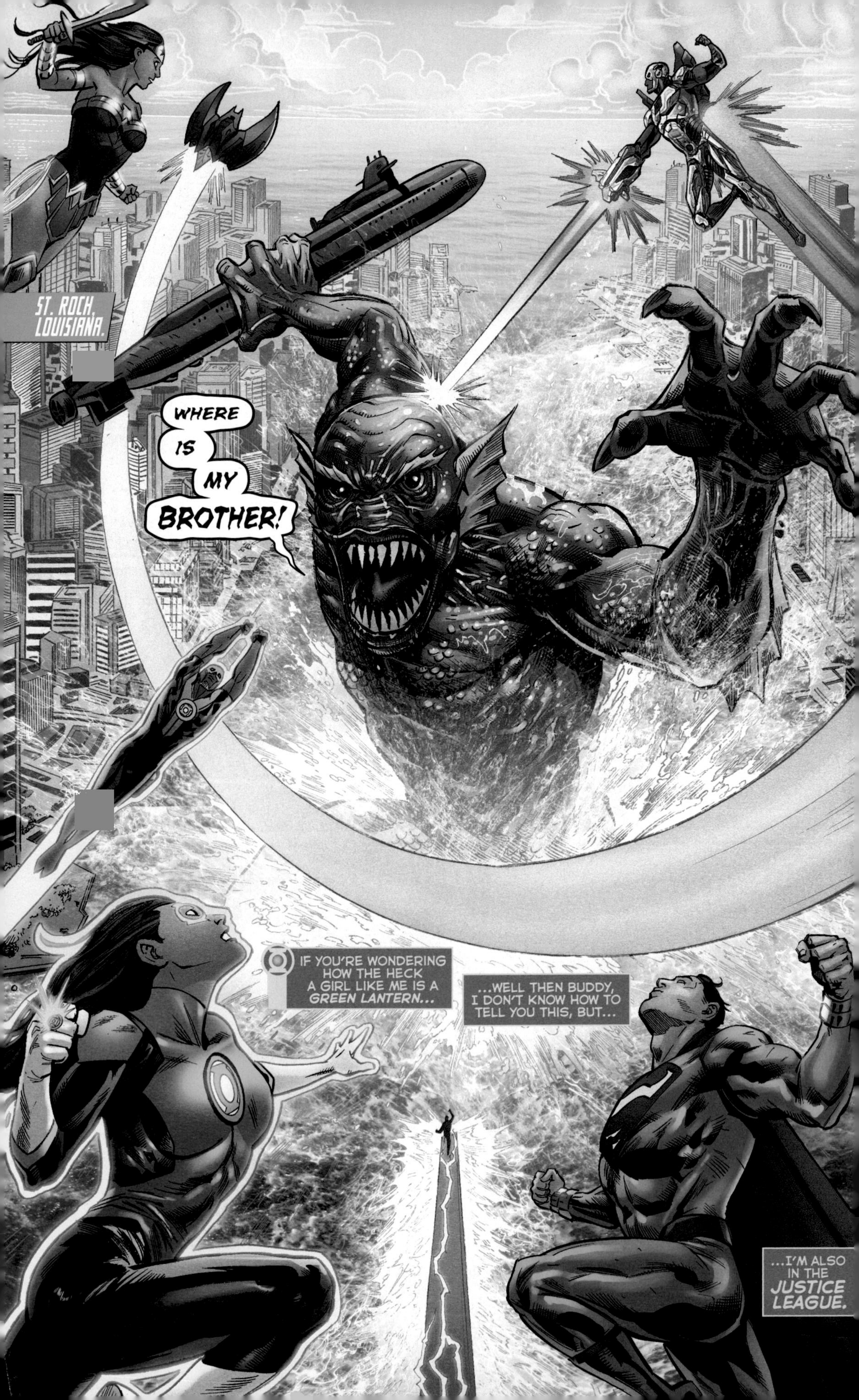
ST. ROCH, LOUISIANA.
WHERE IS MY BROTHER!
IF YOU'RE WONDERING HOW THE HECK A GIRL LIKE ME IS A GREEN LANTERN...
...WELL THEN BUDDY, I DON'T KNOW HOW TO TELL YOU THIS, BUT...
...I'M ALSO IN THE JUSTICE LEAGUE.

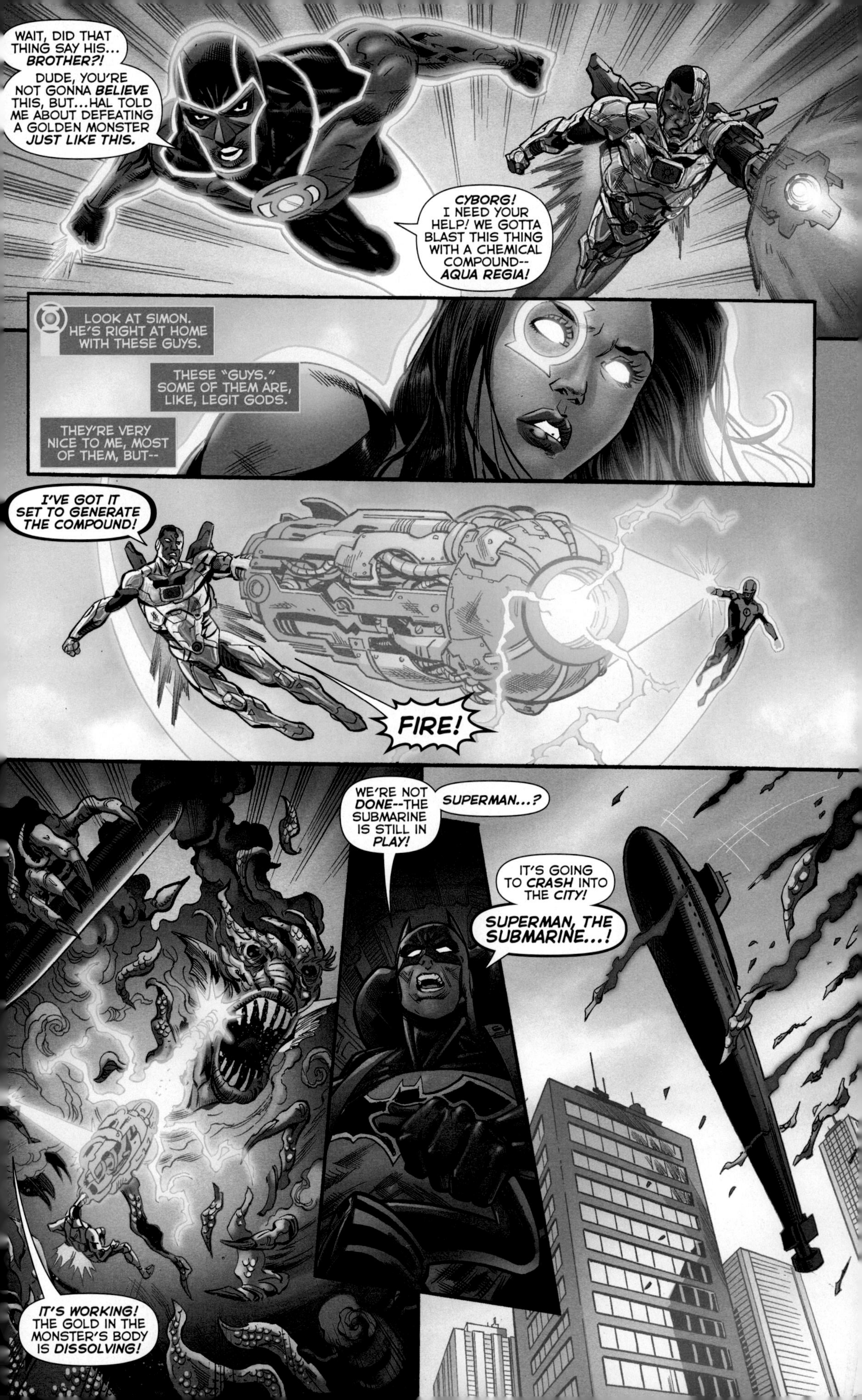
WAIT, DID THAT THING SAY HIS... BROTHER?!
DUDE, YOU'RE NOT GONNA BELIEVE THIS, BUT...HAL TOLD ME ABOUT DEFEATING A GOLDEN MONSTER JUST LIKE THIS.
CYBORG! I NEED YOUR HELP! WE GOTTA BLAST THIS THING WITH A CHEMICAL COMPOUND-- AQUA REGIA!
LOOK AT SIMON. HE'S RIGHT AT HOME WITH THESE GUYS.
THESE "GUYS." SOME OF THEM ARE, LIKE, LEGIT GODS.
THEY'RE VERY NICE TO ME, MOST OF THEM, BUT--
I'VE GOT IT SET TO GENERATE THE COMPOUND!
FIRE!
WE'RE NOT DONE--THE SUBMARINE IS STILL IN PLAY!
SUPERMAN...?
IT'S GOING TO CRASH INTO THE CITY!
SUPERMAN, THE SUBMARINE...!
IT'S WORKING! THE GOLD IN THE MONSTER'S BODY IS DISSOLVING!

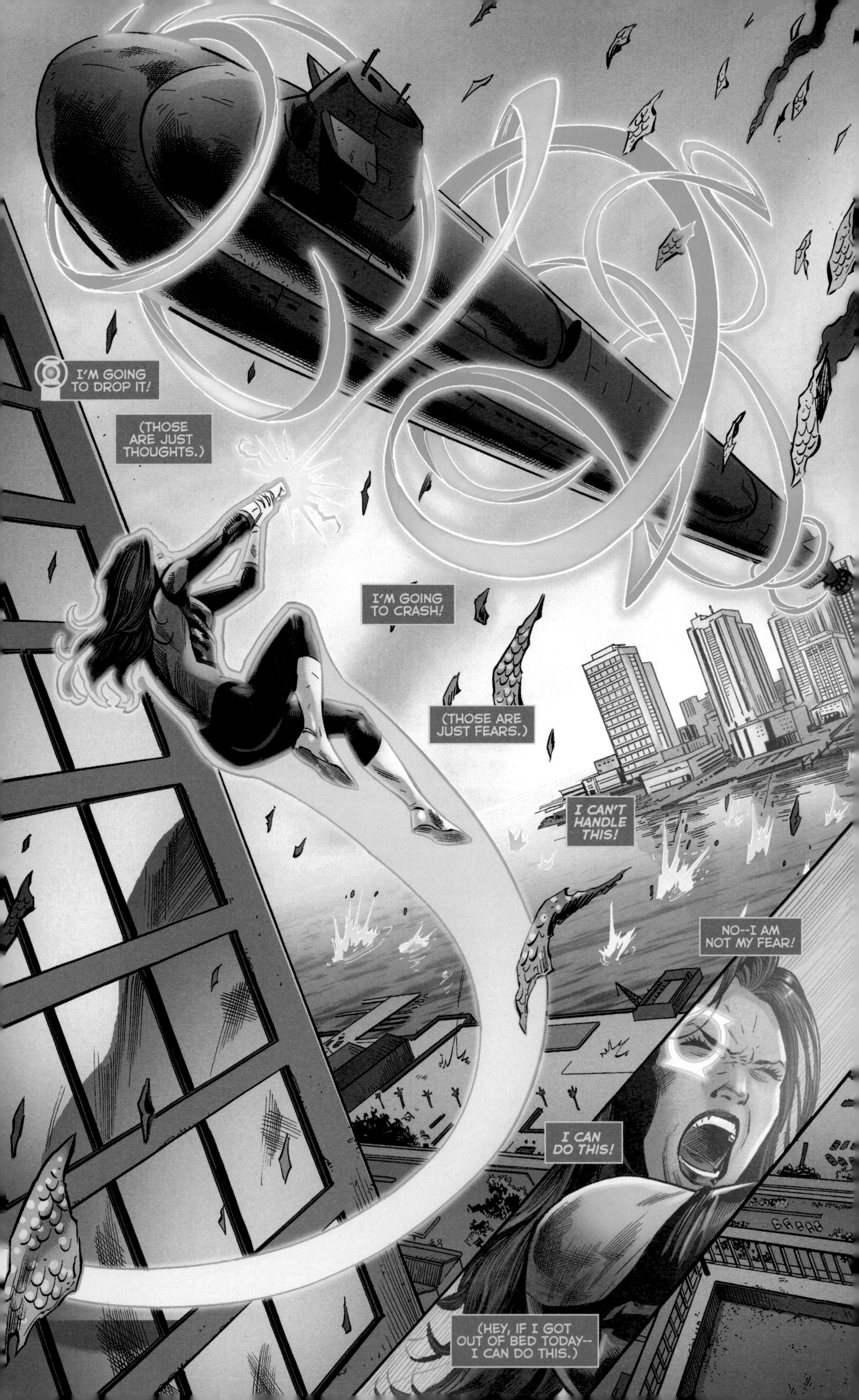
I'M GOING TO DROP IT!
(THOSE ARE JUST THOUGHTS.)
I'M GOING TO CRASH!
(THOSE ARE JUST FEARS.)
I CAN'T HANDLE THIS!
NO--I AM NOT MY FEAR!
I CAN DO THIS!
(HEY, IF I GOT OUT OF BED TODAY-- I CAN DO THIS.)

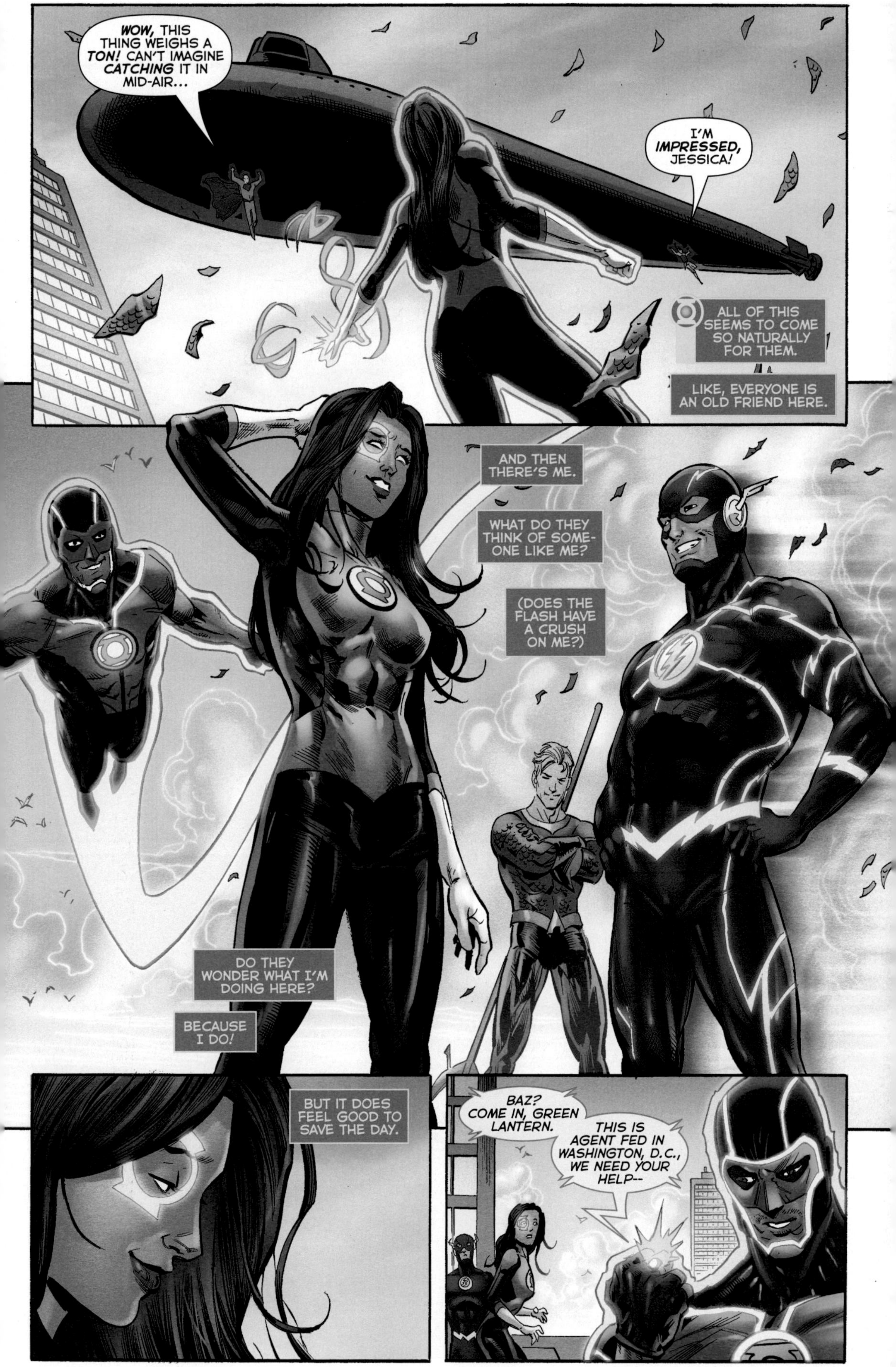

WOW, THIS THING WEIGHS A TON! CAN'T IMAGINE CATCHING IT IN MID-AIR...
I'M IMPRESSED, JESSICA!
ALL OF THIS SEEMS TO COME SO NATURALLY FOR THEM.
LIKE, EVERYONE IS AN OLD FRIEND HERE.
AND THEN THERE'S ME.
WHAT DO THEY THINK OF SOME-ONE LIKE ME?
(DOES THE FLASH HAVE A CRUSH ON ME?)
DO THEY WONDER WHAT I'M DOING HERE?
BECAUSE I DO!
BUT IT DOES FEEL GOOD TO SAVE THE DAY.
BAZ? COME IN, GREEN LANTERN.
THIS IS AGENT FED IN WASHINGTON, D.C., WE NEED YOUR HELP--

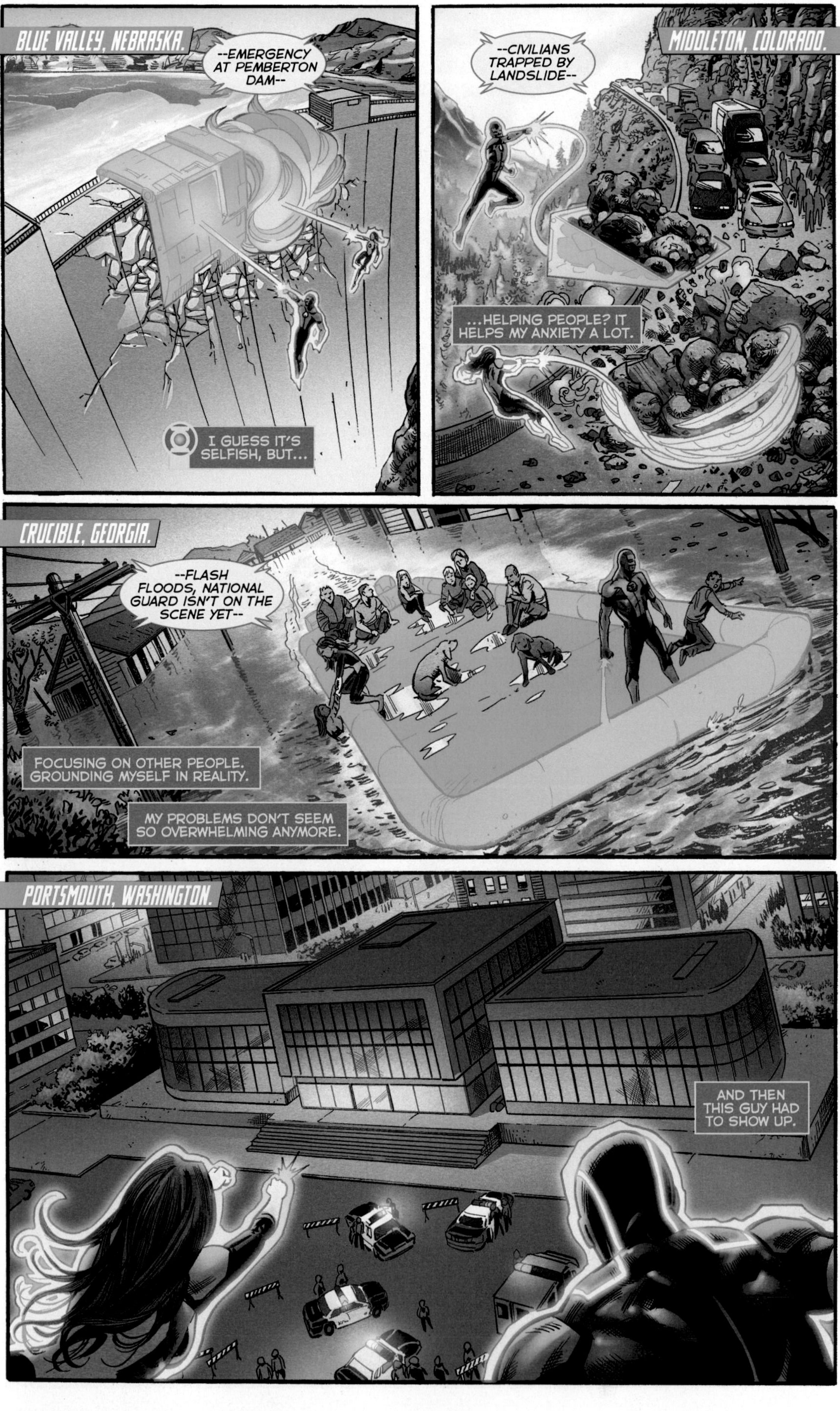
BLUE VALLEY, NEBRASKA.
--EMERGENCY AT PEMBERTON DAM--
I GUESS IT'S SELFISH, BUT...
MIDDLETON, COLORADO.
--CIVILIANS TRAPPED BY LANDSLIDE--
...HELPING PEOPLE? IT HELPS MY ANXIETY A LOT.
CRUCIBLE, GEORGIA.
--FLASH FLOODS, NATIONAL GUARD ISN'T ON THE SCENE YET--
FOCUSING ON OTHER PEOPLE. GROUNDING MYSELF IN REALITY.
MY PROBLEMS DON'T SEEM SO OVERWHELMING ANYMORE.
PORTSMOUTH, WASHINGTON.
AND THEN THIS GUY HAD TO SHOW UP.

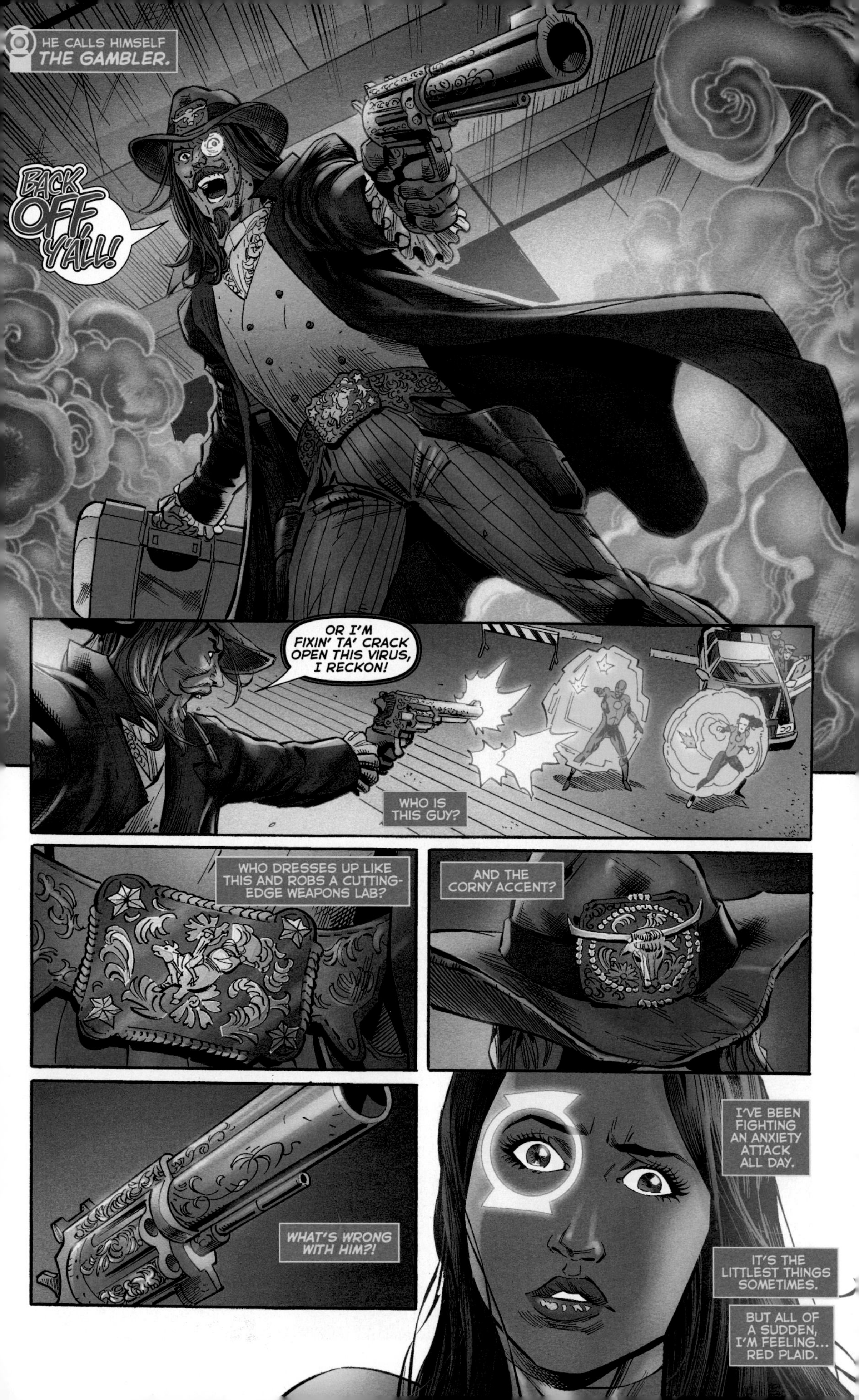
HE CALLS HIMSELF THE GAMBLER.
BACK OFF, Y'ALL!
OR I'M FIXIN' TA' CRACK OPEN THIS VIRUS, I RECKON!
WHO IS THIS GUY?
WHO DRESSES UP LIKE THIS AND ROBS A CUTTING-EDGE WEAPONS LAB?
AND THE CORNY ACCENT?
WHAT'S WRONG WITH HIM?!
I'VE BEEN FIGHTING AN ANXIETY ATTACK ALL DAY.
IT'S THE LITTLEST THINGS SOMETIMES.
BUT ALL OF A SUDDEN, I'M FEELING... RED PLAID.

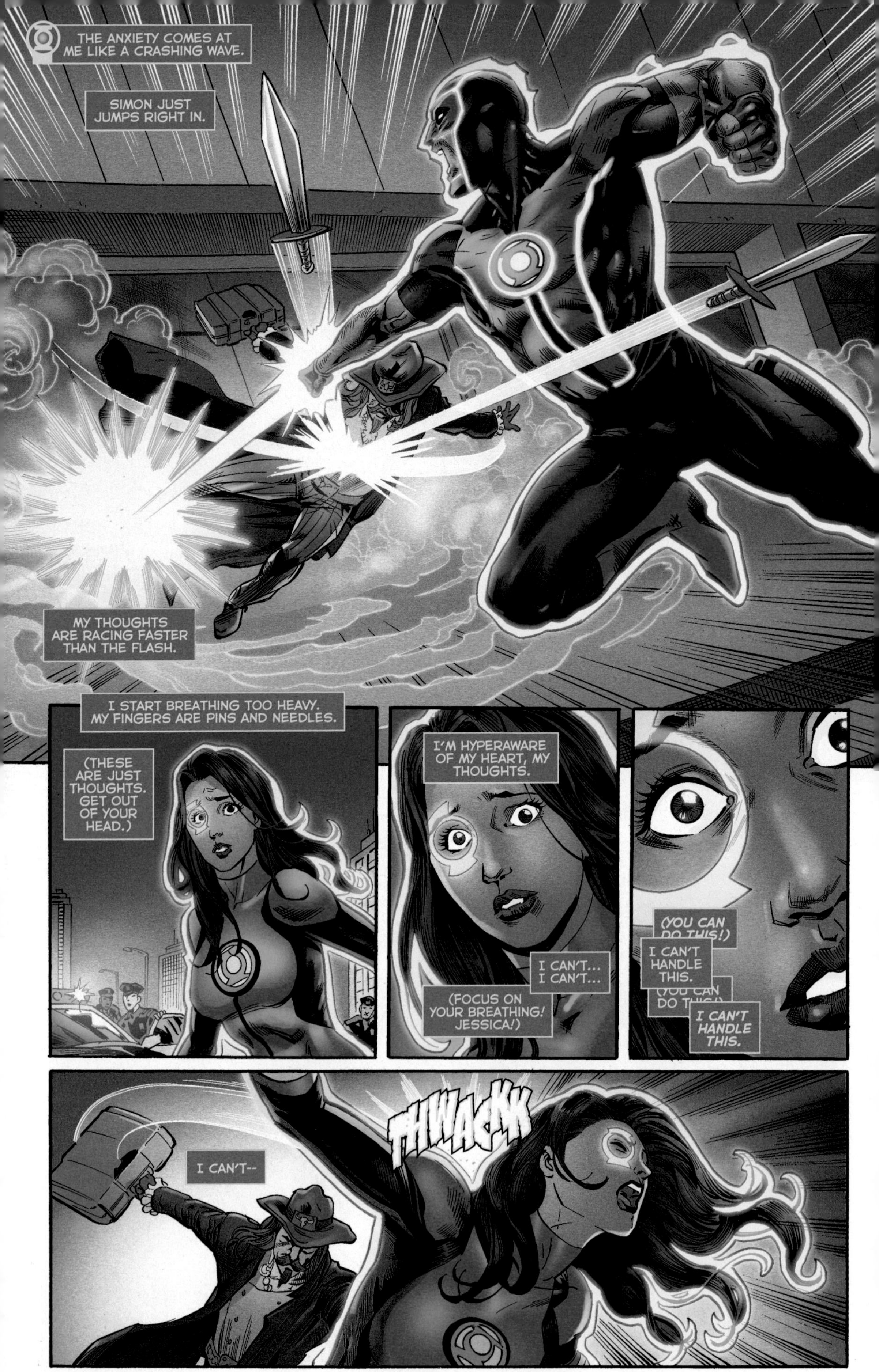
THE ANXIETY COMES AT ME LIKE A CRASHING WAVE.
SIMON JUST JUMPS RIGHT IN.
MY THOUGHTS ARE RACING FASTER THAN THE FLASH.
I START BREATHING TOO HEAVY. MY FINGERS ARE PINS AND NEEDLES.
(THESE ARE JUST THOUGHTS. GET OUT OF YOUR HEAD.)
I'M HYPERAWARE OF MY HEART, MY THOUGHTS.
I CAN'T... I CAN'T...
(FOCUS ON YOUR BREATHING! JESSICA!)
(YOU CAN DO THIS!)
I CAN'T HANDLE THIS.
I CAN'T HANDLE THIS.
THWACKK
I CAN'T--

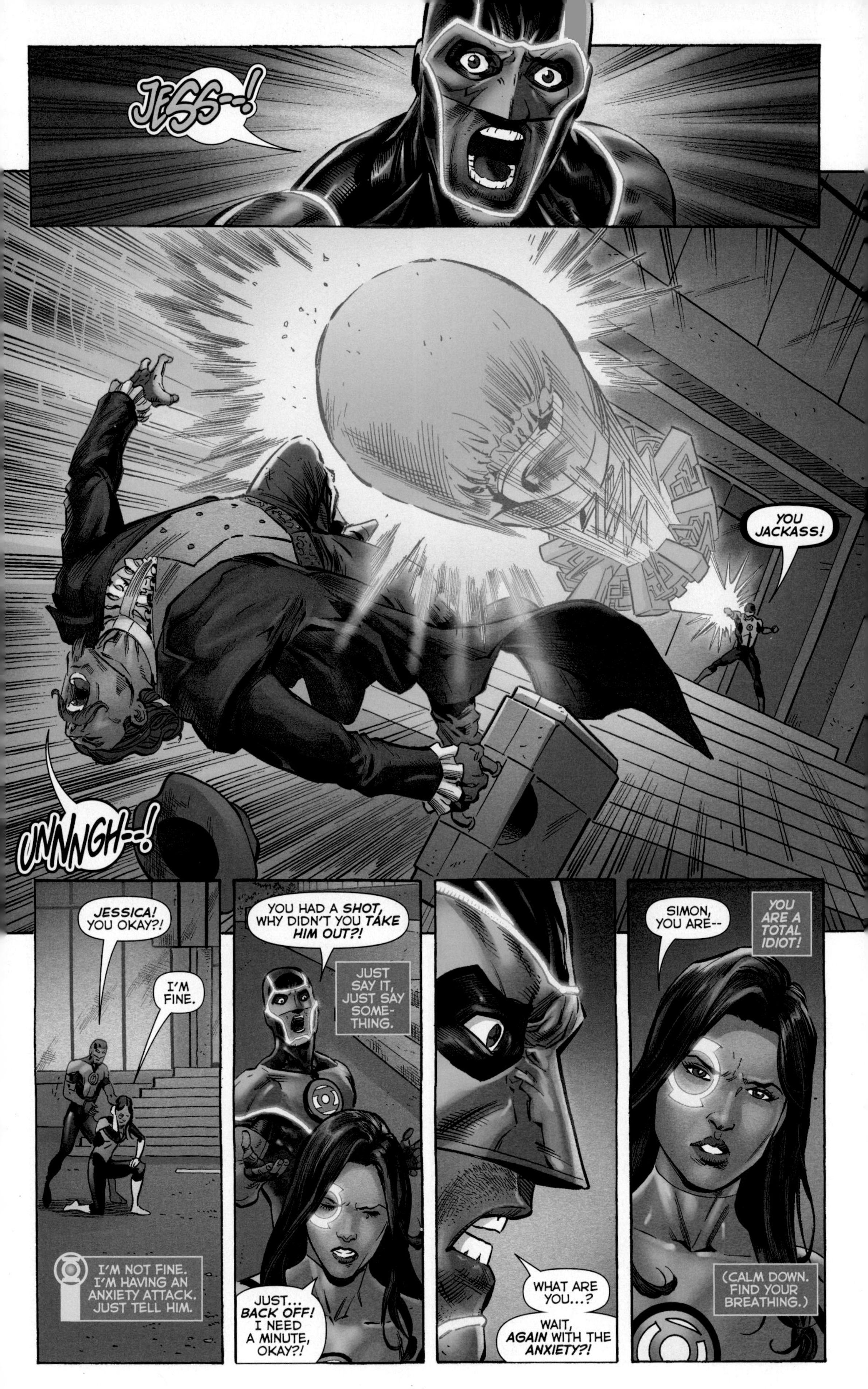
JESS--!
YOU JACKASS!
UNNNGH--!
JESSICA! YOU OKAY?!
I'M FINE.
I'M NOT FINE. I'M HAVING AN ANXIETY ATTACK. JUST TELL HIM.
YOU HAD A SHOT, WHY DIDN'T YOU TAKE HIM OUT?!
JUST SAY IT, JUST SAY SOME-THING.
JUST... BACK OFF! I NEED A MINUTE, OKAY?!
WHAT ARE YOU...?
WAIT, AGAIN WITH THE ANXIETY?!
SIMON, YOU ARE--
YOU ARE A TOTAL IDIOT!
(CALM DOWN. FIND YOUR BREATHING.)

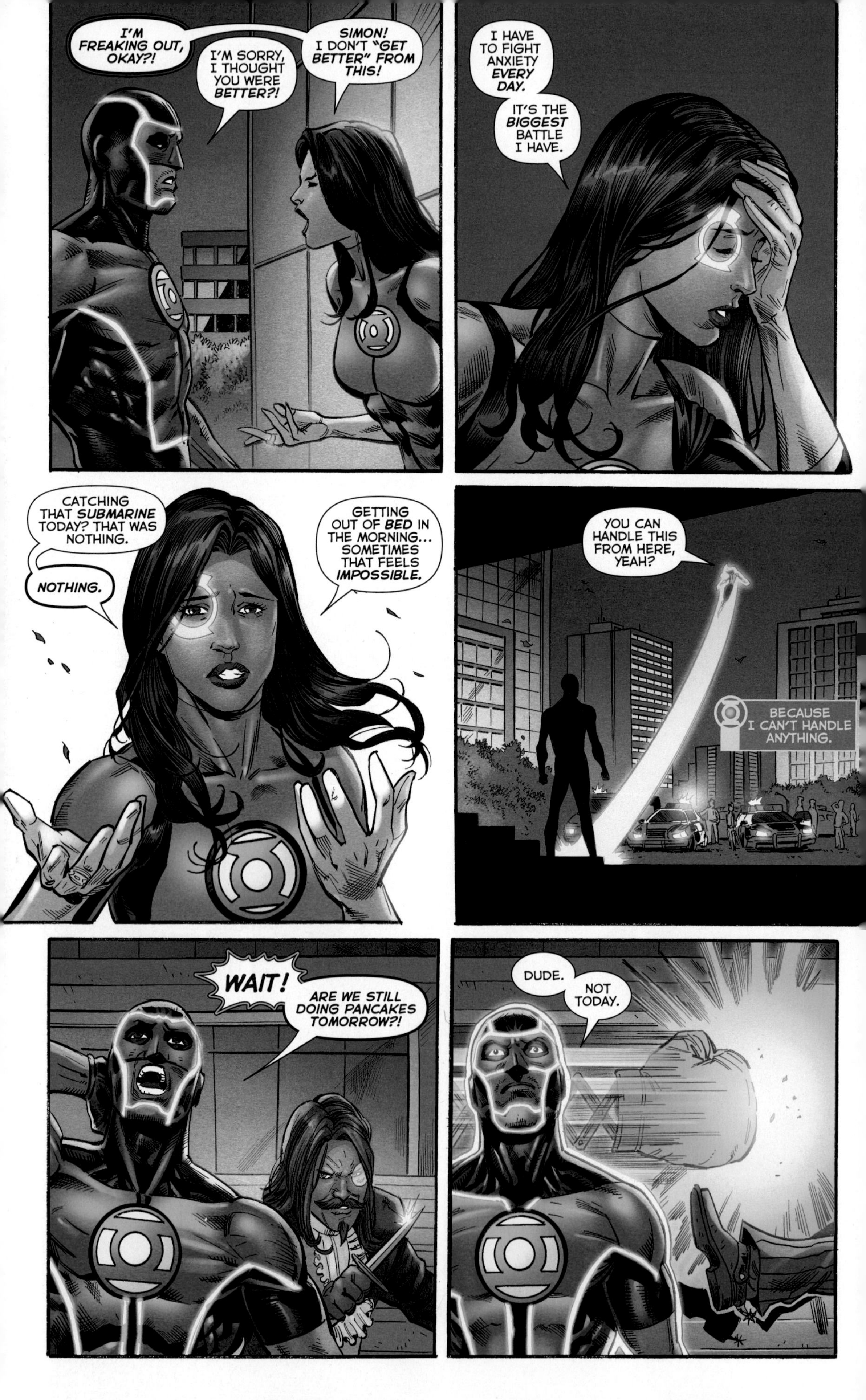
I'M FREAKING OUT, OKAY?!
I'M SORRY, I THOUGHT YOU WERE BETTER?!
SIMON! I DON'T "GET BETTER" FROM THIS!
I HAVE TO FIGHT ANXIETY EVERY DAY.
IT'S THE BIGGEST BATTLE I HAVE.
CATCHING THAT SUBMARINE TODAY? THAT WAS NOTHING.
NOTHING.
GETTING OUT OF BED IN THE MORNING... SOMETIMES THAT FEELS IMPOSSIBLE.
YOU CAN HANDLE THIS FROM HERE, YEAH?
BECAUSE I CAN'T HANDLE ANYTHING.
WAIT!
ARE WE STILL DOING PANCAKES TOMORROW?!
DUDE.
NOT TODAY.

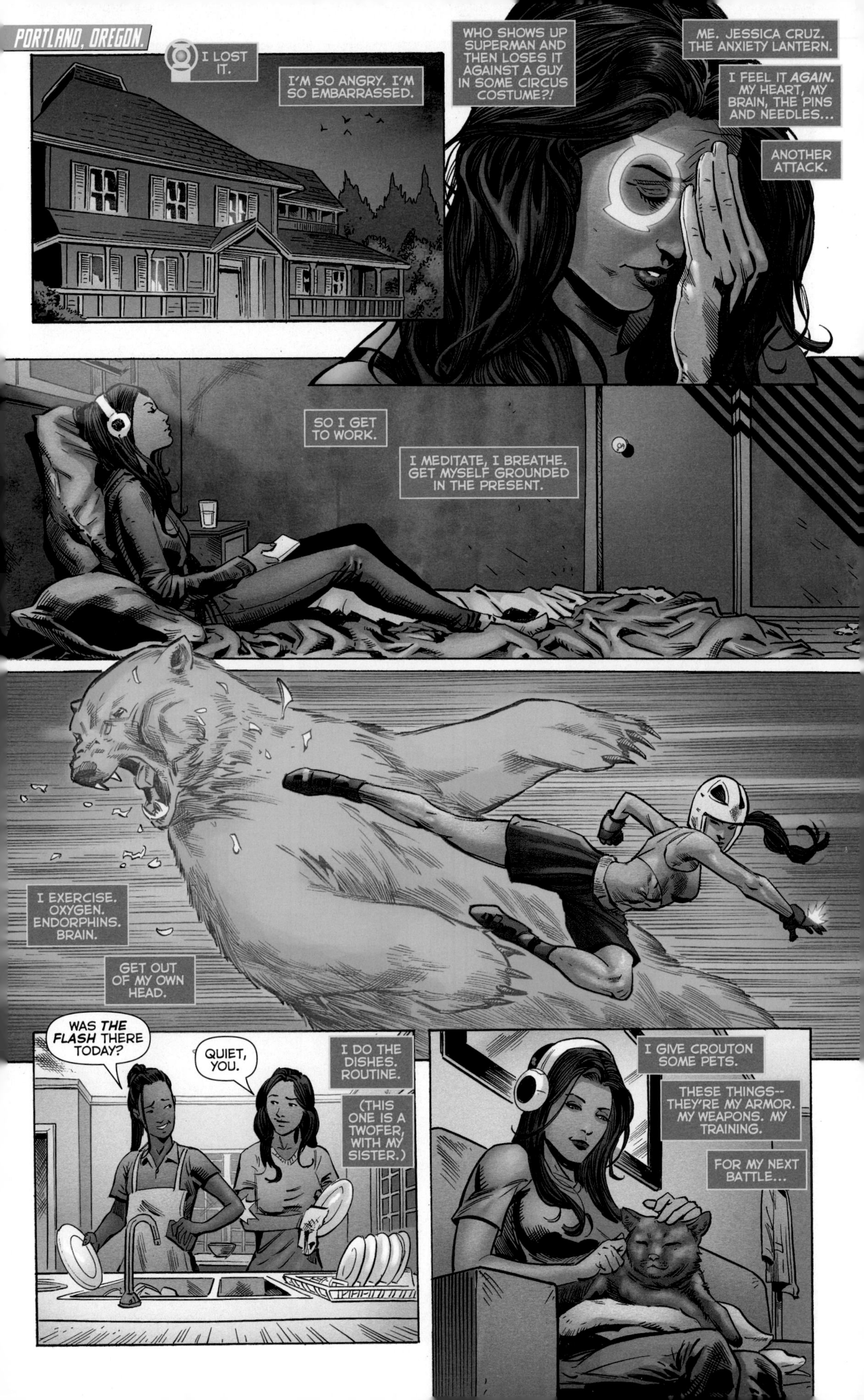
PORTLAND, OREGON.
I LOST IT.
I'M SO ANGRY. I'M SO EMBARRASSED.
WHO SHOWS UP SUPERMAN AND THEN LOSES IT AGAINST A GUY IN SOME CIRCUS COSTUME?!
ME. JESSICA CRUZ. THE ANXIETY LANTERN.
I FEEL IT *AGAIN.* MY HEART, MY BRAIN, THE PINS AND NEEDLES...
ANOTHER ATTACK.
SO I GET TO WORK.
I MEDITATE, I BREATHE. GET MYSELF GROUNDED IN THE PRESENT.
I EXERCISE. OXYGEN. ENDORPHINS. BRAIN.
GET OUT OF MY OWN HEAD.
WAS *THE FLASH* THERE TODAY?
QUIET, YOU.
I DO THE DISHES. ROUTINE.
(THIS ONE IS A TWOFER, WITH MY SISTER.)
I GIVE CROUTON SOME PETS.
THESE THINGS-- THEY'RE MY ARMOR. MY WEAPONS. MY TRAINING.
FOR MY NEXT BATTLE...

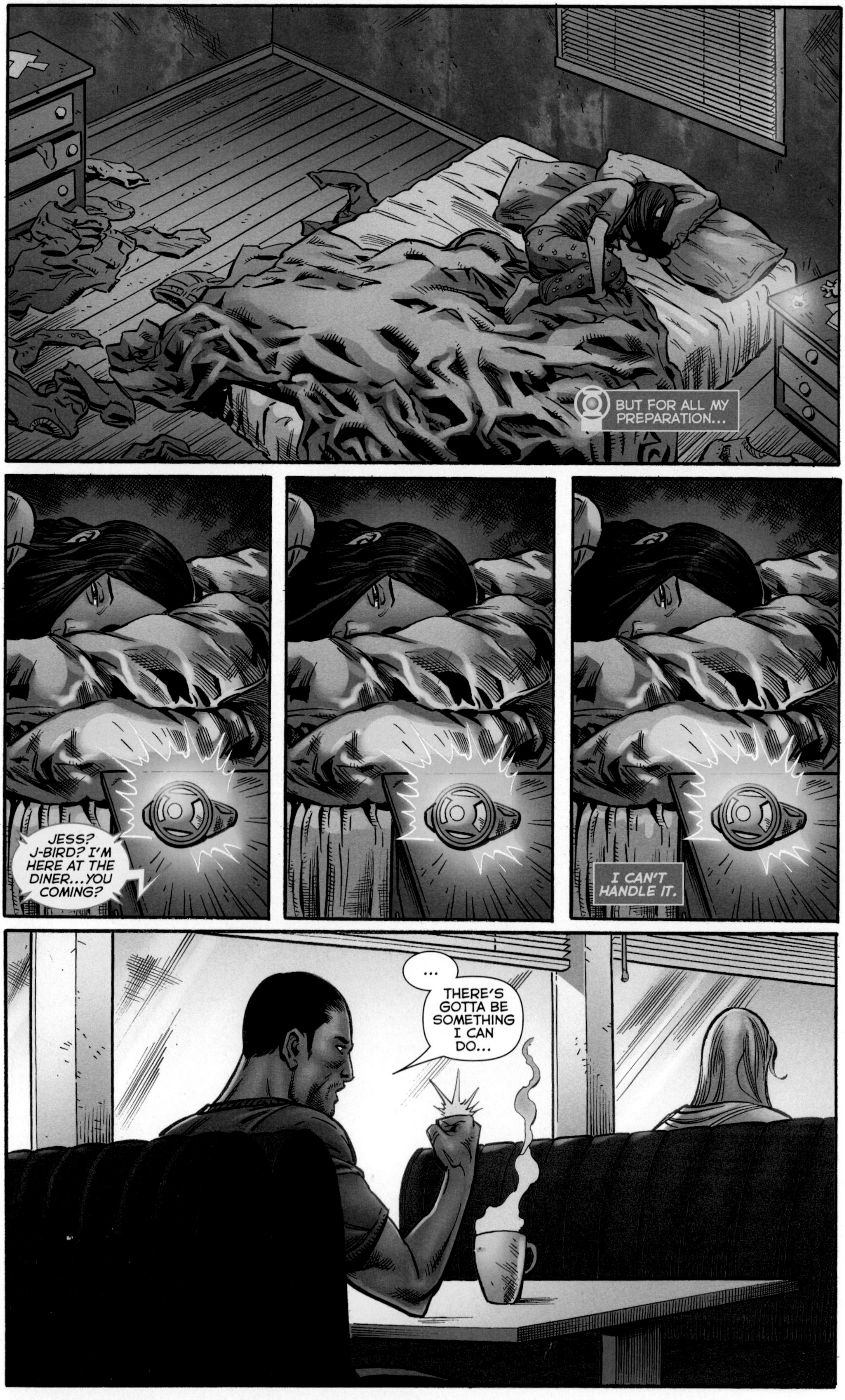
BUT FOR ALL MY PREPARATION...
JESS? J-BIRD? I'M HERE AT THE DINER...YOU COMING?
I CAN'T HANDLE IT.
...
THERE'S GOTTA BE SOMETHING I CAN DO...

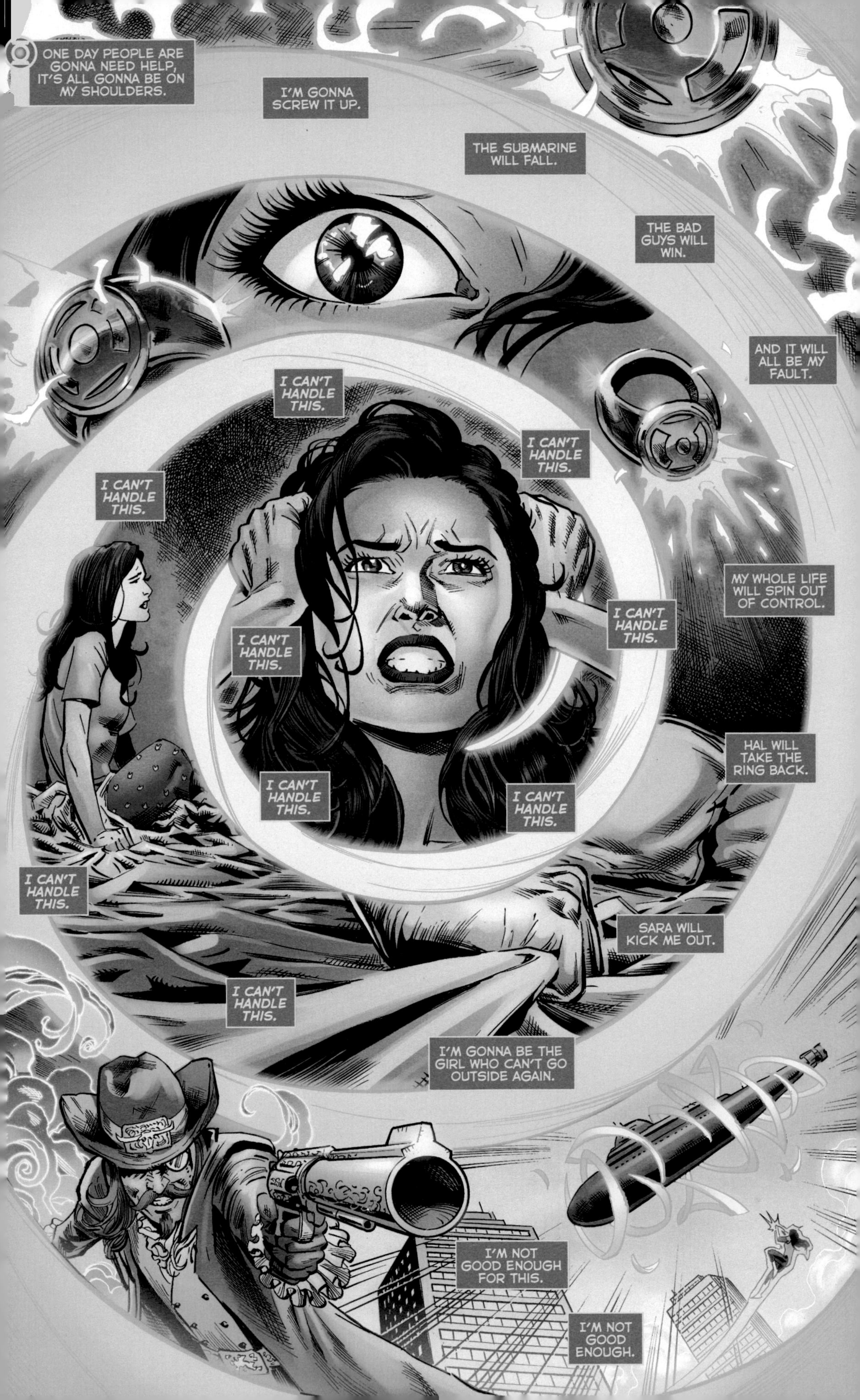
ONE DAY PEOPLE ARE GONNA NEED HELP, IT'S ALL GONNA BE ON MY SHOULDERS.
I'M GONNA SCREW IT UP.
THE SUBMARINE WILL FALL.
THE BAD GUYS WILL WIN.
AND IT WILL ALL BE MY FAULT.
I CAN'T HANDLE THIS.
I CAN'T HANDLE THIS.
I CAN'T HANDLE THIS.
MY WHOLE LIFE WILL SPIN OUT OF CONTROL.
I CAN'T HANDLE THIS.
I CAN'T HANDLE THIS.
HAL WILL TAKE THE RING BACK.
I CAN'T HANDLE THIS.
I CAN'T HANDLE THIS.
I CAN'T HANDLE THIS.
SARA WILL KICK ME OUT.
I CAN'T HANDLE THIS.
I'M GONNA BE THE GIRL WHO CAN'T GO OUTSIDE AGAIN.
I'M NOT GOOD ENOUGH FOR THIS.
I'M NOT GOOD ENOUGH.

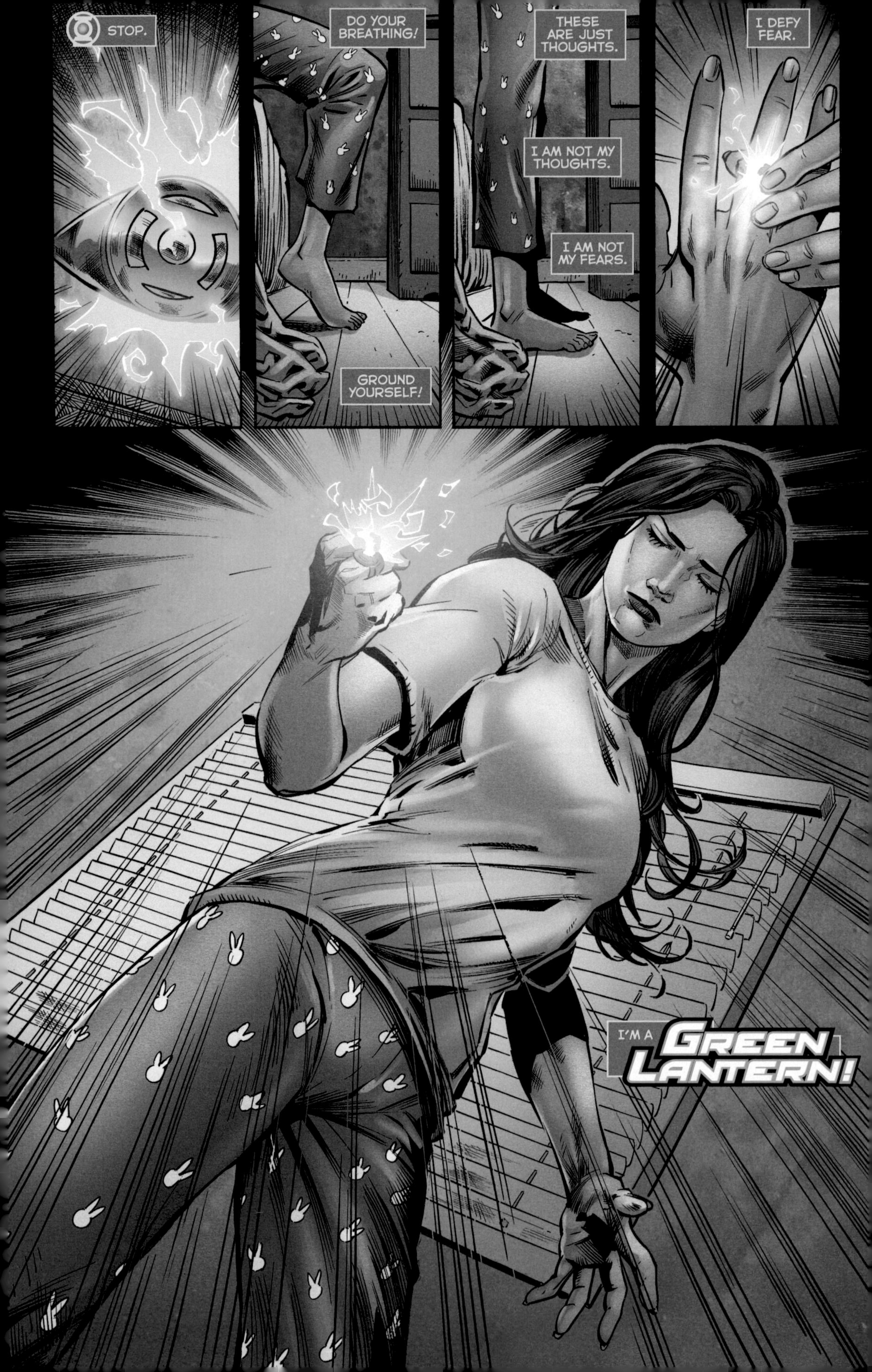

STOP.
DO YOUR BREATHING!
GROUND YOURSELF!
THESE ARE JUST THOUGHTS.
I AM NOT MY THOUGHTS.
I AM NOT MY FEARS.
I DEFY FEAR.
I'M A GREEN LANTERN!

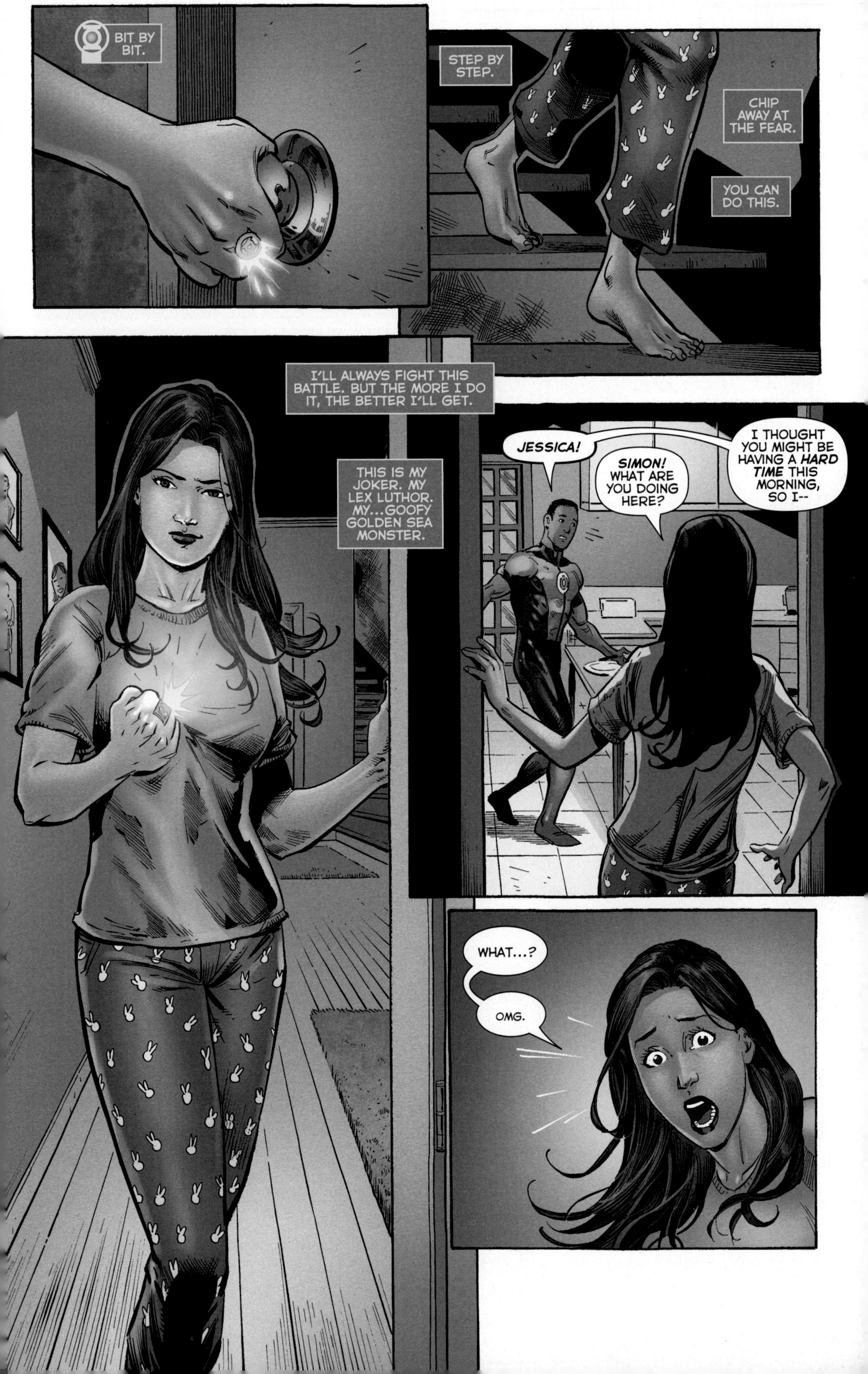
BIT BY BIT.
STEP BY STEP.
CHIP AWAY AT THE FEAR.
YOU CAN DO THIS.
I'LL ALWAYS FIGHT THIS BATTLE. BUT THE MORE I DO IT, THE BETTER I'LL GET.
THIS IS MY JOKER. MY LEX LUTHOR. MY...GOOFY GOLDEN SEA MONSTER.
JESSICA!
SIMON! WHAT ARE YOU DOING HERE?
I THOUGHT YOU MIGHT BE HAVING A HARD TIME THIS MORNING, SO I--
WHAT...?
OMG.

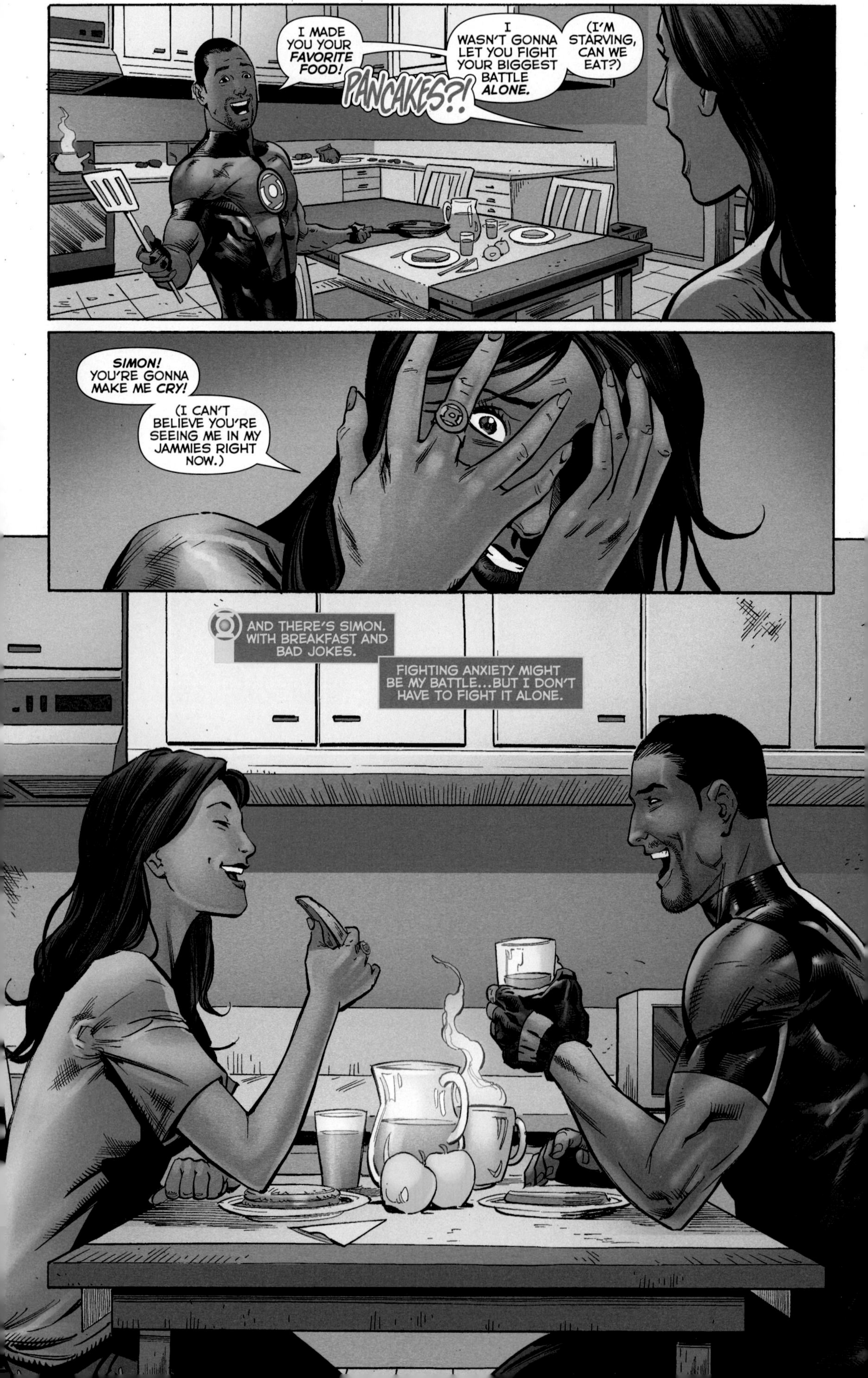
I MADE YOU YOUR FAVORITE FOOD!
PANCAKES?!
I WASN'T GONNA LET YOU FIGHT YOUR BIGGEST BATTLE ALONE.
(I'M STARVING, CAN WE EAT?)
SIMON! YOU'RE GONNA MAKE ME CRY!
(I CAN'T BELIEVE YOU'RE SEEING ME IN MY JAMMIES RIGHT NOW.)
AND THERE'S SIMON. WITH BREAKFAST AND BAD JOKES.
FIGHTING ANXIETY MIGHT BE MY BATTLE...BUT I DON'T HAVE TO FIGHT IT ALONE.

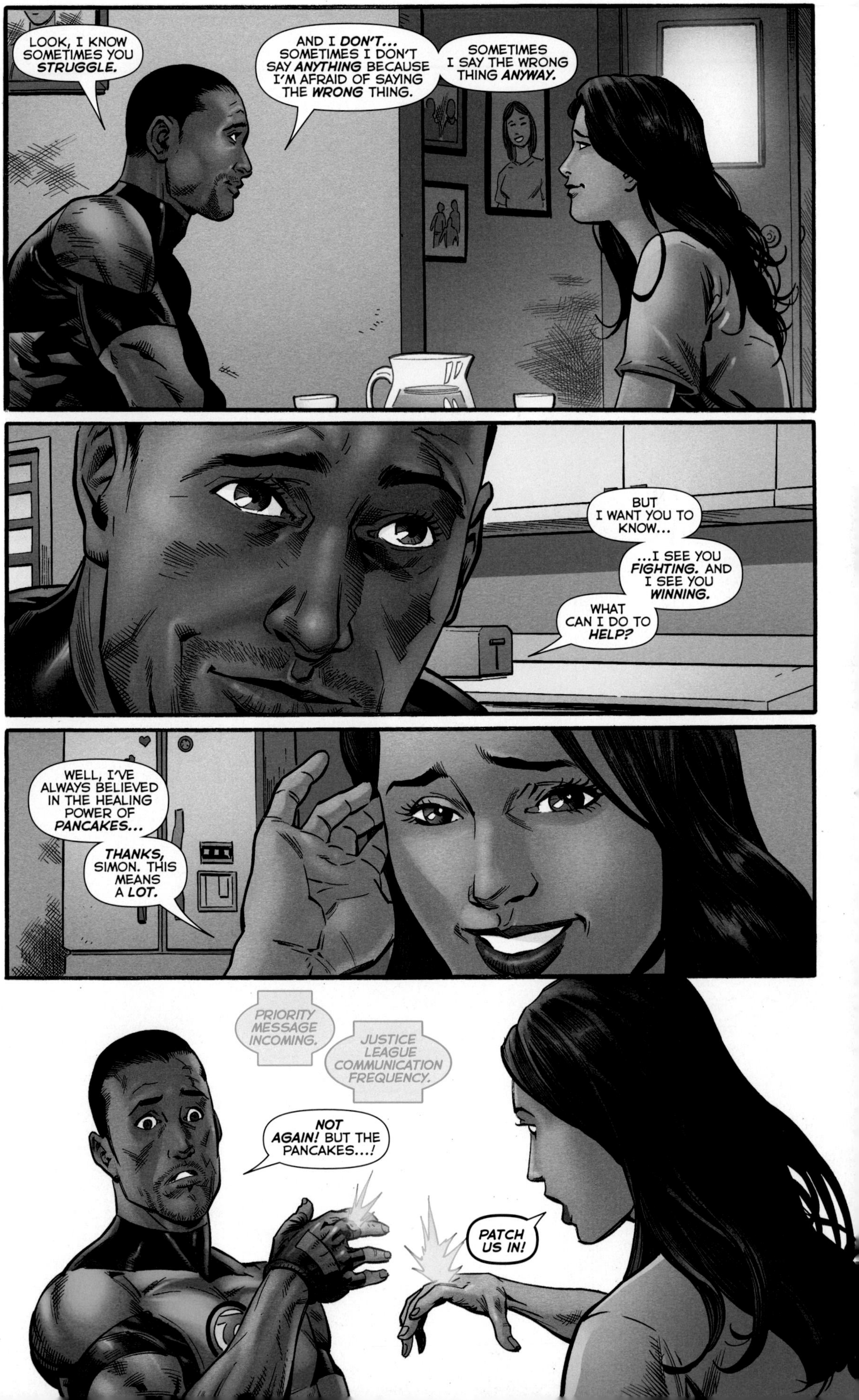

LOOK, I KNOW SOMETIMES YOU STRUGGLE.
AND I DON'T... SOMETIMES I DON'T SAY ANYTHING BECAUSE I'M AFRAID OF SAYING THE WRONG THING.
SOMETIMES I SAY THE WRONG THING ANYWAY.
BUT I WANT YOU TO KNOW...
...I SEE YOU FIGHTING. AND I SEE YOU WINNING.
WHAT CAN I DO TO HELP?
WELL, I'VE ALWAYS BELIEVED IN THE HEALING POWER OF PANCAKES...
THANKS, SIMON. THIS MEANS A LOT.
PRIORITY MESSAGE INCOMING.
JUSTICE LEAGUE COMMUNICATION FREQUENCY.
NOT AGAIN! BUT THE PANCAKES...!
PATCH US IN!

GREEN LANTERNS.

BATMAN! GET OVER HERE. WE GOT PANCAKES!

LISTEN TO ME. BOTH OF YOU.

THE WAY I SAW YOU TWO OPERATE OUT THERE YESTERDAY...THE WAY YOU HANDLE FEAR. IT MADE ME THINK.

I'VE GOT A SITUATION HERE. AND I DON'T HAVE TIME TO WORK IT OUT ON MY OWN.

YOU NEED OUR HELP?!

JUST US?!

IS THIS THE BATMAN/GREEN LANTERNS TEAM-UP I'VE BEEN WAITING FOR?!

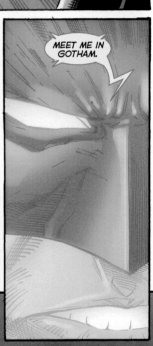

MEET ME IN GOTHAM.

"I'LL LEAVE THE LIGHT ON FOR YOU."

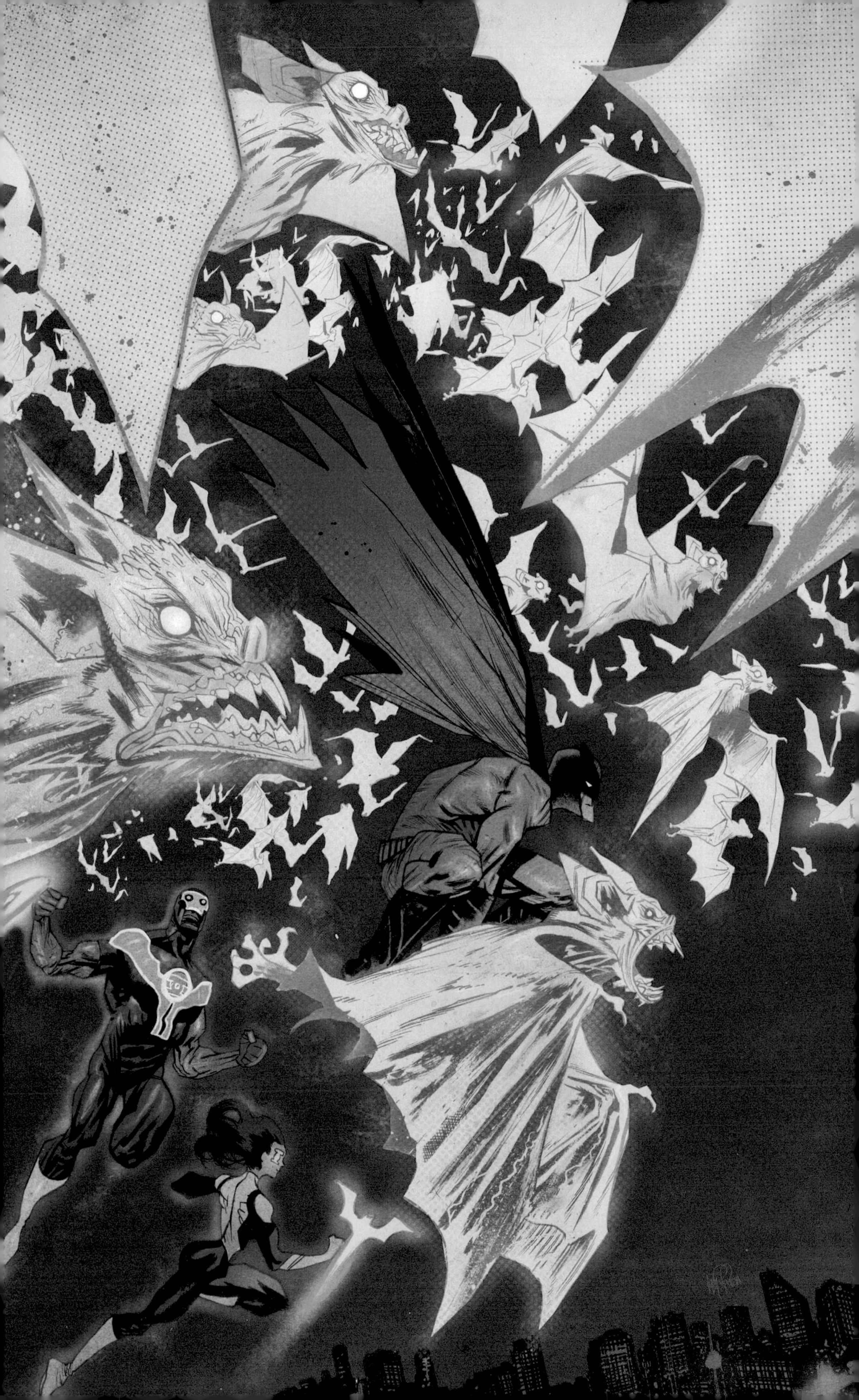

"DARKEST KNIGHTS PART 1"

NEIL EDWARDS penciller * JAY LEISTEN KEITH CHAMPAGNE Inkers
Cover by JAMES HARREN

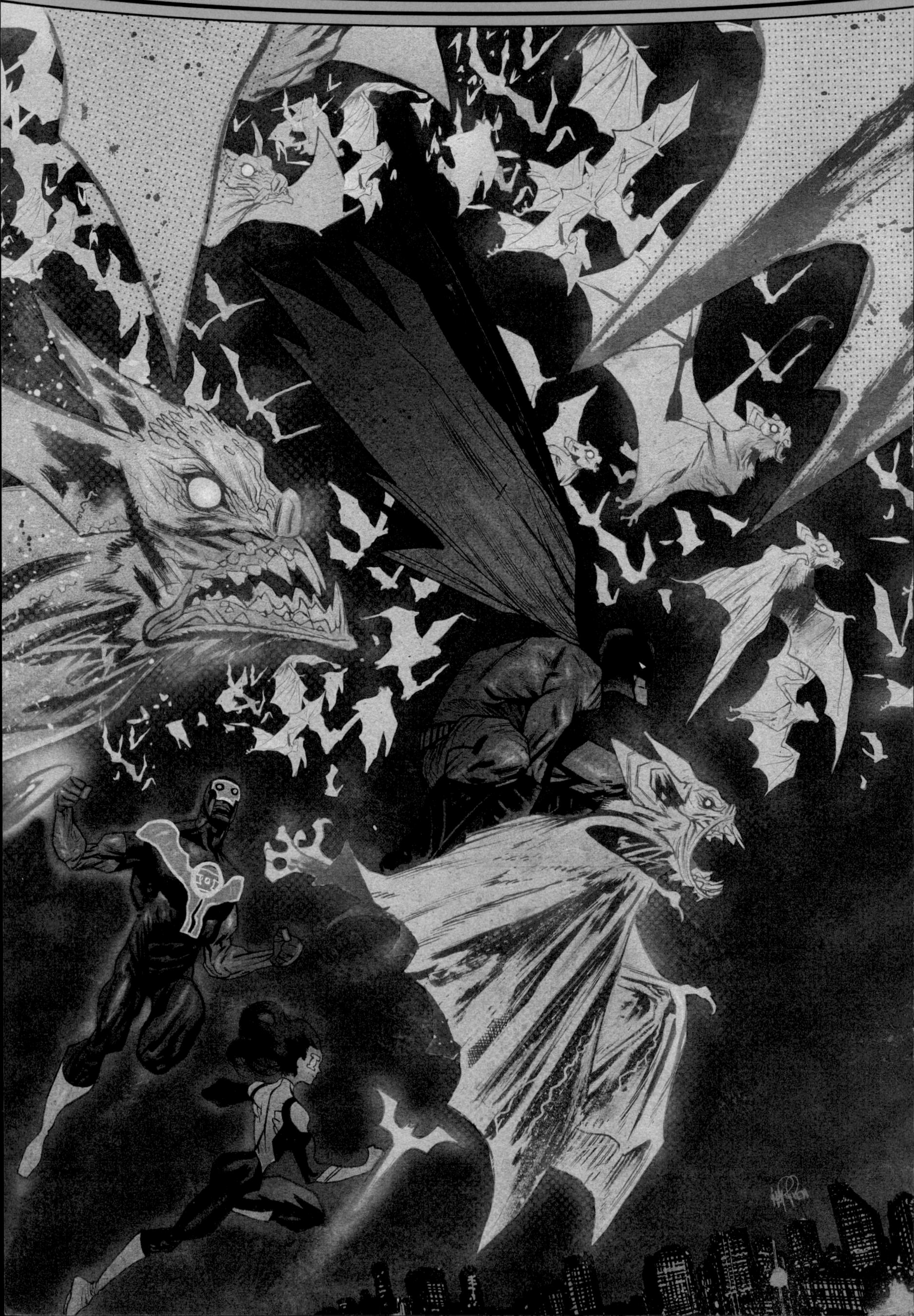

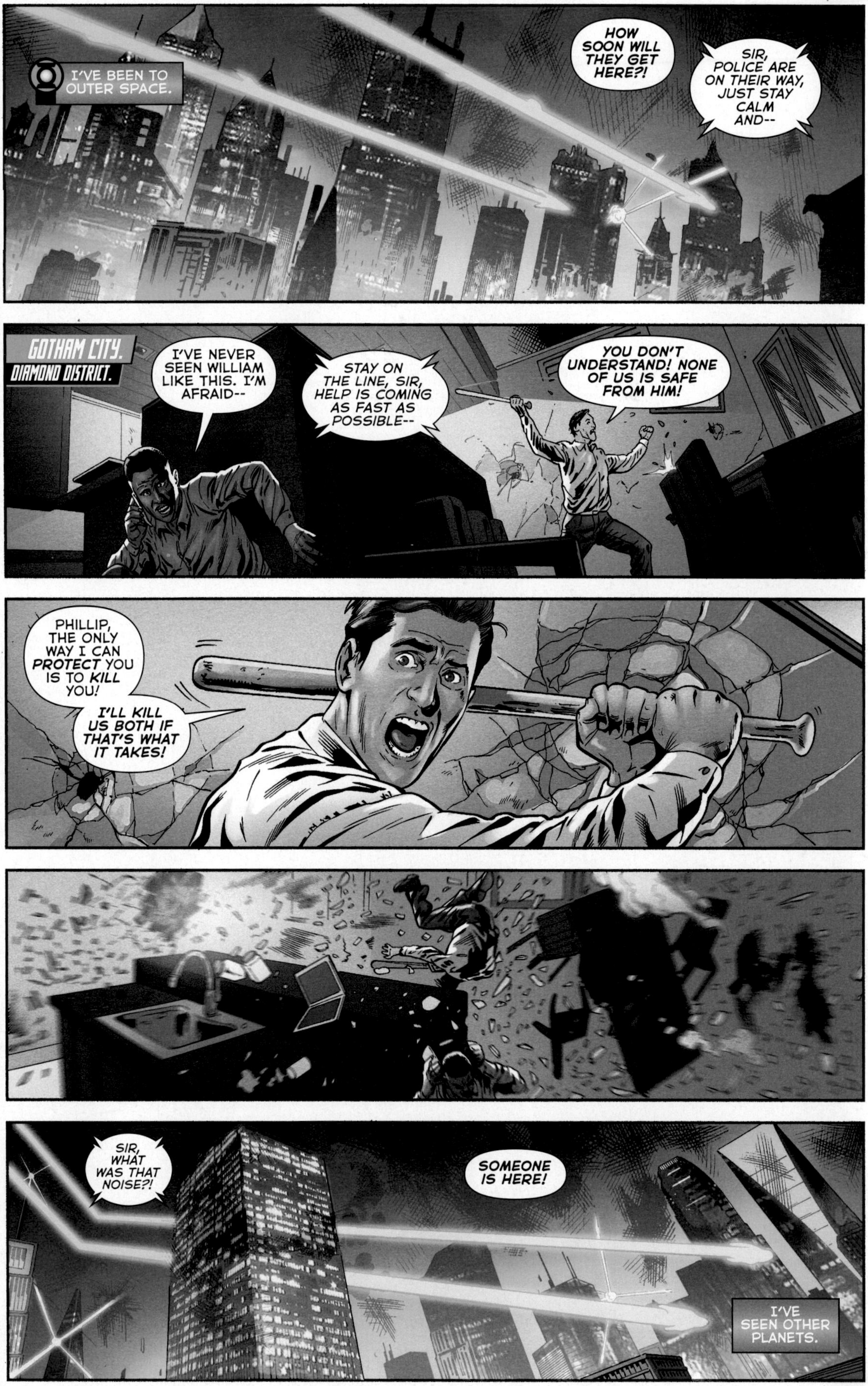
I'VE BEEN TO OUTER SPACE.
HOW SOON WILL THEY GET HERE?!
SIR, POLICE ARE ON THEIR WAY, JUST STAY CALM AND--
GOTHAM CITY.
DIAMOND DISTRICT.
I'VE NEVER SEEN WILLIAM LIKE THIS. I'M AFRAID--
STAY ON THE LINE, SIR, HELP IS COMING AS FAST AS POSSIBLE--
YOU DON'T UNDERSTAND! NONE OF US IS SAFE FROM HIM!
PHILLIP, THE ONLY WAY I CAN PROTECT YOU IS TO KILL YOU!
I'LL KILL US BOTH IF THAT'S WHAT IT TAKES!
SIR, WHAT WAS THAT NOISE?!
SOMEONE IS HERE!
I'VE SEEN OTHER PLANETS.

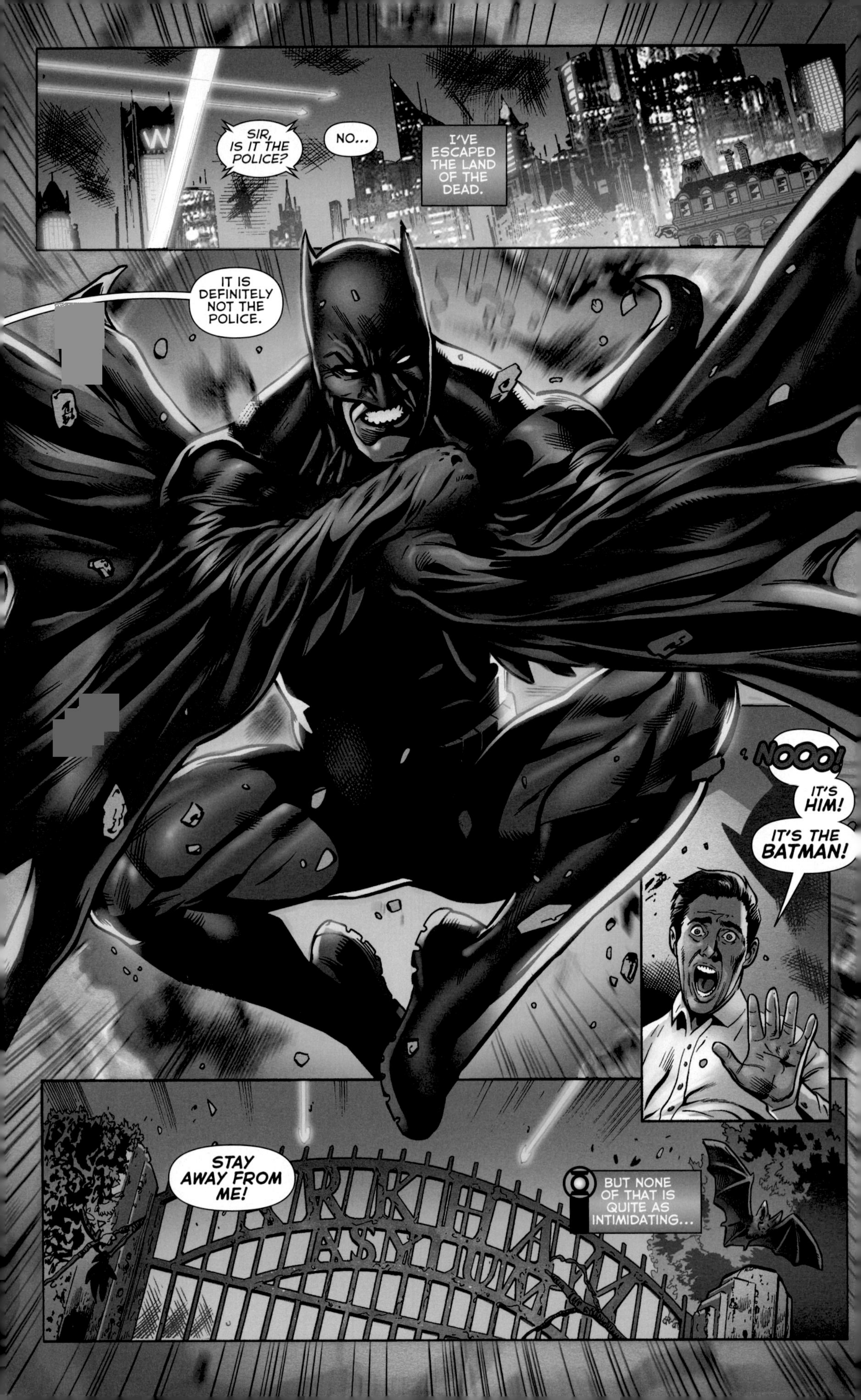
SIR, IS IT THE POLICE?
NO...
I'VE ESCAPED THE LAND OF THE DEAD.
IT IS DEFINITELY NOT THE POLICE.
NOOO!
IT'S HIM!
IT'S THE BATMAN!
STAY AWAY FROM ME!
BUT NONE OF THAT IS QUITE AS INTIMIDATING...

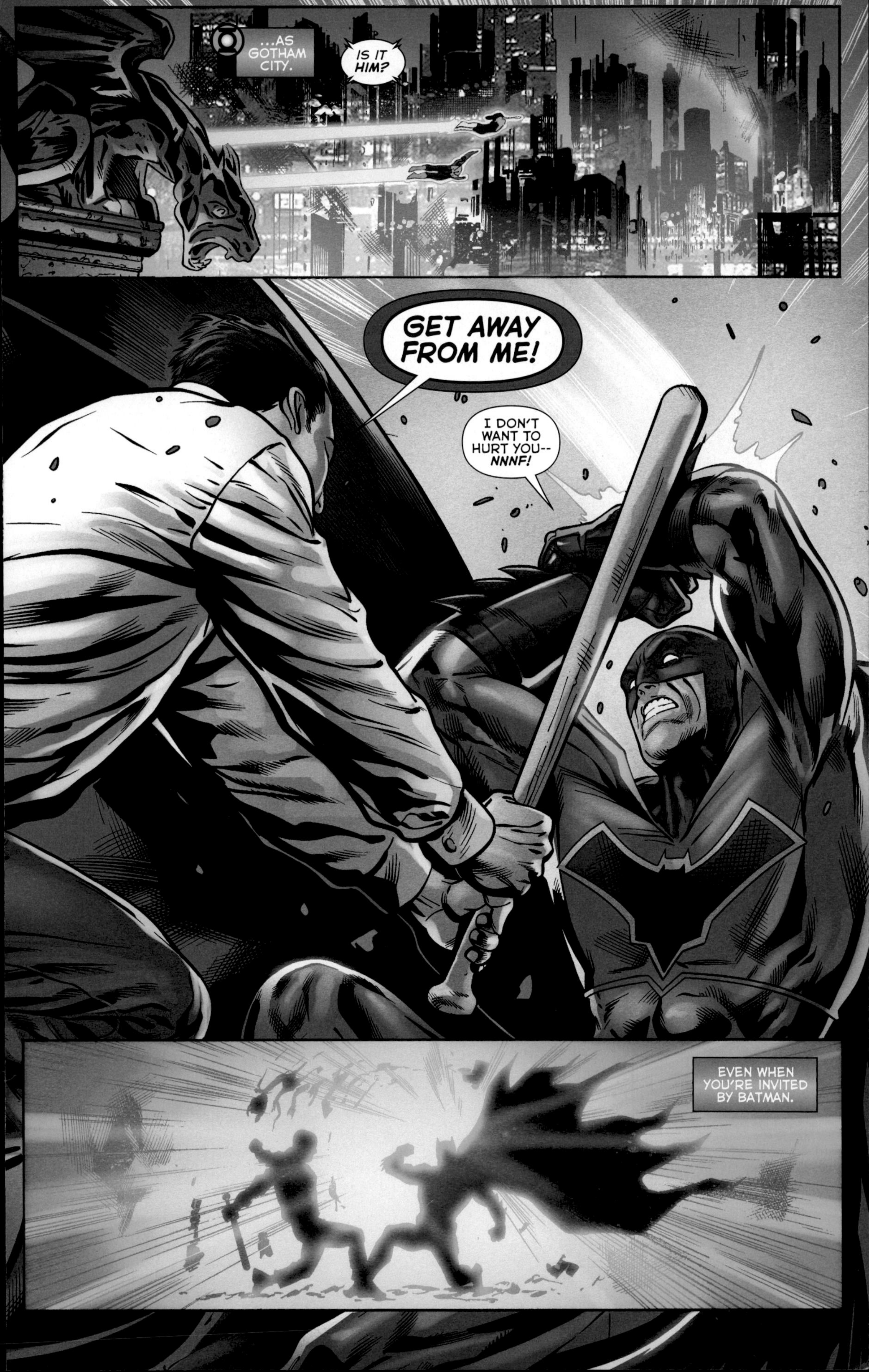
...AS GOTHAM CITY.
IS IT HIM?
GET AWAY FROM ME!
I DON'T WANT TO HURT YOU-- NNNF!
EVEN WHEN YOU'RE INVITED BY BATMAN.

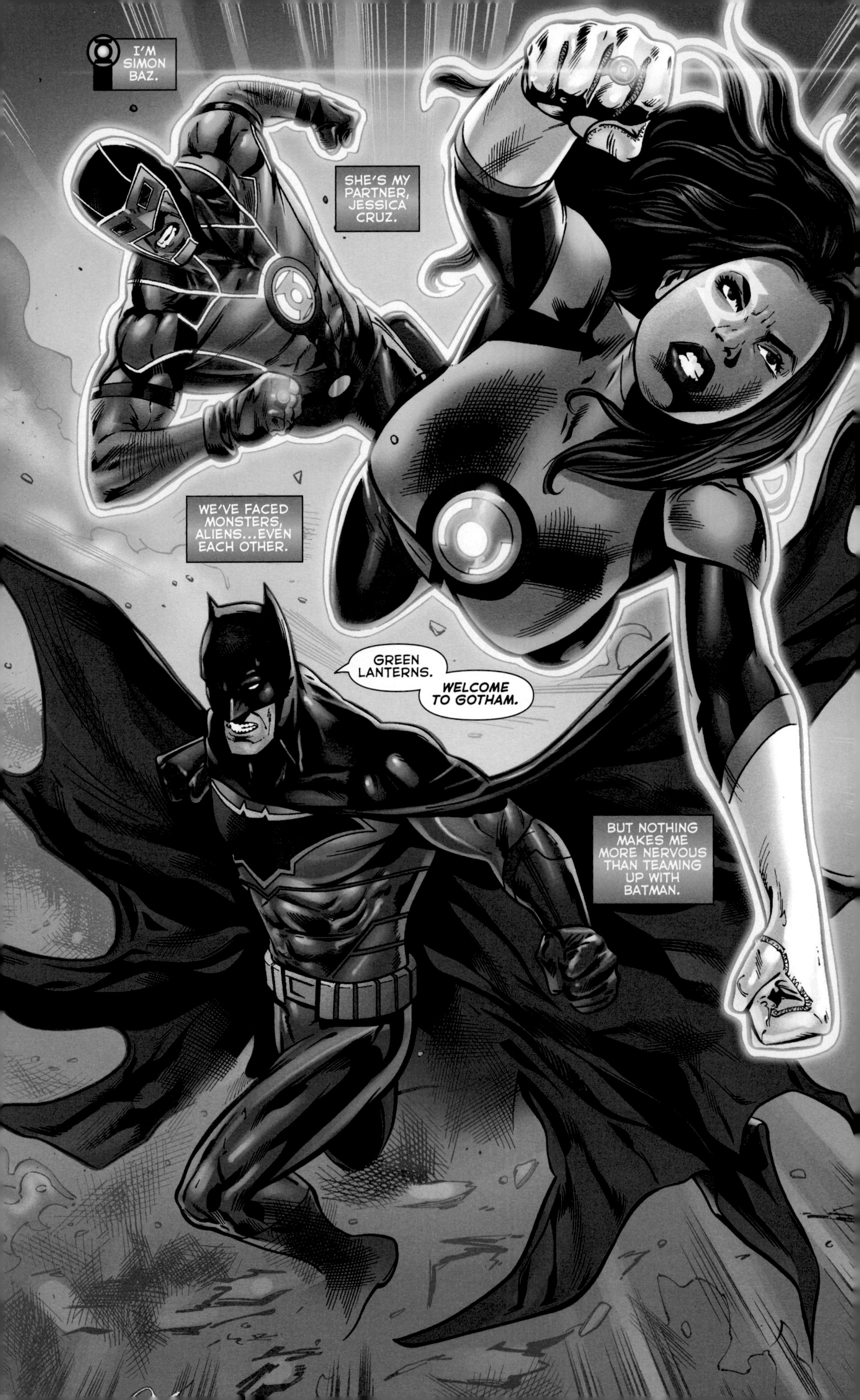

I'M SIMON BAZ.
SHE'S MY PARTNER, JESSICA CRUZ.
WE'VE FACED MONSTERS, ALIENS...EVEN EACH OTHER.
GREEN LANTERNS. *WELCOME TO GOTHAM.*
BUT NOTHING MAKES ME MORE NERVOUS THAN TEAMING UP WITH BATMAN.

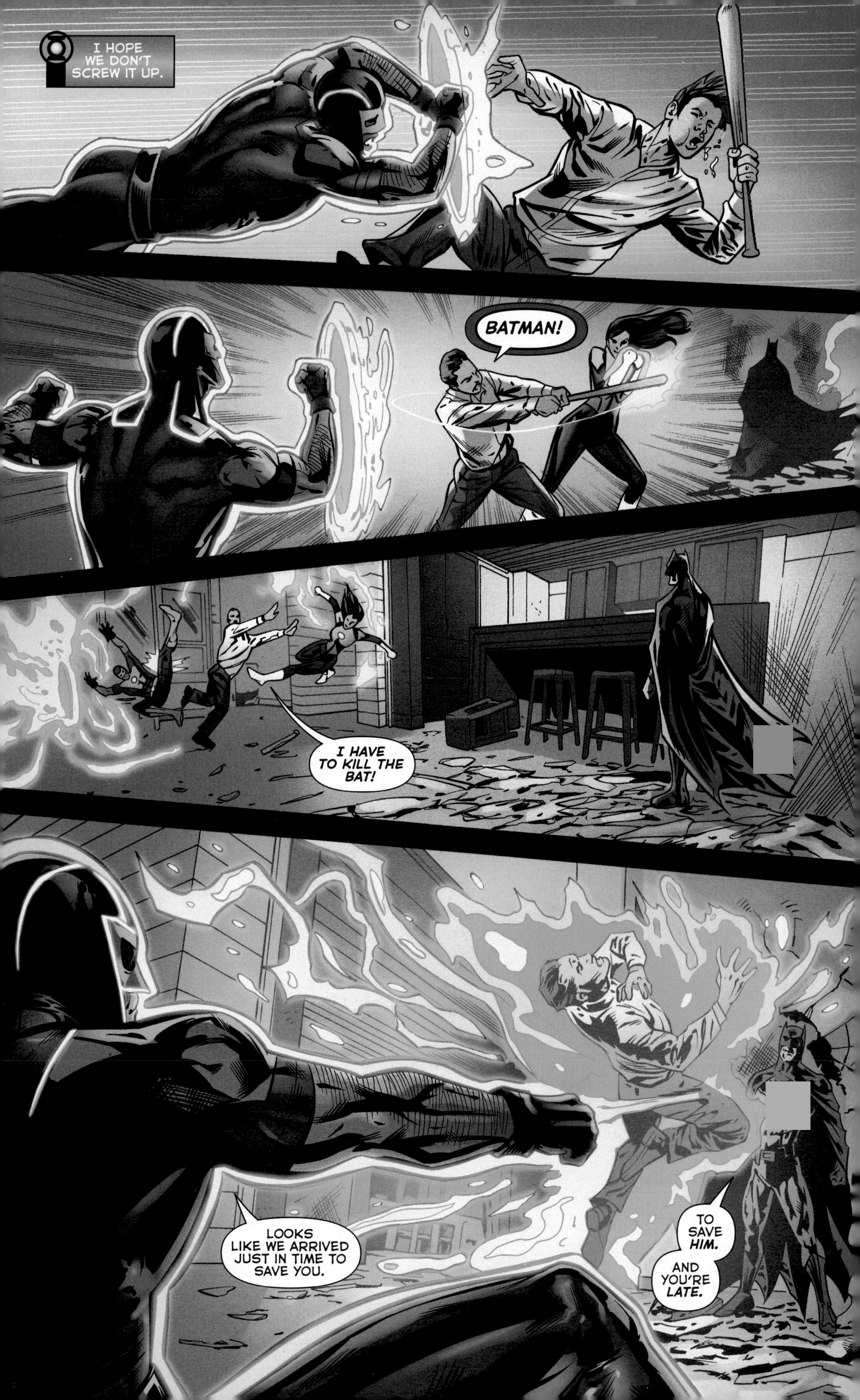
I HOPE WE DON'T SCREW IT UP.
BATMAN!
I HAVE TO KILL THE BAT!
LOOKS LIKE WE ARRIVED JUST IN TIME TO SAVE YOU.
TO SAVE *HIM.*
AND YOU'RE *LATE.*

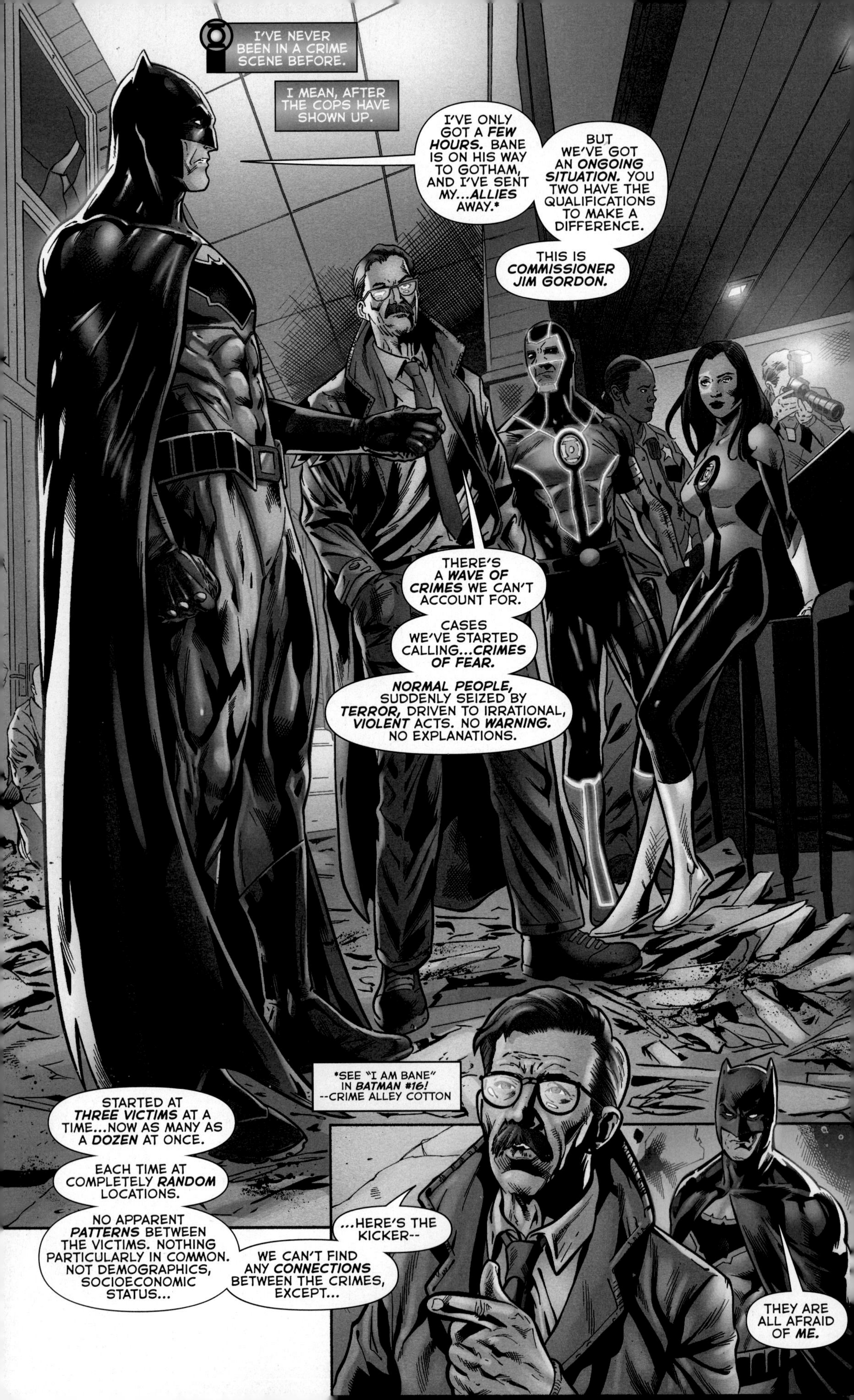
I'VE NEVER BEEN IN A CRIME SCENE BEFORE.
I MEAN, AFTER THE COPS HAVE SHOWN UP.
I'VE ONLY GOT A FEW HOURS. BANE IS ON HIS WAY TO GOTHAM, AND I'VE SENT MY...ALLIES AWAY.*
BUT WE'VE GOT AN ONGOING SITUATION. YOU TWO HAVE THE QUALIFICATIONS TO MAKE A DIFFERENCE.
THIS IS COMMISSIONER JIM GORDON.
THERE'S A WAVE OF CRIMES WE CAN'T ACCOUNT FOR.
CASES WE'VE STARTED CALLING...CRIMES OF FEAR.
NORMAL PEOPLE, SUDDENLY SEIZED BY TERROR, DRIVEN TO IRRATIONAL, VIOLENT ACTS. NO WARNING. NO EXPLANATIONS.
*SEE "I AM BANE" IN BATMAN #16! --CRIME ALLEY COTTON
STARTED AT THREE VICTIMS AT A TIME...NOW AS MANY AS A DOZEN AT ONCE.
EACH TIME AT COMPLETELY RANDOM LOCATIONS.
NO APPARENT PATTERNS BETWEEN THE VICTIMS. NOTHING PARTICULARLY IN COMMON. NOT DEMOGRAPHICS, SOCIOECONOMIC STATUS...
WE CAN'T FIND ANY CONNECTIONS BETWEEN THE CRIMES, EXCEPT...
...HERE'S THE KICKER--
THEY ARE ALL AFRAID OF ME.

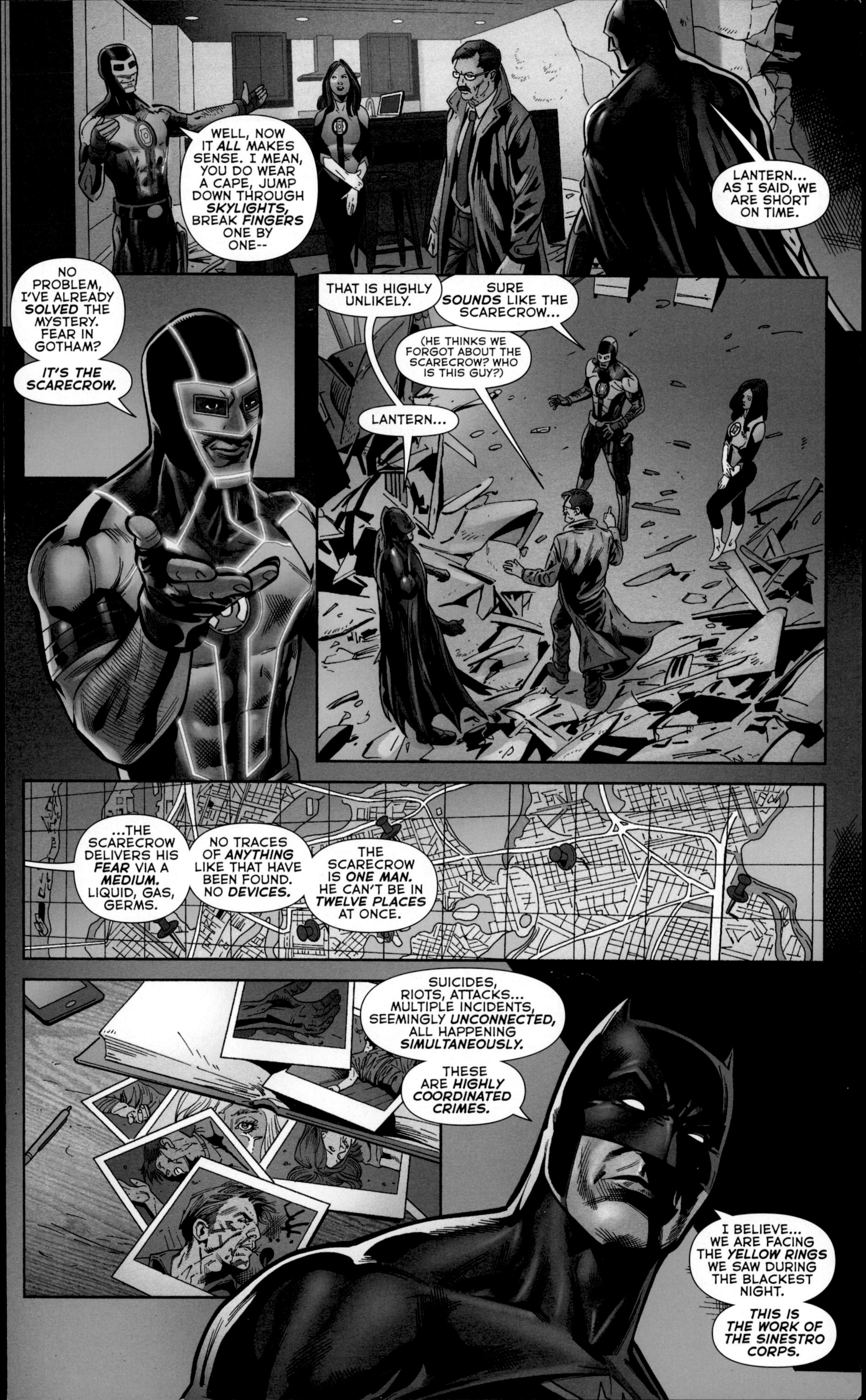
WELL, NOW IT ALL MAKES SENSE. I MEAN, YOU DO WEAR A CAPE, JUMP DOWN THROUGH SKYLIGHTS, BREAK FINGERS ONE BY ONE--
LANTERN... AS I SAID, WE ARE SHORT ON TIME.
NO PROBLEM, I'VE ALREADY SOLVED THE MYSTERY. FEAR IN GOTHAM?
IT'S THE SCARECROW.
THAT IS HIGHLY UNLIKELY.
SURE SOUNDS LIKE THE SCARECROW...
(HE THINKS WE FORGOT ABOUT THE SCARECROW? WHO IS THIS GUY?)
LANTERN...
...THE SCARECROW DELIVERS HIS FEAR VIA A MEDIUM. LIQUID, GAS, GERMS.
NO TRACES OF ANYTHING LIKE THAT HAVE BEEN FOUND. NO DEVICES.
THE SCARECROW IS ONE MAN. HE CAN'T BE IN TWELVE PLACES AT ONCE.
SUICIDES, RIOTS, ATTACKS... MULTIPLE INCIDENTS, SEEMINGLY UNCONNECTED, ALL HAPPENING SIMULTANEOUSLY.
THESE ARE HIGHLY COORDINATED CRIMES.
I BELIEVE... WE ARE FACING THE YELLOW RINGS WE SAW DURING THE BLACKEST NIGHT.
THIS IS THE WORK OF THE SINESTRO CORPS.

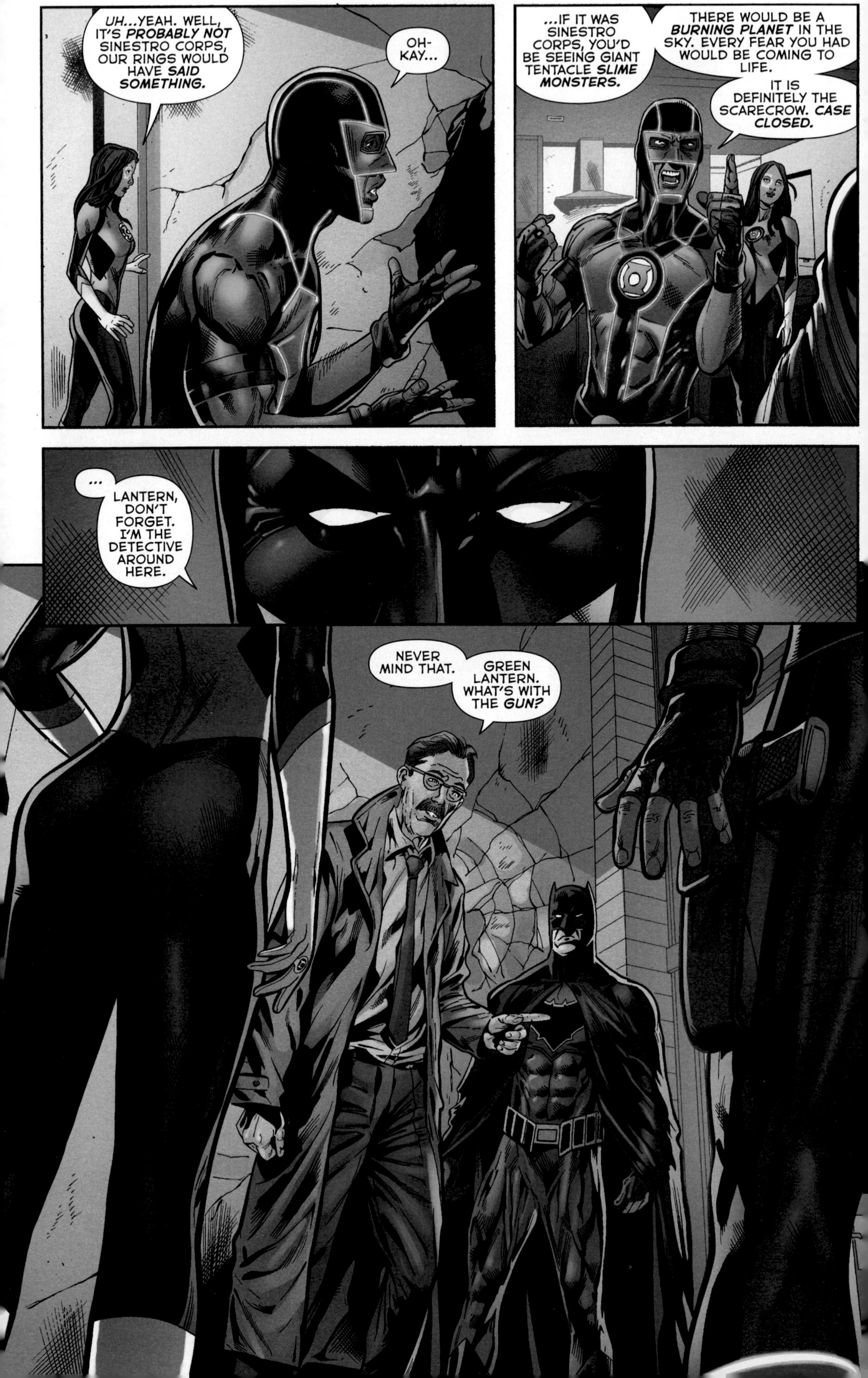
UH...YEAH. WELL, IT'S PROBABLY NOT SINESTRO CORPS, OUR RINGS WOULD HAVE SAID SOMETHING.
OH-KAY...
...IF IT WAS SINESTRO CORPS, YOU'D BE SEEING GIANT TENTACLE SLIME MONSTERS.
THERE WOULD BE A BURNING PLANET IN THE SKY. EVERY FEAR YOU HAD WOULD BE COMING TO LIFE.
IT IS DEFINITELY THE SCARECROW. CASE CLOSED.
...
LANTERN, DON'T FORGET. I'M THE DETECTIVE AROUND HERE.
NEVER MIND THAT.
GREEN LANTERN. WHAT'S WITH THE GUN?

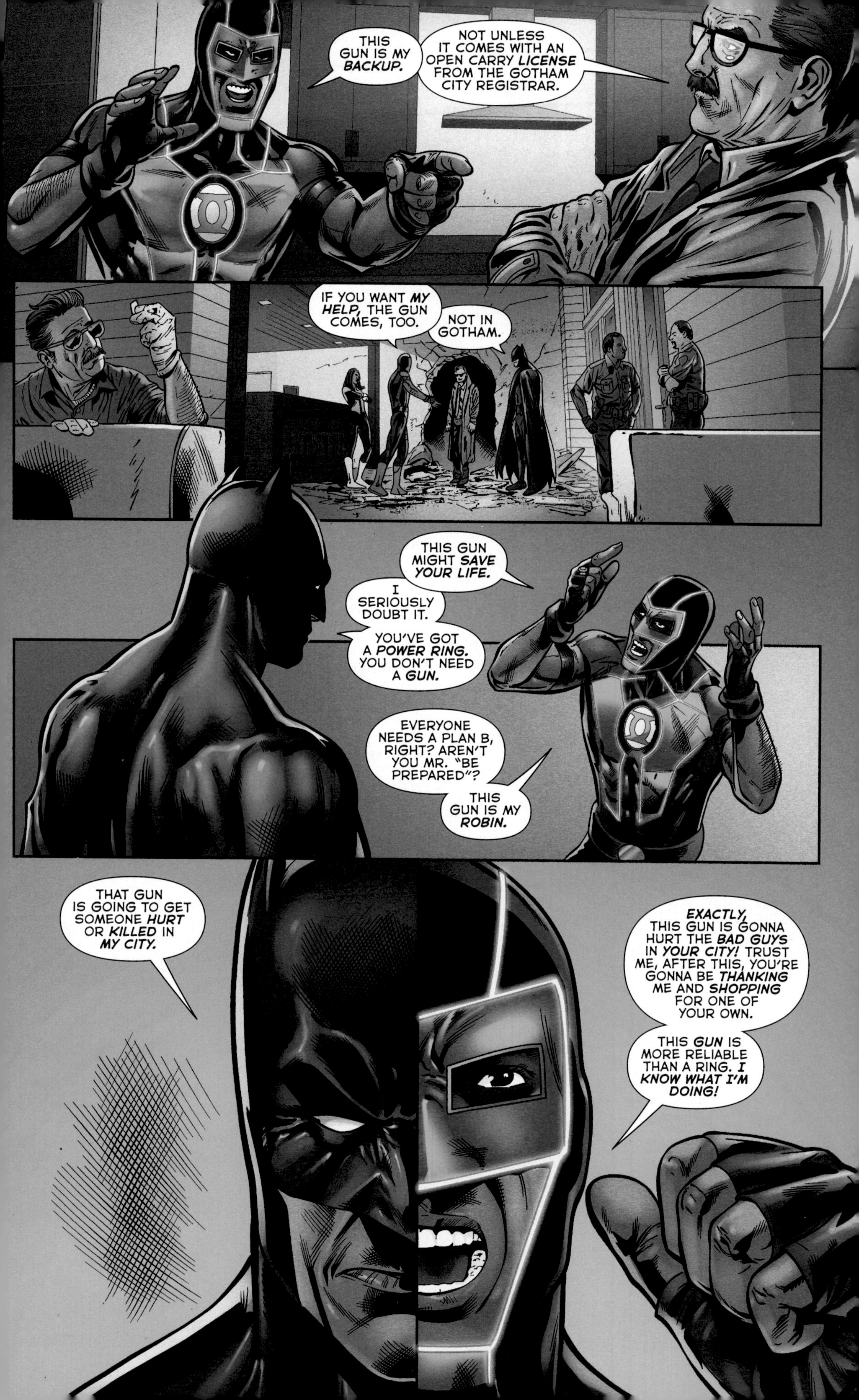
THIS GUN IS MY *BACKUP.*
NOT UNLESS IT COMES WITH AN OPEN CARRY *LICENSE* FROM THE GOTHAM CITY REGISTRAR.
IF YOU WANT *MY HELP,* THE GUN COMES, TOO.
NOT IN GOTHAM.
THIS GUN MIGHT *SAVE YOUR LIFE.*
I SERIOUSLY DOUBT IT.
YOU'VE GOT A *POWER RING.* YOU DON'T NEED A *GUN.*
EVERYONE NEEDS A PLAN B, RIGHT? AREN'T YOU MR. "BE PREPARED"?
THIS GUN IS MY *ROBIN.*
THAT GUN IS GOING TO GET SOMEONE *HURT* OR *KILLED* IN *MY CITY.*
EXACTLY, THIS GUN IS GONNA HURT THE *BAD GUYS* IN *YOUR CITY!* TRUST ME, AFTER THIS, YOU'RE GONNA BE *THANKING* ME AND *SHOPPING* FOR ONE OF YOUR OWN.
THIS *GUN* IS MORE RELIABLE THAN A RING. *I KNOW WHAT I'M DOING!*

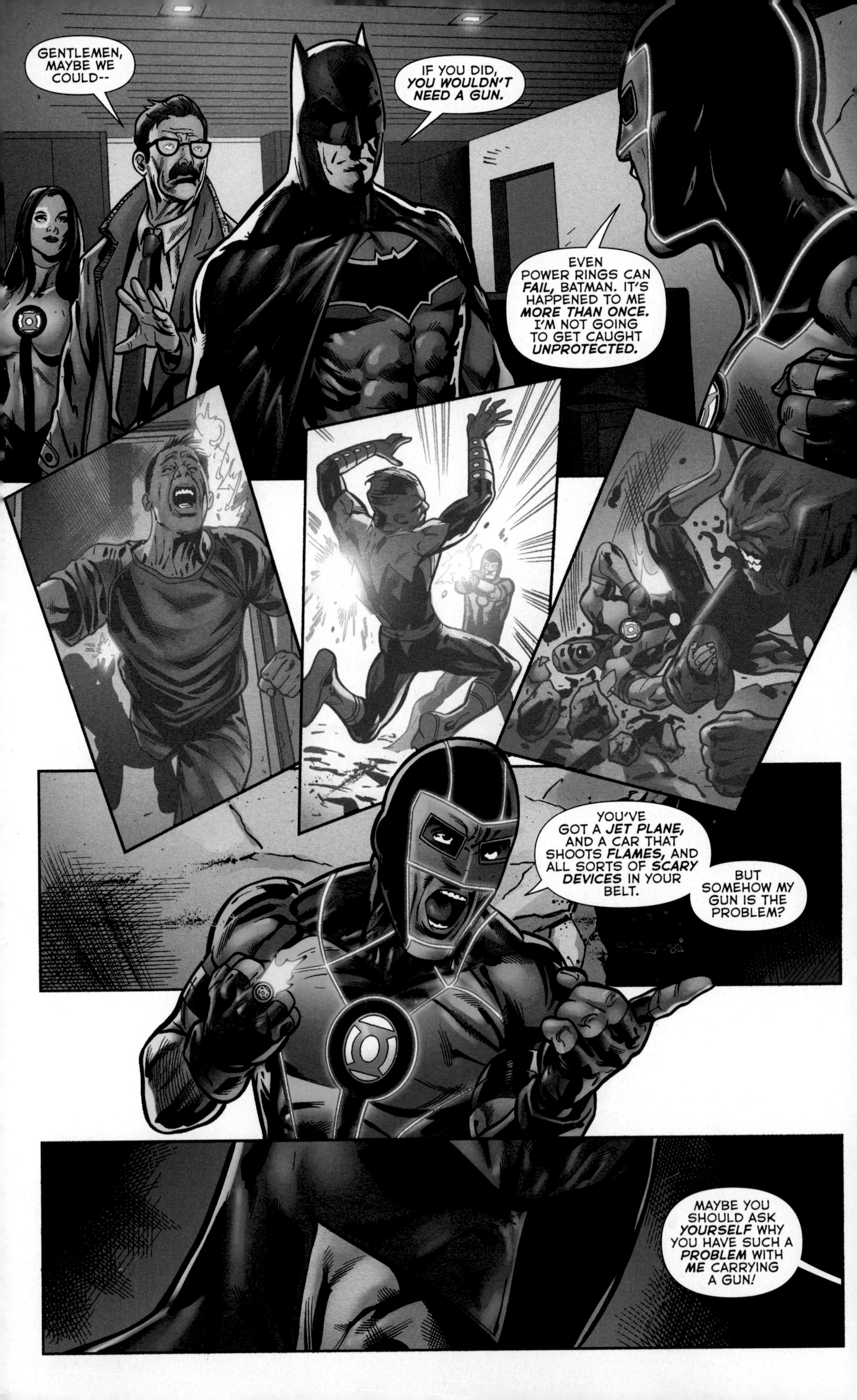
GENTLEMEN, MAYBE WE COULD--
IF YOU DID, YOU WOULDN'T NEED A GUN.
EVEN POWER RINGS CAN FAIL, BATMAN. IT'S HAPPENED TO ME MORE THAN ONCE. I'M NOT GOING TO GET CAUGHT UNPROTECTED.
YOU'VE GOT A JET PLANE, AND A CAR THAT SHOOTS FLAMES, AND ALL SORTS OF SCARY DEVICES IN YOUR BELT.
BUT SOMEHOW MY GUN IS THE PROBLEM?
MAYBE YOU SHOULD ASK YOURSELF WHY YOU HAVE SUCH A PROBLEM WITH ME CARRYING A GUN!

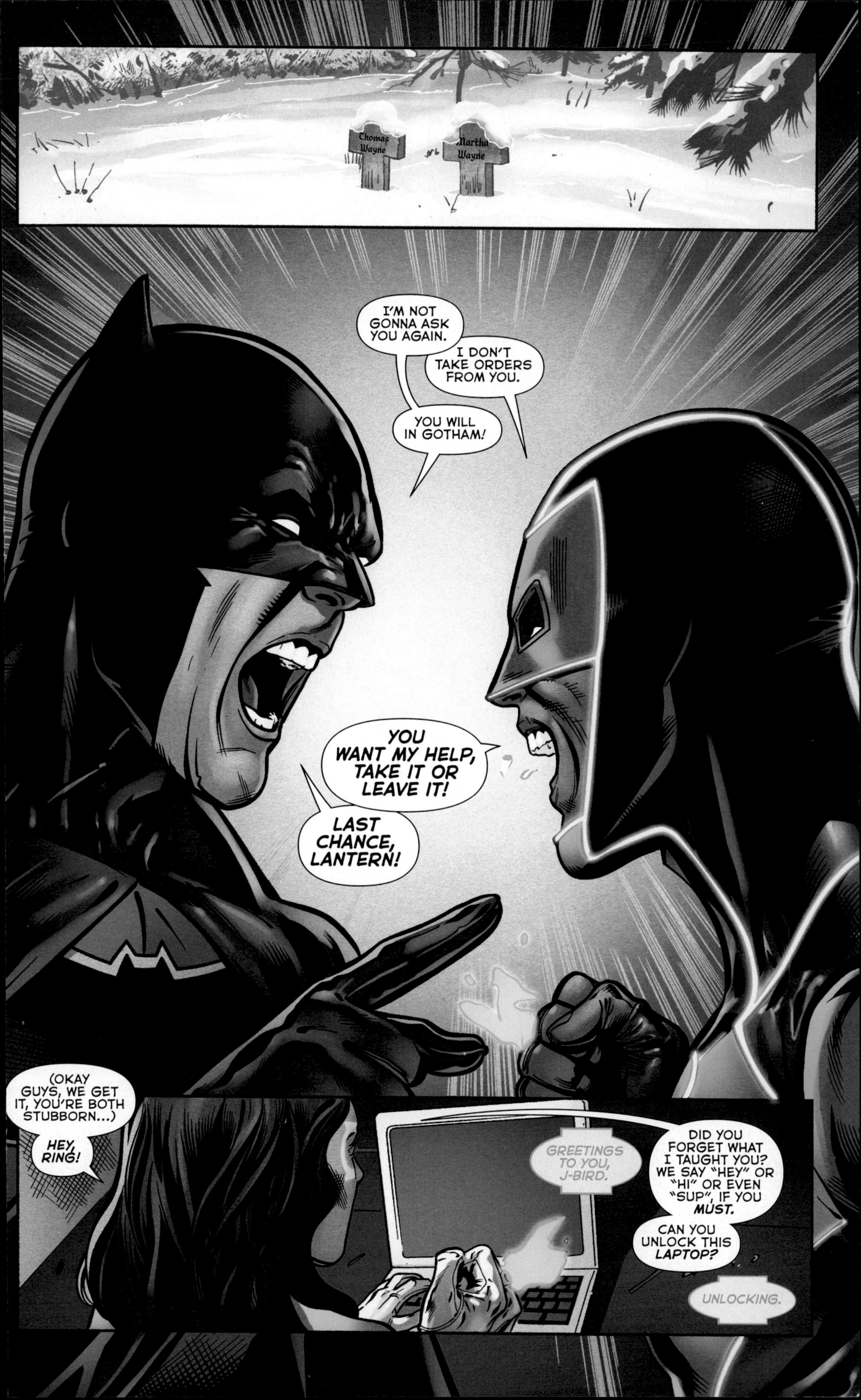
Thomas Wayne
Martha Wayne
I'M NOT GONNA ASK YOU AGAIN.
I DON'T TAKE ORDERS FROM YOU.
YOU WILL IN GOTHAM!
YOU WANT MY HELP, TAKE IT OR LEAVE IT!
LAST CHANCE, LANTERN!
(OKAY GUYS, WE GET IT, YOU'RE BOTH STUBBORN...)
HEY, RING!
GREETINGS TO YOU, J-BIRD.
DID YOU FORGET WHAT I TAUGHT YOU? WE SAY "HEY" OR "HI" OR EVEN "SUP", IF YOU MUST.
CAN YOU UNLOCK THIS LAPTOP?
UNLOCKING.

HEY, I'VE SEEN THESE VIDEOS!

BATMAN IS A THREAT TO YOUR FAMILY!

BATMAN: SPYING ON YOU???

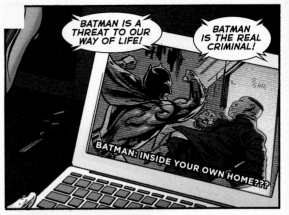

BATMAN IS A THREAT TO OUR WAY OF LIFE!

BATMAN IS THE REAL CRIMINAL!

BATMAN: INSIDE YOUR OWN HOME???

WHAT IS THIS UGLY-ASS VIDEO?

YEAH, THESE "BAD BATMAN" VIDEOS ARE REALLY POPULAR RIGHT NOW.

I'VE SEEN A BUNCH OF THEM...

I MEAN... UH...

WELL, I'VE HEARD OF THEM! ON A BLOG! NOT THAT I EVER READ BLOGS, I JUST...

DON'T WORRY BATMAN, I STILL THINK YOU'RE COOL.

ALERT!

(PHEW.)

ABERRATIONS DETECTED IN THE EMOTIONAL SPECTRUM!

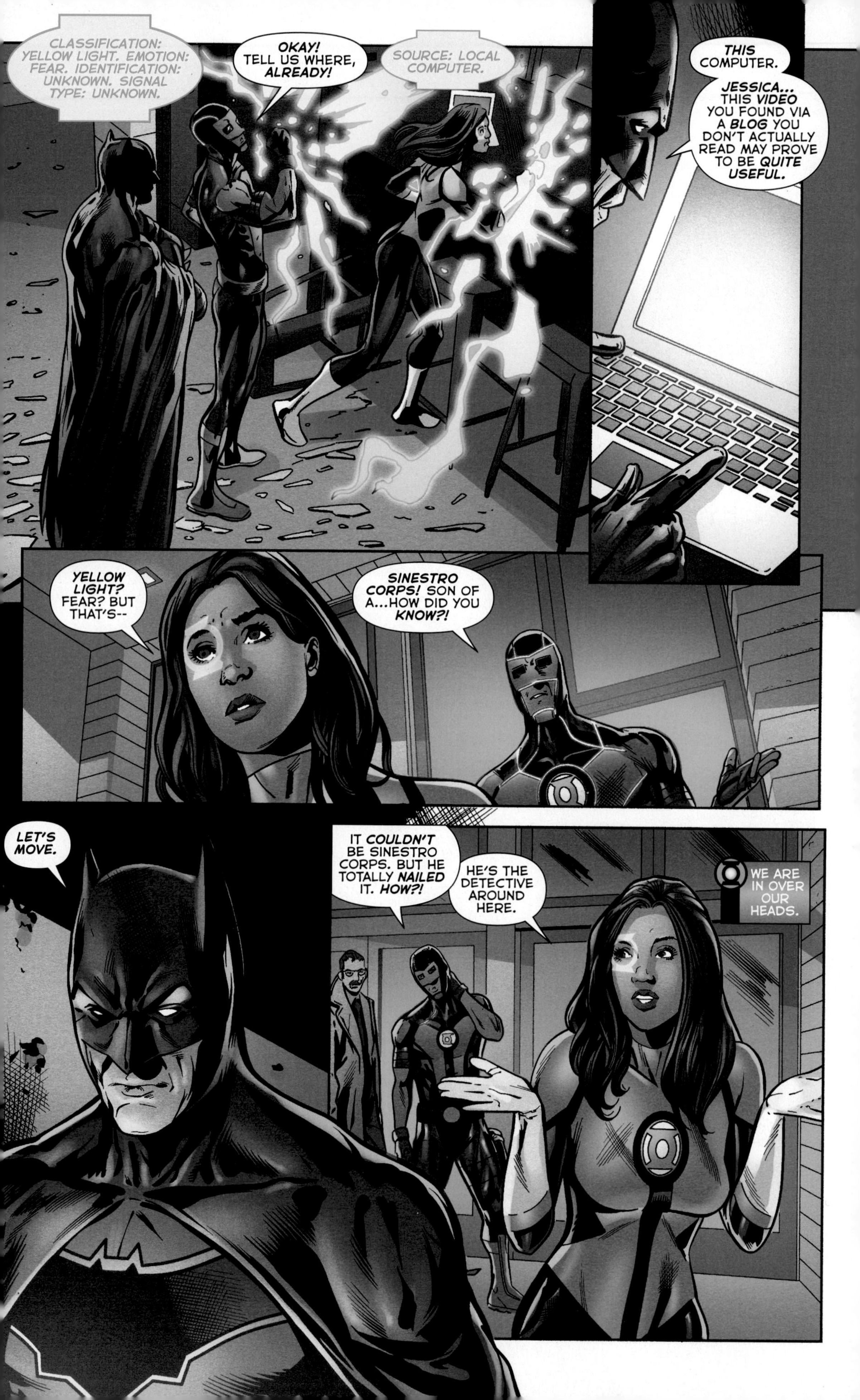
CLASSIFICATION: YELLOW LIGHT. EMOTION: FEAR. IDENTIFICATION: UNKNOWN. SIGNAL TYPE: UNKNOWN.
OKAY! TELL US WHERE, ALREADY!
SOURCE: LOCAL COMPUTER.
THIS COMPUTER.
JESSICA... THIS VIDEO YOU FOUND VIA A BLOG YOU DON'T ACTUALLY READ MAY PROVE TO BE QUITE USEFUL.
YELLOW LIGHT? FEAR? BUT THAT'S--
SINESTRO CORPS! SON OF A...HOW DID YOU KNOW?!
LET'S MOVE.
IT COULDN'T BE SINESTRO CORPS. BUT HE TOTALLY NAILED IT. HOW?!
HE'S THE DETECTIVE AROUND HERE.
WE ARE IN OVER OUR HEADS.

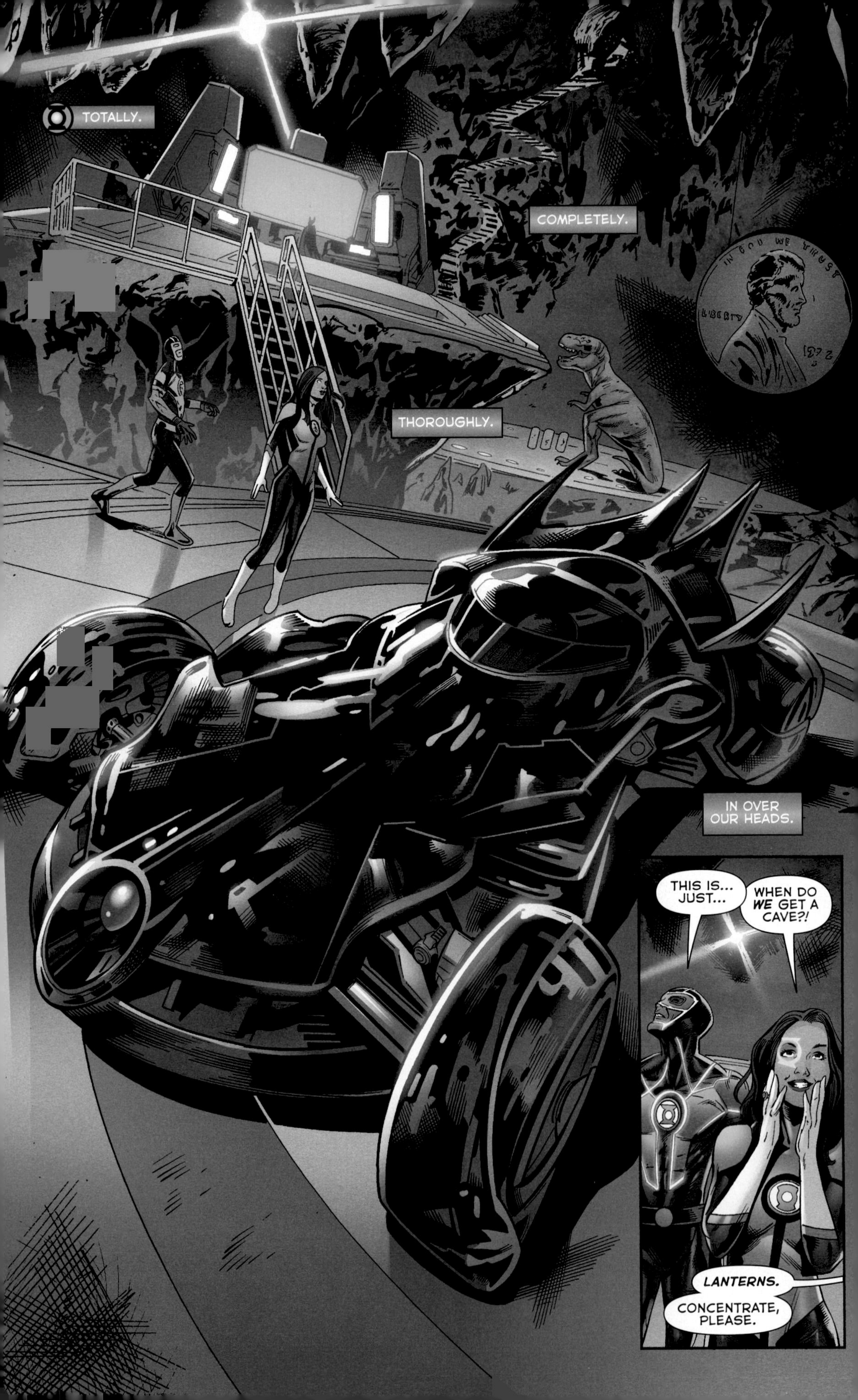
TOTALLY.
COMPLETELY.
THOROUGHLY.
IN OVER OUR HEADS.
THIS IS... JUST...
WHEN DO *WE* GET A CAVE?!
LANTERNS.
CONCENTRATE, PLEASE.

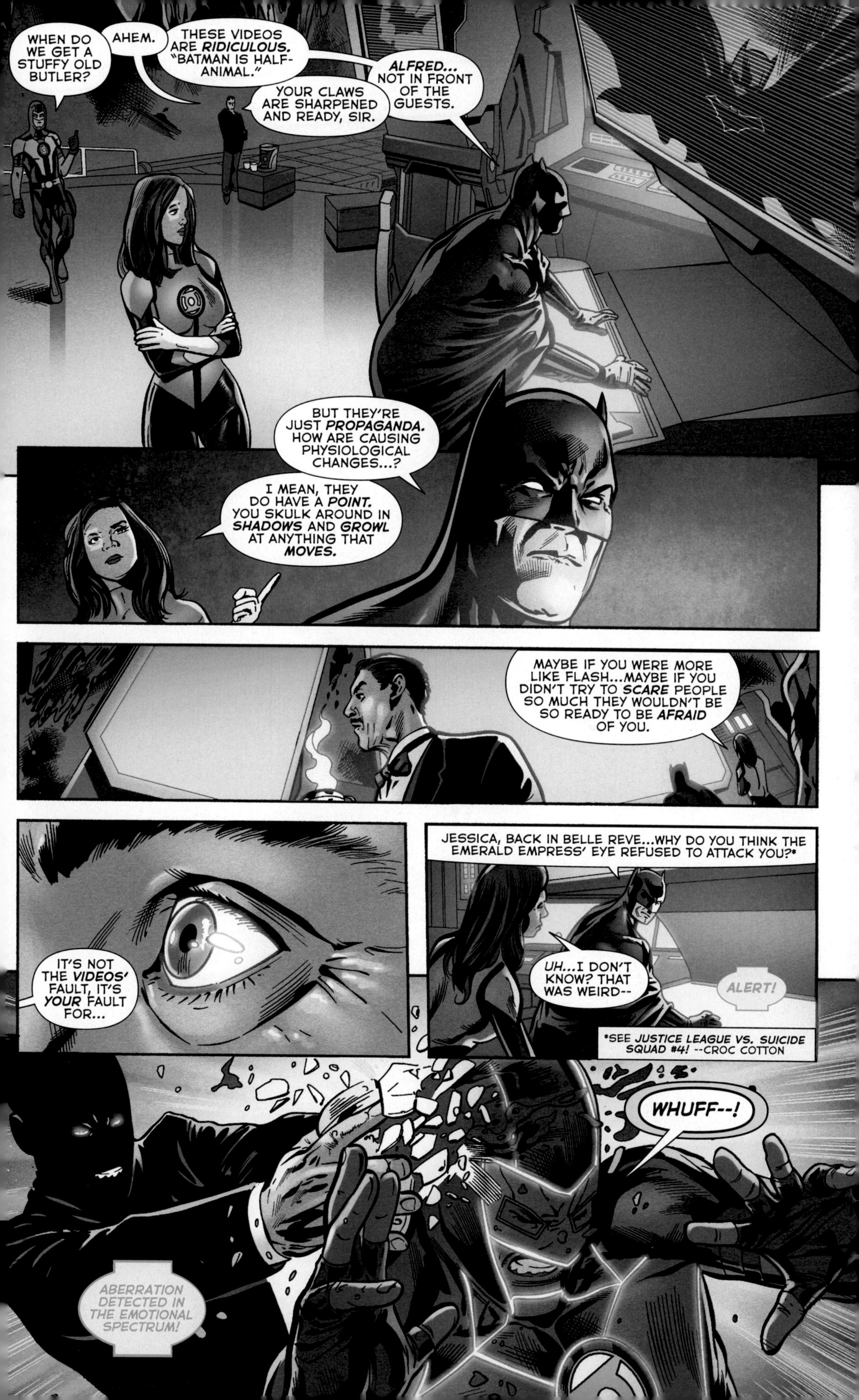

WHEN DO WE GET A STUFFY OLD BUTLER?
AHEM.
THESE VIDEOS ARE *RIDICULOUS.* "BATMAN IS HALF-ANIMAL."
YOUR CLAWS ARE SHARPENED AND READY, SIR.
ALFRED... NOT IN FRONT OF THE GUESTS.
BUT THEY'RE JUST *PROPAGANDA.* HOW ARE CAUSING PHYSIOLOGICAL CHANGES...?
I MEAN, THEY DO HAVE A *POINT.* YOU SKULK AROUND IN *SHADOWS* AND *GROWL* AT ANYTHING THAT *MOVES.*
MAYBE IF YOU WERE MORE LIKE FLASH...MAYBE IF YOU DIDN'T TRY TO *SCARE* PEOPLE SO MUCH THEY WOULDN'T BE SO READY TO BE *AFRAID* OF YOU.
IT'S NOT THE *VIDEOS'* FAULT, IT'S *YOUR* FAULT FOR...
JESSICA, BACK IN BELLE REVE...WHY DO YOU THINK THE EMERALD EMPRESS' EYE REFUSED TO ATTACK YOU?*
*UH...*I DON'T KNOW? THAT WAS WEIRD--
ALERT!
*SEE *JUSTICE LEAGUE VS. SUICIDE SQUAD #4!* --CROC COTTON
WHUFF--!
ABERRATION DETECTED IN THE EMOTIONAL SPECTRUM!

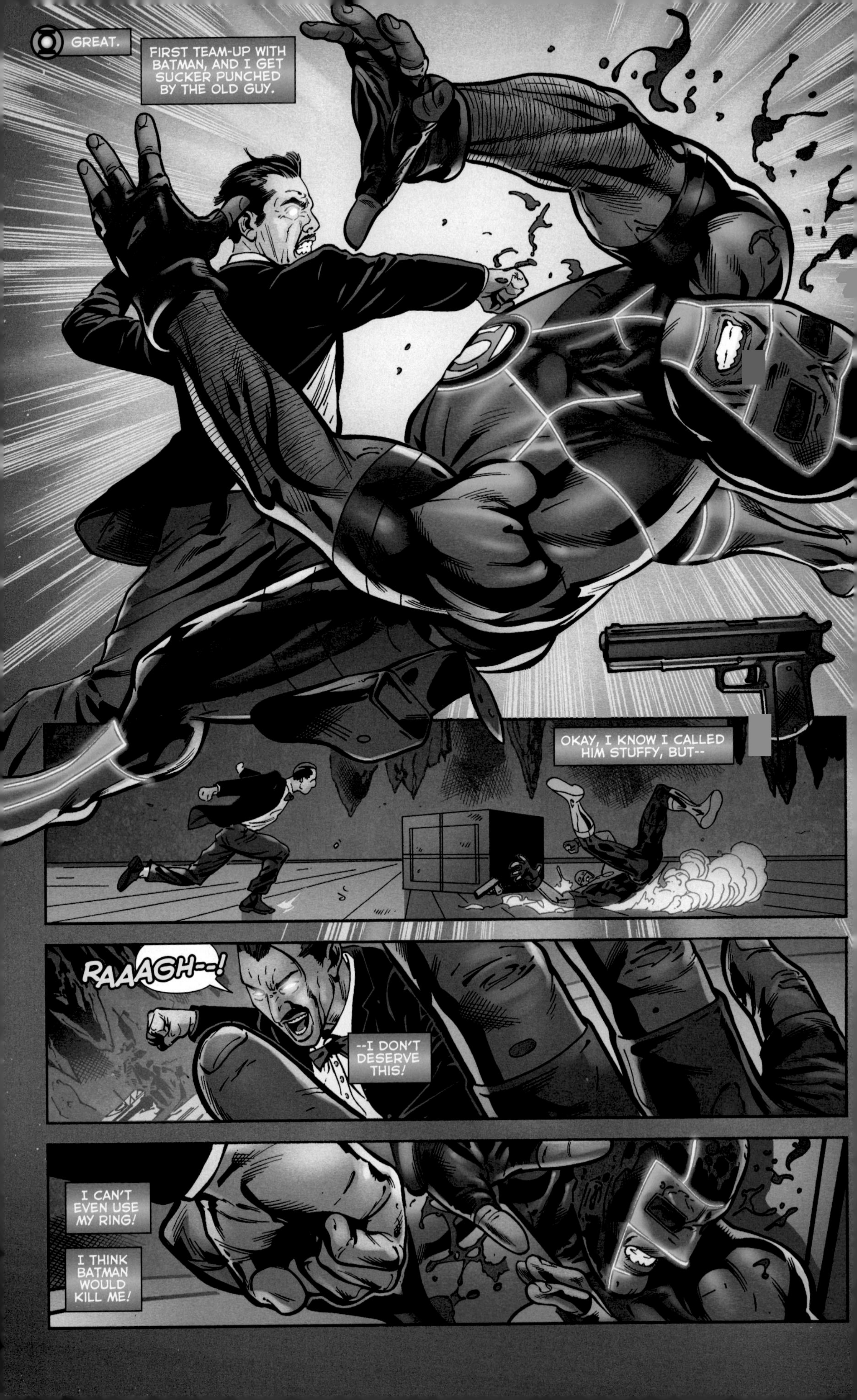
GREAT.
FIRST TEAM-UP WITH BATMAN, AND I GET SUCKER PUNCHED BY THE OLD GUY.
OKAY, I KNOW I CALLED HIM STUFFY, BUT--
RAAAGH--!
--I DON'T DESERVE THIS!
I CAN'T EVEN USE MY RING!
I THINK BATMAN WOULD KILL ME!

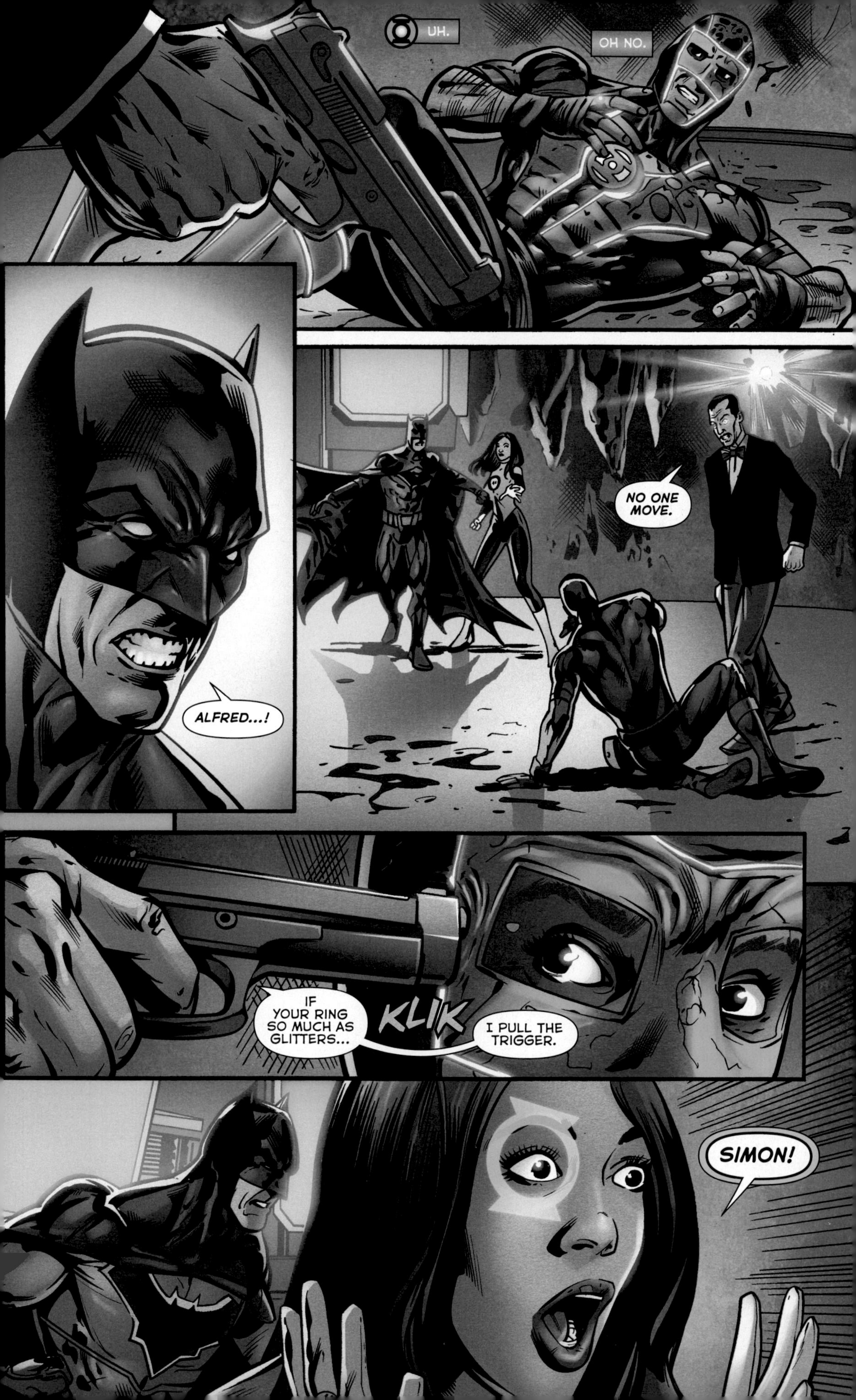

UH.
OH NO.
ALFRED...!
NO ONE MOVE.
IF YOUR RING SO MUCH AS GLITTERS...
KLIK
I PULL THE TRIGGER.
SIMON!

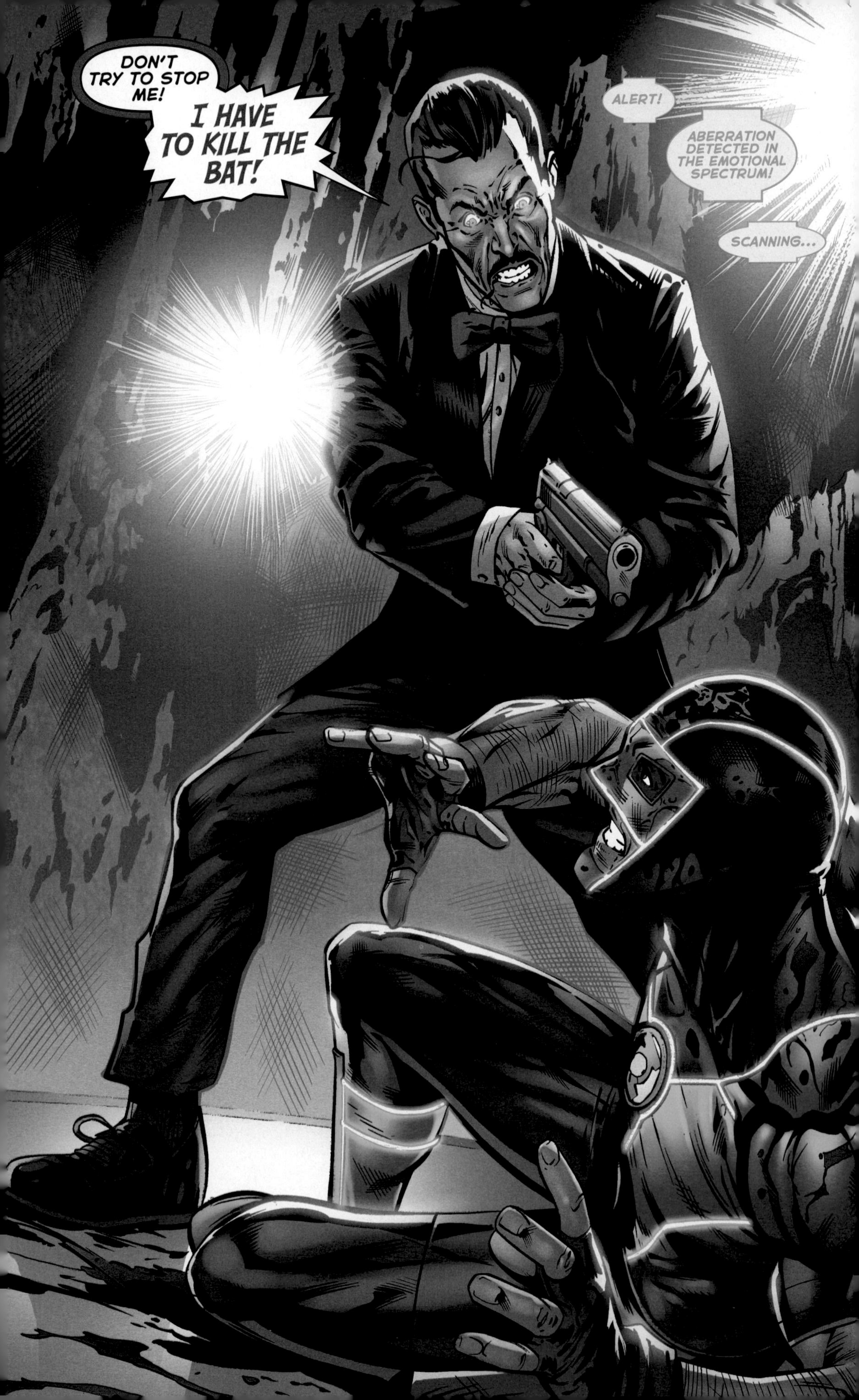
DON'T TRY TO STOP ME!
I HAVE TO KILL THE BAT!
ALERT!
ABERRATION DETECTED IN THE EMOTIONAL SPECTRUM!
SCANNING...

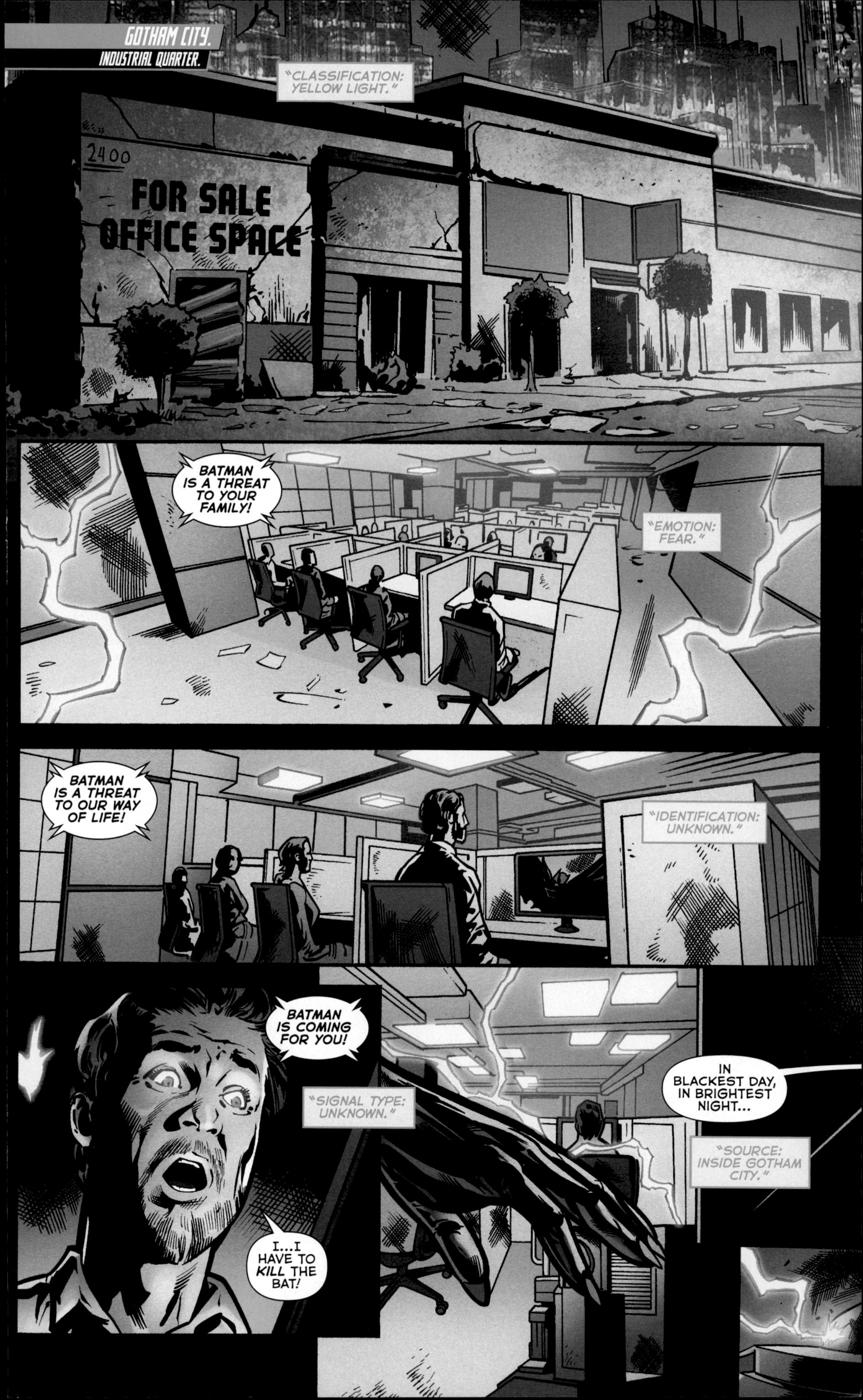
GOTHAM CITY.
INDUSTRIAL QUARTER.
"CLASSIFICATION: YELLOW LIGHT."
2400
FOR SALE OFFICE SPACE
BATMAN IS A THREAT TO YOUR FAMILY!
"EMOTION: FEAR."
BATMAN IS A THREAT TO OUR WAY OF LIFE!
"IDENTIFICATION: UNKNOWN."
BATMAN IS COMING FOR YOU!
"SIGNAL TYPE: UNKNOWN."
IN BLACKEST DAY, IN BRIGHTEST NIGHT...
"SOURCE: INSIDE GOTHAM CITY."
I...I HAVE TO KILL THE BAT!

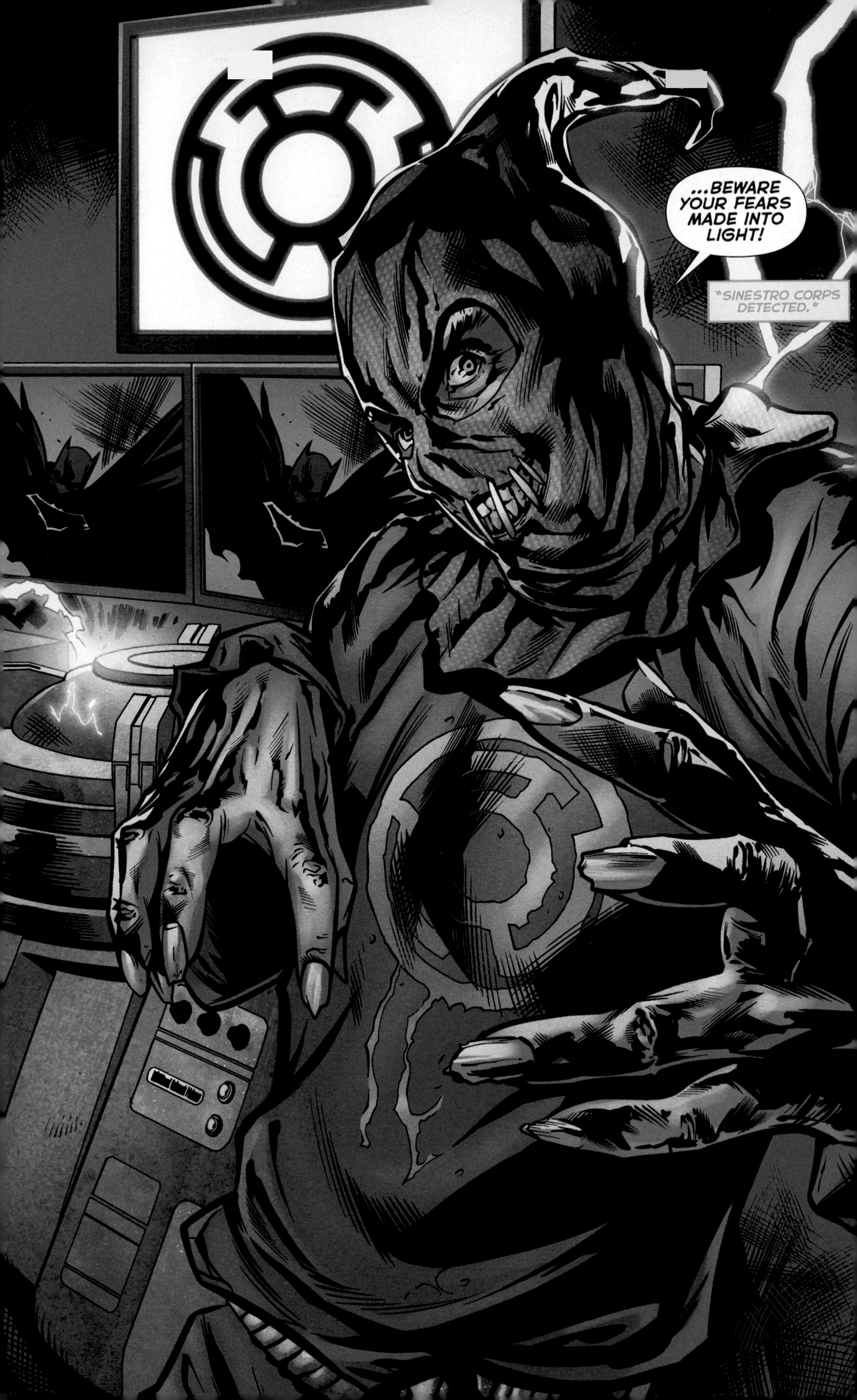
...BEWARE YOUR FEARS MADE INTO LIGHT!
"SINESTRO CORPS DETECTED."

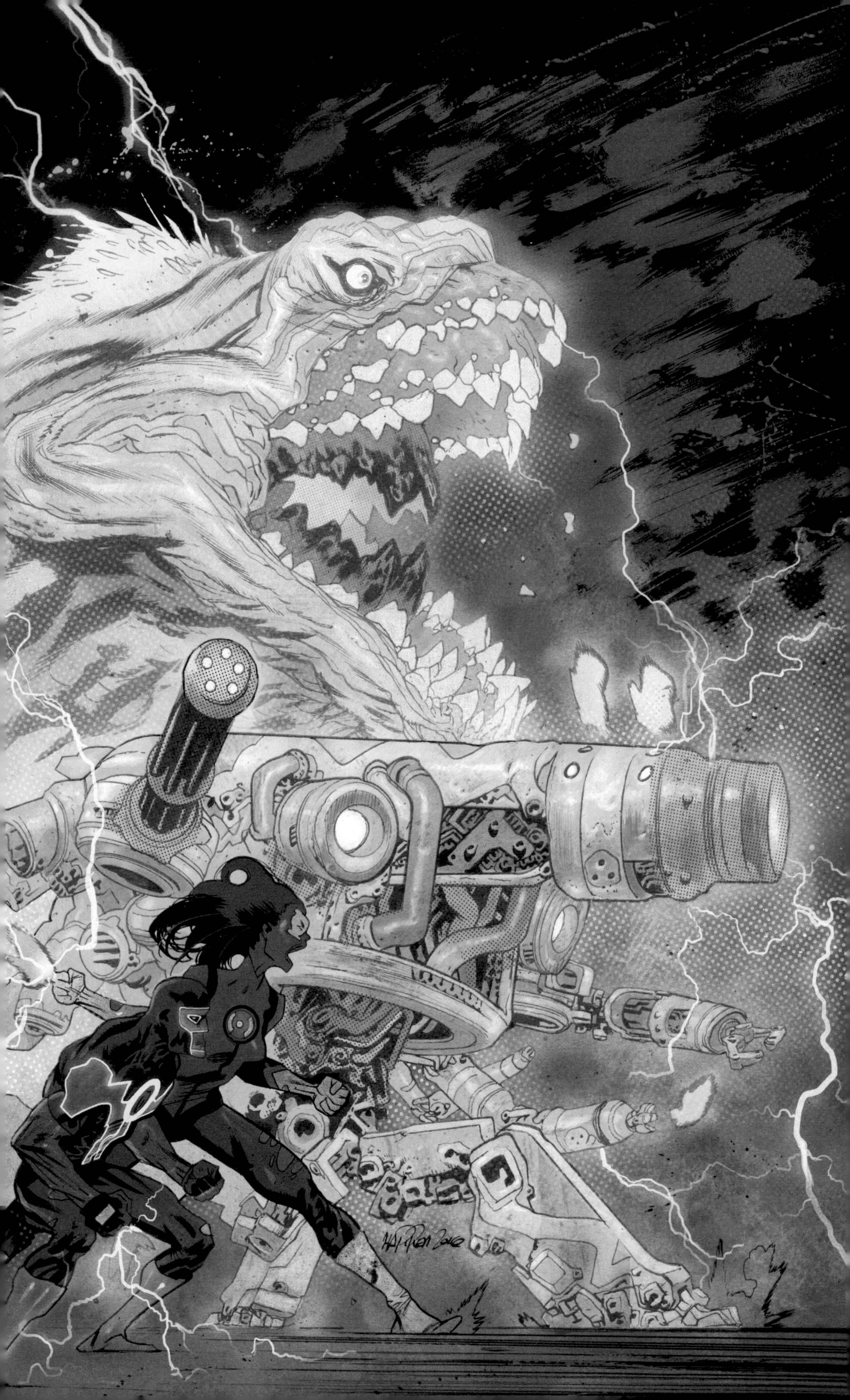

"DARKEST KNIGHTS PART 2"

EDUARDO PANSICA penciller * JULIO FERREIRA inker

Cover by JAMES HARREN

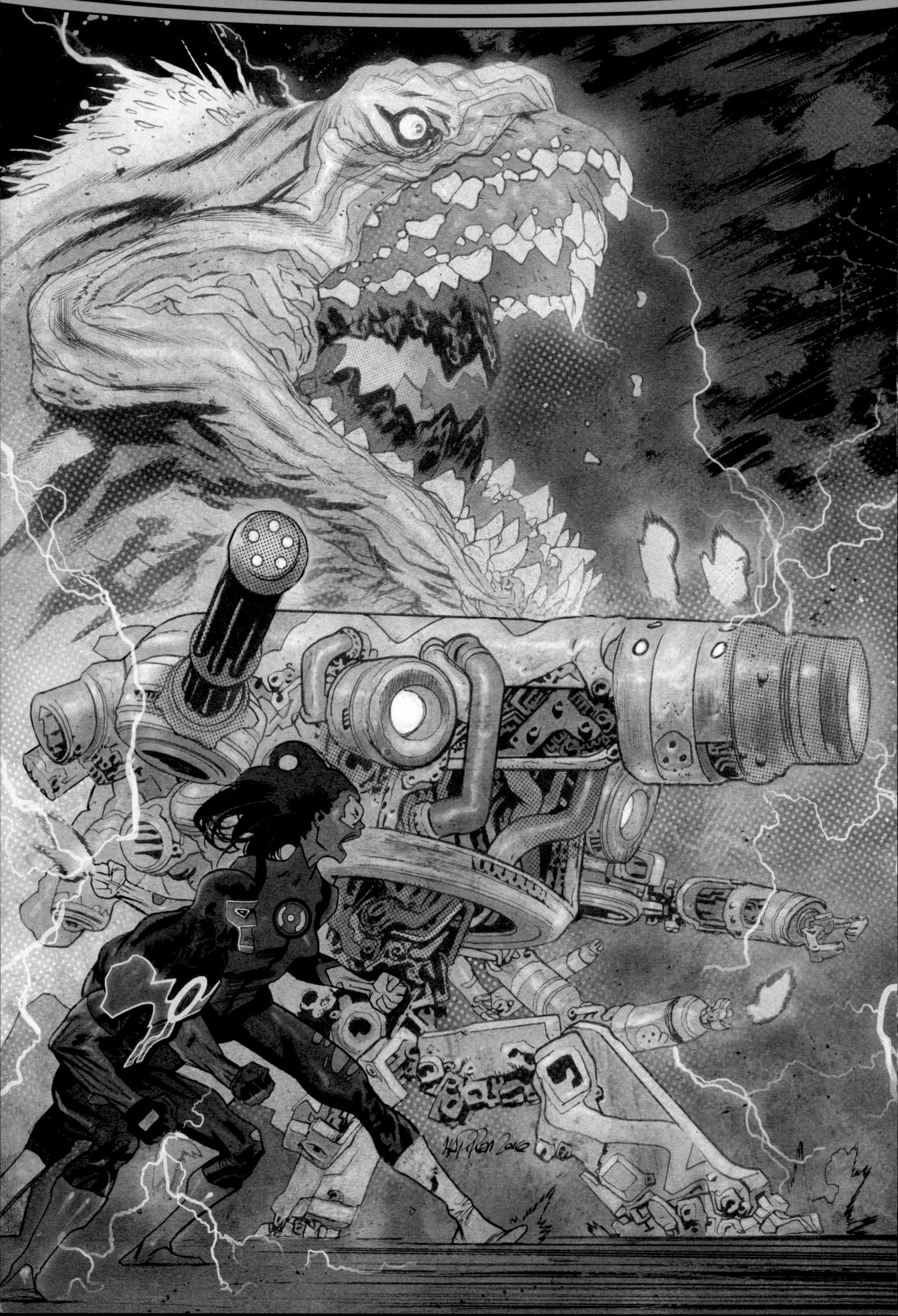

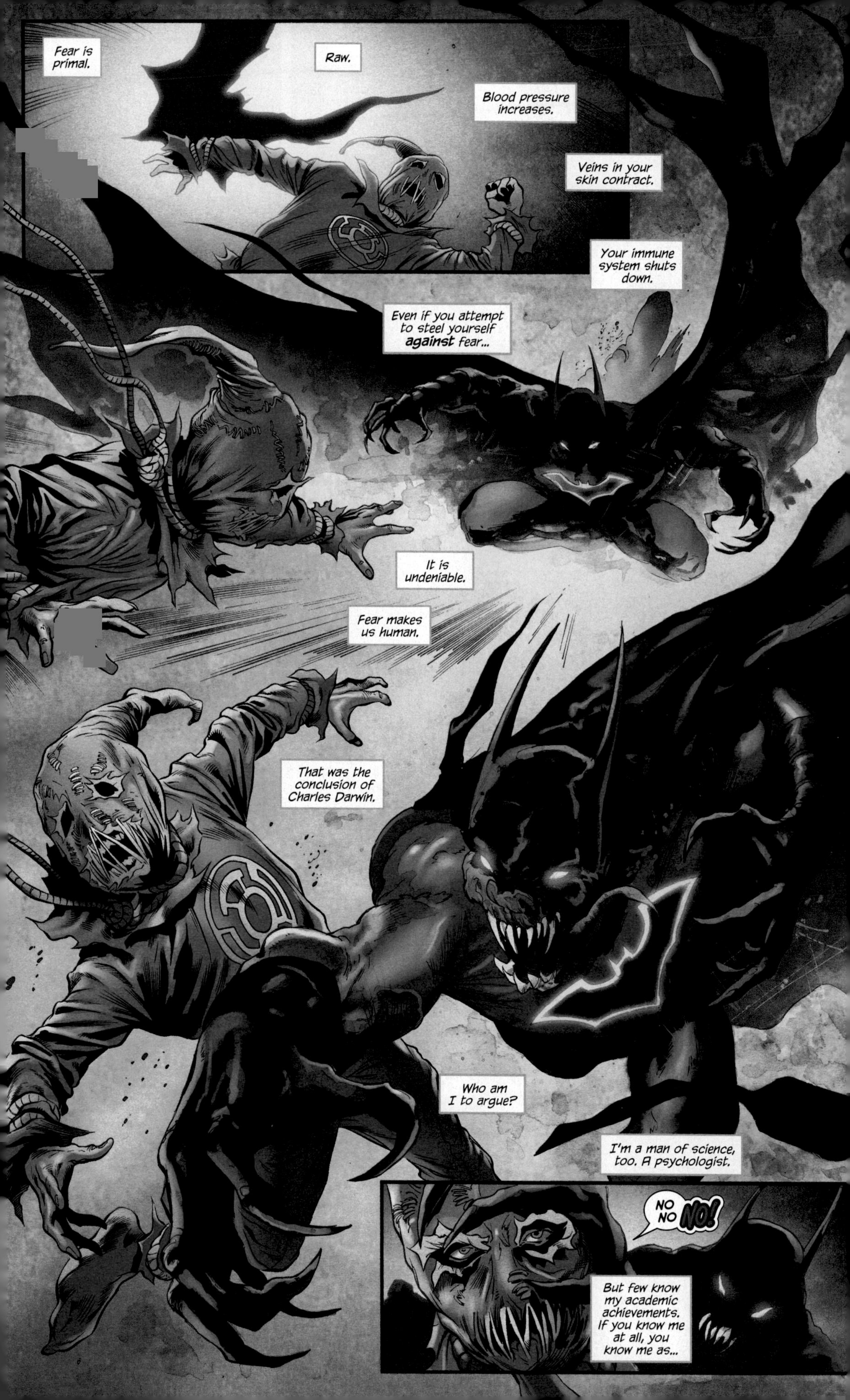

Fear is primal.
Raw.
Blood pressure increases.
Veins in your skin contract.
Your immune system shuts down.
Even if you attempt to steel yourself **against** fear...
It is undeniable.
Fear makes us human.
That was the conclusion of Charles Darwin.
Who am I to argue?
I'm a man of science, too. A psychologist.
NO NO NO!
But few know my academic achievements. If you know me at all, you know me as...

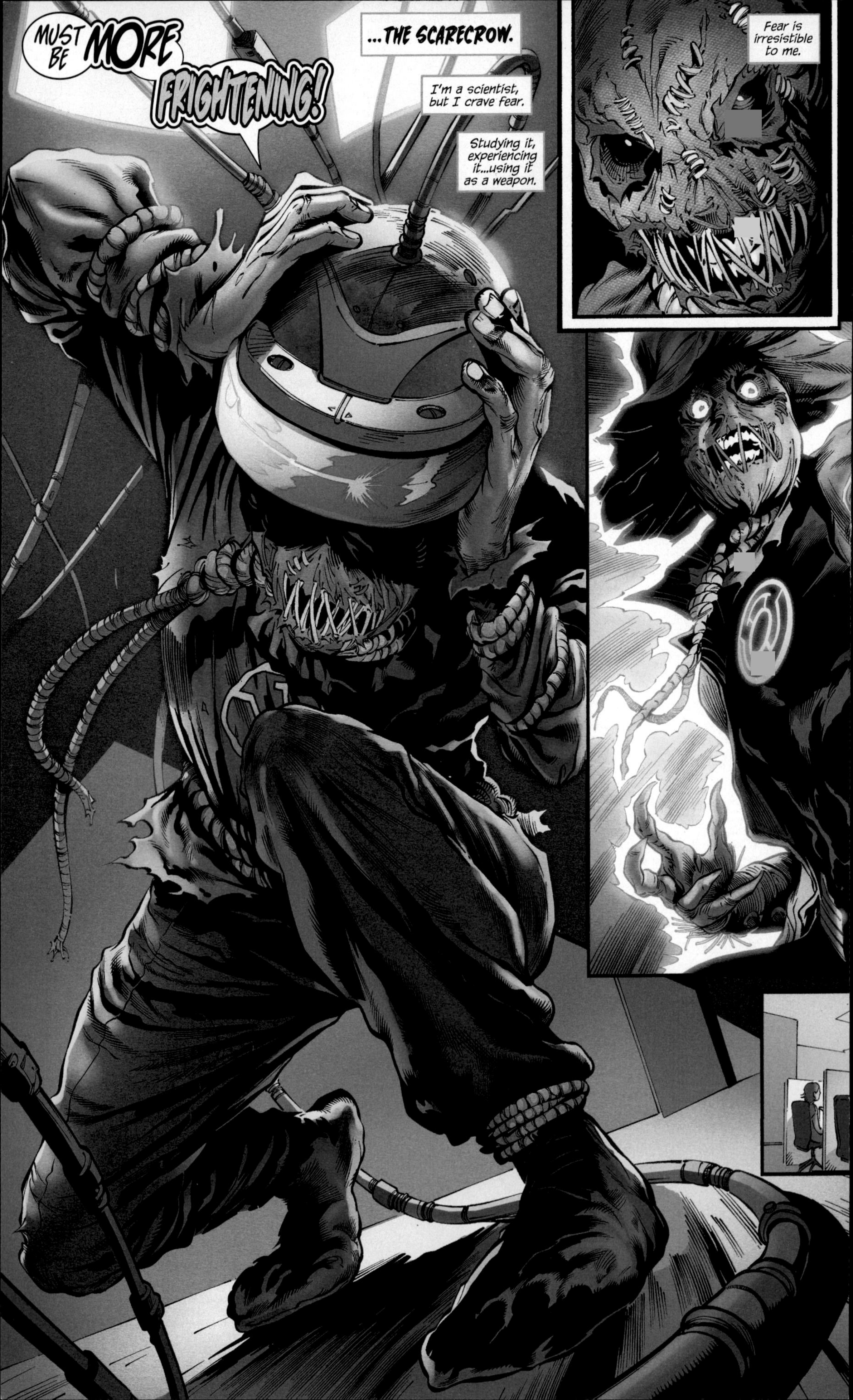

MUST BE MORE FRIGHTENING!
...THE SCARECROW.
I'm a scientist, but I crave fear.
Studying it, experiencing it...using it as a weapon.
Fear is irresistible to me.

CORTICOTROPIN
CORTICOTROPIN
EPINEPHRINE
EPINEPHRINE
It is my drink. My romance. My gambling.
But then I overdosed. Burned out.
I couldn't feel it anymore.
I became a shell. A shadow of a human.
No relief from the pain of being fearless.
Until the ring came for me.
Can you imagine what that was like? A weapon powered by terror!
I wasn't just feeling fear... I was wielding it.
So I stole a moment to study it. To learn as much as possible.
It was endlessly complex. A combination of emotion and light.
Its full potential was beyond me. But I learned enough. And when the ring left me a second time...
I was prepared. I was like the caveman who found the burning branch. It ignited the fire within me.
After weeks of experiments... I can use it to scare them.
But it isn't enough. Not for me to feel fear again.
I must try again... I must keep trying.
YAAAAAGH!
AAAAUGH!
Until I perfect it.
Until I am whole again.
Until I am consumed by FEAR.

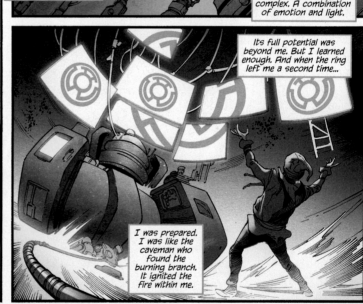

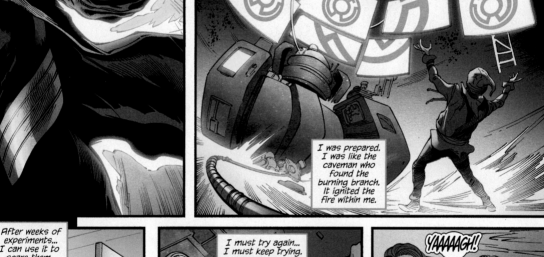

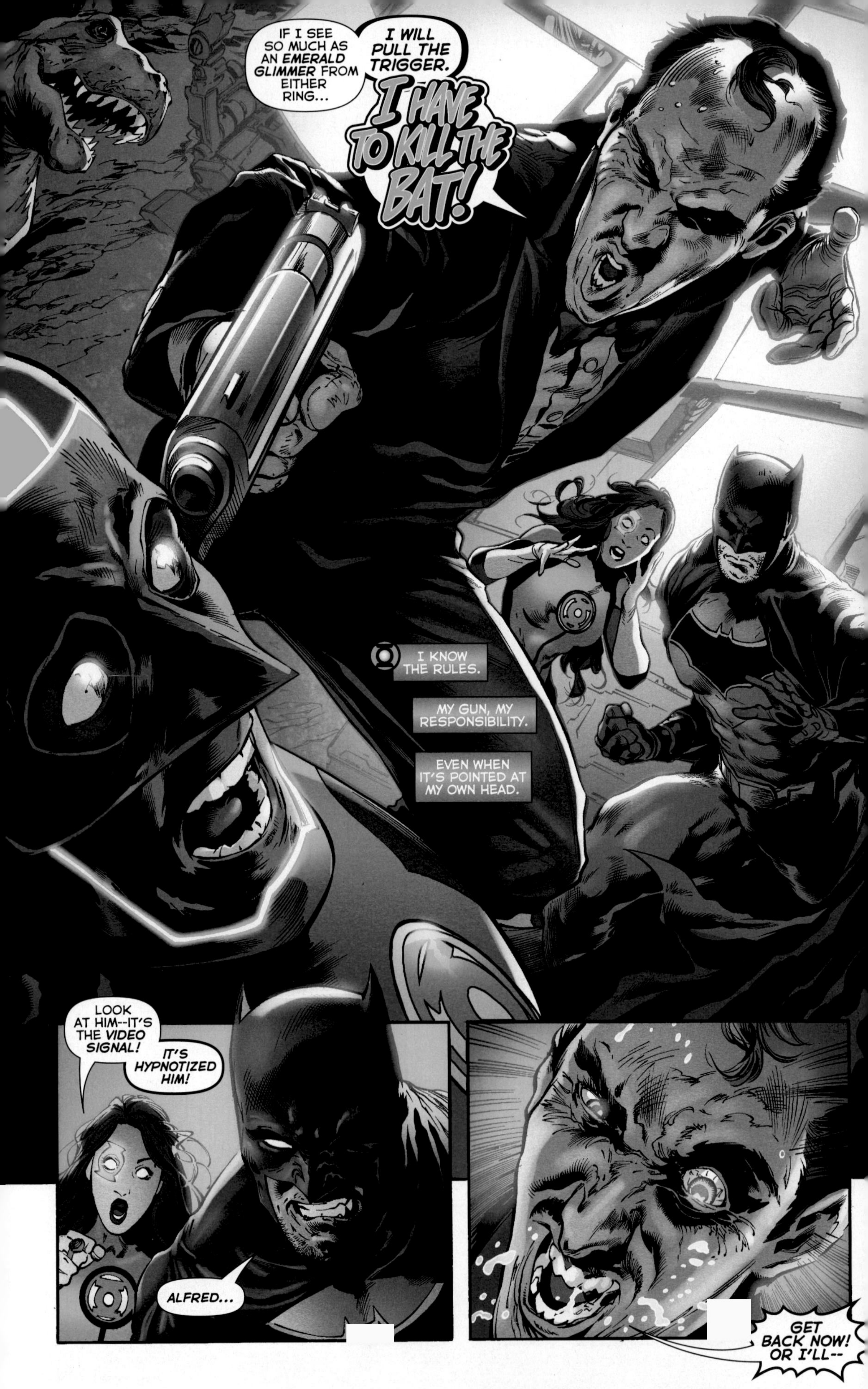
IF I SEE SO MUCH AS AN EMERALD GLIMMER FROM EITHER RING...
I WILL PULL THE TRIGGER.
I HAVE TO KILL THE BAT!
I KNOW THE RULES.
MY GUN, MY RESPONSIBILITY.
EVEN WHEN IT'S POINTED AT MY OWN HEAD.
LOOK AT HIM--IT'S THE VIDEO SIGNAL!
IT'S HYPNOTIZED HIM!
ALFRED...
GET BACK NOW! OR I'LL--

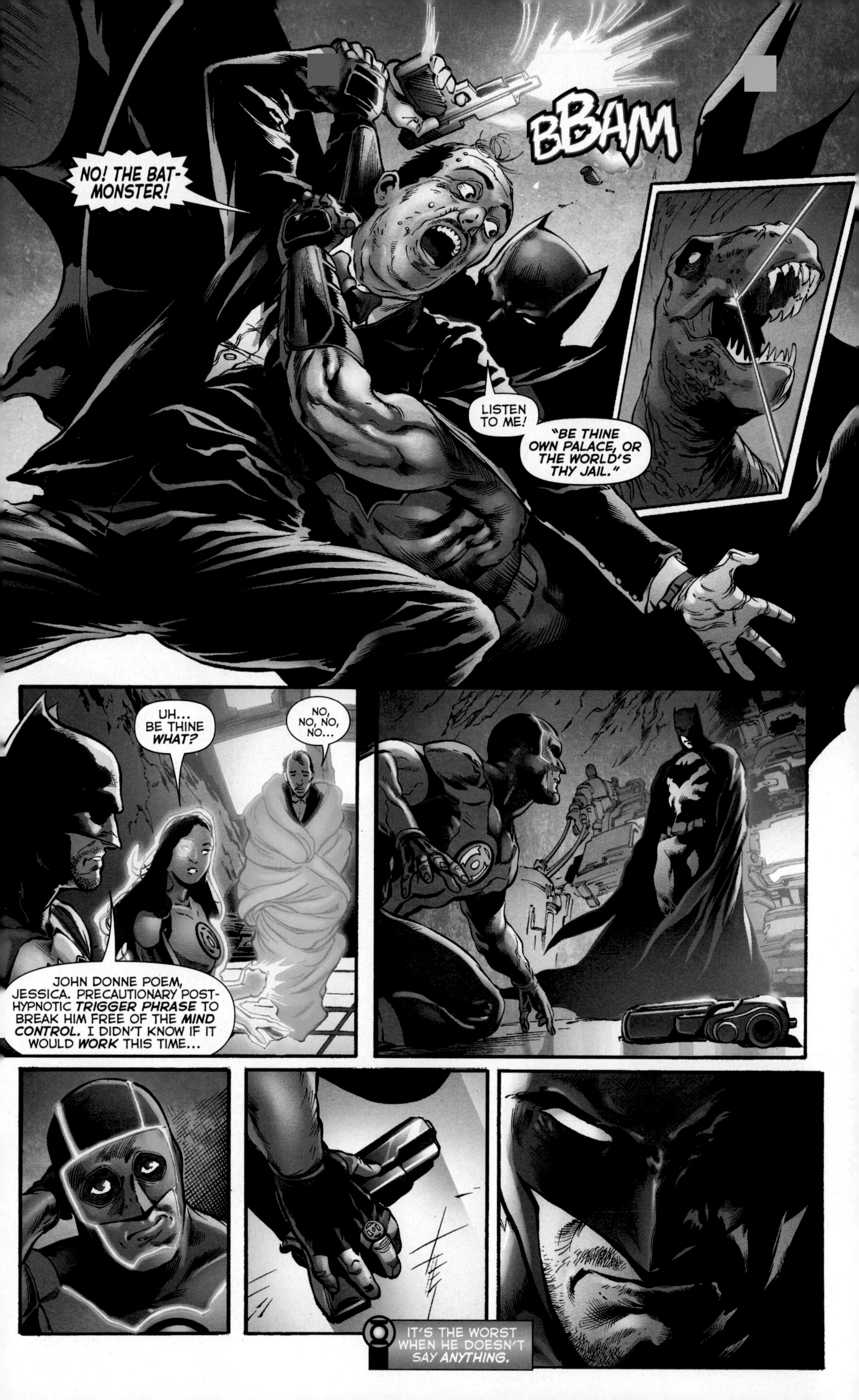
BBAM
NO! THE BAT-MONSTER!
LISTEN TO ME!
"BE THINE OWN PALACE, OR THE WORLD'S THY JAIL."
UH... BE THINE WHAT?
NO, NO, NO, NO...
JOHN DONNE POEM, JESSICA. PRECAUTIONARY POST-HYPNOTIC TRIGGER PHRASE TO BREAK HIM FREE OF THE MIND CONTROL. I DIDN'T KNOW IF IT WOULD WORK THIS TIME...
IT'S THE WORST WHEN HE DOESN'T SAY ANYTHING.

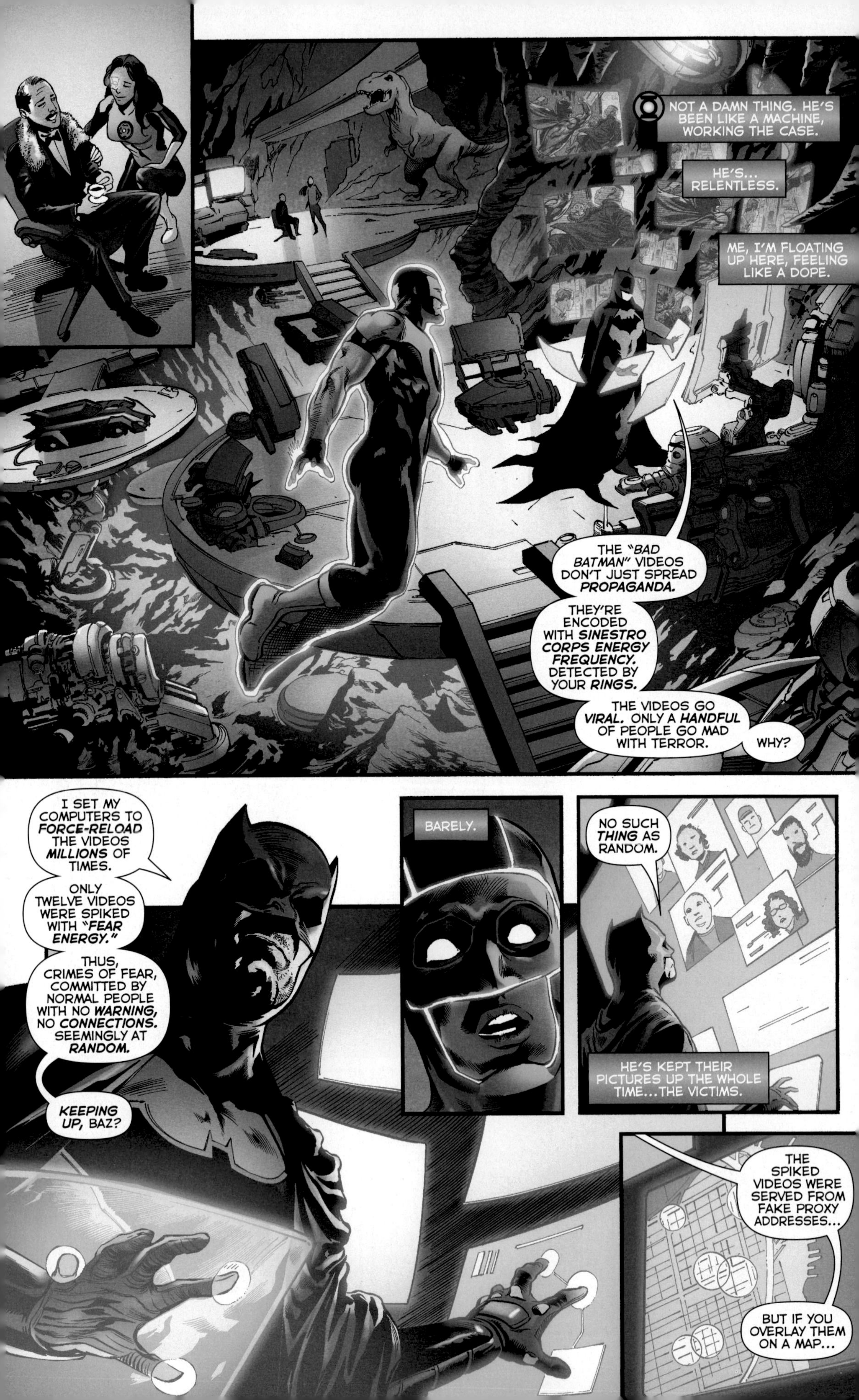
NOT A DAMN THING. HE'S BEEN LIKE A MACHINE, WORKING THE CASE.
HE'S... RELENTLESS.
ME, I'M FLOATING UP HERE, FEELING LIKE A DOPE.
THE "BAD BATMAN" VIDEOS DON'T JUST SPREAD PROPAGANDA.
THEY'RE ENCODED WITH SINESTRO CORPS ENERGY FREQUENCY. DETECTED BY YOUR RINGS.
THE VIDEOS GO VIRAL. ONLY A HANDFUL OF PEOPLE GO MAD WITH TERROR.
WHY?
I SET MY COMPUTERS TO FORCE-RELOAD THE VIDEOS MILLIONS OF TIMES.
ONLY TWELVE VIDEOS WERE SPIKED WITH "FEAR ENERGY."
THUS, CRIMES OF FEAR, COMMITTED BY NORMAL PEOPLE WITH NO WARNING, NO CONNECTIONS. SEEMINGLY AT RANDOM.
KEEPING UP, BAZ?
BARELY.
NO SUCH THING AS RANDOM.
HE'S KEPT THEIR PICTURES UP THE WHOLE TIME...THE VICTIMS.
THE SPIKED VIDEOS WERE SERVED FROM FAKE PROXY ADDRESSES...
BUT IF YOU OVERLAY THEM ON A MAP...

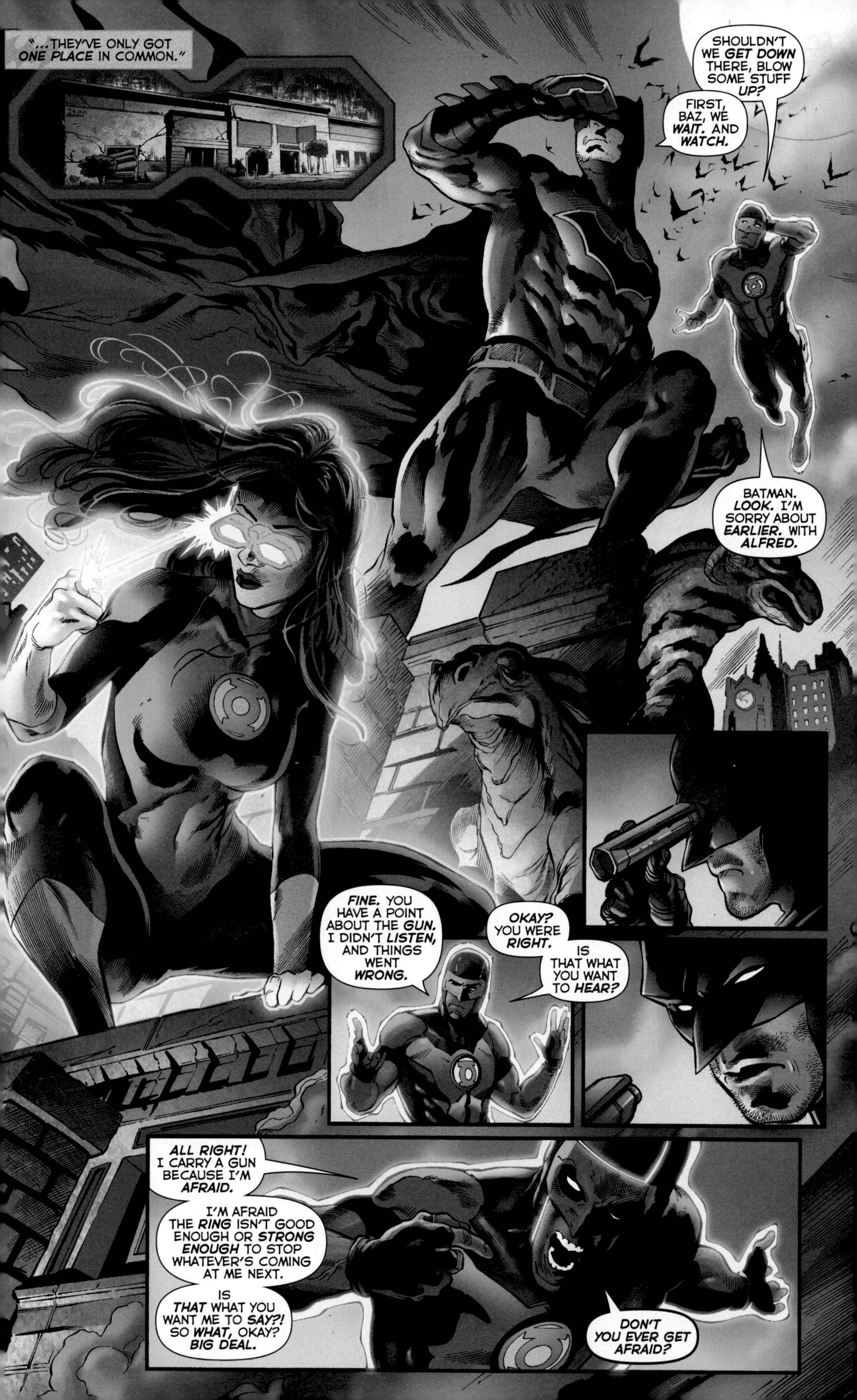
"...THEY'VE ONLY GOT ONE PLACE IN COMMON."
2400
SHOULDN'T WE GET DOWN THERE, BLOW SOME STUFF UP?
FIRST, BAZ, WE WAIT. AND WATCH.
BATMAN. LOOK. I'M SORRY ABOUT EARLIER. WITH ALFRED.
FINE. YOU HAVE A POINT ABOUT THE GUN. I DIDN'T LISTEN, AND THINGS WENT WRONG.
OKAY? YOU WERE RIGHT.
IS THAT WHAT YOU WANT TO HEAR?
ALL RIGHT! I CARRY A GUN BECAUSE I'M AFRAID.
I'M AFRAID THE RING ISN'T GOOD ENOUGH OR STRONG ENOUGH TO STOP WHATEVER'S COMING AT ME NEXT.
IS THAT WHAT YOU WANT ME TO SAY?! SO WHAT, OKAY? BIG DEAL.
DON'T YOU EVER GET AFRAID?

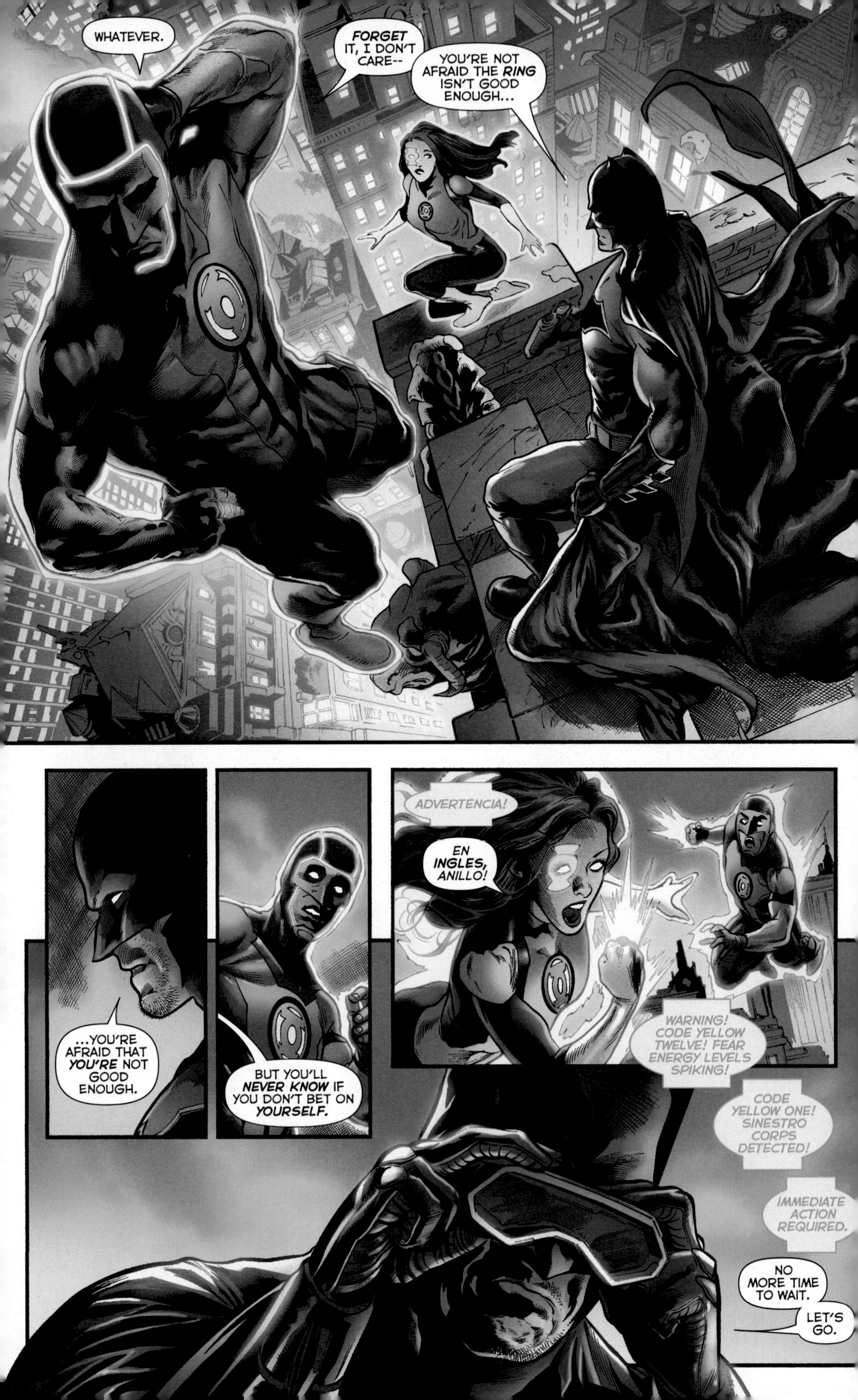
WHATEVER.
FORGET IT, I DON'T CARE--
YOU'RE NOT AFRAID THE RING ISN'T GOOD ENOUGH...
...YOU'RE AFRAID THAT YOU'RE NOT GOOD ENOUGH.
BUT YOU'LL NEVER KNOW IF YOU DON'T BET ON YOURSELF.
ADVERTENCIA!
EN INGLES, ANILLO!
WARNING! CODE YELLOW TWELVE! FEAR ENERGY LEVELS SPIKING!
CODE YELLOW ONE! SINESTRO CORPS DETECTED!
IMMEDIATE ACTION REQUIRED.
NO MORE TIME TO WAIT.
LET'S GO.

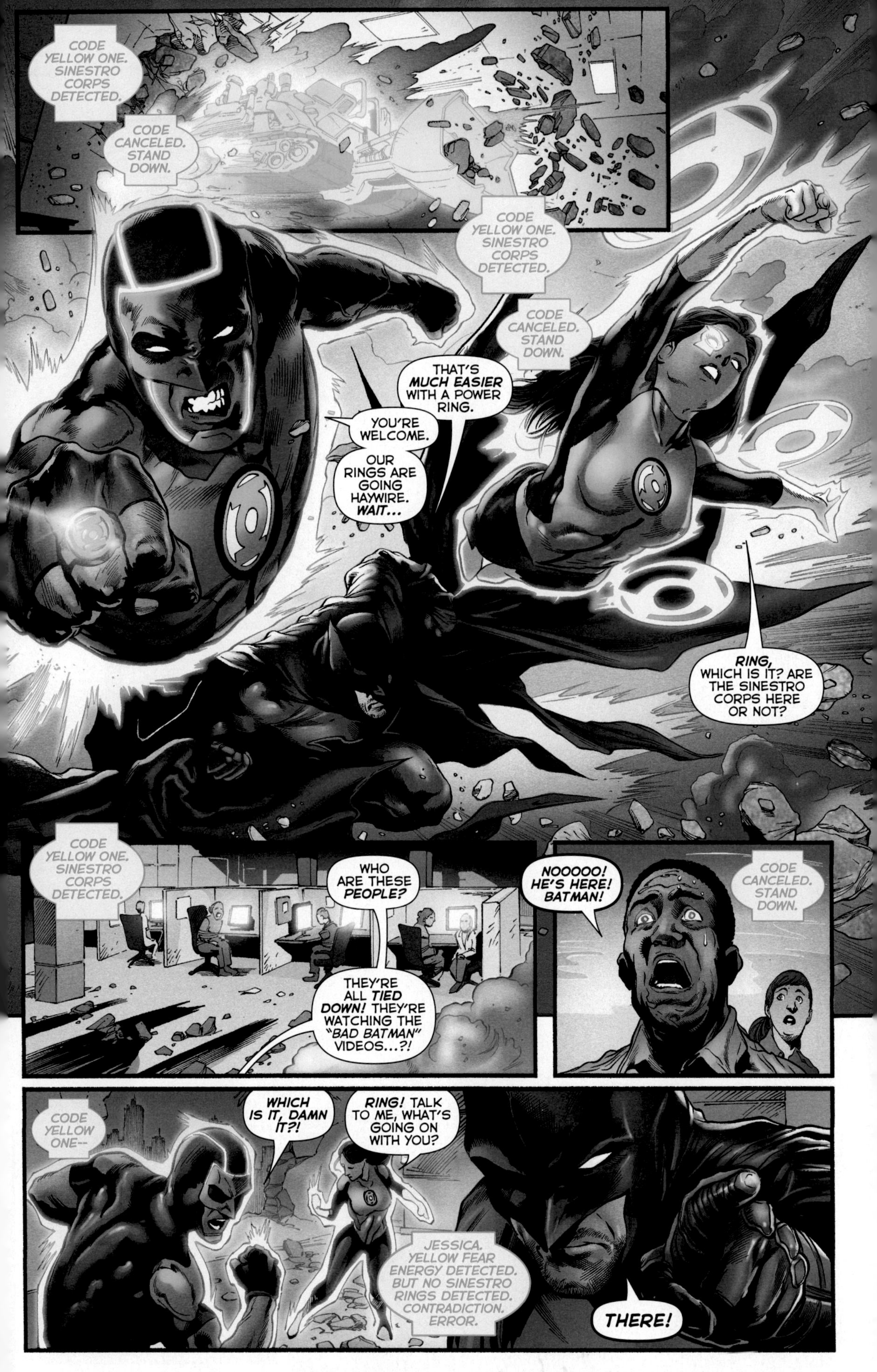
CODE YELLOW ONE. SINESTRO CORPS DETECTED.
CODE CANCELED. STAND DOWN.
CODE YELLOW ONE. SINESTRO CORPS DETECTED.
CODE CANCELED. STAND DOWN.
THAT'S MUCH EASIER WITH A POWER RING.
YOU'RE WELCOME.
OUR RINGS ARE GOING HAYWIRE. WAIT...
RING, WHICH IS IT? ARE THE SINESTRO CORPS HERE OR NOT?
CODE YELLOW ONE. SINESTRO CORPS DETECTED.
WHO ARE THESE PEOPLE?
THEY'RE ALL TIED DOWN! THEY'RE WATCHING THE "BAD BATMAN" VIDEOS...?!
NOOOOO! HE'S HERE! BATMAN!
CODE CANCELED. STAND DOWN.
CODE YELLOW ONE--
WHICH IS IT, DAMN IT?!
RING! TALK TO ME, WHAT'S GOING ON WITH YOU?
JESSICA. YELLOW FEAR ENERGY DETECTED. BUT NO SINESTRO RINGS DETECTED. CONTRADICTION. ERROR.
THERE!

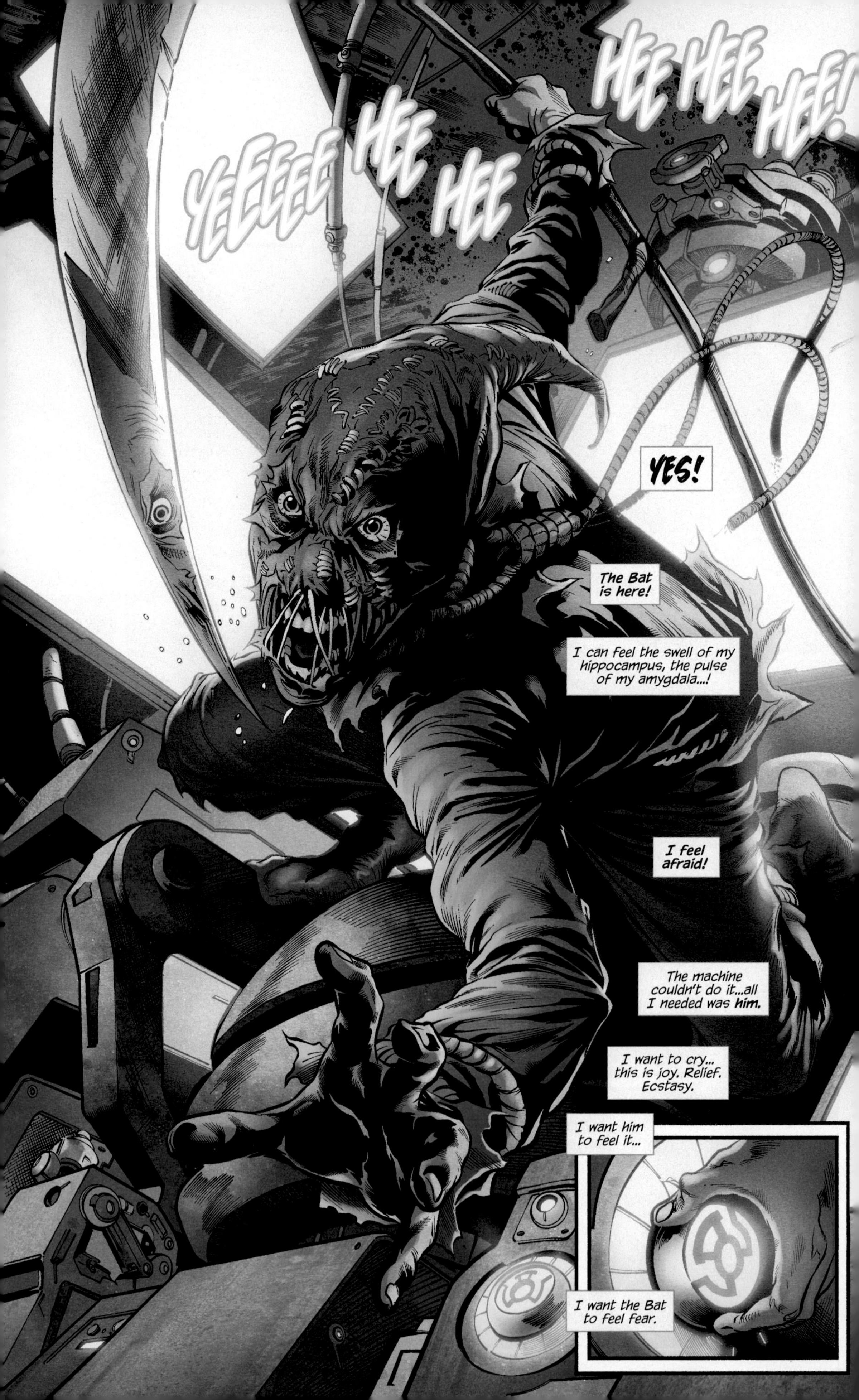
YEEEEEE HEE HEE
HEE HEE HEE!
YES!
The Bat is here!
I can feel the swell of my hippocampus, the pulse of my amygdala...!
I feel afraid!
The machine couldn't do it...all I needed was **him.**
I want to cry... this is joy. Relief. Ecstasy.
I want him to feel it...
I want the Bat to feel fear.

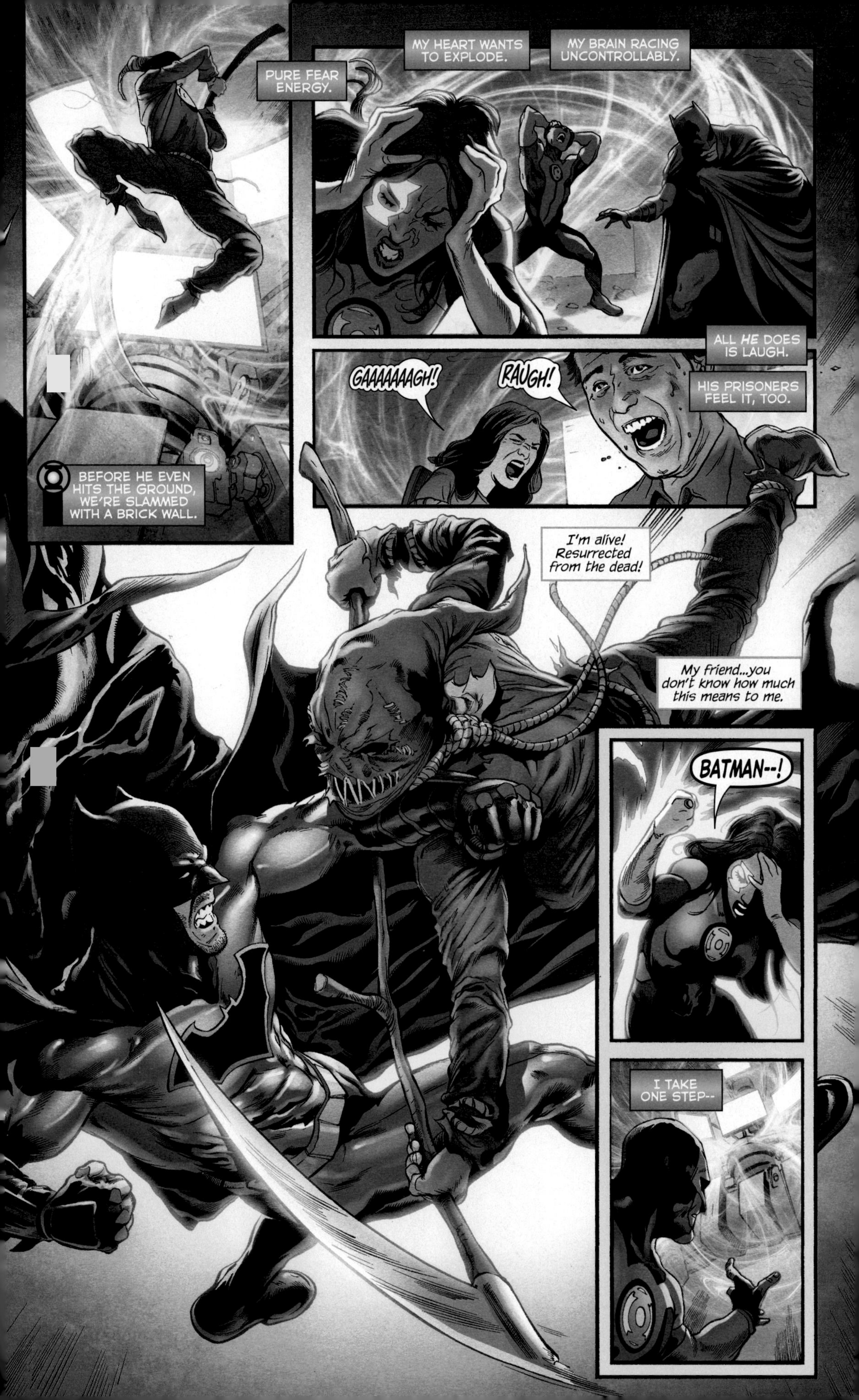
BEFORE HE EVEN HITS THE GROUND, WE'RE SLAMMED WITH A BRICK WALL.
PURE FEAR ENERGY.
MY HEART WANTS TO EXPLODE.
MY BRAIN RACING UNCONTROLLABLY.
ALL HE DOES IS LAUGH.
HIS PRISONERS FEEL IT, TOO.
GAAAAAAAGH!
RAUGH!
I'm alive! Resurrected from the dead!
My friend...you don't know how much this means to me.
BATMAN--!
I TAKE ONE STEP--

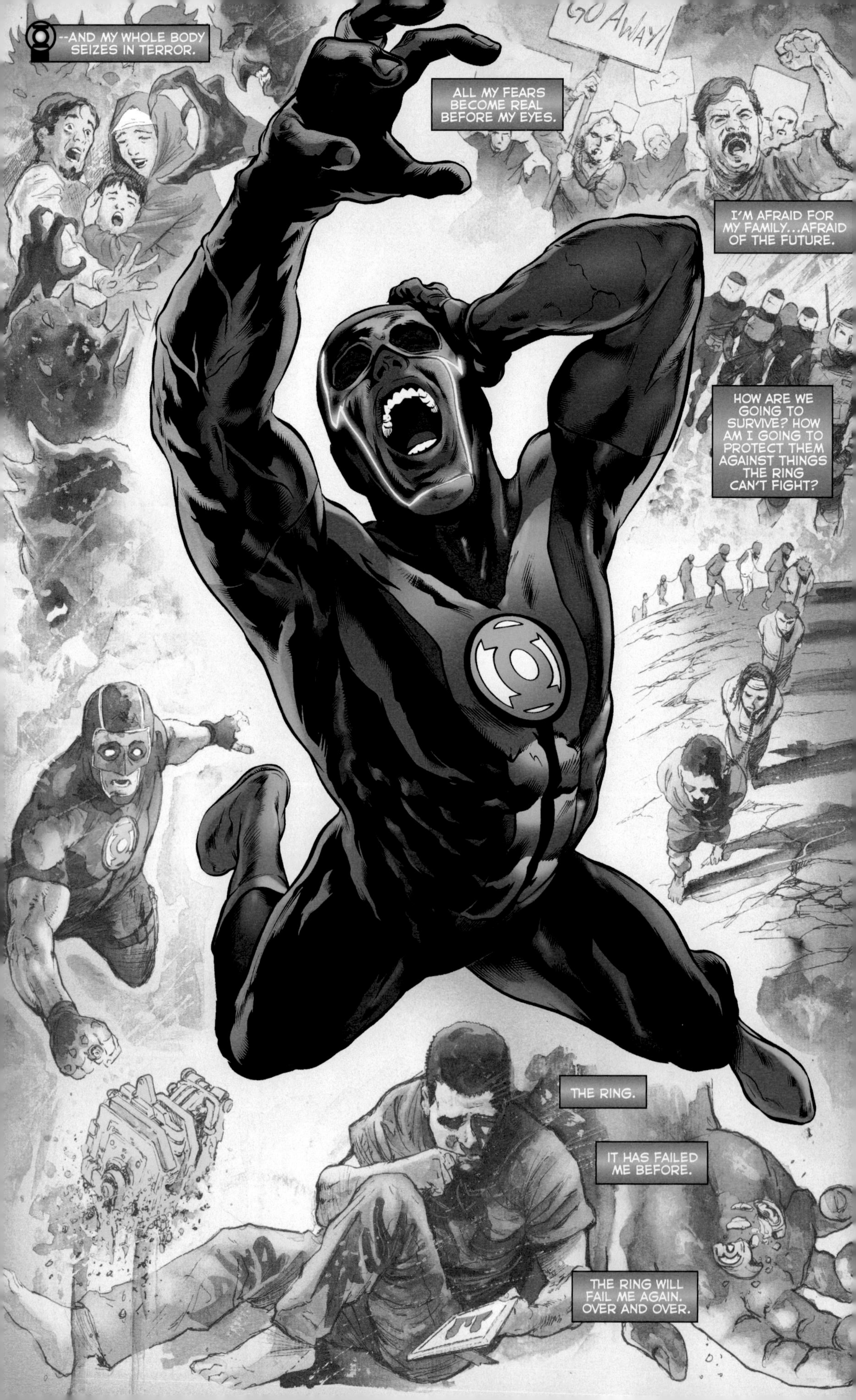
--AND MY WHOLE BODY SEIZES IN TERROR.
GO AWAY!
ALL MY FEARS BECOME REAL BEFORE MY EYES.
I'M AFRAID FOR MY FAMILY...AFRAID OF THE FUTURE.
HOW ARE WE GOING TO SURVIVE? HOW AM I GOING TO PROTECT THEM AGAINST THINGS THE RING CAN'T FIGHT?
THE RING.
IT HAS FAILED ME BEFORE.
THE RING WILL FAIL ME AGAIN. OVER AND OVER.

INSUFFICIENT WILLPOWER.
IT'S FAILING ME NOW.
IN THE FACE OF FEAR...
THE RING IS NOTHING.
WHAT IS HE DOING? HE'LL KILL US ALL!
USE THE RING, NOT THE GUN!
ONLY THE GUN CAN SAVE US NOW.
THE RING...IT'S ONLY AS POWERFUL AS ITS BEARER.
IT'S ONLY AS STRONG AS I MAKE IT.
AM I LISTENING TO MY FEAR?
THE RING WILL ONLY FAIL IF I FAIL.
I CANNOT LISTEN TO MY FEAR.

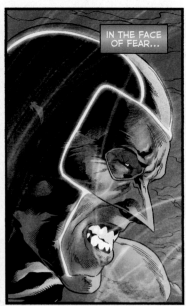

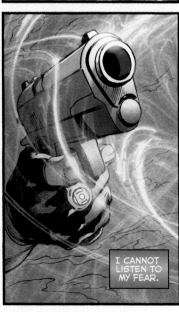

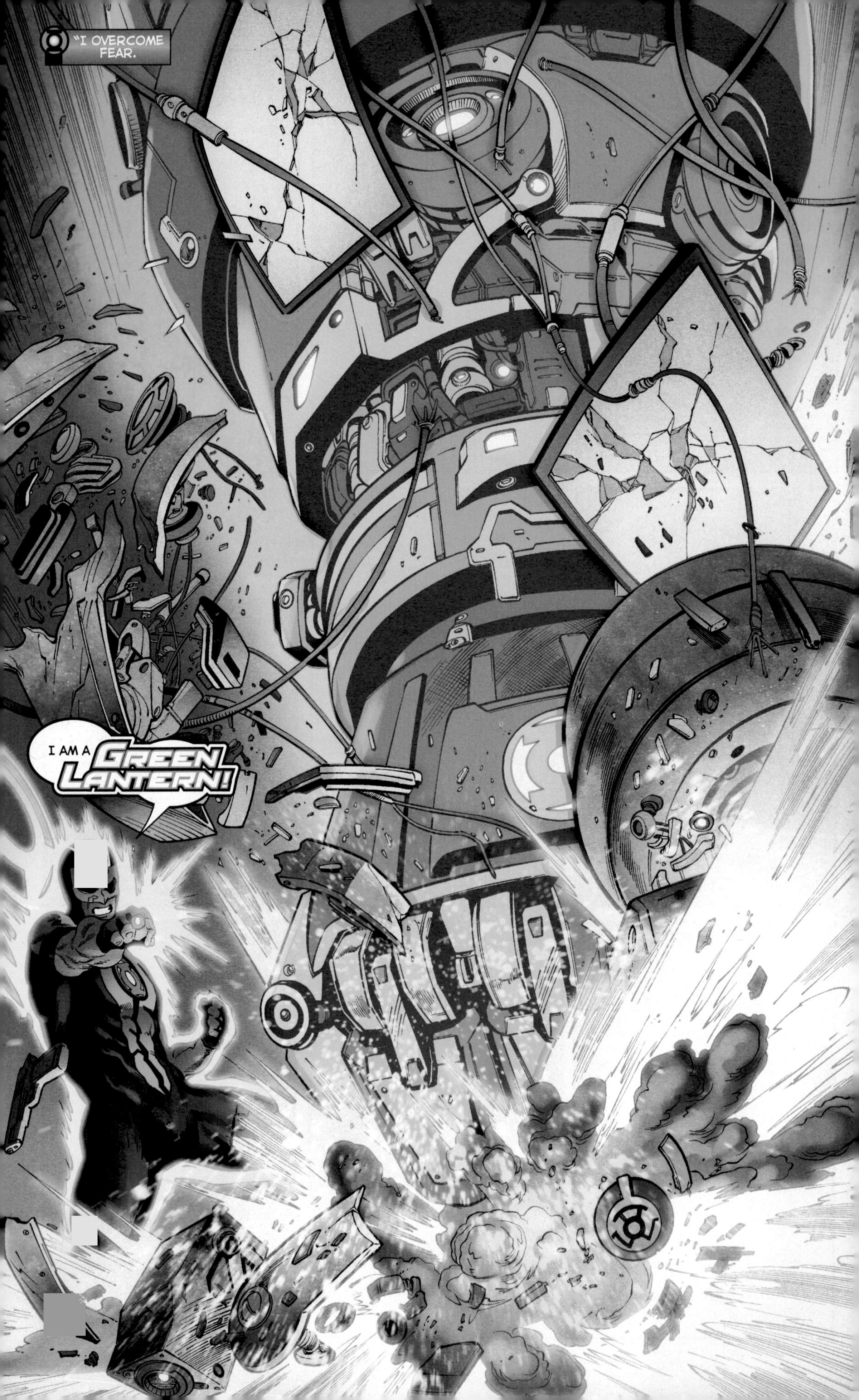
"I OVERCOME FEAR.
I AM A GREEN LANTERN!

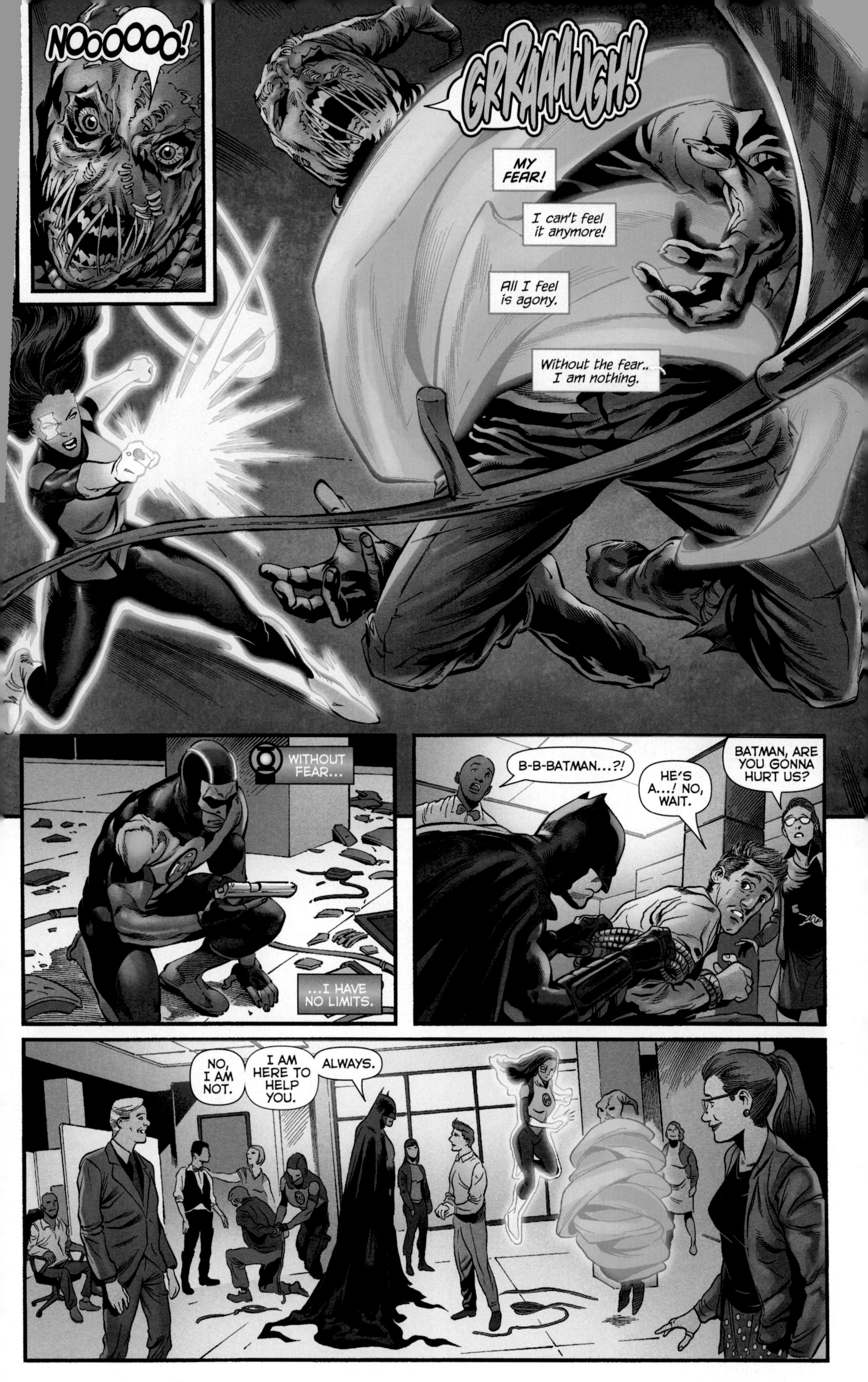
NOOOOOO!
GRRAAAUGH!
MY FEAR!
I can't feel it anymore!
All I feel is agony.
Without the fear.. I am nothing.
WITHOUT FEAR...
...I HAVE NO LIMITS.
B-B-BATMAN...?!
HE'S A...! NO, WAIT.
BATMAN, ARE YOU GONNA HURT US?
NO, I AM NOT.
I AM HERE TO HELP YOU.
ALWAYS.

STRAIGHT BACK TO ARKHAM?

DON'T ASK ME.

LANTERNS, GOTHAM *OFFICIALLY* THANKS *YOU* FOR YOUR *HELP.*

NOW GET THE HELL OUT OF MY CITY WITH THOSE WEIRD RINGS.

WHAT, NO KEY TO THE CITY?

WHO KNOWS HOW MANY *VICTIMS* GOT SCREWED UP BY THE SCARECROW...HE NEEDS TO BE LOCKED UP FOR A *LONG* TIME.

NO.

HE'S AN *ADDICT.* HE NEEDS *HELP...*

WHAT YOU SAID EARLIER, LANTERN...I'M NOT ALL ABOUT USING *FEAR* AS A WEAPON. I KNOW WHAT IT'S LIKE TO BE *AFRAID.*

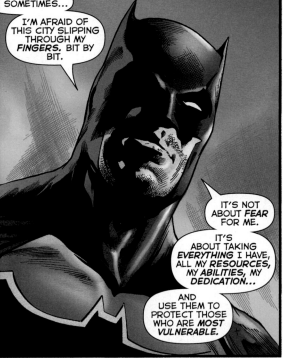

SOMETIMES...

I'M AFRAID OF THIS CITY SLIPPING THROUGH MY *FINGERS.* BIT BY BIT.

IT'S NOT ABOUT *FEAR* FOR ME.

IT'S ABOUT TAKING *EVERYTHING* I HAVE, ALL MY *RESOURCES,* MY *ABILITIES,* MY *DEDICATION...*

AND USE THEM TO PROTECT THOSE WHO ARE *MOST* VULNERABLE.

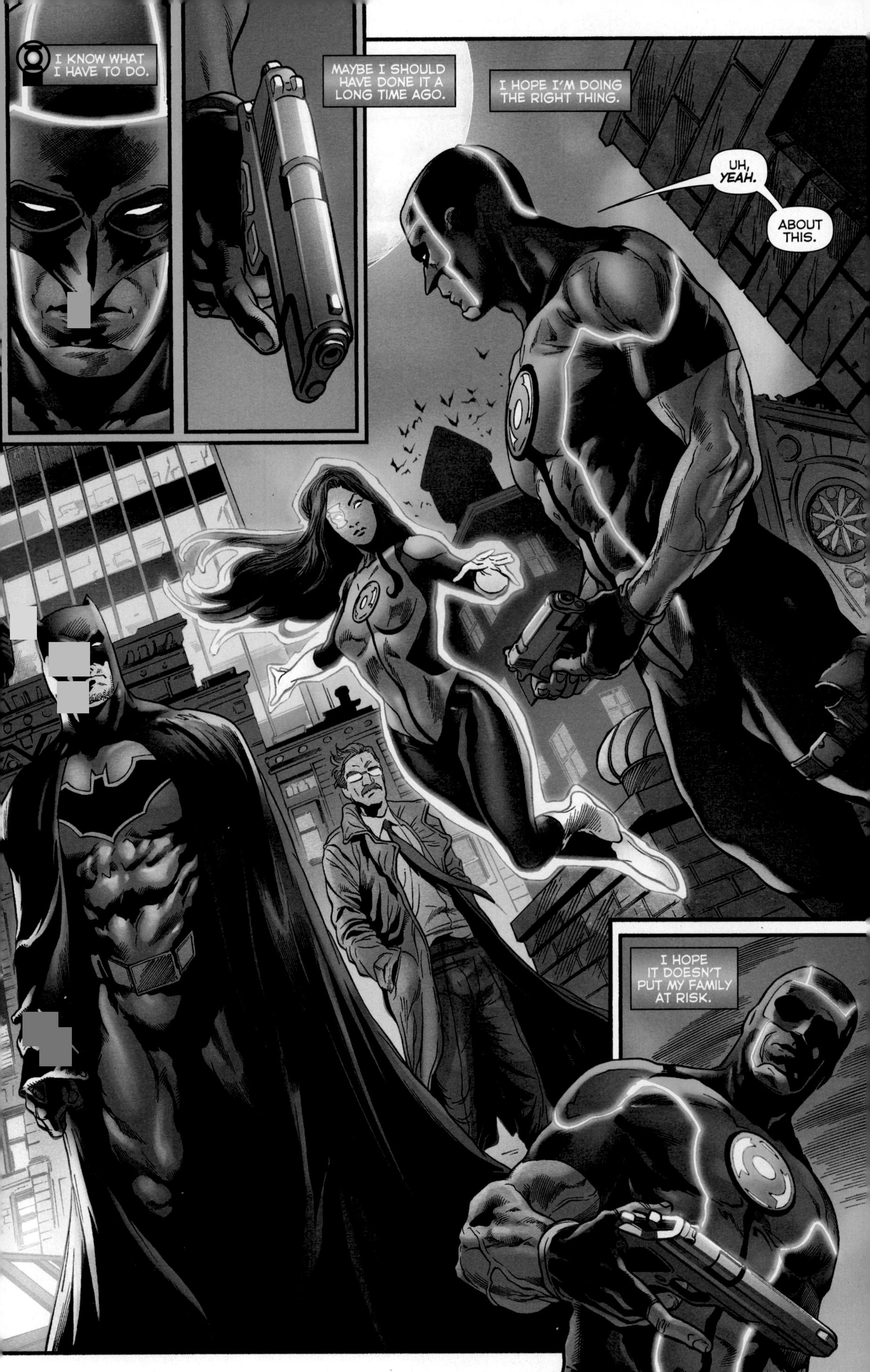
I KNOW WHAT I HAVE TO DO.
MAYBE I SHOULD HAVE DONE IT A LONG TIME AGO.
I HOPE I'M DOING THE RIGHT THING.
UH, YEAH.
ABOUT THIS.
I HOPE IT DOESN'T PUT MY FAMILY AT RISK.

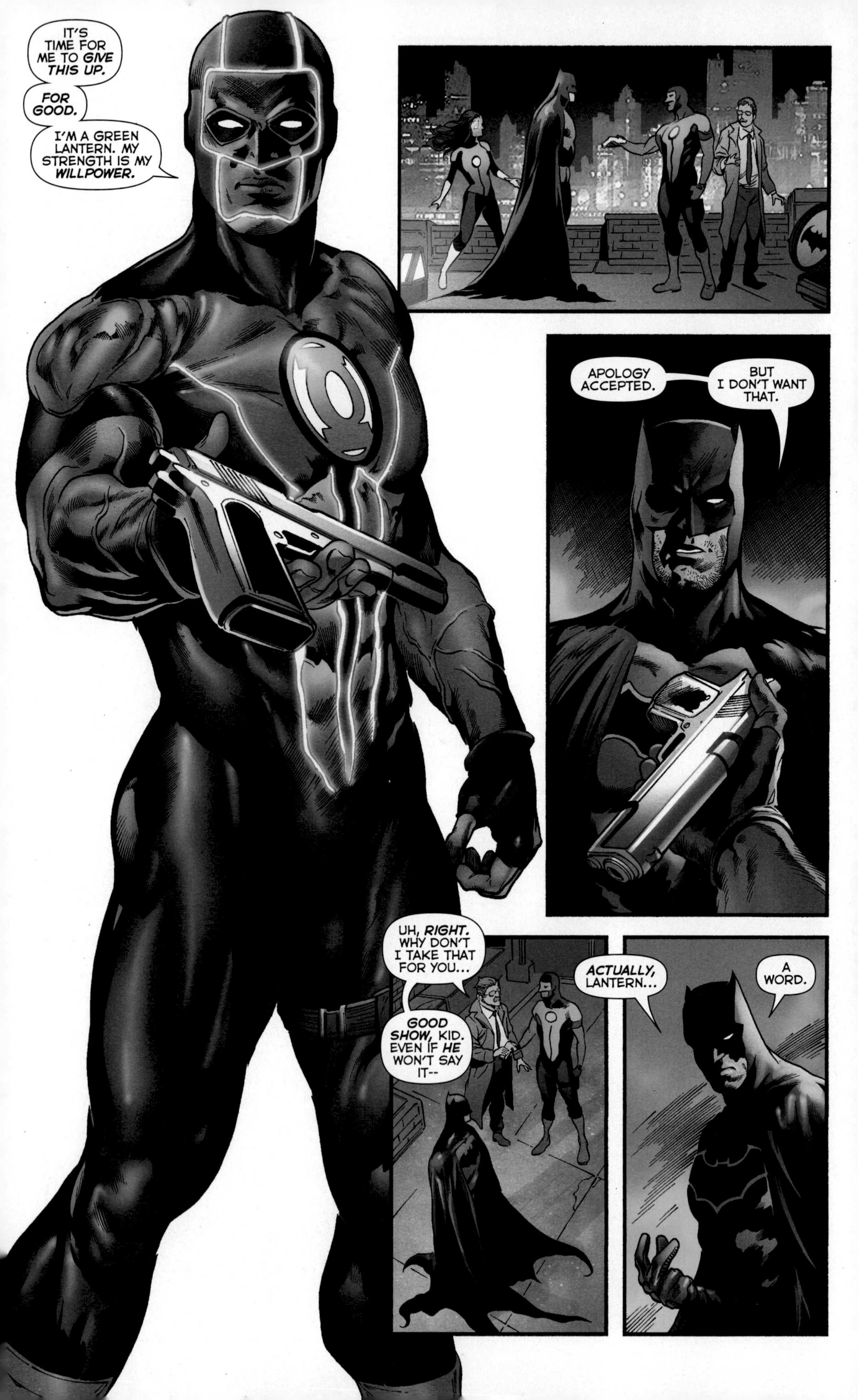
IT'S TIME FOR ME TO GIVE THIS UP.
FOR GOOD.
I'M A GREEN LANTERN. MY STRENGTH IS MY WILLPOWER.
APOLOGY ACCEPTED.
BUT I DON'T WANT THAT.
UH, RIGHT. WHY DON'T I TAKE THAT FOR YOU...
GOOD SHOW, KID. EVEN IF HE WON'T SAY IT--
ACTUALLY, LANTERN...
A WORD.

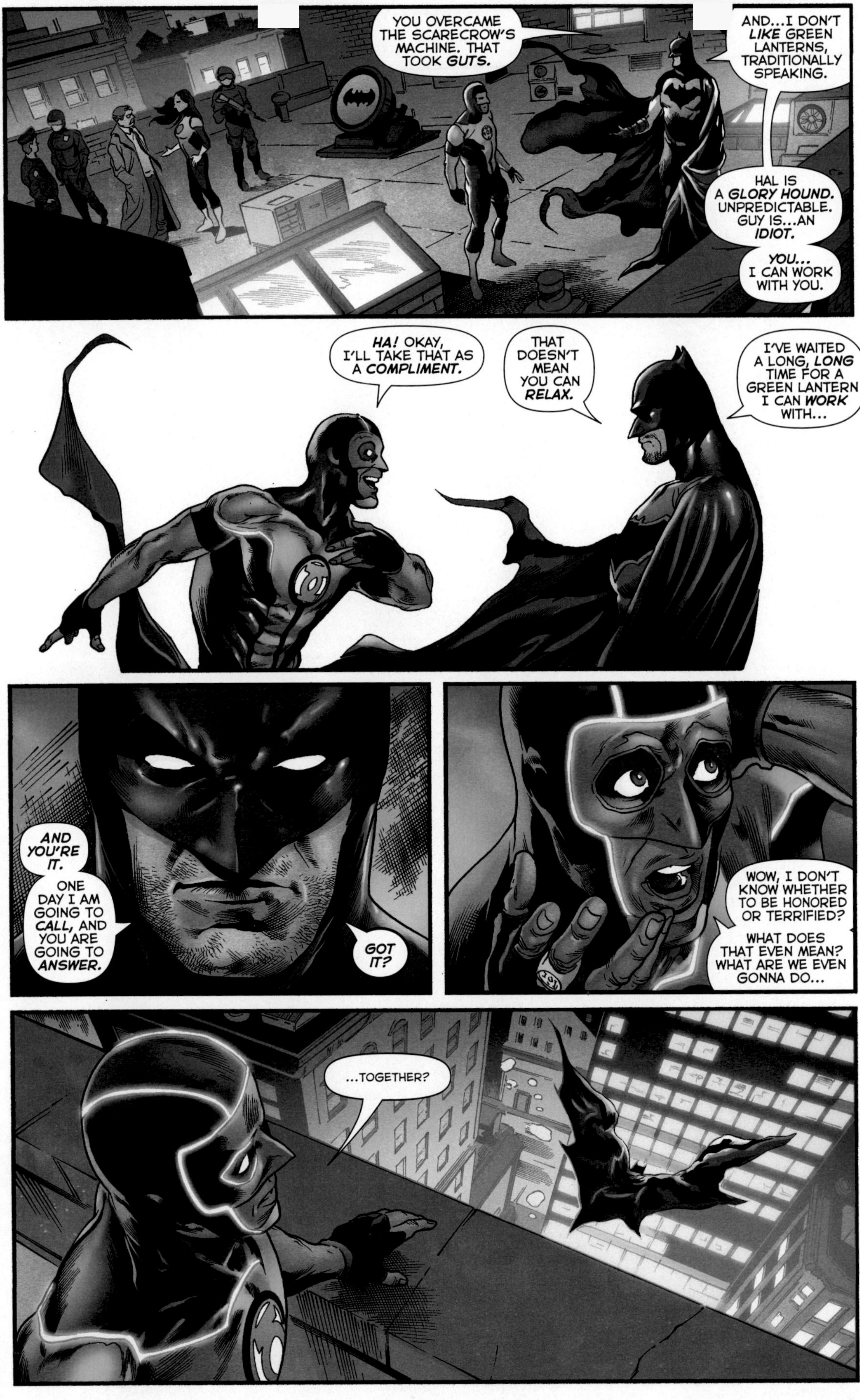
YOU OVERCAME THE SCARECROW'S MACHINE. THAT TOOK GUTS.
AND...I DON'T LIKE GREEN LANTERNS, TRADITIONALLY SPEAKING.
HAL IS A GLORY HOUND. UNPREDICTABLE. GUY IS...AN IDIOT.
YOU... I CAN WORK WITH YOU.
HA! OKAY, I'LL TAKE THAT AS A COMPLIMENT.
THAT DOESN'T MEAN YOU CAN RELAX.
I'VE WAITED A LONG, LONG TIME FOR A GREEN LANTERN I CAN WORK WITH...
AND YOU'RE IT.
ONE DAY I AM GOING TO CALL, AND YOU ARE GOING TO ANSWER.
GOT IT?
WOW, I DON'T KNOW WHETHER TO BE HONORED OR TERRIFIED?
WHAT DOES THAT EVEN MEAN? WHAT ARE WE EVEN GONNA DO...
...TOGETHER?

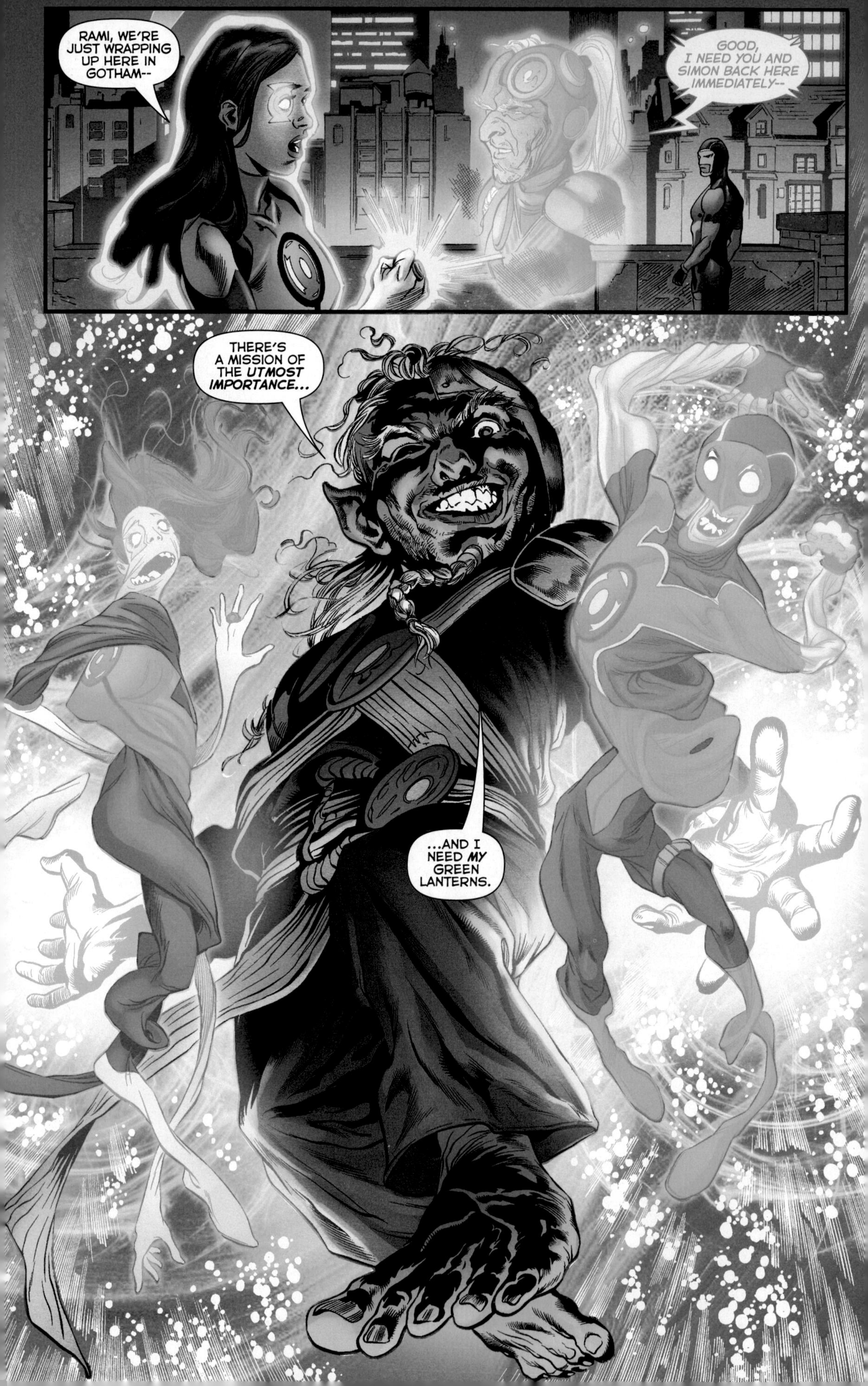
RAMI, WE'RE JUST WRAPPING UP HERE IN GOTHAM--
GOOD, I NEED YOU AND SIMON BACK HERE IMMEDIATELY--
THERE'S A MISSION OF THE *UTMOST IMPORTANCE*...
...AND I NEED *MY* GREEN LANTERNS.

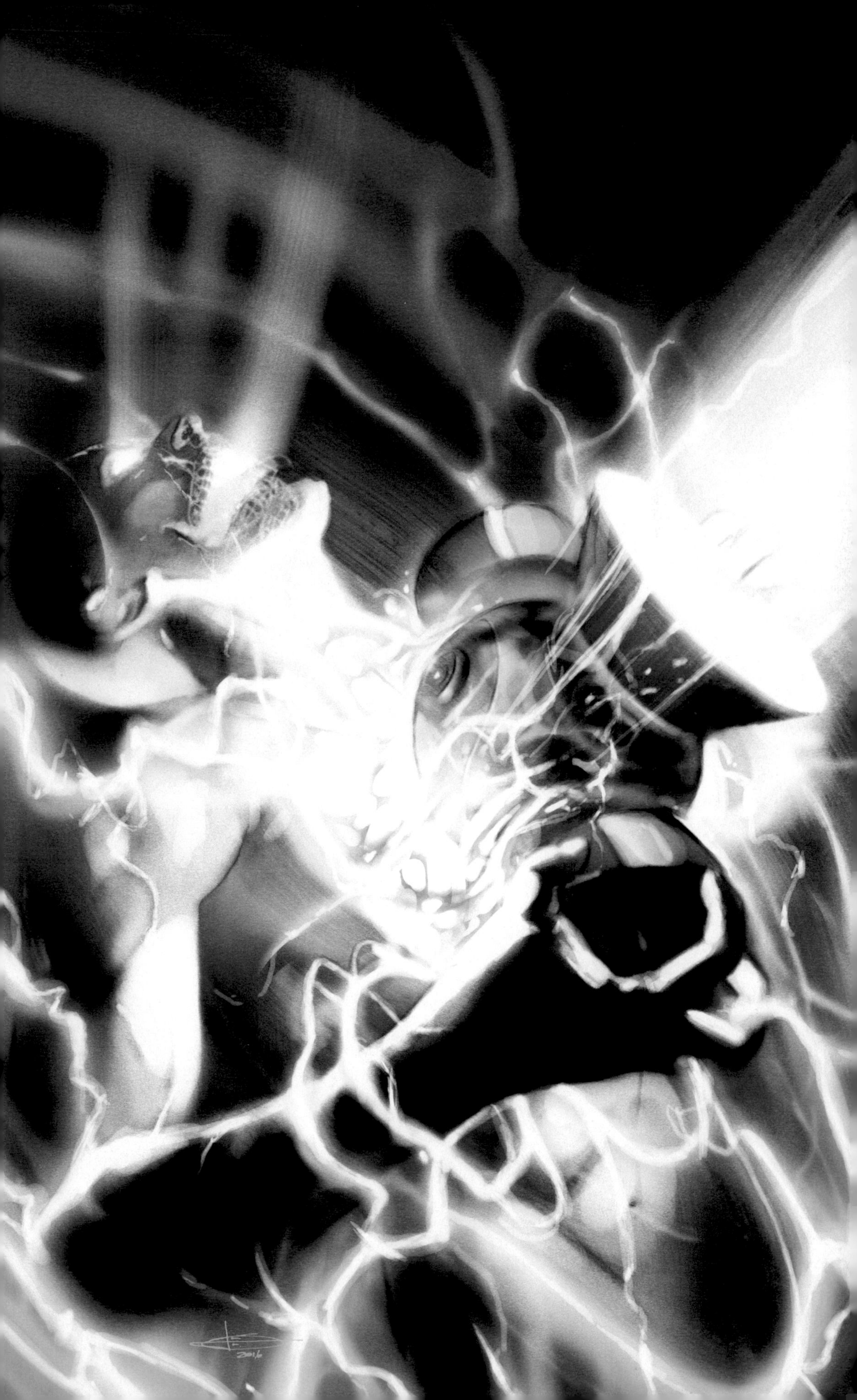

"THE LAST TESTAMENT OF THE FIRST LANTERN"

ROBSON ROCHA penciller * DANIEL HENRIQUES inker

Cover by LEO MANCO

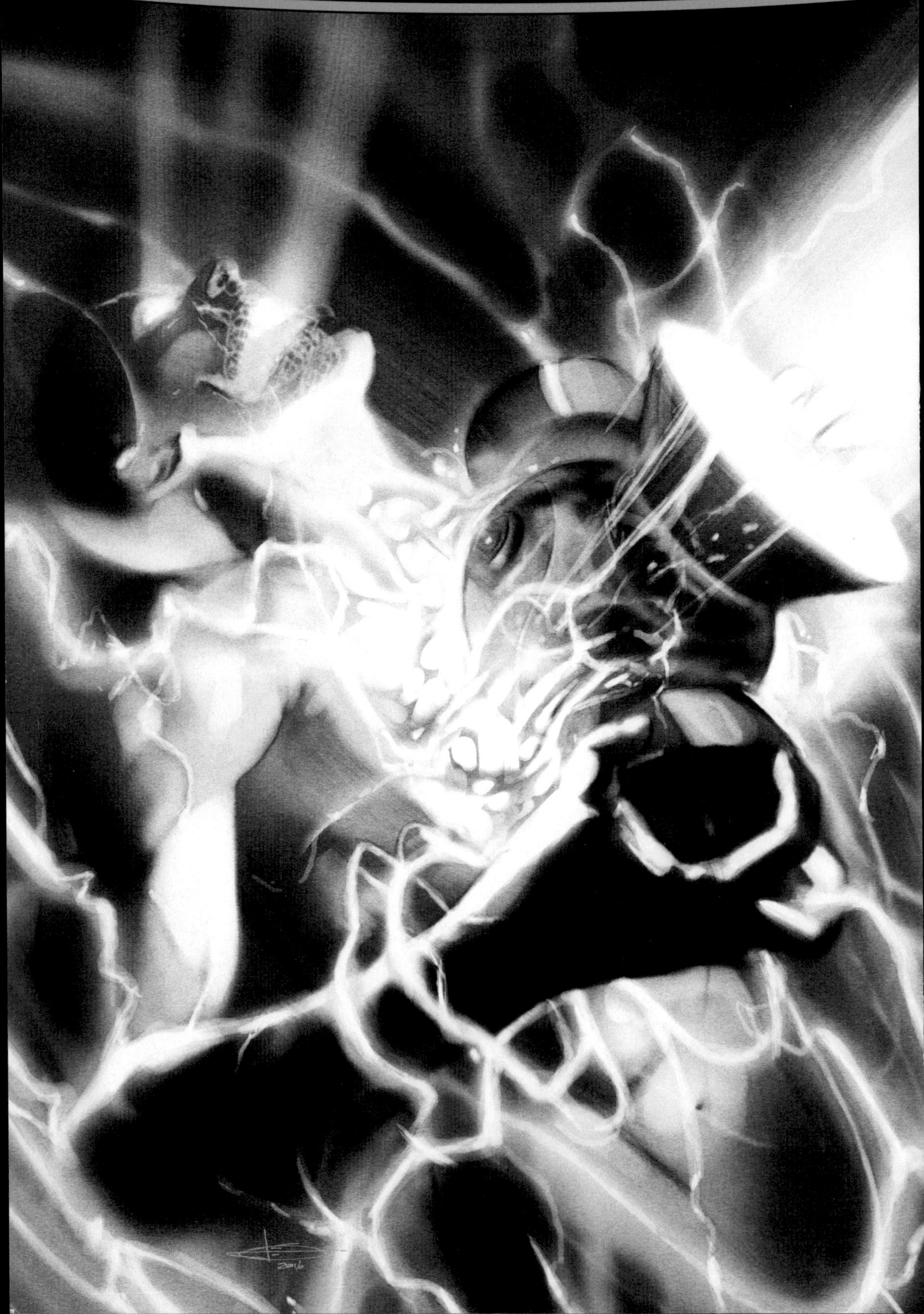

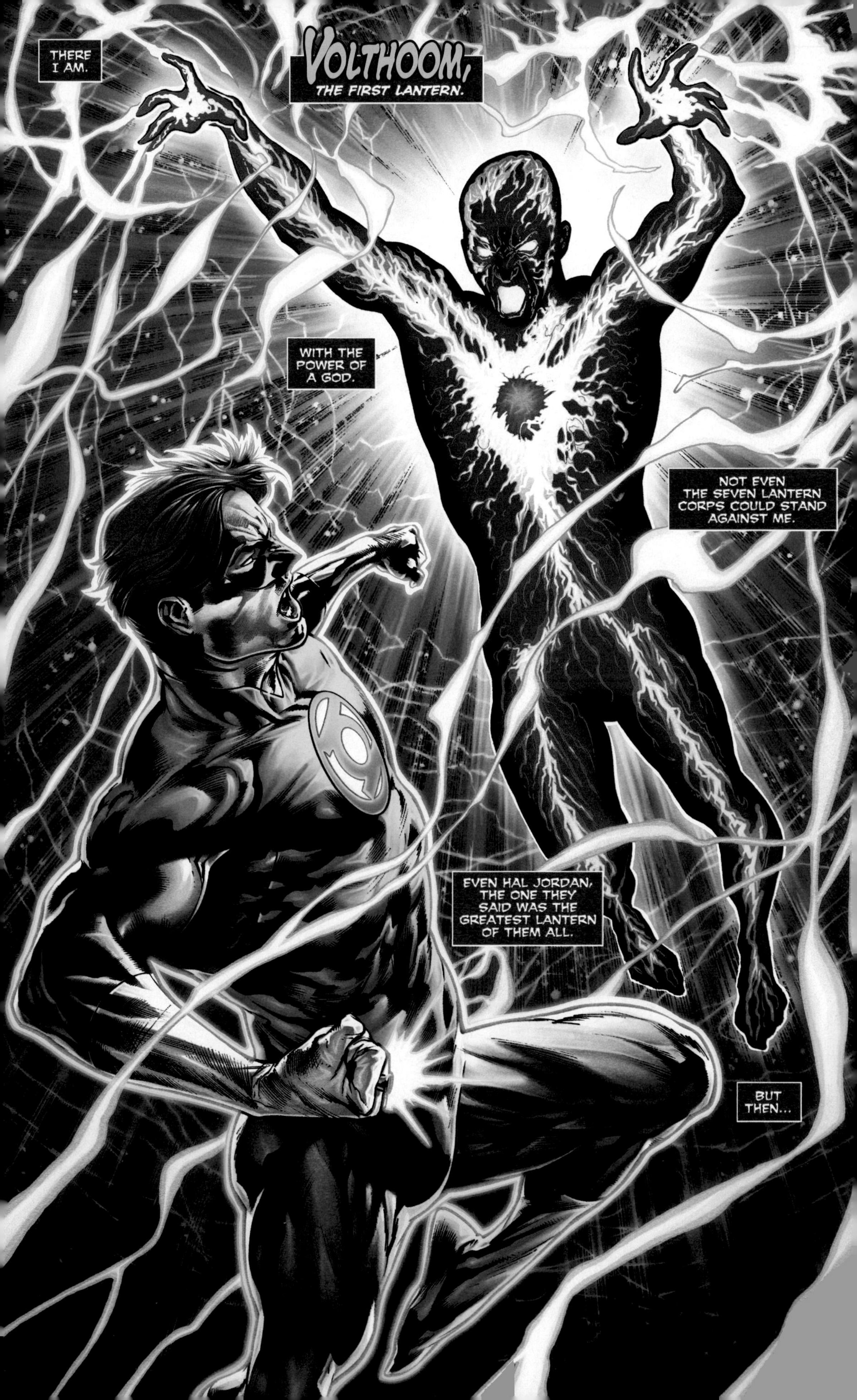
THERE I AM.
VOLTHOOM, THE FIRST LANTERN.
WITH THE POWER OF A GOD.
NOT EVEN THE SEVEN LANTERN CORPS COULD STAND AGAINST ME.
EVEN HAL JORDAN, THE ONE THEY SAID WAS THE GREATEST LANTERN OF THEM ALL.
BUT THEN...

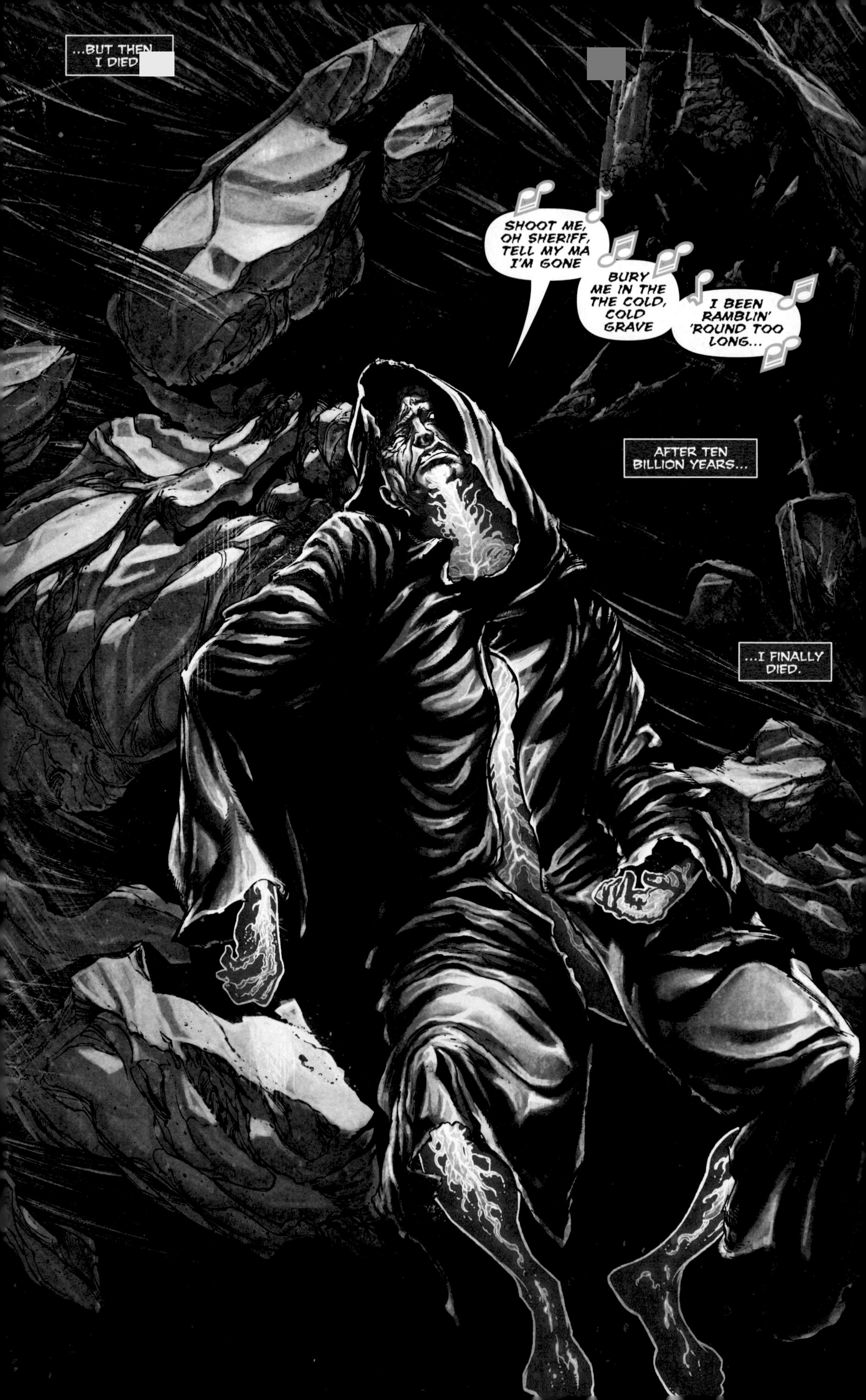
...BUT THEN
I DIED
SHOOT ME, OH SHERIFF, TELL MY MA I'M GONE
BURY ME IN THE THE COLD, COLD GRAVE
I BEEN RAMBLIN' 'ROUND TOO LONG...
AFTER TEN BILLION YEARS...
...I FINALLY DIED.

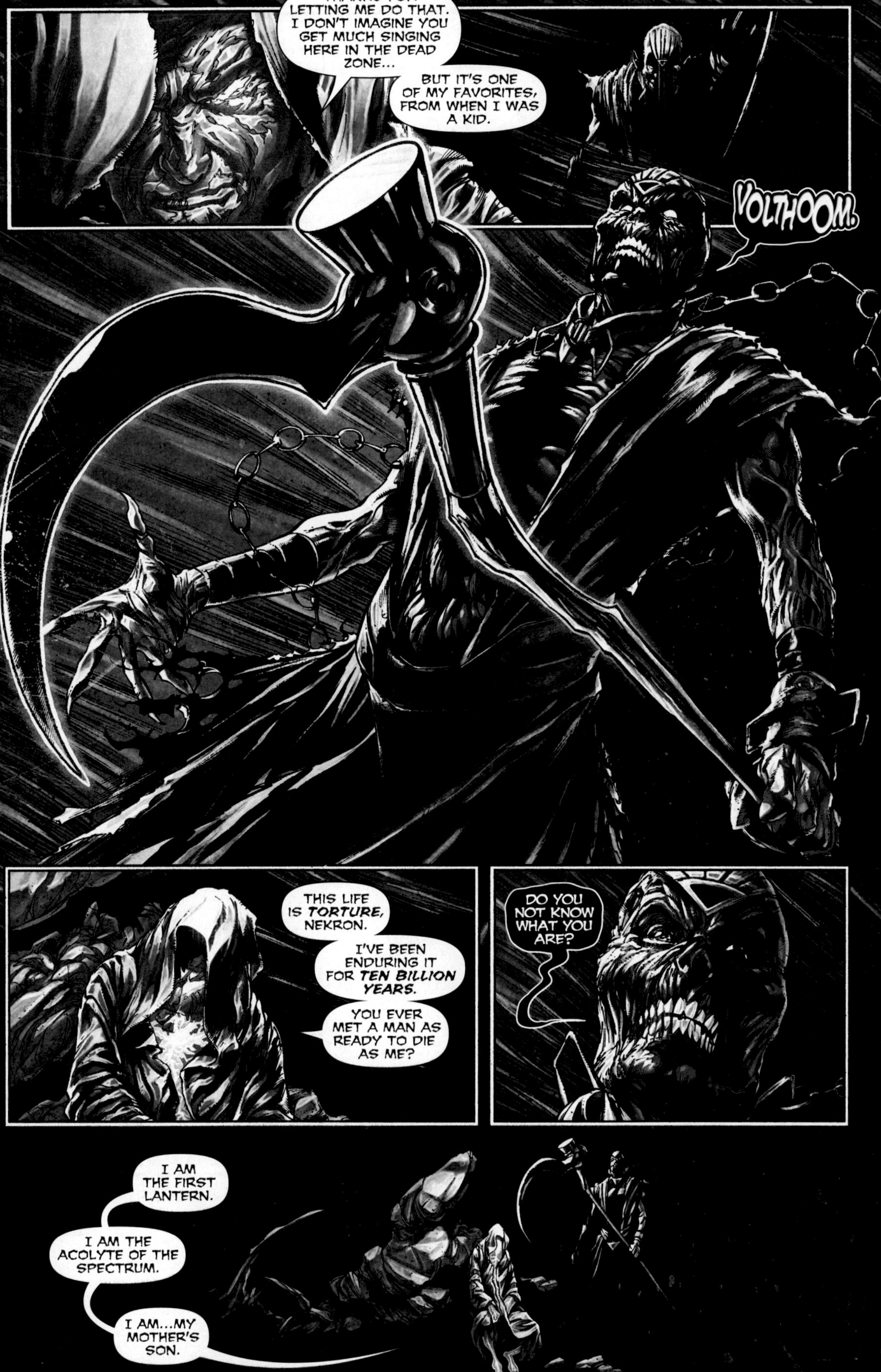
THANKS FOR LETTING ME DO THAT. I DON'T IMAGINE YOU GET MUCH SINGING HERE IN THE DEAD ZONE...
BUT IT'S ONE OF MY FAVORITES, FROM WHEN I WAS A KID.
VOLTHOOM.
THIS LIFE IS TORTURE, NEKRON.
I'VE BEEN ENDURING IT FOR TEN BILLION YEARS.
YOU EVER MET A MAN AS READY TO DIE AS ME?
DO YOU NOT KNOW WHAT YOU ARE?
I AM THE FIRST LANTERN.
I AM THE ACOLYTE OF THE SPECTRUM.
I AM...MY MOTHER'S SON.

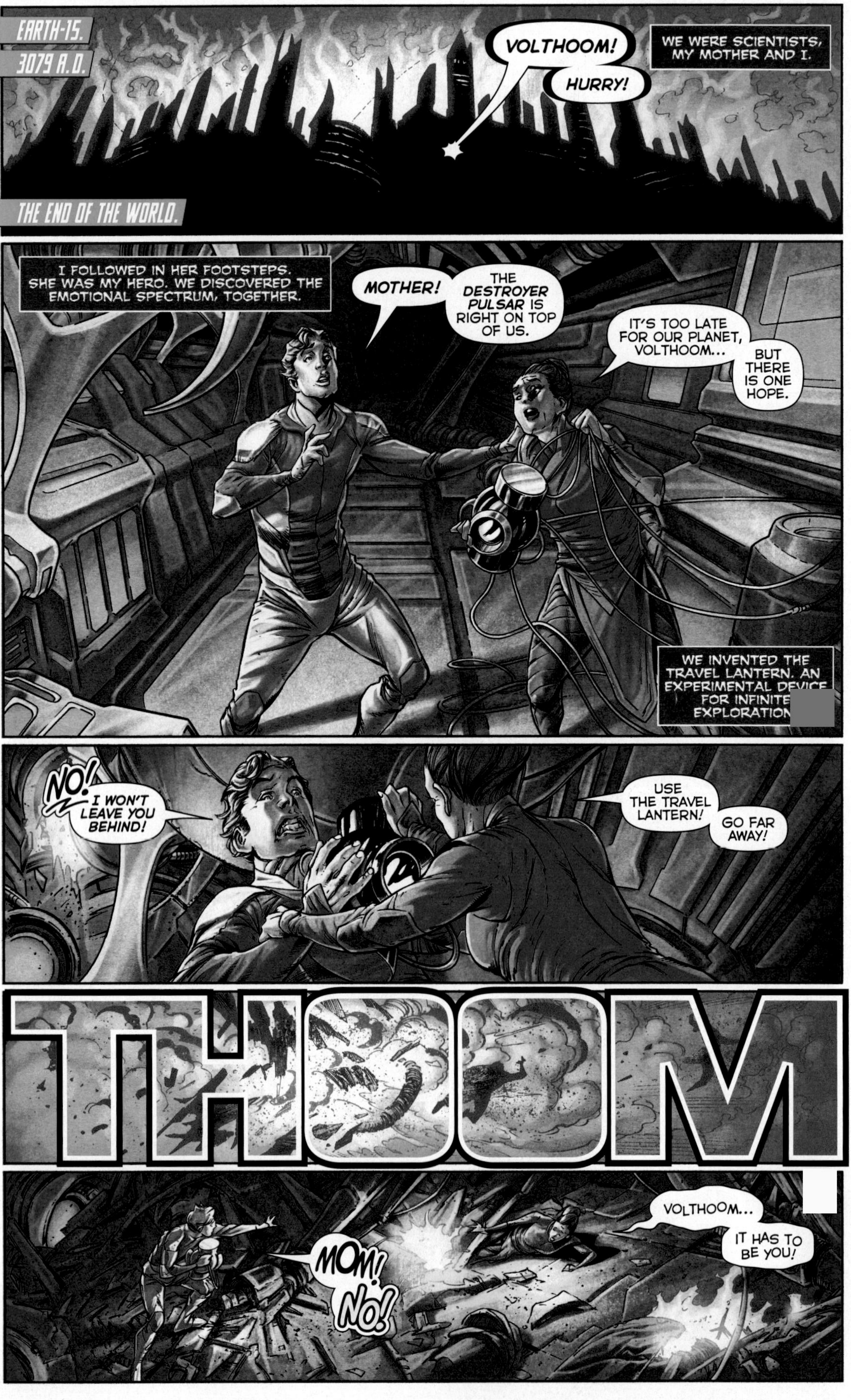
EARTH-15.
3079 A.D.
VOLTHOOM!
HURRY!
WE WERE SCIENTISTS, MY MOTHER AND I.
THE END OF THE WORLD.
I FOLLOWED IN HER FOOTSTEPS. SHE WAS MY HERO. WE DISCOVERED THE EMOTIONAL SPECTRUM, TOGETHER.
MOTHER!
THE *DESTROYER PULSAR* IS RIGHT ON TOP OF US.
IT'S TOO LATE FOR OUR PLANET, VOLTHOOM...
BUT THERE IS ONE HOPE.
WE INVENTED THE TRAVEL LANTERN. AN EXPERIMENTAL DEVICE FOR INFINITE EXPLORATION
NO! I WON'T LEAVE YOU BEHIND!
USE THE TRAVEL LANTERN!
GO FAR AWAY!
THOOM
MOM! NO!
VOLTHOOM...
IT HAS TO BE YOU!

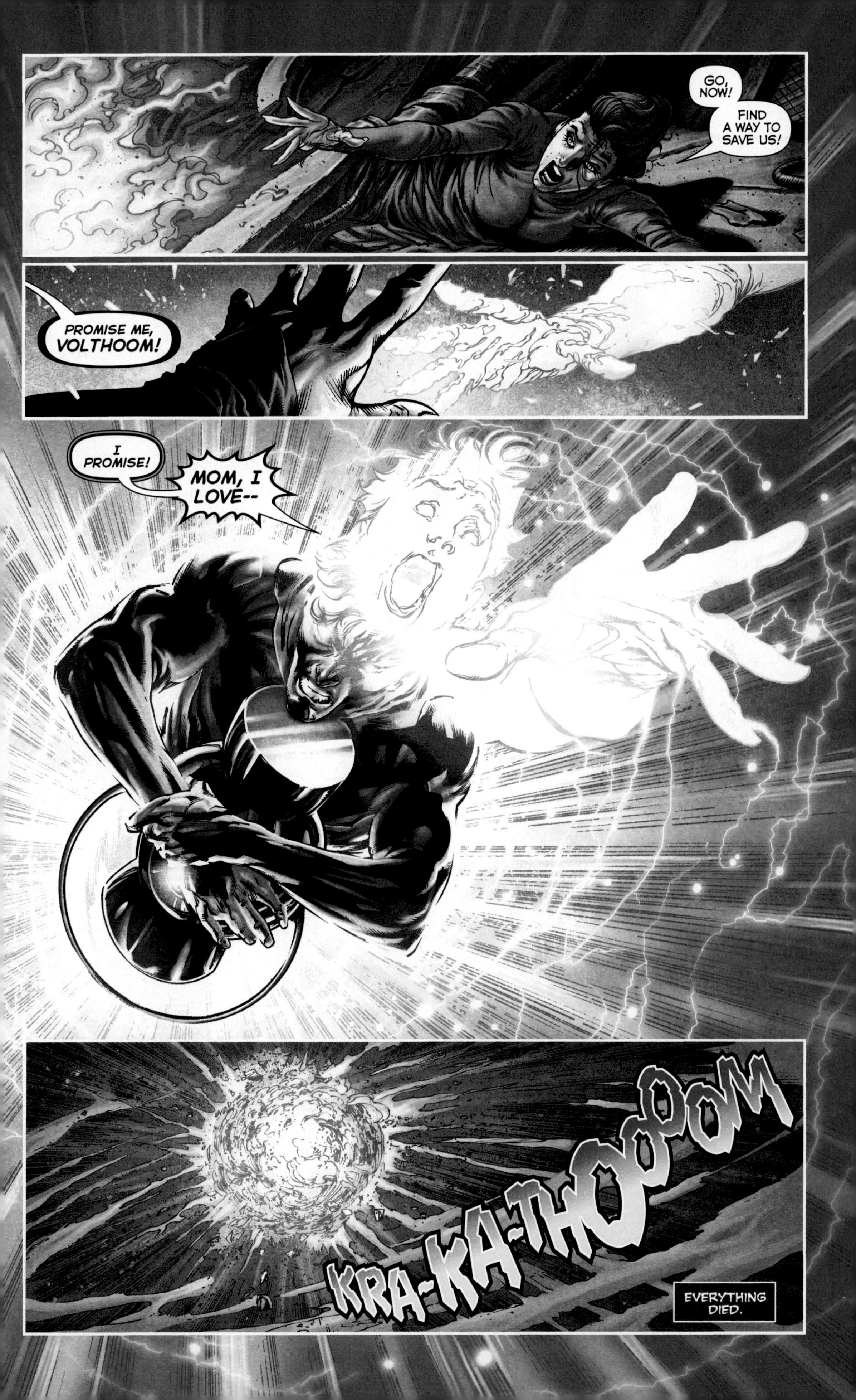
GO, NOW!
FIND A WAY TO SAVE US!
PROMISE ME, VOLTHOOM!
I PROMISE!
MOM, I LOVE--
KRA-KA-THOOOOM
EVERYTHING DIED.

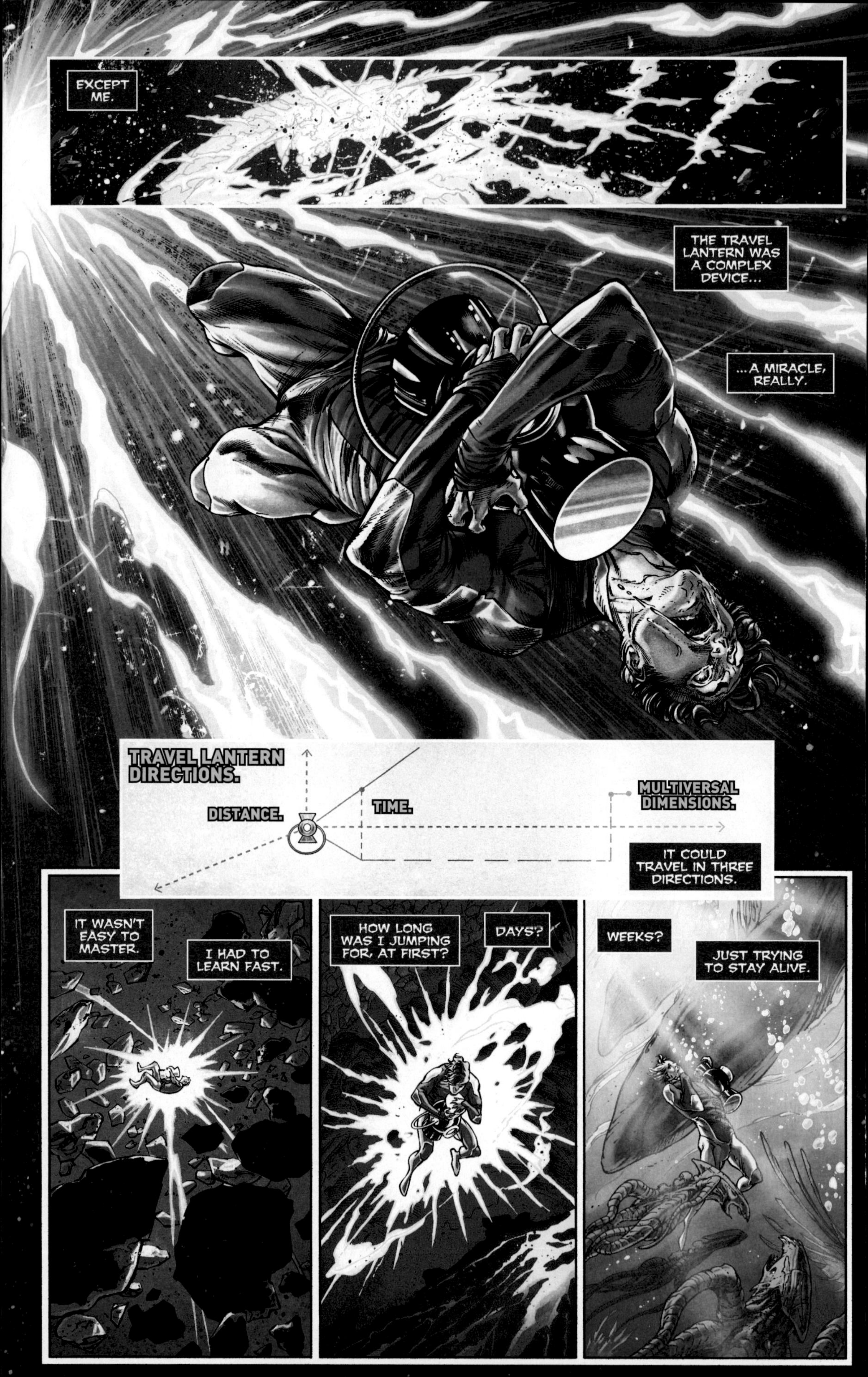
EXCEPT ME.
THE TRAVEL LANTERN WAS A COMPLEX DEVICE...
...A MIRACLE, REALLY.
TRAVEL LANTERN DIRECTIONS.
DISTANCE.
TIME.
MULTIVERSAL DIMENSIONS.
IT COULD TRAVEL IN THREE DIRECTIONS.
IT WASN'T EASY TO MASTER.
I HAD TO LEARN FAST.
HOW LONG WAS I JUMPING FOR, AT FIRST?
DAYS?
WEEKS?
JUST TRYING TO STAY ALIVE.

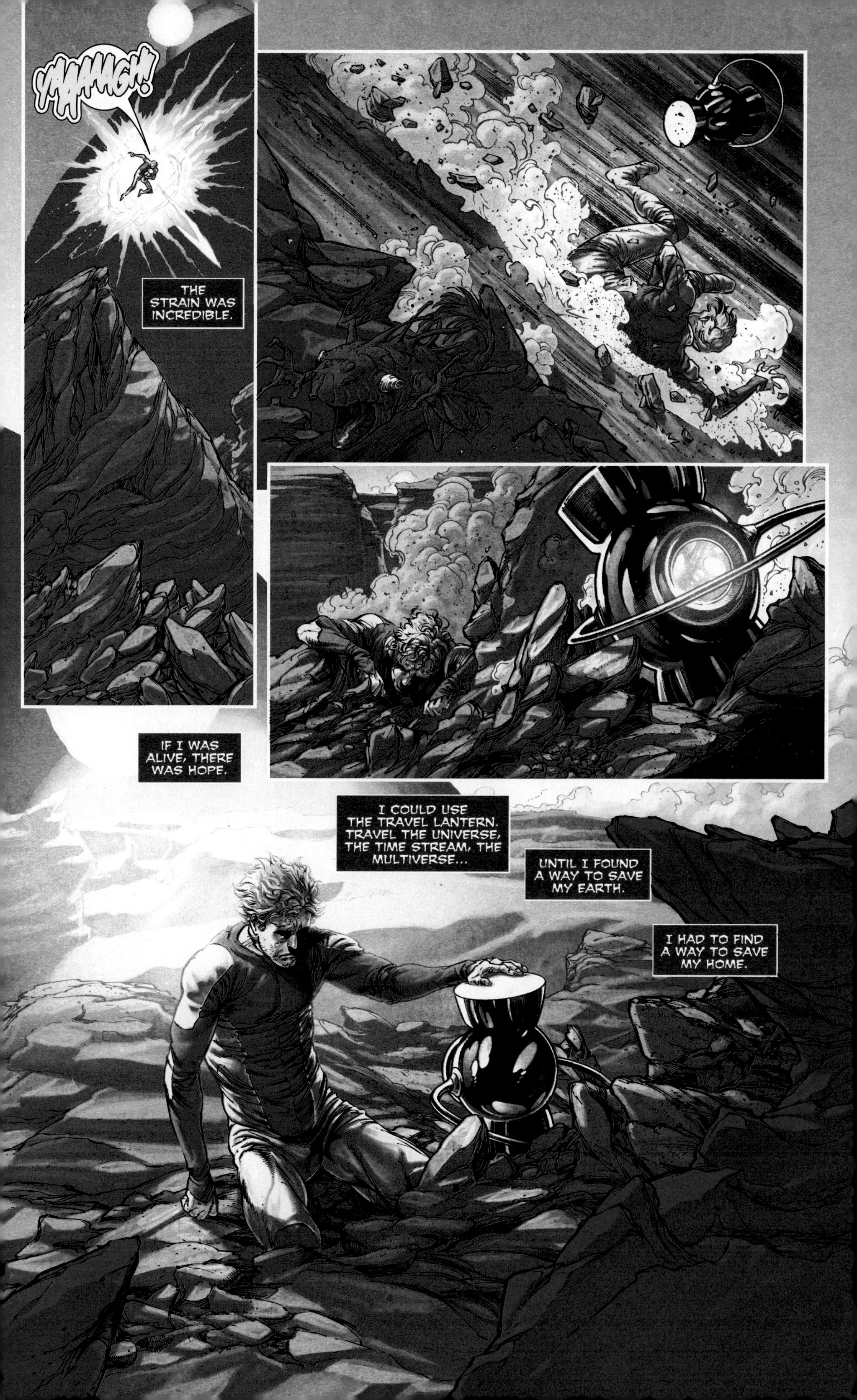
YAAAAAGH!
THE STRAIN WAS INCREDIBLE.
IF I WAS ALIVE, THERE WAS HOPE.
I COULD USE THE TRAVEL LANTERN. TRAVEL THE UNIVERSE, THE TIME STREAM, THE MULTIVERSE...
UNTIL I FOUND A WAY TO SAVE MY EARTH.
I HAD TO FIND A WAY TO SAVE MY HOME.

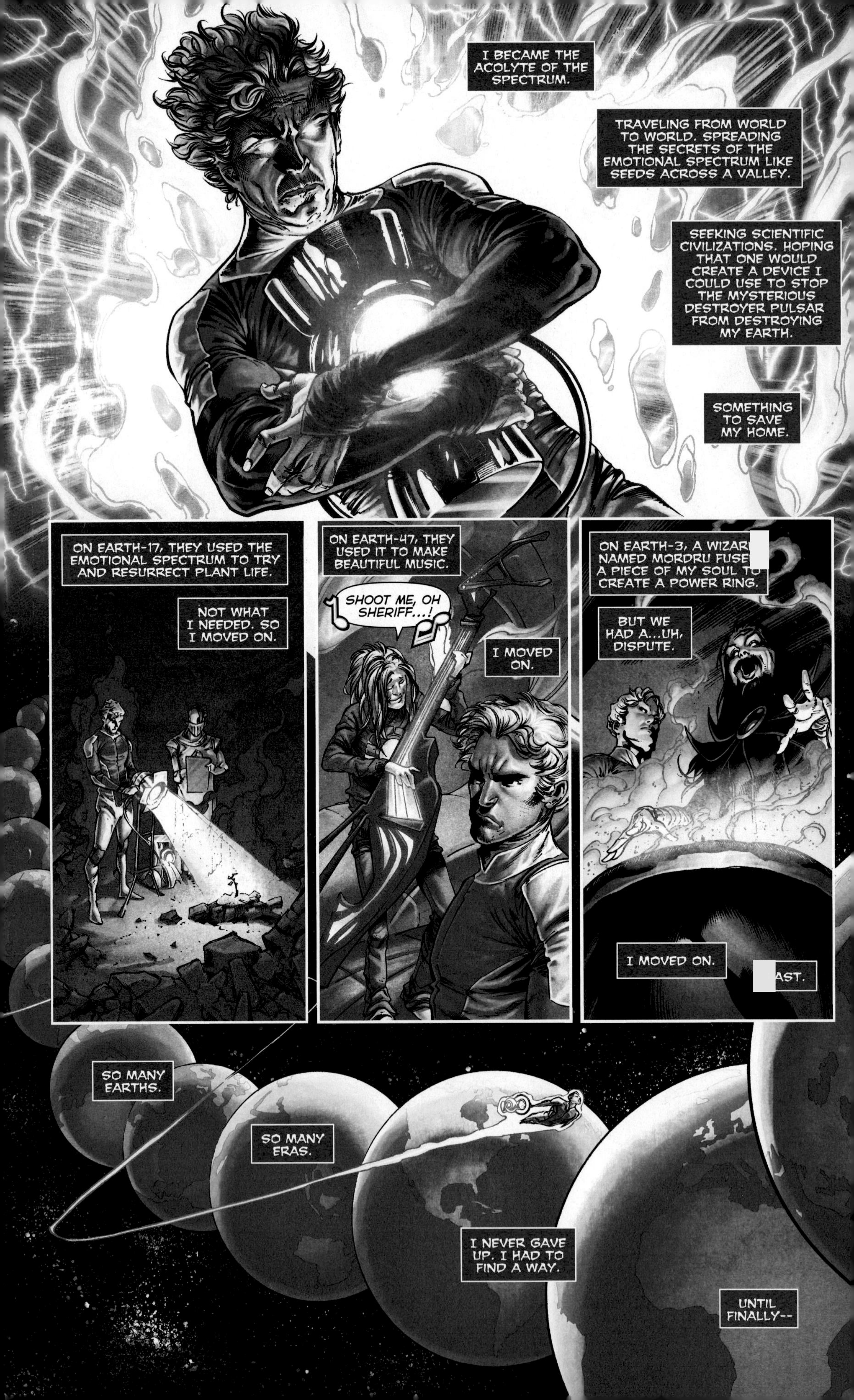
I BECAME THE ACOLYTE OF THE SPECTRUM.
TRAVELING FROM WORLD TO WORLD. SPREADING THE SECRETS OF THE EMOTIONAL SPECTRUM LIKE SEEDS ACROSS A VALLEY.
SEEKING SCIENTIFIC CIVILIZATIONS. HOPING THAT ONE WOULD CREATE A DEVICE I COULD USE TO STOP THE MYSTERIOUS DESTROYER PULSAR FROM DESTROYING MY EARTH.
SOMETHING TO SAVE MY HOME.
ON EARTH-17, THEY USED THE EMOTIONAL SPECTRUM TO TRY AND RESURRECT PLANT LIFE.
NOT WHAT I NEEDED. SO I MOVED ON.
ON EARTH-47, THEY USED IT TO MAKE BEAUTIFUL MUSIC.
SHOOT ME, OH SHERIFF...!
I MOVED ON.
ON EARTH-3, A WIZAR NAMED MORDRU FUSE A PIECE OF MY SOUL TO CREATE A POWER RING.
BUT WE HAD A...UH, DISPUTE.
I MOVED ON.
AST.
SO MANY EARTHS.
SO MANY ERAS.
I NEVER GAVE UP. I HAD TO FIND A WAY.
UNTIL FINALLY--

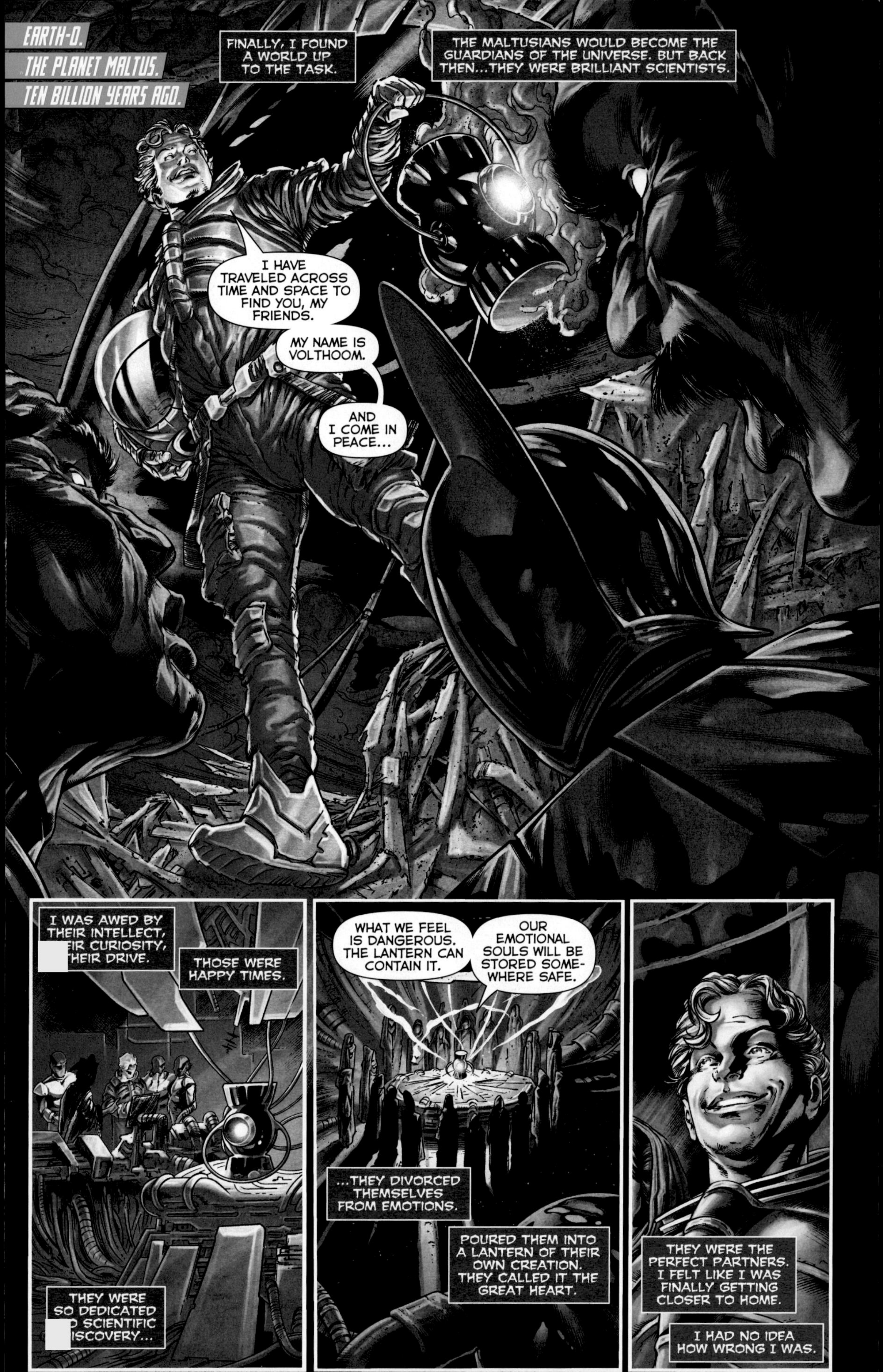
EARTH-0.
THE PLANET MALTUS.
TEN BILLION YEARS AGO.
FINALLY, I FOUND A WORLD UP TO THE TASK.
THE MALTUSIANS WOULD BECOME THE GUARDIANS OF THE UNIVERSE. BUT BACK THEN...THEY WERE BRILLIANT SCIENTISTS.
I HAVE TRAVELED ACROSS TIME AND SPACE TO FIND YOU, MY FRIENDS.
MY NAME IS VOLTHOOM.
AND I COME IN PEACE...
I WAS AWED BY THEIR INTELLECT, EIR CURIOSITY, THEIR DRIVE.
THOSE WERE HAPPY TIMES.
THEY WERE SO DEDICATED O SCIENTIFIC ISCOVERY...
WHAT WE FEEL IS DANGEROUS. THE LANTERN CAN CONTAIN IT.
OUR EMOTIONAL SOULS WILL BE STORED SOME-WHERE SAFE.
...THEY DIVORCED THEMSELVES FROM EMOTIONS.
POURED THEM INTO A LANTERN OF THEIR OWN CREATION. THEY CALLED IT THE GREAT HEART.
THEY WERE THE PERFECT PARTNERS. I FELT LIKE I WAS FINALLY GETTING CLOSER TO HOME.
I HAD NO IDEA HOW WRONG I WAS.

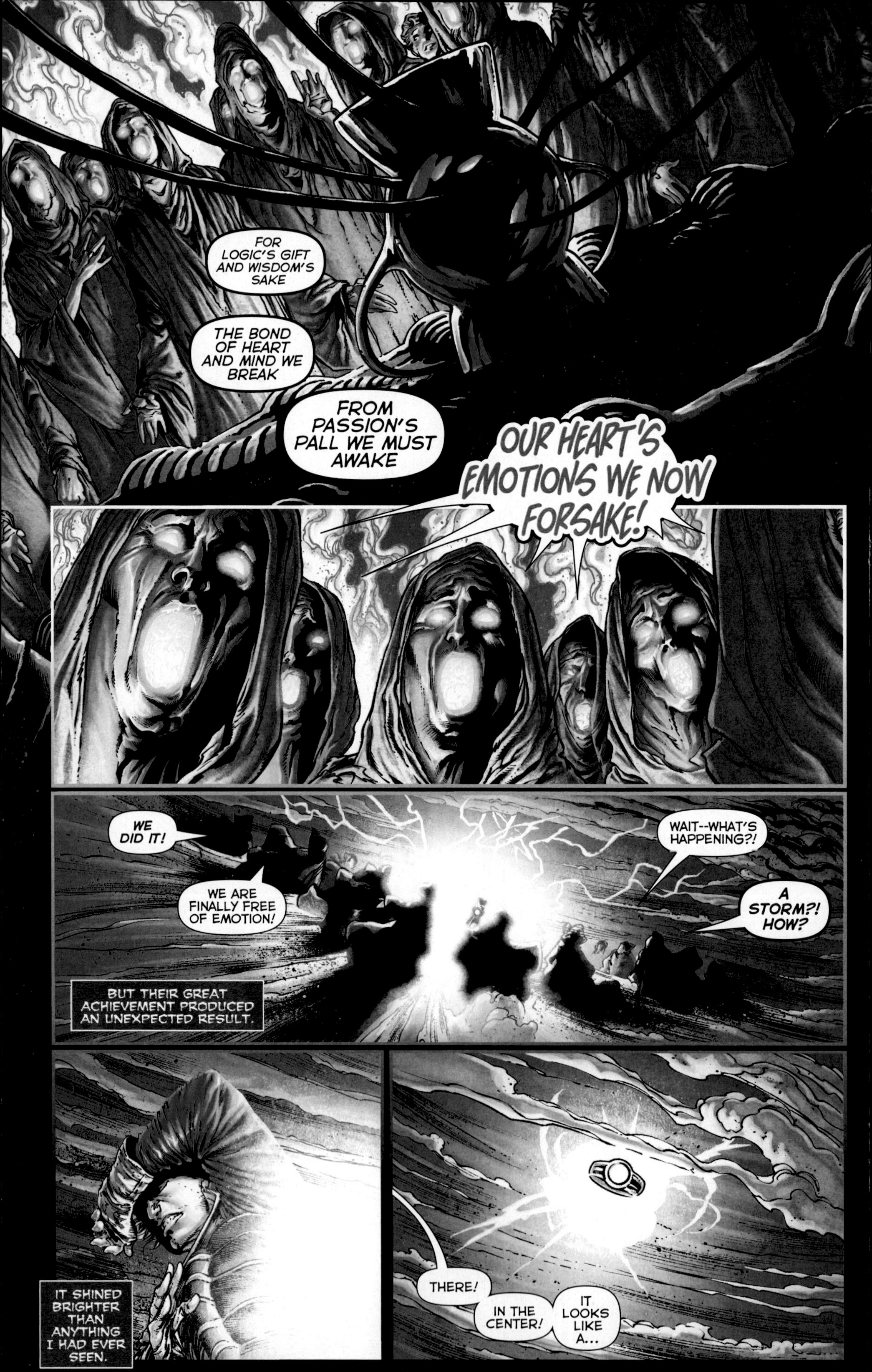
FOR LOGIC'S GIFT AND WISDOM'S SAKE
THE BOND OF HEART AND MIND WE BREAK
FROM PASSION'S PALL WE MUST AWAKE
OUR HEART'S EMOTIONS WE NOW FORSAKE!
WE DID IT!
WE ARE FINALLY FREE OF EMOTION!
WAIT--WHAT'S HAPPENING?!
A STORM?! HOW?
BUT THEIR GREAT ACHIEVEMENT PRODUCED AN UNEXPECTED RESULT.
IT SHINED BRIGHTER THAN ANYTHING I HAD EVER SEEN.
THERE!
IN THE CENTER!
IT LOOKS LIKE A...

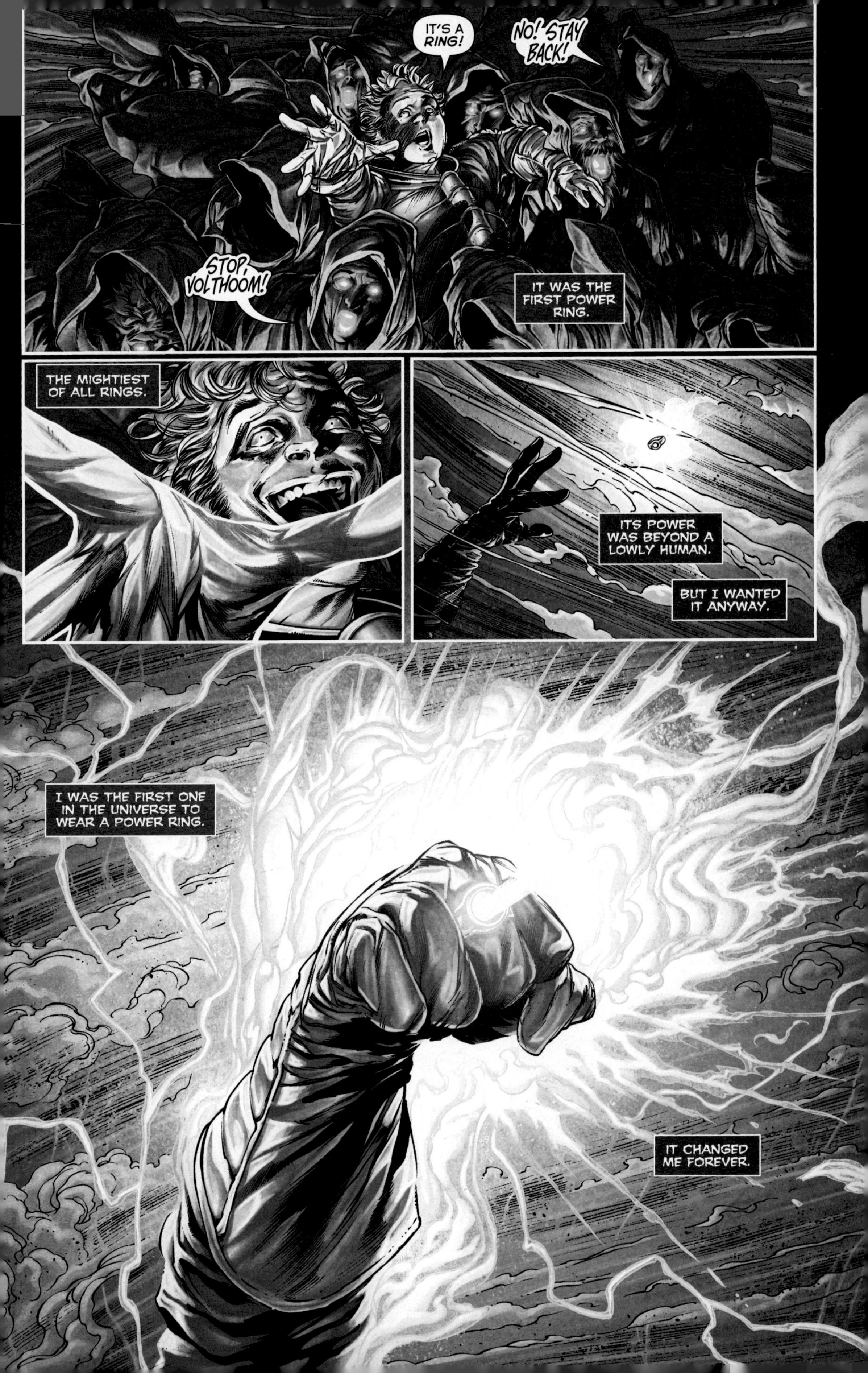
IT'S A RING!
NO! STAY BACK!
STOP, VOLTHOOM!
IT WAS THE FIRST POWER RING.
THE MIGHTIEST OF ALL RINGS.
ITS POWER WAS BEYOND A LOWLY HUMAN.
BUT I WANTED IT ANYWAY.
I WAS THE FIRST ONE IN THE UNIVERSE TO WEAR A POWER RING.
IT CHANGED ME FOREVER.

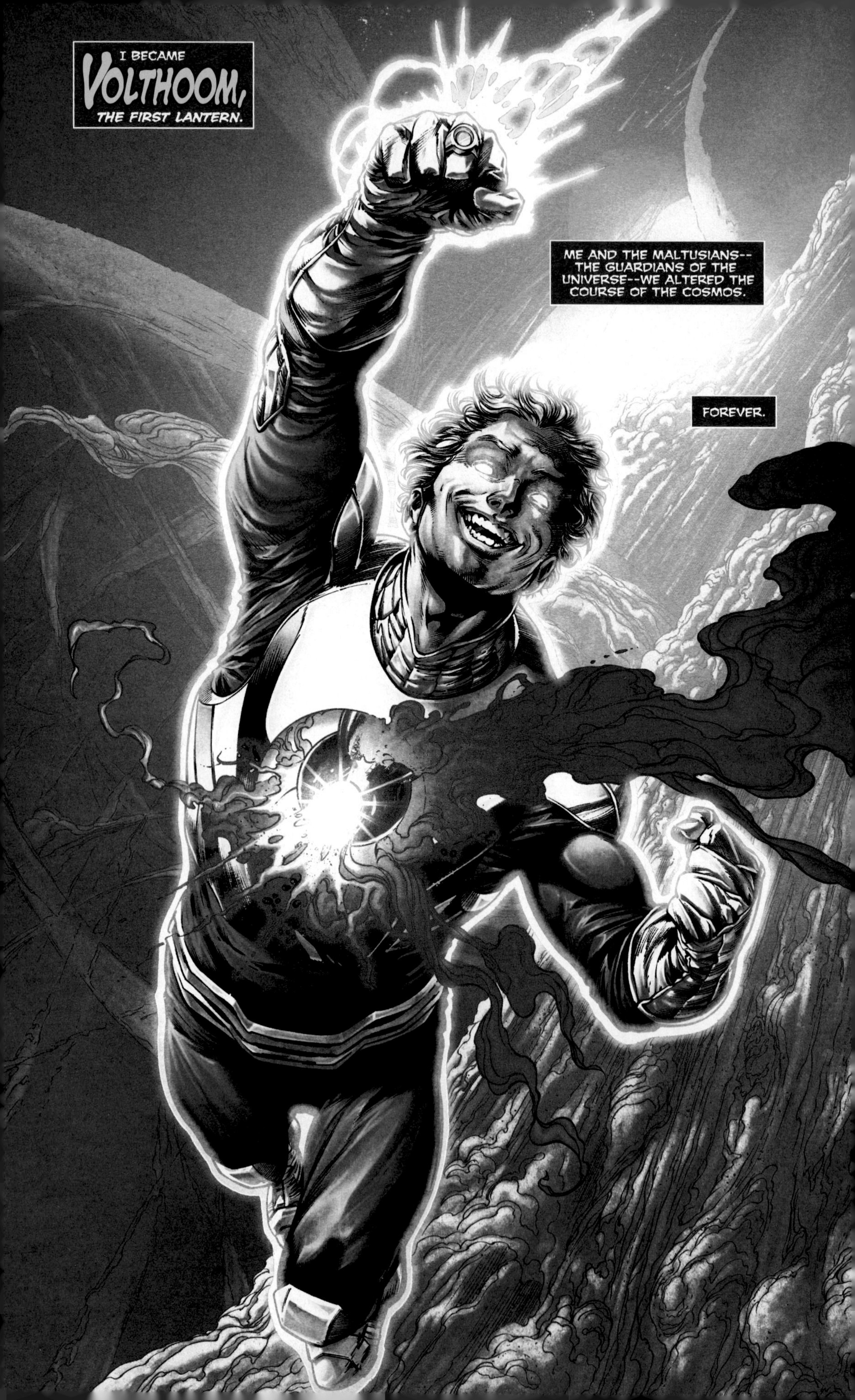
I BECAME
VOLTHOOM,
THE FIRST LANTERN.
ME AND THE MALTUSIANS--THE GUARDIANS OF THE UNIVERSE--WE ALTERED THE COURSE OF THE COSMOS.
FOREVER.

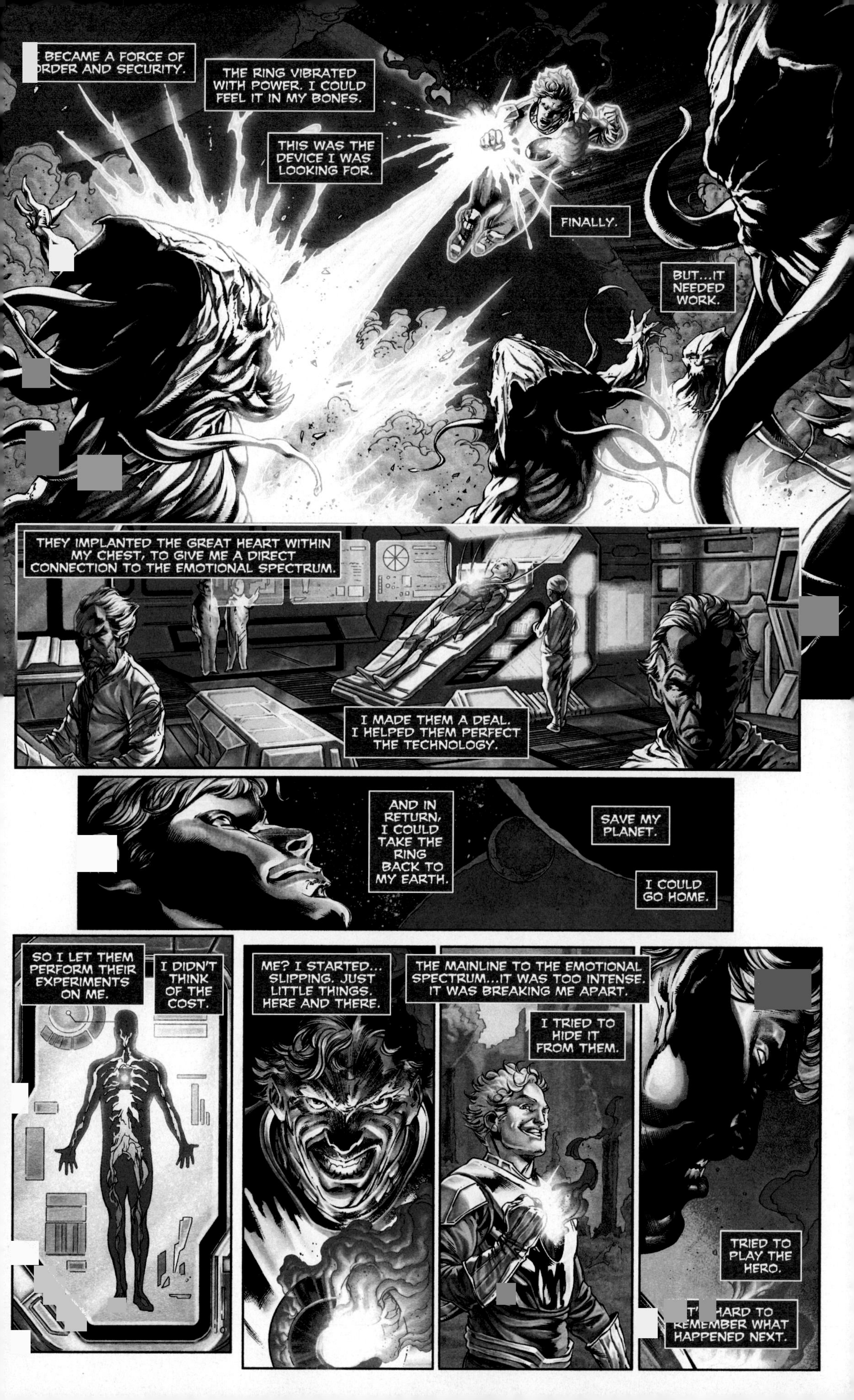
BECAME A FORCE OF
RDER AND SECURITY.
THE RING VIBRATED WITH POWER. I COULD FEEL IT IN MY BONES.
THIS WAS THE DEVICE I WAS LOOKING FOR.
FINALLY.
BUT...IT NEEDED WORK.
THEY IMPLANTED THE GREAT HEART WITHIN MY CHEST, TO GIVE ME A DIRECT CONNECTION TO THE EMOTIONAL SPECTRUM.
I MADE THEM A DEAL. I HELPED THEM PERFECT THE TECHNOLOGY.
AND IN RETURN, I COULD TAKE THE RING BACK TO MY EARTH.
SAVE MY PLANET.
I COULD GO HOME.
SO I LET THEM PERFORM THEIR EXPERIMENTS ON ME.
I DIDN'T THINK OF THE COST.
ME? I STARTED... SLIPPING. JUST LITTLE THINGS. HERE AND THERE.
THE MAINLINE TO THE EMOTIONAL SPECTRUM...IT WAS TOO INTENSE. IT WAS BREAKING ME APART.
I TRIED TO HIDE IT FROM THEM.
TRIED TO PLAY THE HERO.
T'S HARD TO
EMEMBER WHAT
HAPPENED NEXT.

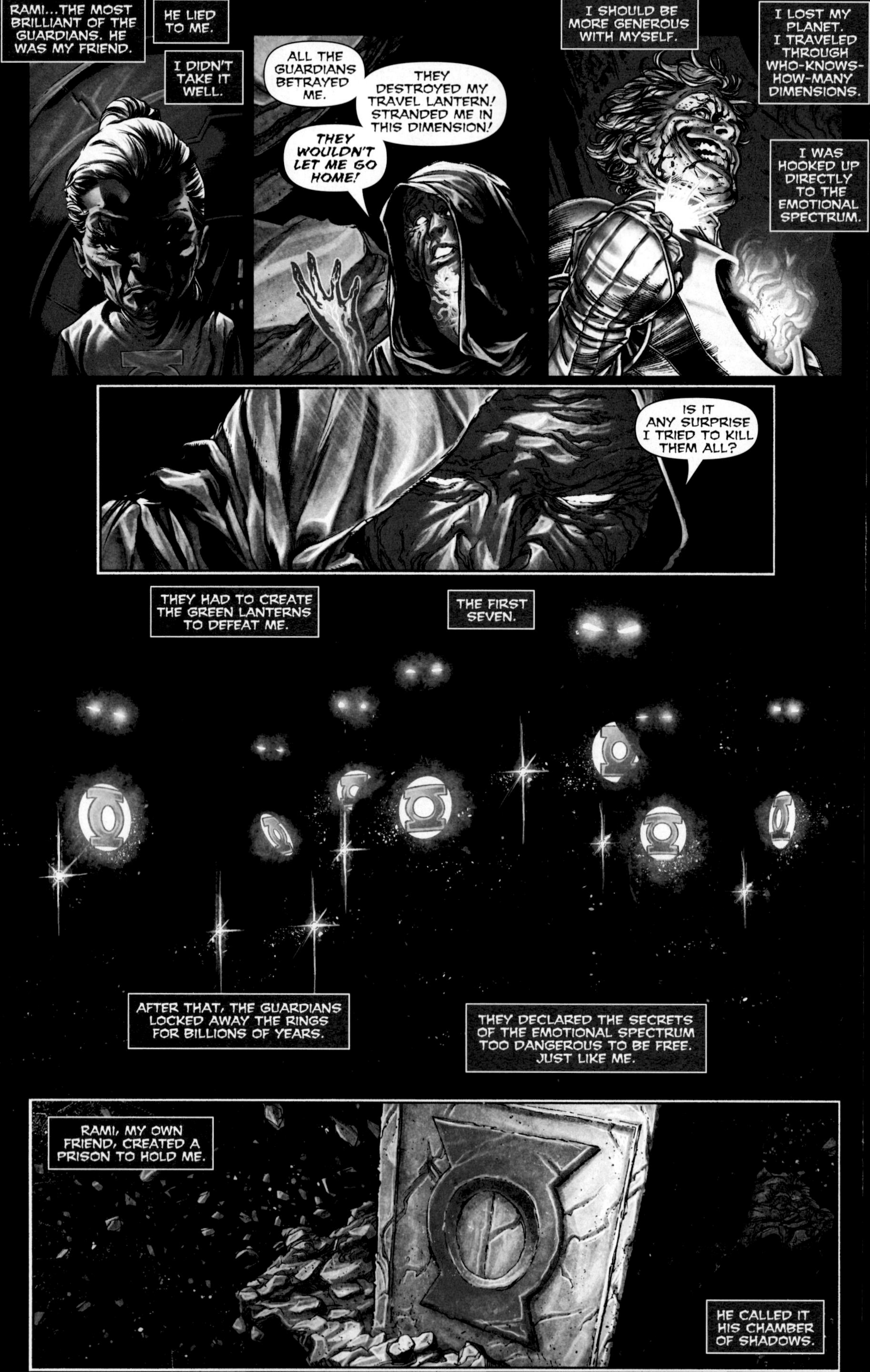
RAMI...THE MOST BRILLIANT OF THE GUARDIANS. HE WAS MY FRIEND.
HE LIED TO ME.
I DIDN'T TAKE IT WELL.
ALL THE GUARDIANS BETRAYED ME.
THEY DESTROYED MY TRAVEL LANTERN! STRANDED ME IN THIS DIMENSION!
THEY WOULDN'T LET ME GO HOME!
I SHOULD BE MORE GENEROUS WITH MYSELF.
I LOST MY PLANET. I TRAVELED THROUGH WHO-KNOWS-HOW-MANY DIMENSIONS.
I WAS HOOKED UP DIRECTLY TO THE EMOTIONAL SPECTRUM.
IS IT ANY SURPRISE I TRIED TO KILL THEM ALL?
THEY HAD TO CREATE THE GREEN LANTERNS TO DEFEAT ME.
THE FIRST SEVEN.
AFTER THAT, THE GUARDIANS LOCKED AWAY THE RINGS FOR BILLIONS OF YEARS.
THEY DECLARED THE SECRETS OF THE EMOTIONAL SPECTRUM TOO DANGEROUS TO BE FREE. JUST LIKE ME.
RAMI, MY OWN FRIEND, CREATED A PRISON TO HOLD ME.
HE CALLED IT HIS CHAMBER OF SHADOWS.

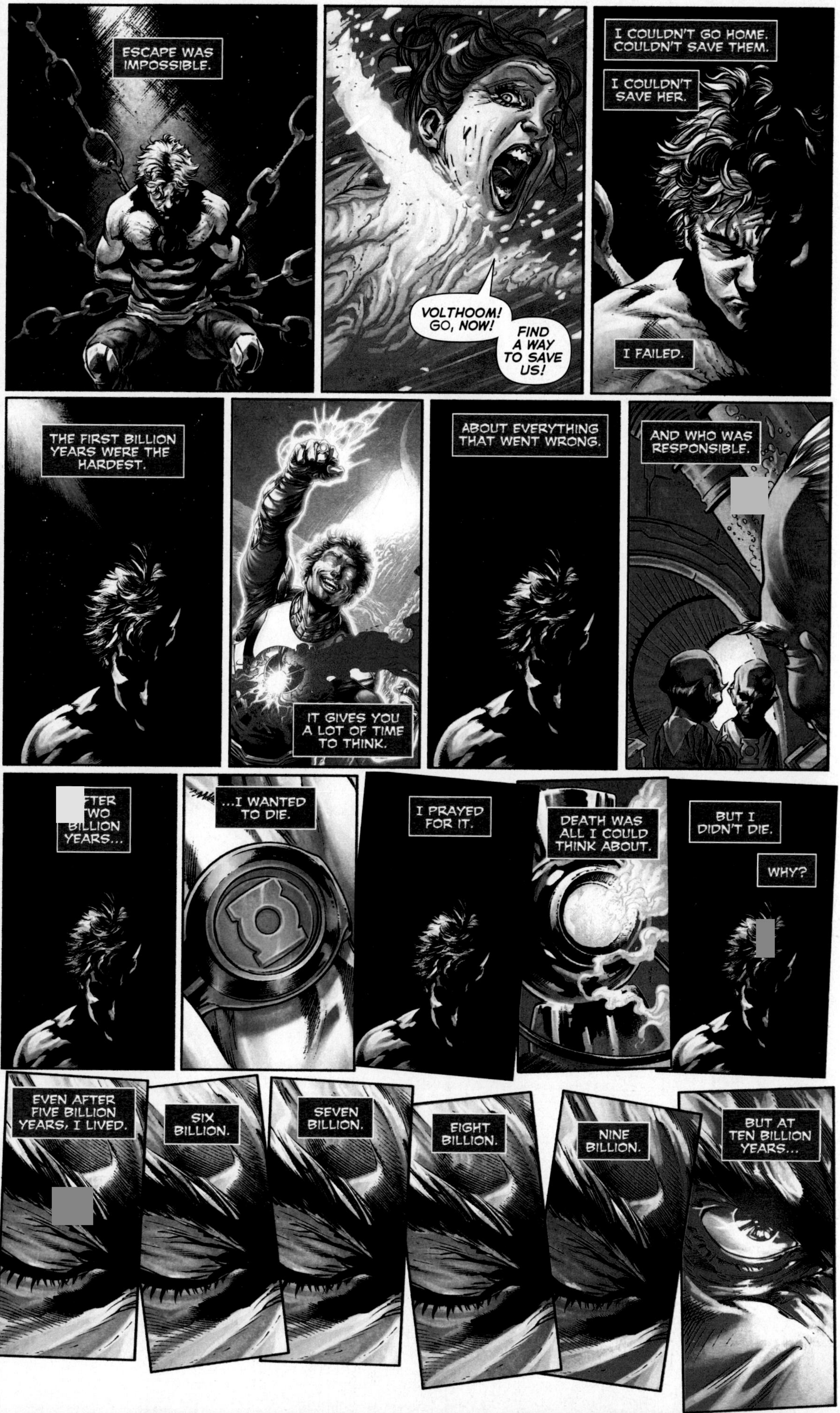
ESCAPE WAS IMPOSSIBLE.
VOLTHOOM! GO, NOW!
FIND A WAY TO SAVE US!
I COULDN'T GO HOME. COULDN'T SAVE THEM.
I COULDN'T SAVE HER.
I FAILED.
THE FIRST BILLION YEARS WERE THE HARDEST.
IT GIVES YOU A LOT OF TIME TO THINK.
ABOUT EVERYTHING THAT WENT WRONG.
AND WHO WAS RESPONSIBLE.
FTER WO BILLION YEARS...
...I WANTED TO DIE.
I PRAYED FOR IT.
DEATH WAS ALL I COULD THINK ABOUT.
BUT I DIDN'T DIE.
WHY?
EVEN AFTER FIVE BILLION YEARS, I LIVED.
SIX BILLION.
SEVEN BILLION.
EIGHT BILLION.
NINE BILLION.
BUT AT TEN BILLION YEARS...

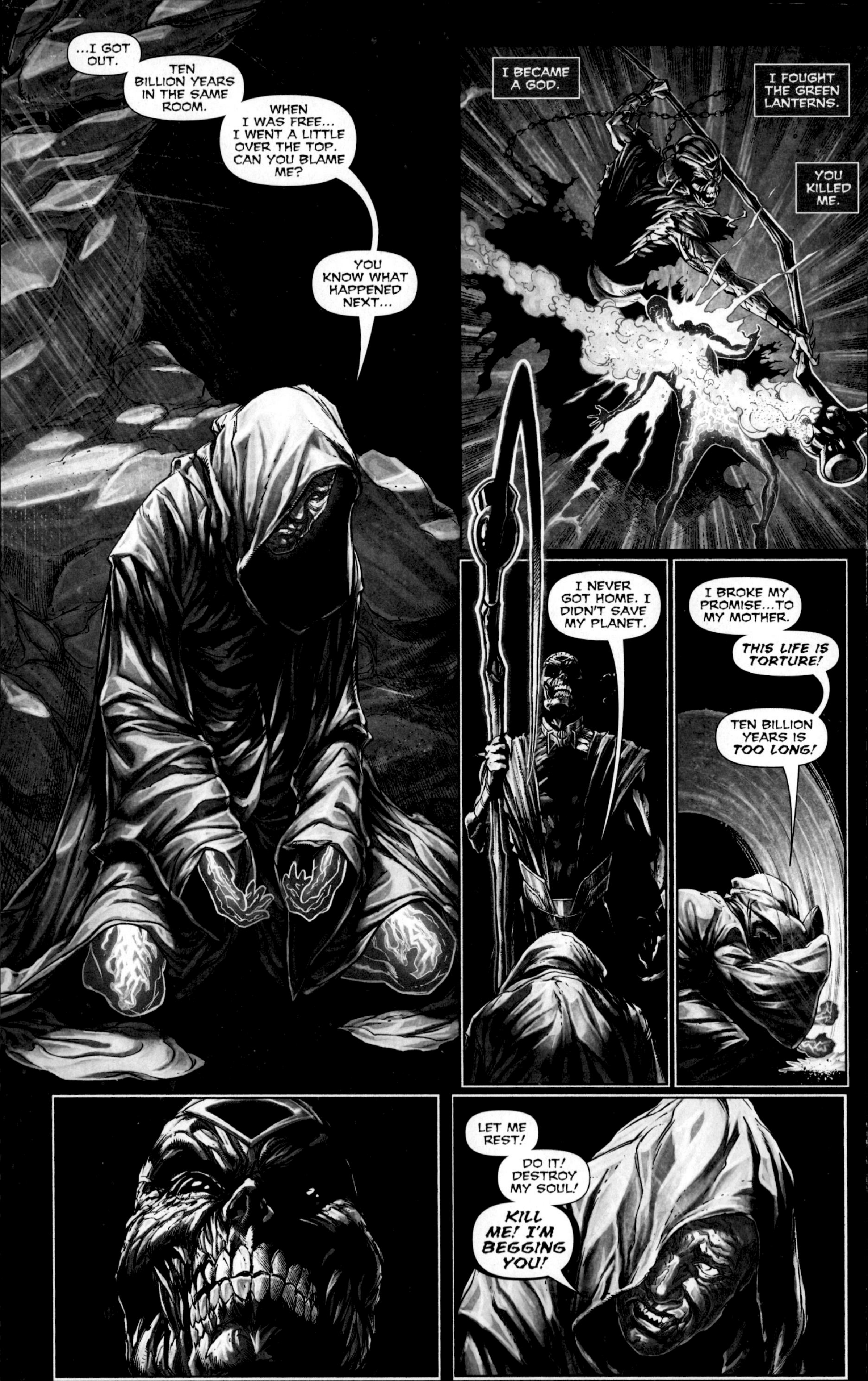
...I GOT OUT.
TEN BILLION YEARS IN THE SAME ROOM.
WHEN I WAS FREE... I WENT A LITTLE OVER THE TOP. CAN YOU BLAME ME?
YOU KNOW WHAT HAPPENED NEXT...
I BECAME A GOD.
I FOUGHT THE GREEN LANTERNS.
YOU KILLED ME.
I NEVER GOT HOME. I DIDN'T SAVE MY PLANET.
I BROKE MY PROMISE...TO MY MOTHER.
THIS LIFE IS TORTURE!
TEN BILLION YEARS IS TOO LONG!
LET ME REST!
DO IT! DESTROY MY SOUL!
KILL ME! I'M BEGGING YOU!

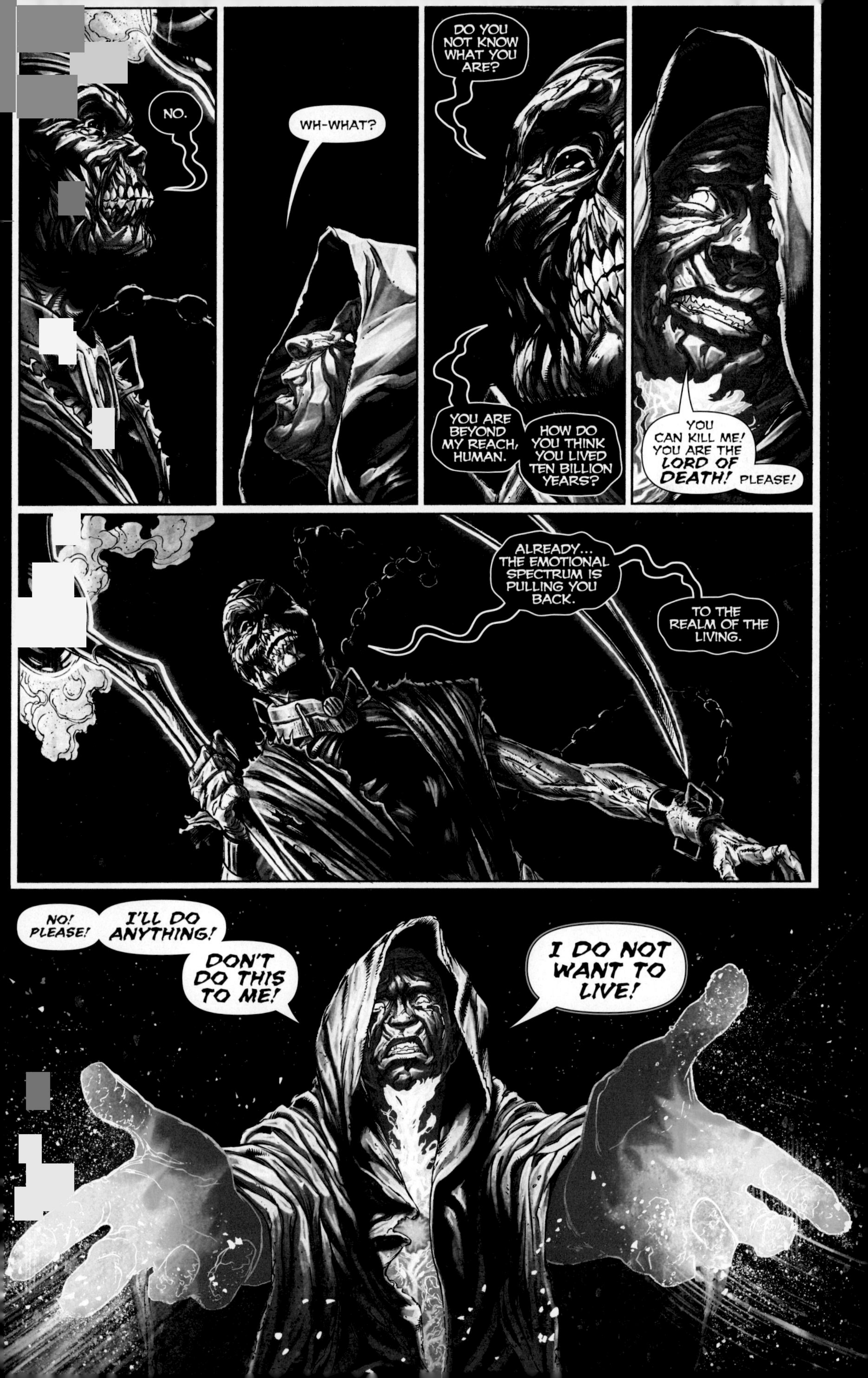
NO.
WH-WHAT?
DO YOU NOT KNOW WHAT YOU ARE?
YOU ARE BEYOND MY REACH, HUMAN.
HOW DO YOU THINK YOU LIVED TEN BILLION YEARS?
YOU CAN KILL ME! YOU ARE THE LORD OF DEATH! PLEASE!
ALREADY... THE EMOTIONAL SPECTRUM IS PULLING YOU BACK.
TO THE REALM OF THE LIVING.
NO! PLEASE!
I'LL DO ANYTHING!
DON'T DO THIS TO ME!
I DO NOT WANT TO LIVE!

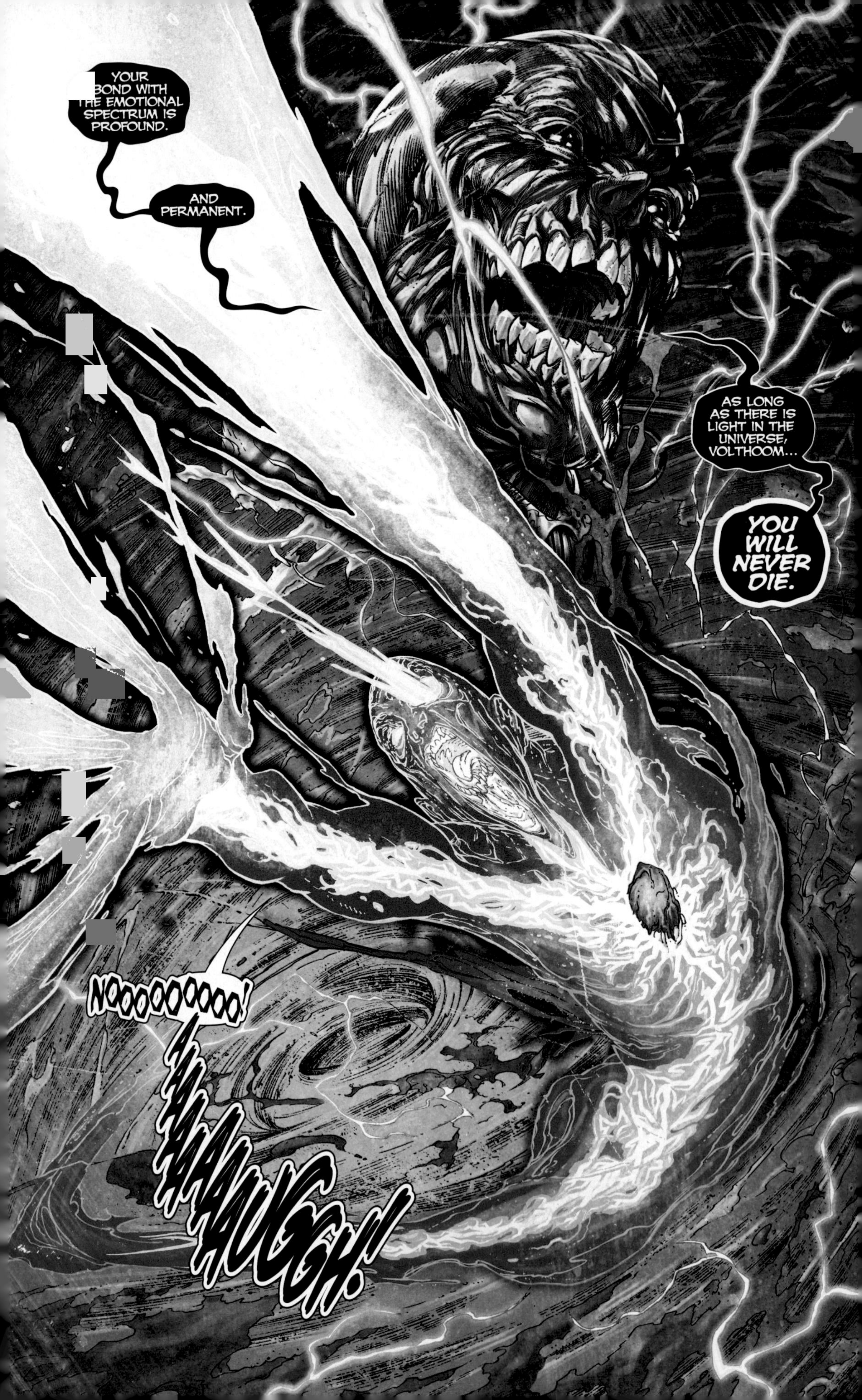
YOUR BOND WITH THE EMOTIONAL SPECTRUM IS PROFOUND.
AND PERMANENT.
AS LONG AS THERE IS LIGHT IN THE UNIVERSE, VOLTHOOM...
YOU WILL NEVER DIE.
NOOOOOOOOOO!
AAAAAAAUGGH!

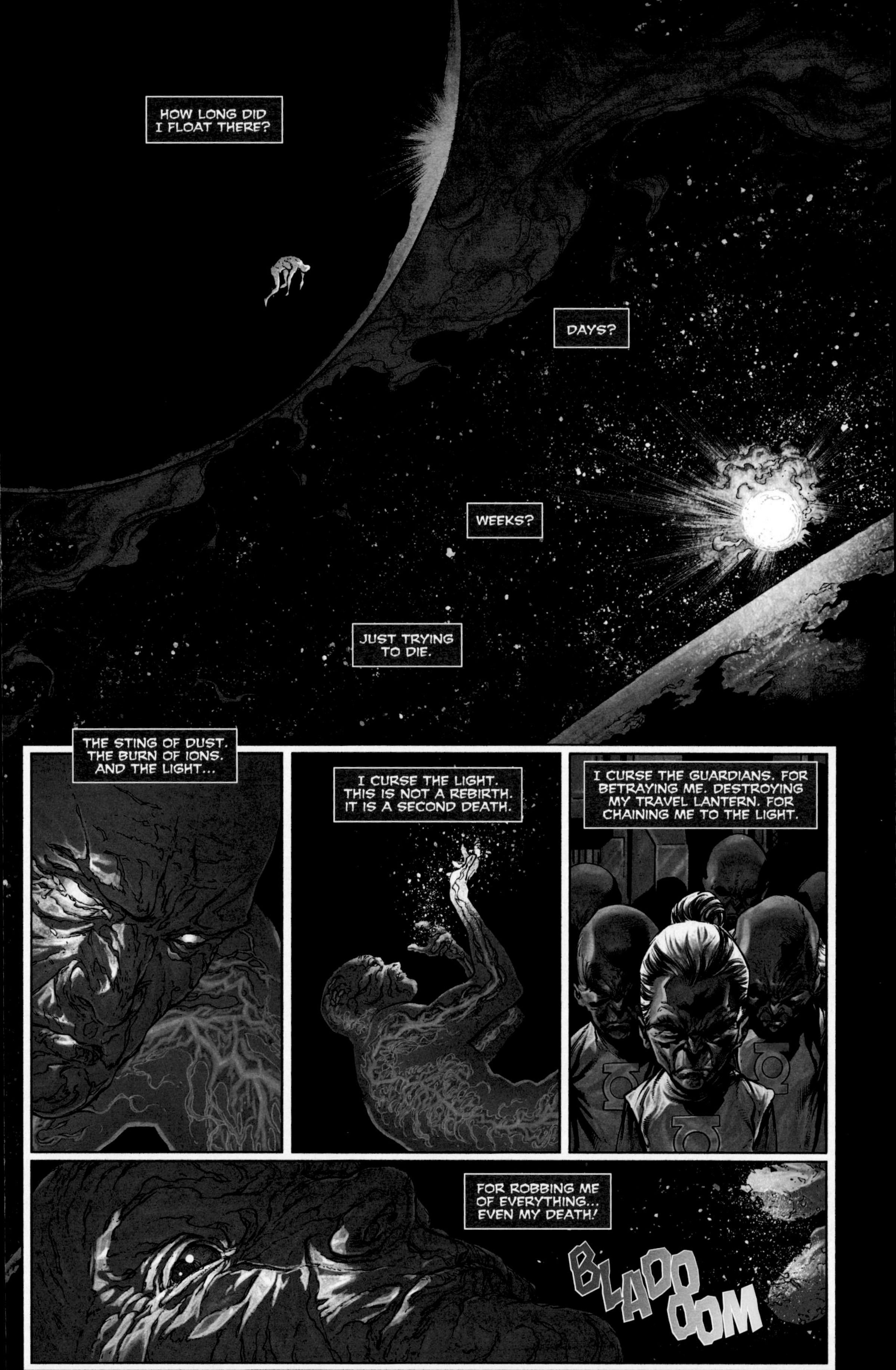
HOW LONG DID I FLOAT THERE?
DAYS?
WEEKS?
JUST TRYING TO DIE.
THE STING OF DUST. THE BURN OF IONS. AND THE LIGHT...
I CURSE THE LIGHT. THIS IS NOT A REBIRTH. IT IS A SECOND DEATH.
I CURSE THE GUARDIANS. FOR BETRAYING ME. DESTROYING MY TRAVEL LANTERN. FOR CHAINING ME TO THE LIGHT.
FOR ROBBING ME OF EVERYTHING... EVEN MY DEATH!
BLADOOOM

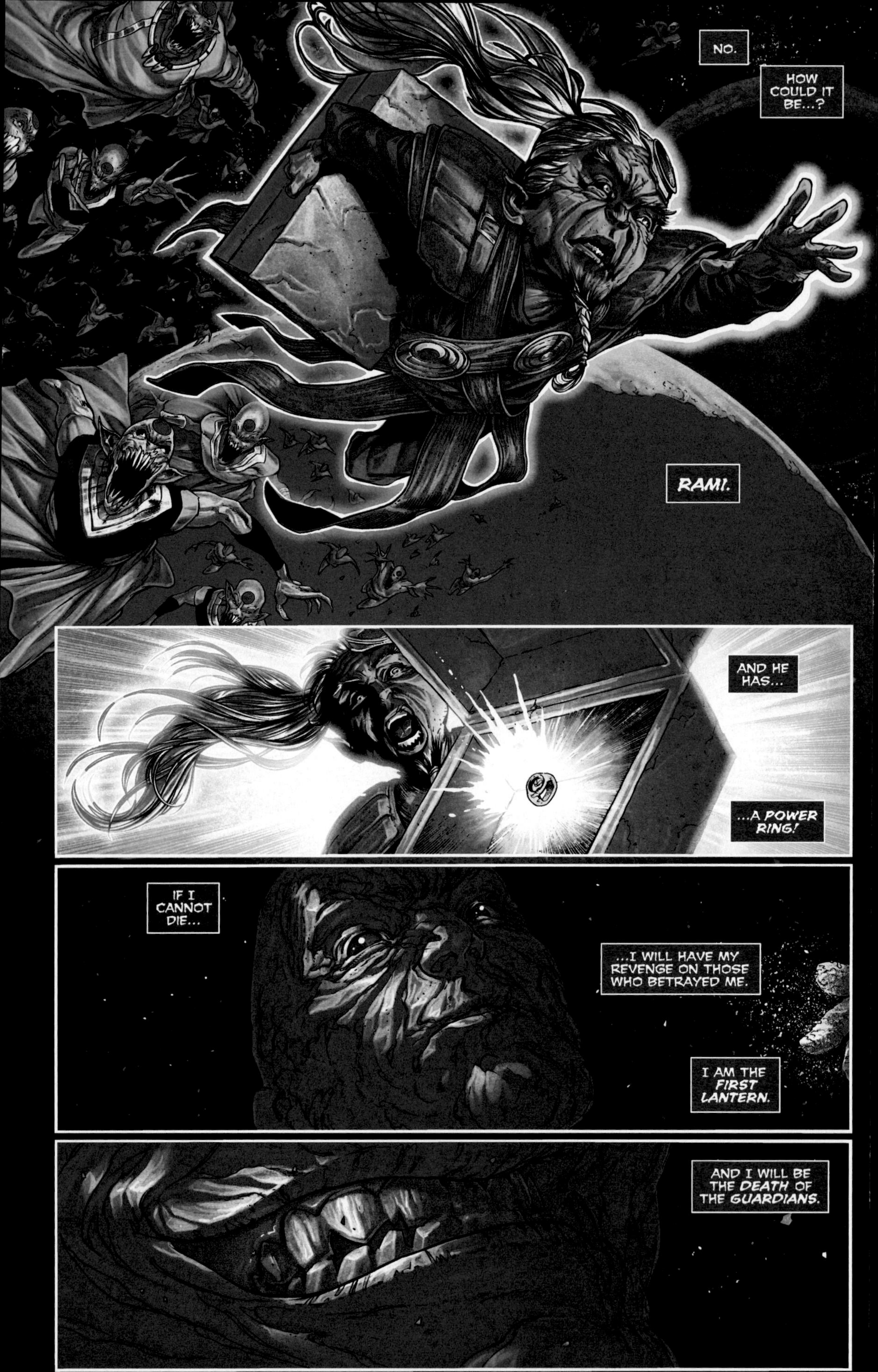
NO.
HOW COULD IT BE...?
RAMI.
AND HE HAS...
...A POWER RING!
IF I CANNOT DIE...
...I WILL HAVE MY REVENGE ON THOSE WHO BETRAYED ME.
I AM THE FIRST LANTERN.
AND I WILL BE THE DEATH OF THE GUARDIANS.

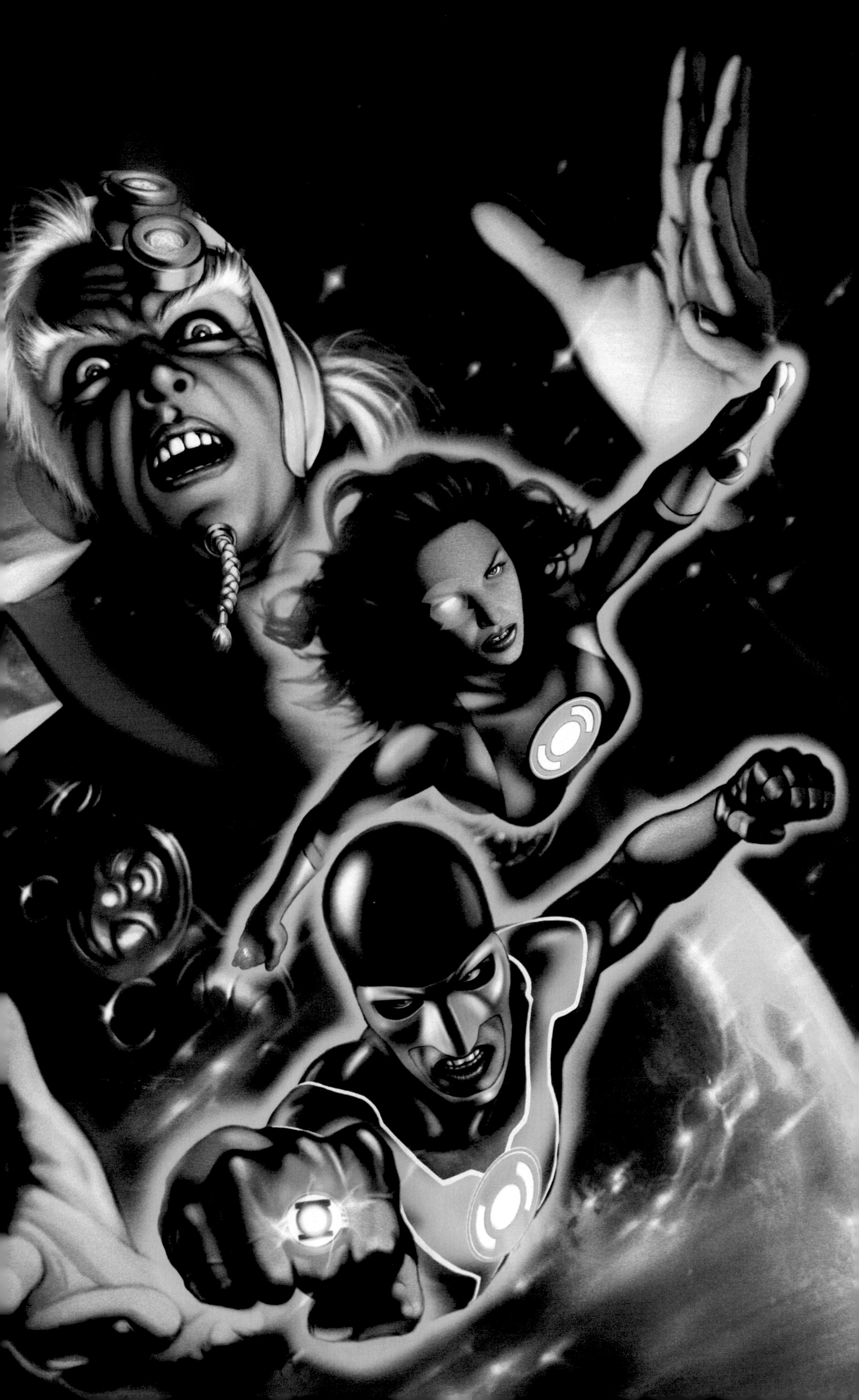

"POLARITY CHAPTER ONE"

RONAN CLIQUET artist

Cover by LEO MANCO

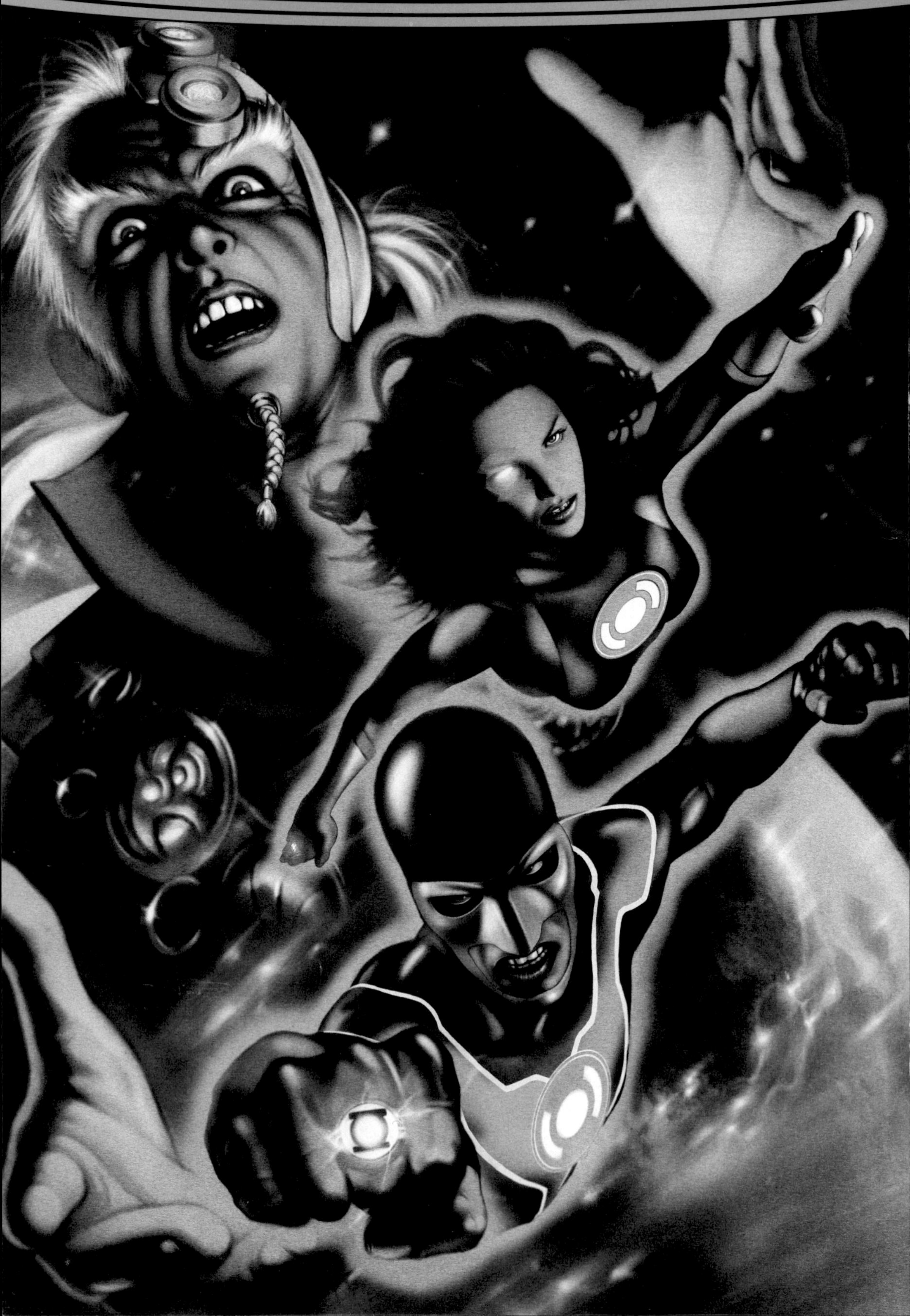

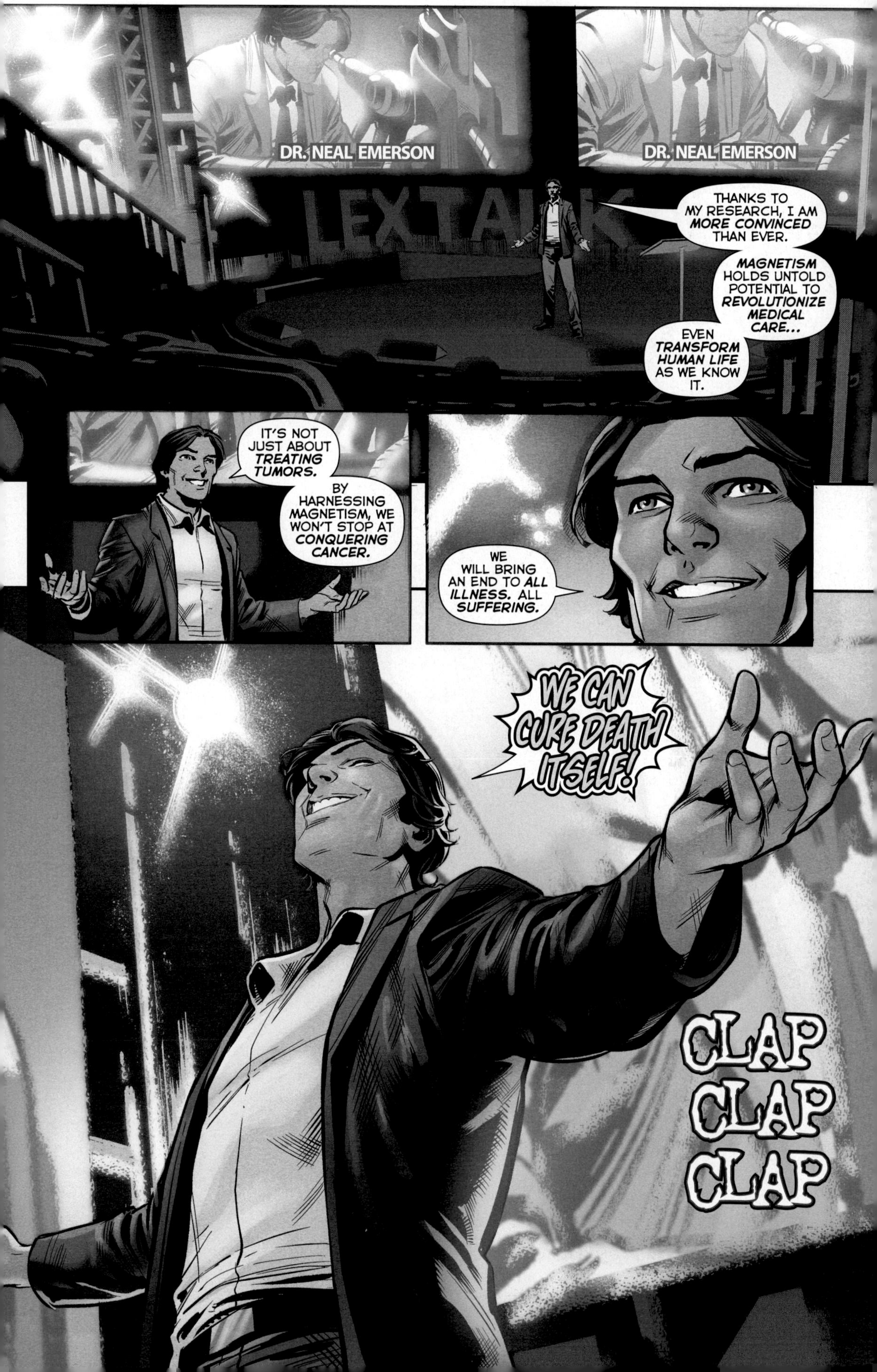
DR. NEAL EMERSON
DR. NEAL EMERSON
LEXTALK
THANKS TO MY RESEARCH, I AM MORE CONVINCED THAN EVER.
MAGNETISM HOLDS UNTOLD POTENTIAL TO REVOLUTIONIZE MEDICAL CARE...
EVEN TRANSFORM HUMAN LIFE AS WE KNOW IT.
IT'S NOT JUST ABOUT TREATING TUMORS.
BY HARNESSING MAGNETISM, WE WON'T STOP AT CONQUERING CANCER.
WE WILL BRING AN END TO ALL ILLNESS. ALL SUFFERING.
WE CAN CURE DEATH ITSELF!
CLAP
CLAP
CLAP

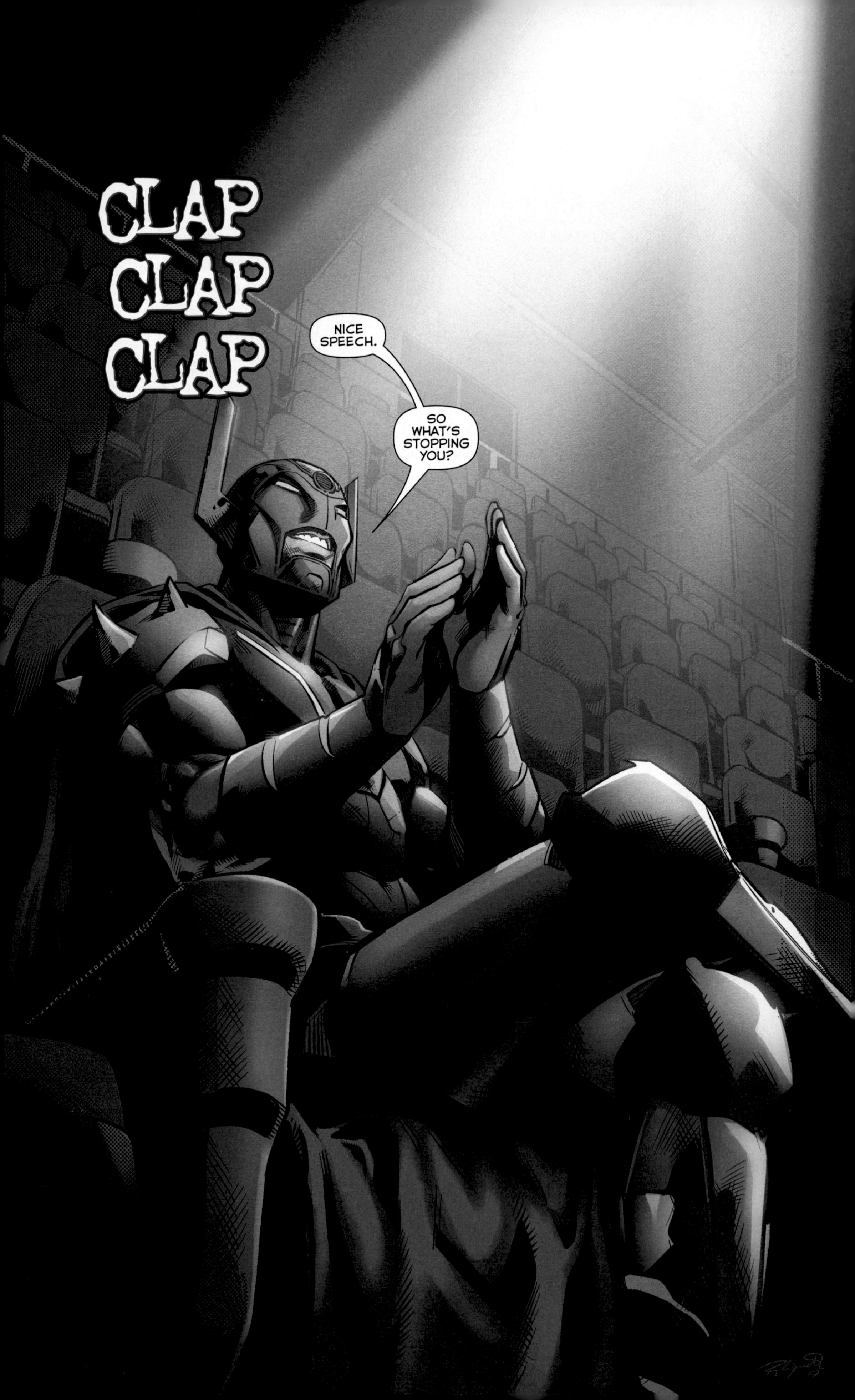

CLAP CLAP CLAP
NICE SPEECH.
SO WHAT'S STOPPING YOU?

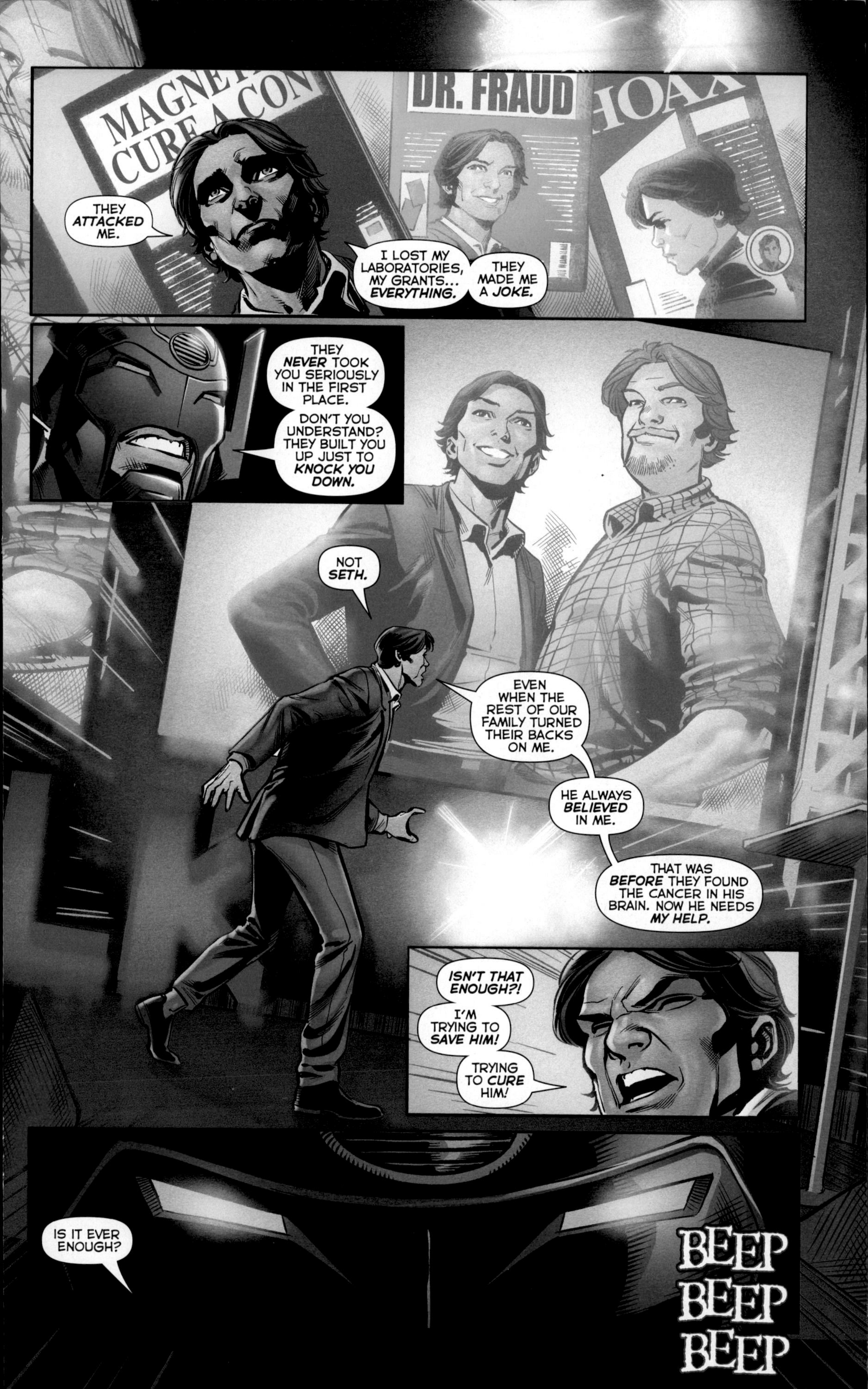
MAGNET… CURE A CON
DR. FRAUD
HOAX
THEY ATTACKED ME.
I LOST MY LABORATORIES, MY GRANTS... EVERYTHING.
THEY MADE ME A JOKE.
THEY NEVER TOOK YOU SERIOUSLY IN THE FIRST PLACE.
DON'T YOU UNDERSTAND? THEY BUILT YOU UP JUST TO KNOCK YOU DOWN.
NOT SETH.
EVEN WHEN THE REST OF OUR FAMILY TURNED THEIR BACKS ON ME.
HE ALWAYS BELIEVED IN ME.
THAT WAS BEFORE THEY FOUND THE CANCER IN HIS BRAIN. NOW HE NEEDS MY HELP.
ISN'T THAT ENOUGH?!
I'M TRYING TO SAVE HIM!
TRYING TO CURE HIM!
IS IT EVER ENOUGH?
BEEP BEEP BEEP

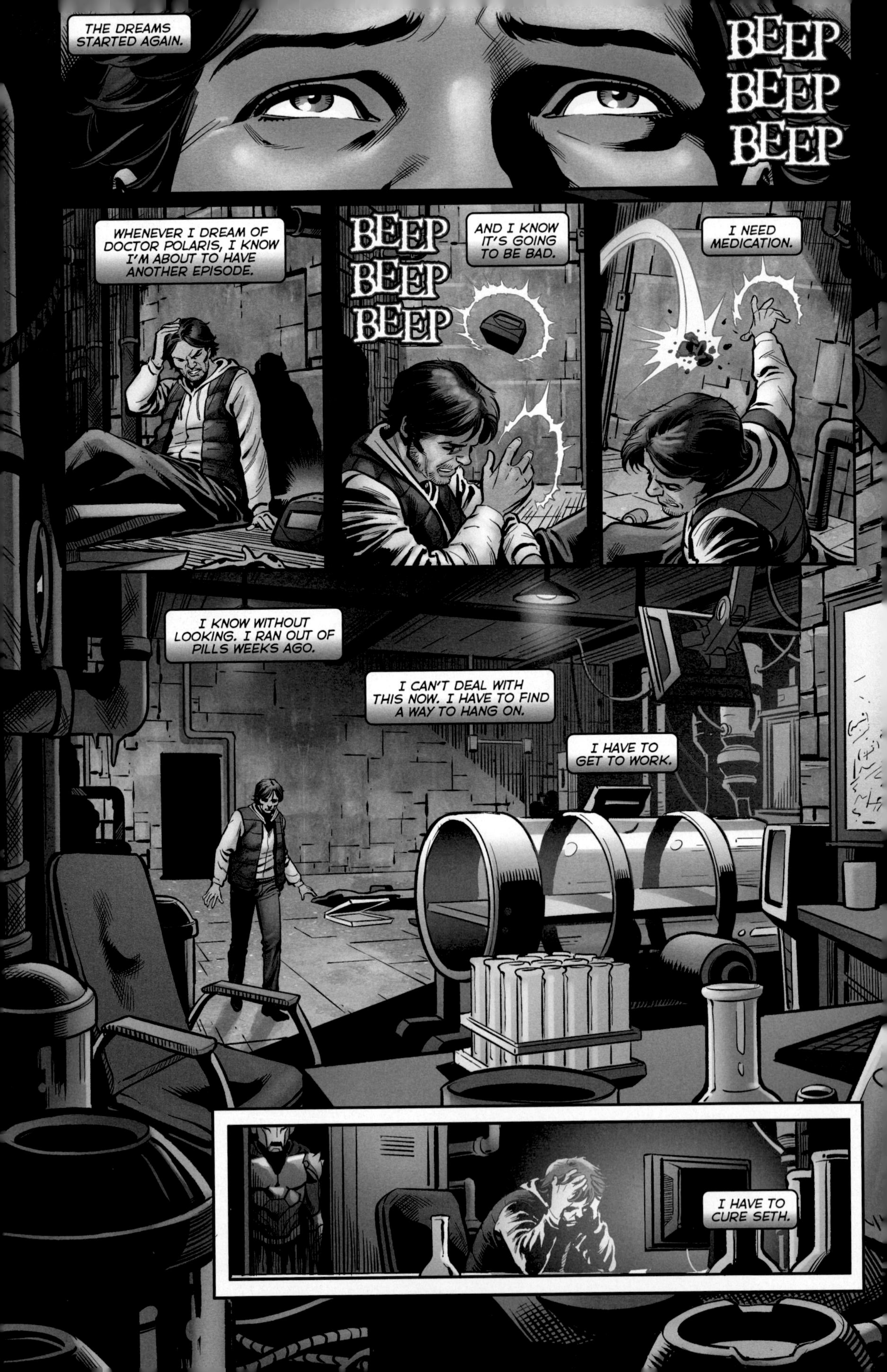
THE DREAMS STARTED AGAIN.
BEEP BEEP BEEP
WHENEVER I DREAM OF DOCTOR POLARIS, I KNOW I'M ABOUT TO HAVE ANOTHER EPISODE.
BEEP BEEP BEEP
AND I KNOW IT'S GOING TO BE BAD.
I NEED MEDICATION.
I KNOW WITHOUT LOOKING. I RAN OUT OF PILLS WEEKS AGO.
I CAN'T DEAL WITH THIS NOW. I HAVE TO FIND A WAY TO HANG ON.
I HAVE TO GET TO WORK.
I HAVE TO CURE SETH.

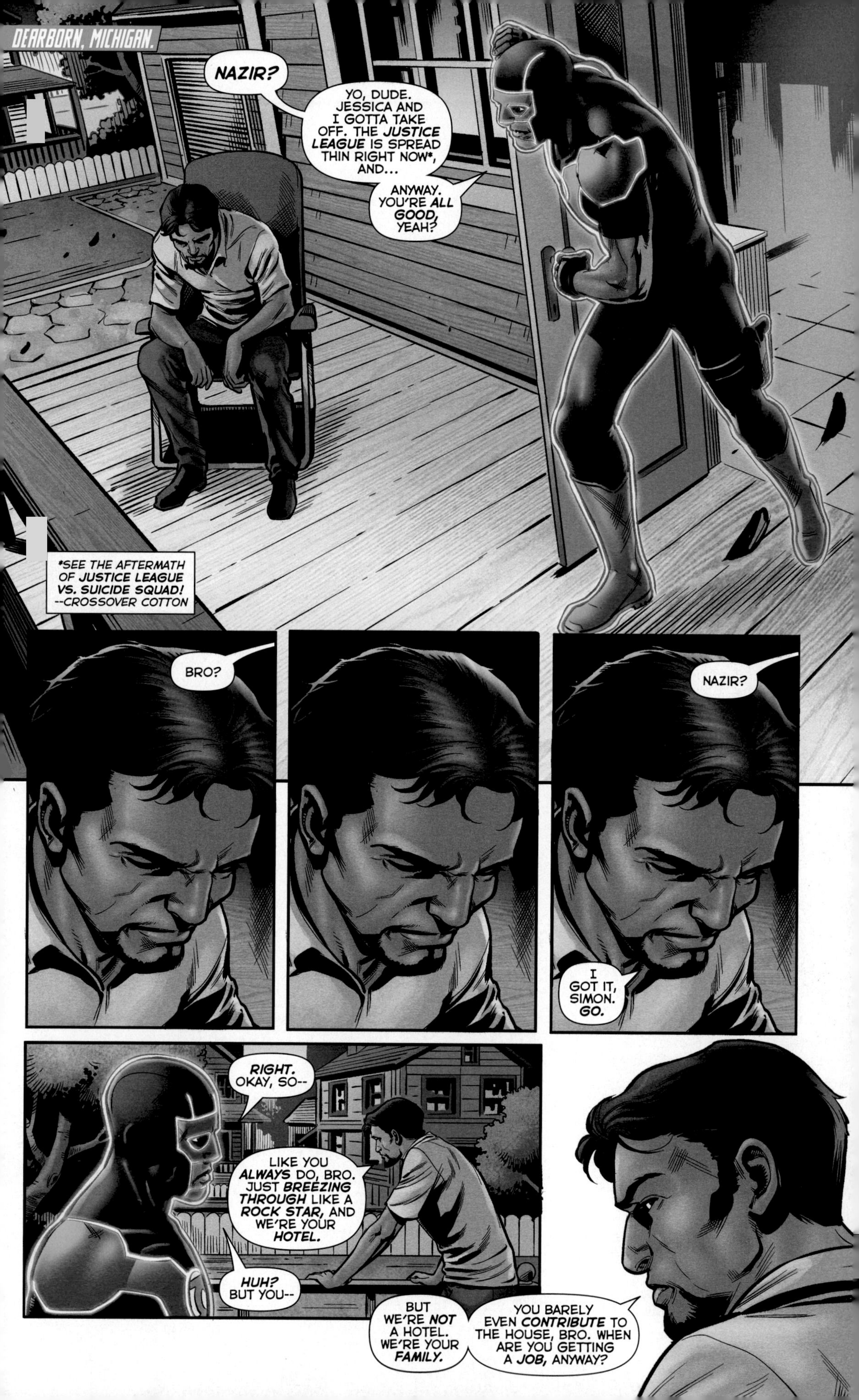
DEARBORN, MICHIGAN.
NAZIR?
YO, DUDE. JESSICA AND I GOTTA TAKE OFF. THE JUSTICE LEAGUE IS SPREAD THIN RIGHT NOW*, AND...
ANYWAY. YOU'RE ALL GOOD, YEAH?
*SEE THE AFTERMATH OF JUSTICE LEAGUE VS. SUICIDE SQUAD! --CROSSOVER COTTON
BRO?
NAZIR?
I GOT IT, SIMON. GO.
RIGHT. OKAY, SO--
LIKE YOU ALWAYS DO, BRO. JUST BREEZING THROUGH LIKE A ROCK STAR, AND WE'RE YOUR HOTEL.
HUH? BUT YOU--
BUT WE'RE NOT A HOTEL. WE'RE YOUR FAMILY.
YOU BARELY EVEN CONTRIBUTE TO THE HOUSE, BRO. WHEN ARE YOU GETTING A JOB, ANYWAY?

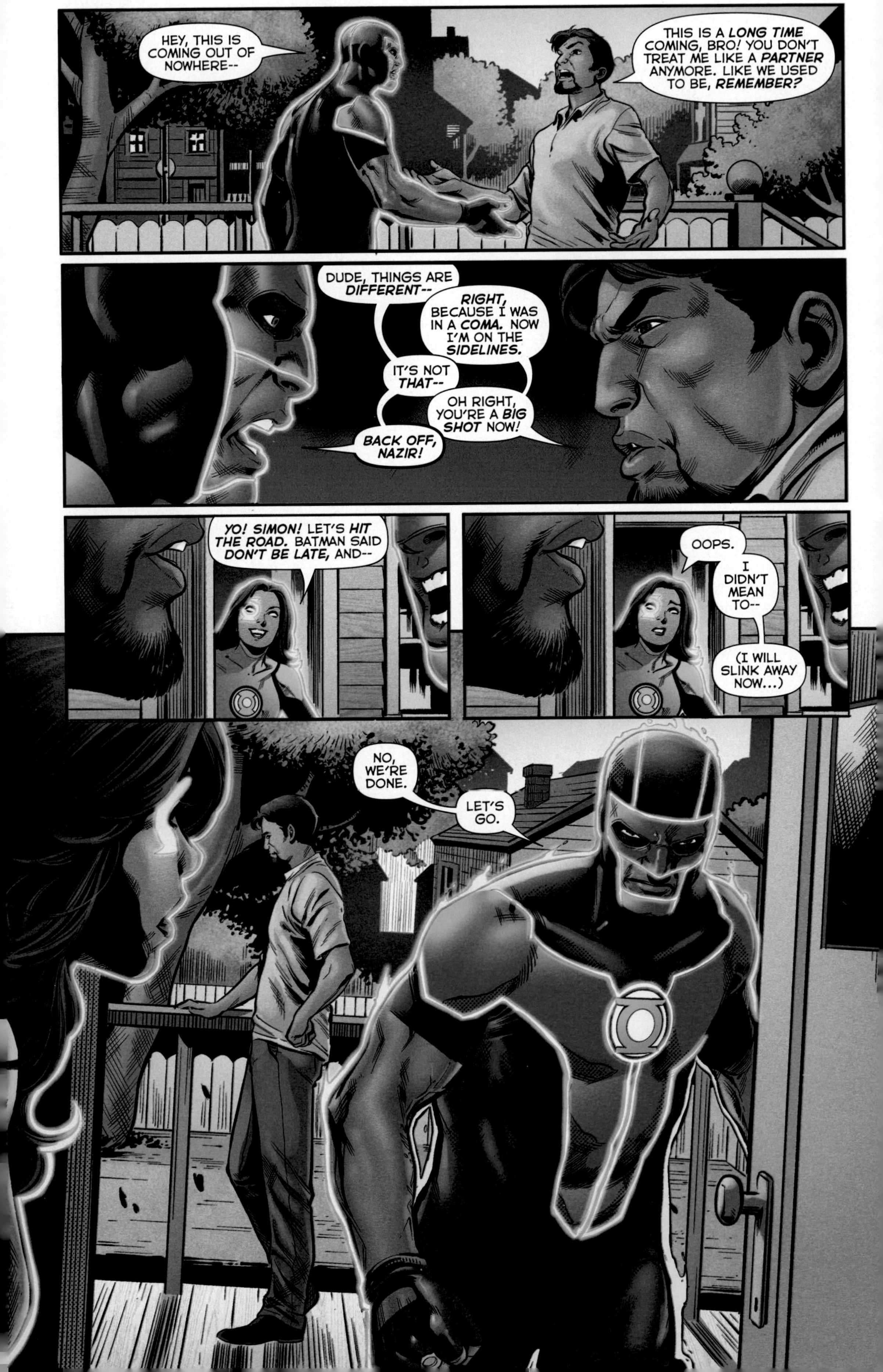
HEY, THIS IS COMING OUT OF NOWHERE--
THIS IS A LONG TIME COMING, BRO! YOU DON'T TREAT ME LIKE A PARTNER ANYMORE. LIKE WE USED TO BE, REMEMBER?
DUDE, THINGS ARE DIFFERENT--
RIGHT, BECAUSE I WAS IN A COMA. NOW I'M ON THE SIDELINES.
IT'S NOT THAT--
OH RIGHT, YOU'RE A BIG SHOT NOW!
BACK OFF, NAZIR!
YO! SIMON! LET'S HIT THE ROAD. BATMAN SAID DON'T BE LATE, AND--
OOPS.
I DIDN'T MEAN TO--
(I WILL SLINK AWAY NOW...)
NO, WE'RE DONE.
LET'S GO.

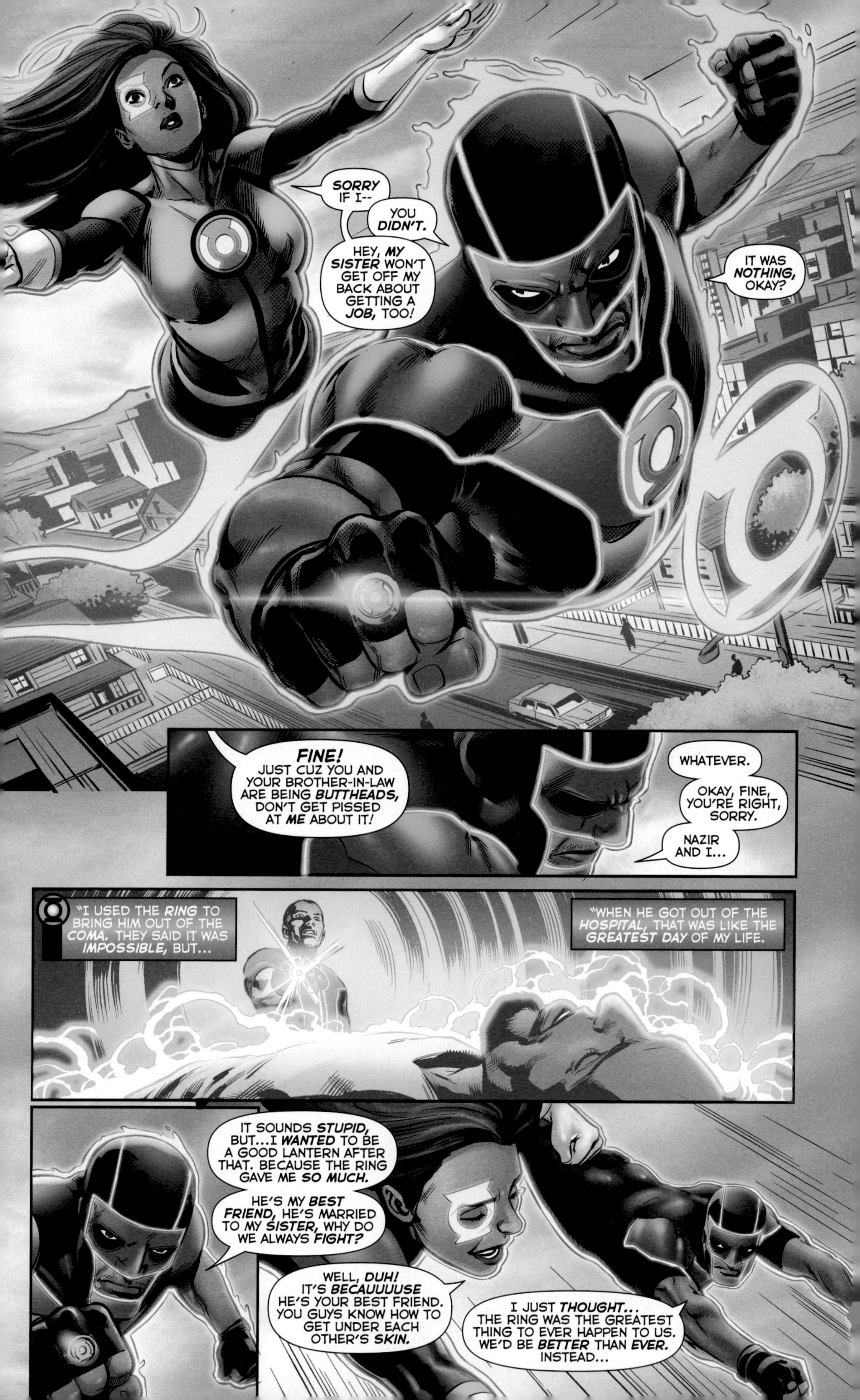
SORRY IF I--
YOU DIDN'T.
HEY, MY SISTER WON'T GET OFF MY BACK ABOUT GETTING A JOB, TOO!
IT WAS NOTHING, OKAY?
FINE! JUST CUZ YOU AND YOUR BROTHER-IN-LAW ARE BEING BUTTHEADS, DON'T GET PISSED AT ME ABOUT IT!
WHATEVER.
OKAY, FINE, YOU'RE RIGHT, SORRY.
NAZIR AND I...
"I USED THE RING TO BRING HIM OUT OF THE COMA. THEY SAID IT WAS IMPOSSIBLE, BUT...
"WHEN HE GOT OUT OF THE HOSPITAL, THAT WAS LIKE THE GREATEST DAY OF MY LIFE.
IT SOUNDS STUPID, BUT...I WANTED TO BE A GOOD LANTERN AFTER THAT. BECAUSE THE RING GAVE ME SO MUCH.
HE'S MY BEST FRIEND, HE'S MARRIED TO MY SISTER, WHY DO WE ALWAYS FIGHT?
WELL, DUH! IT'S BECAUUUUSE HE'S YOUR BEST FRIEND. YOU GUYS KNOW HOW TO GET UNDER EACH OTHER'S SKIN.
I JUST THOUGHT... THE RING WAS THE GREATEST THING TO EVER HAPPEN TO US. WE'D BE BETTER THAN EVER. INSTEAD...

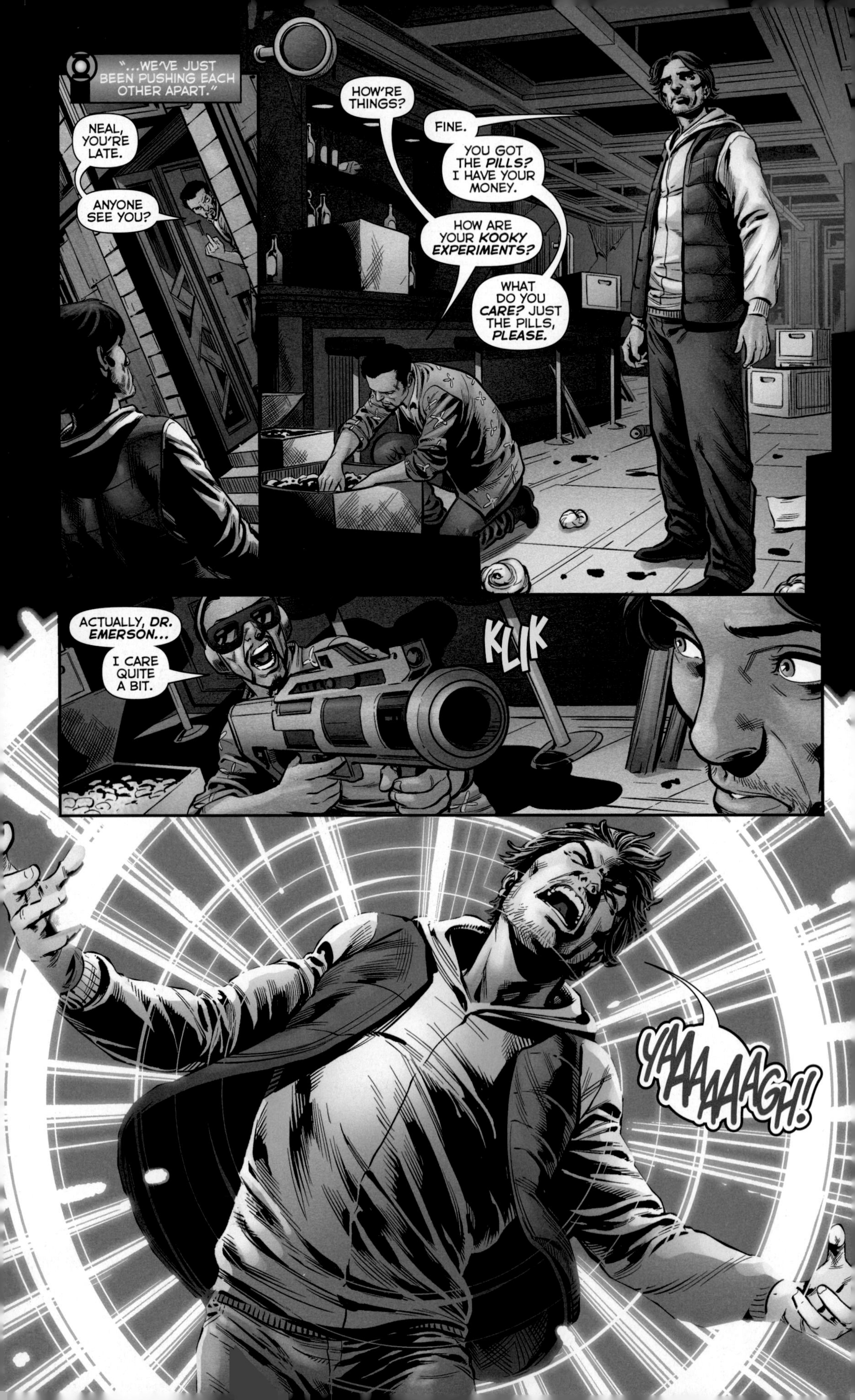

"...WE'VE JUST BEEN PUSHING EACH OTHER APART."
NEAL, YOU'RE LATE.
ANYONE SEE YOU?
HOW'RE THINGS?
FINE.
YOU GOT THE PILLS? I HAVE YOUR MONEY.
HOW ARE YOUR KOOKY EXPERIMENTS?
WHAT DO YOU CARE? JUST THE PILLS, PLEASE.
ACTUALLY, DR. EMERSON...
I CARE QUITE A BIT.
KLIK
YAAAAAAGH!

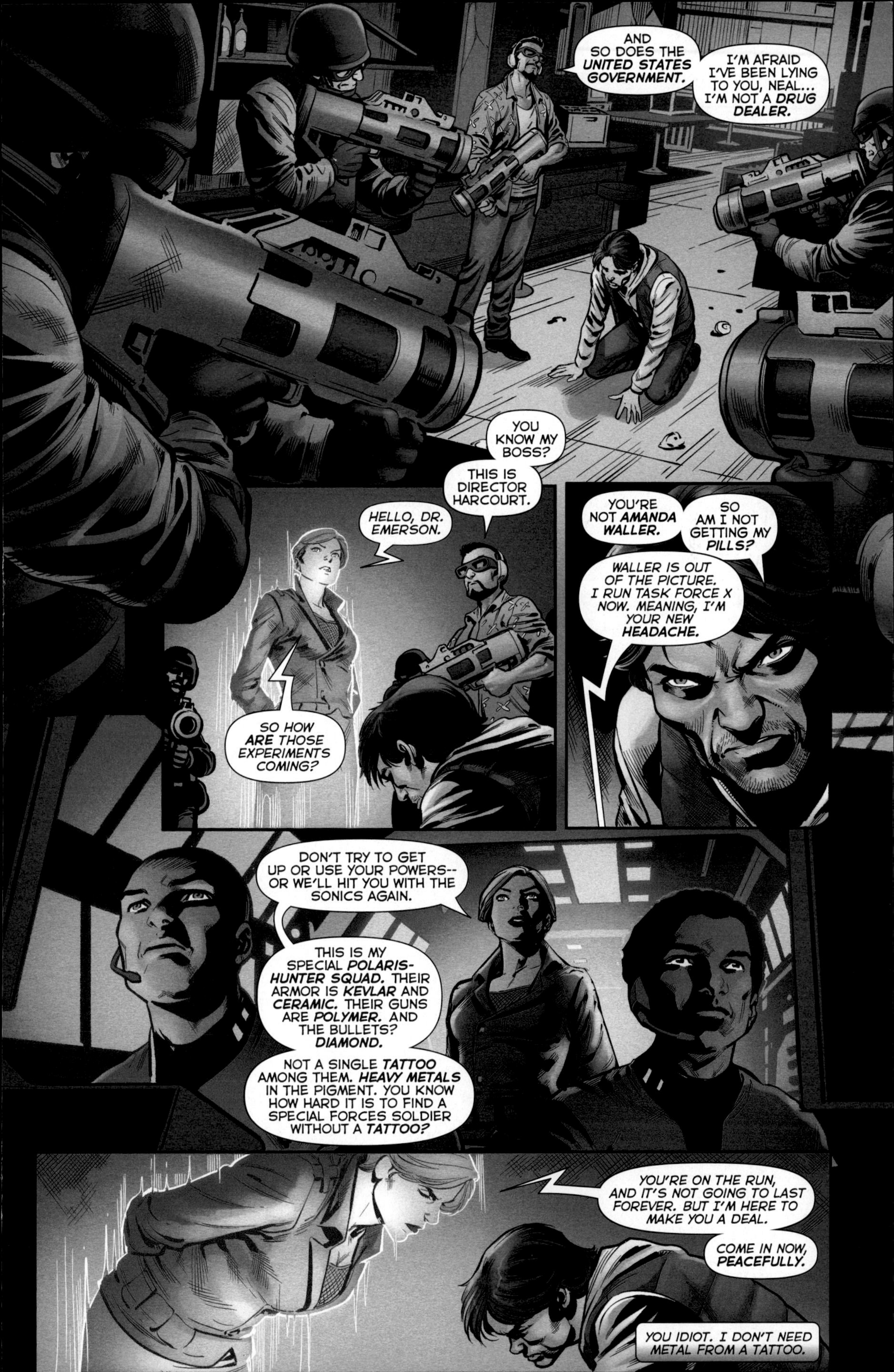
AND SO DOES THE UNITED STATES GOVERNMENT.
I'M AFRAID I'VE BEEN LYING TO YOU, NEAL... I'M NOT A DRUG DEALER.
YOU KNOW MY BOSS?
THIS IS DIRECTOR HARCOURT.
HELLO, DR. EMERSON.
SO HOW ARE THOSE EXPERIMENTS COMING?
YOU'RE NOT AMANDA WALLER.
SO AM I NOT GETTING MY PILLS?
WALLER IS OUT OF THE PICTURE. I RUN TASK FORCE X NOW. MEANING, I'M YOUR NEW HEADACHE.
DON'T TRY TO GET UP OR USE YOUR POWERS-- OR WE'LL HIT YOU WITH THE SONICS AGAIN.
THIS IS MY SPECIAL POLARIS-HUNTER SQUAD. THEIR ARMOR IS KEVLAR AND CERAMIC. THEIR GUNS ARE POLYMER. AND THE BULLETS? DIAMOND.
NOT A SINGLE TATTOO AMONG THEM. HEAVY METALS IN THE PIGMENT. YOU KNOW HOW HARD IT IS TO FIND A SPECIAL FORCES SOLDIER WITHOUT A TATTOO?
YOU'RE ON THE RUN, AND IT'S NOT GOING TO LAST FOREVER. BUT I'M HERE TO MAKE YOU A DEAL.
COME IN NOW, PEACEFULLY.
YOU IDIOT. I DON'T NEED METAL FROM A TATTOO.

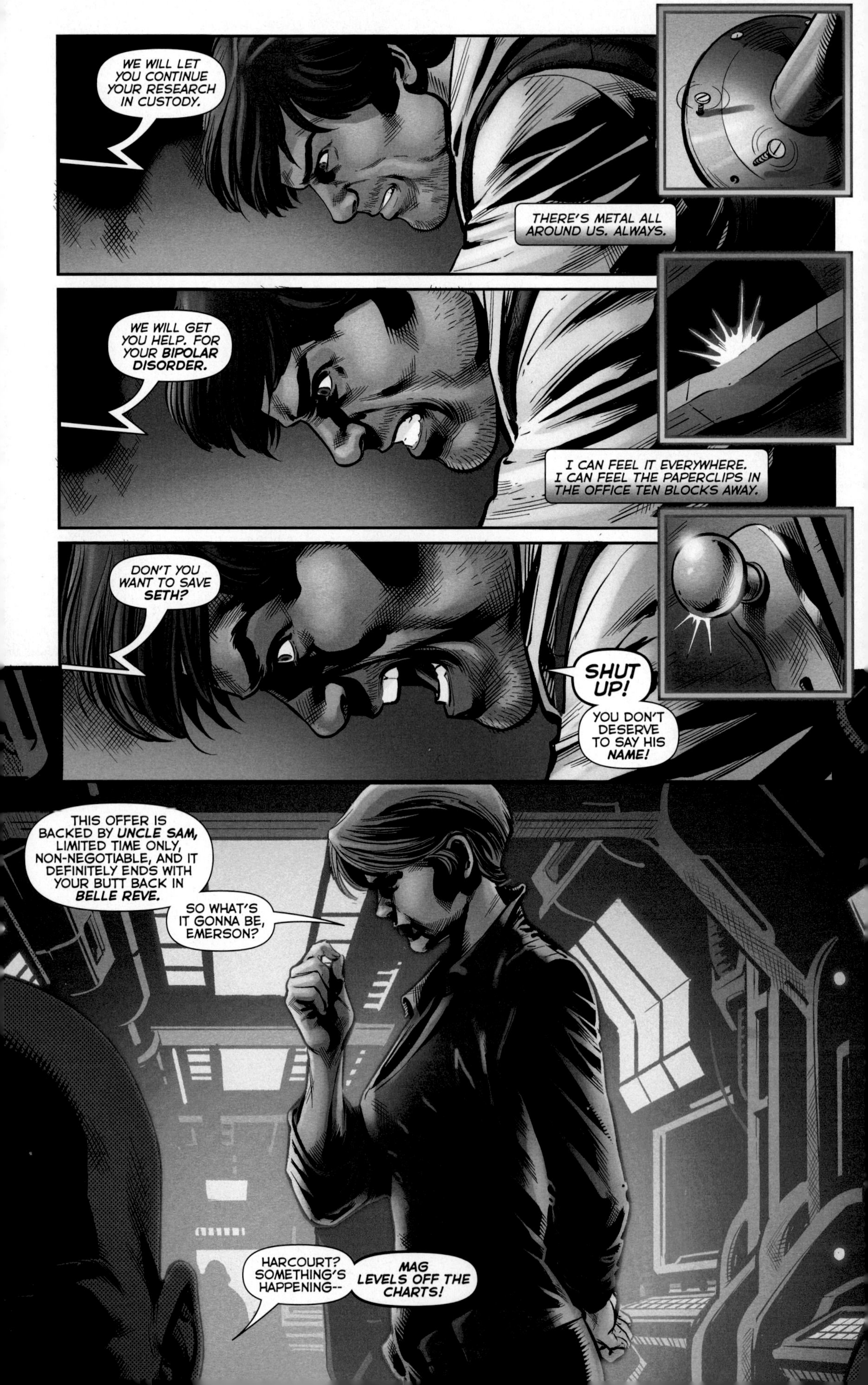
WE WILL LET YOU CONTINUE YOUR RESEARCH IN CUSTODY.
THERE'S METAL ALL AROUND US. ALWAYS.
WE WILL GET YOU HELP. FOR YOUR BIPOLAR DISORDER.
I CAN FEEL IT EVERYWHERE. I CAN FEEL THE PAPERCLIPS IN THE OFFICE TEN BLOCKS AWAY.
DON'T YOU WANT TO SAVE SETH?
SHUT UP!
YOU DON'T DESERVE TO SAY HIS NAME!
THIS OFFER IS BACKED BY UNCLE SAM, LIMITED TIME ONLY, NON-NEGOTIABLE, AND IT DEFINITELY ENDS WITH YOUR BUTT BACK IN BELLE REVE.
SO WHAT'S IT GONNA BE, EMERSON?
HARCOURT? SOMETHING'S HAPPENING--
MAG LEVELS OFF THE CHARTS!

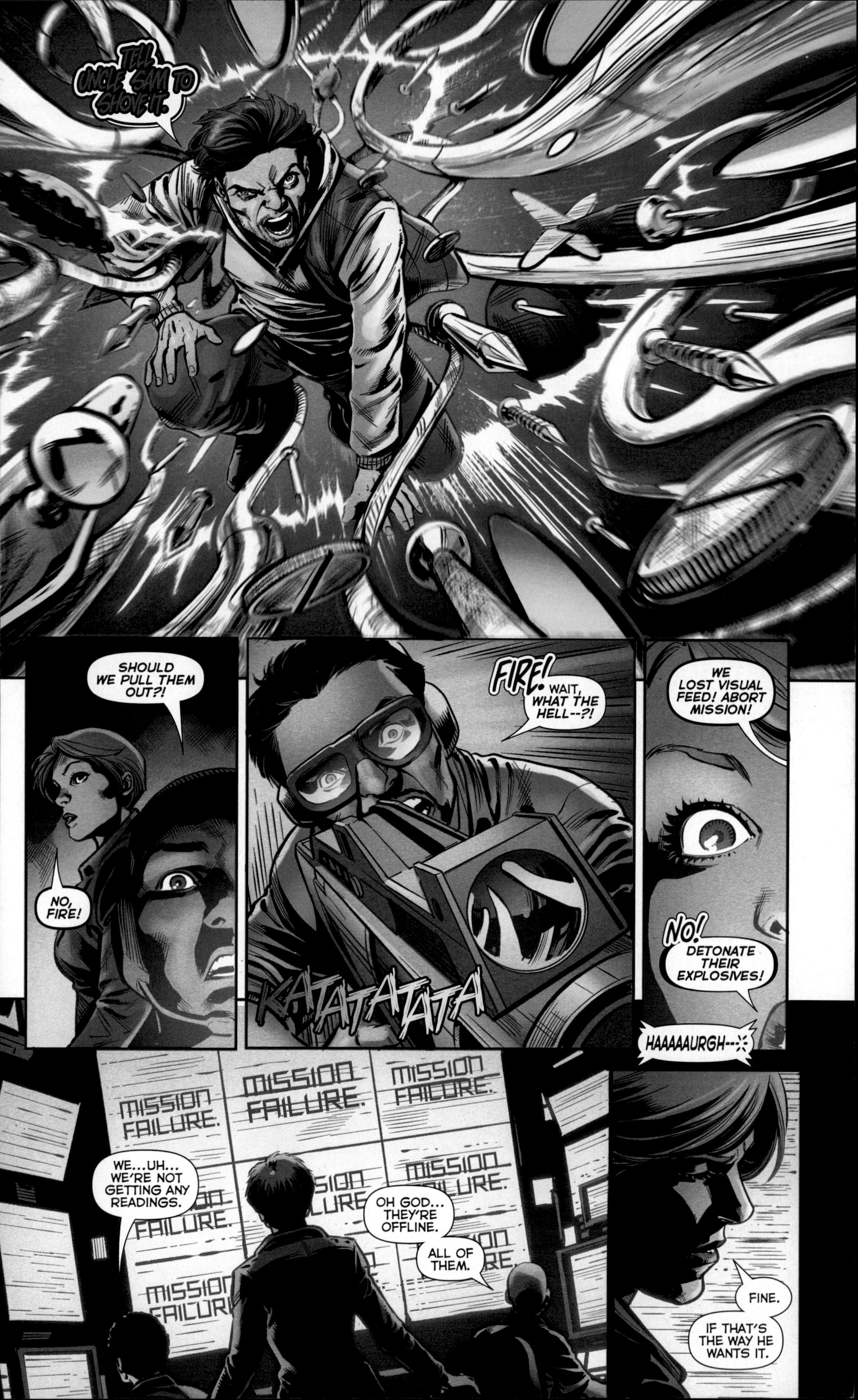
TELL UNCLE SAM TO SHOVE IT.
SHOULD WE PULL THEM OUT?!
NO, FIRE!
FIRE! WAIT, WHAT THE HELL--?!
KATATATATATA
WE LOST VISUAL FEED! ABORT MISSION!
NO! DETONATE THEIR EXPLOSIVES!
HAAAAAURGH--
MISSION FAILURE.
MISSION FAILURE.
MISSION FAILURE.
MISSION FAILURE.
MISSION FAILURE.
MISSION FAILURE.
WE...UH... WE'RE NOT GETTING ANY READINGS.
OH GOD... THEY'RE OFFLINE.
ALL OF THEM.
FINE.
IF THAT'S THE WAY HE WANTS IT.

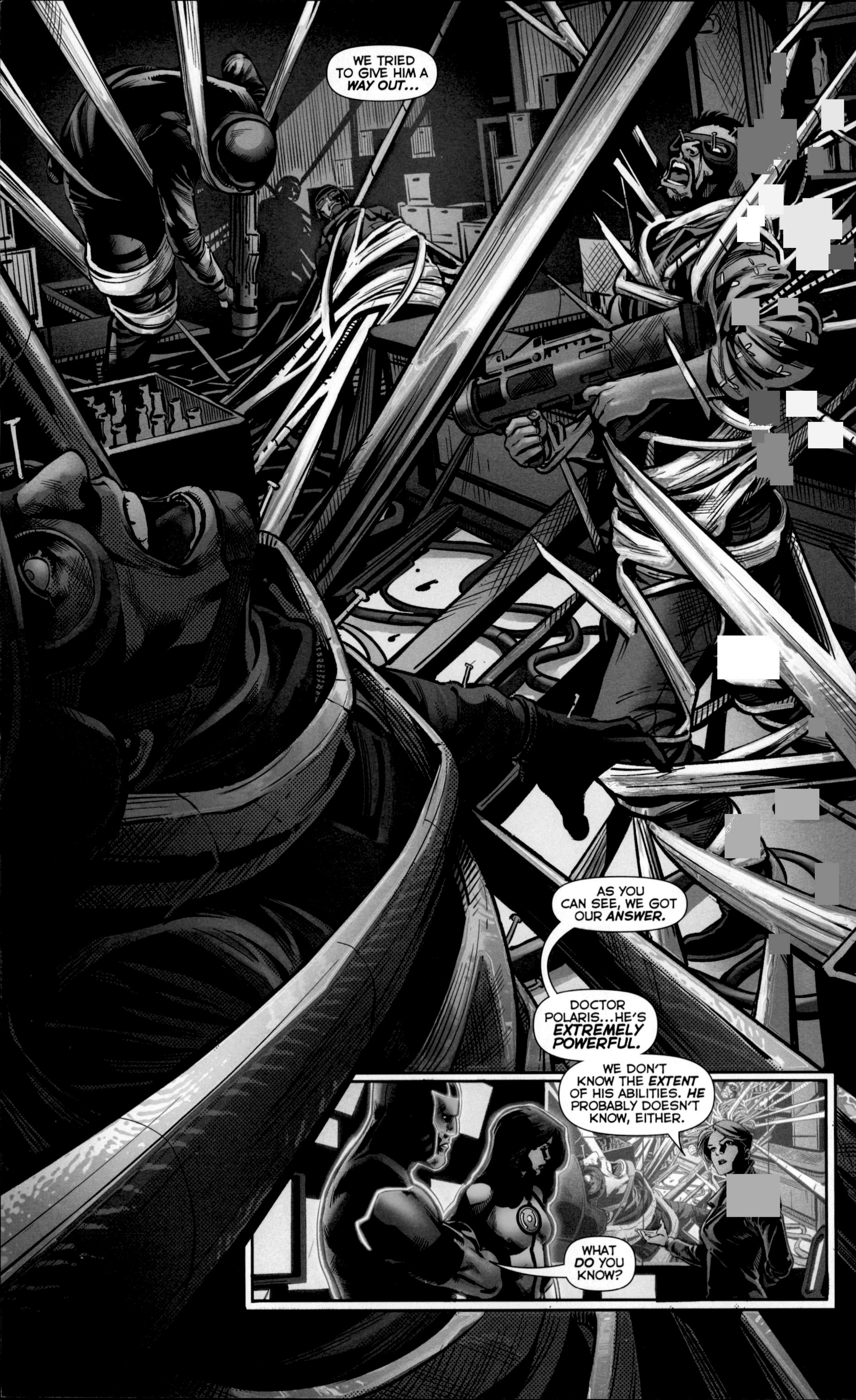
WE TRIED TO GIVE HIM A WAY OUT...
AS YOU CAN SEE, WE GOT OUR ANSWER.
DOCTOR POLARIS...HE'S EXTREMELY POWERFUL.
WE DON'T KNOW THE EXTENT OF HIS ABILITIES. HE PROBABLY DOESN'T KNOW, EITHER.
WHAT DO YOU KNOW?

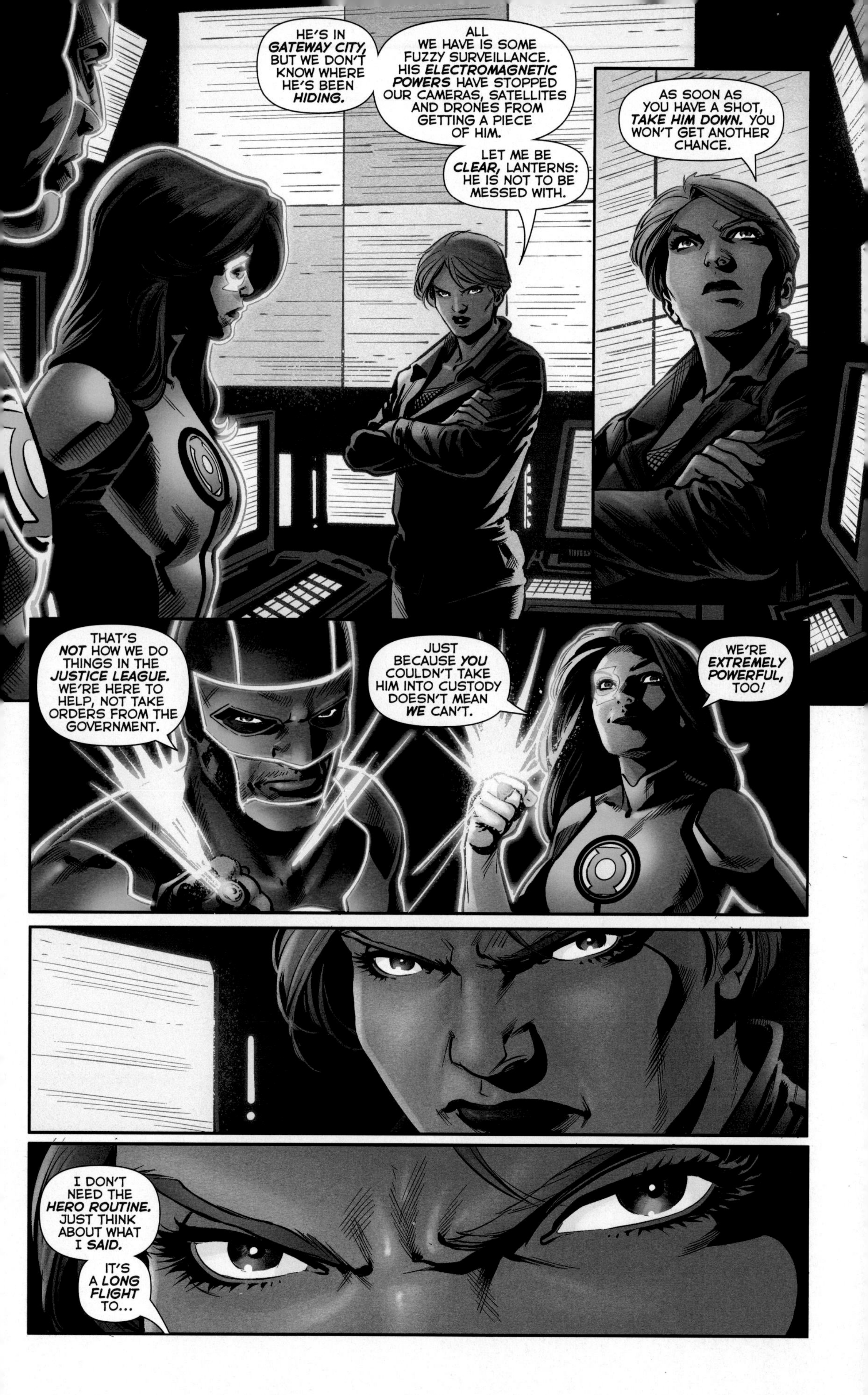
HE'S IN GATEWAY CITY, BUT WE DON'T KNOW WHERE HE'S BEEN HIDING.
ALL WE HAVE IS SOME FUZZY SURVEILLANCE. HIS ELECTROMAGNETIC POWERS HAVE STOPPED OUR CAMERAS, SATELLITES AND DRONES FROM GETTING A PIECE OF HIM.
LET ME BE CLEAR, LANTERNS: HE IS NOT TO BE MESSED WITH.
AS SOON AS YOU HAVE A SHOT, TAKE HIM DOWN. YOU WON'T GET ANOTHER CHANCE.
THAT'S NOT HOW WE DO THINGS IN THE JUSTICE LEAGUE. WE'RE HERE TO HELP, NOT TAKE ORDERS FROM THE GOVERNMENT.
JUST BECAUSE YOU COULDN'T TAKE HIM INTO CUSTODY DOESN'T MEAN WE CAN'T.
WE'RE EXTREMELY POWERFUL, TOO!
I DON'T NEED THE HERO ROUTINE. JUST THINK ABOUT WHAT I SAID.
IT'S A LONG FLIGHT TO...

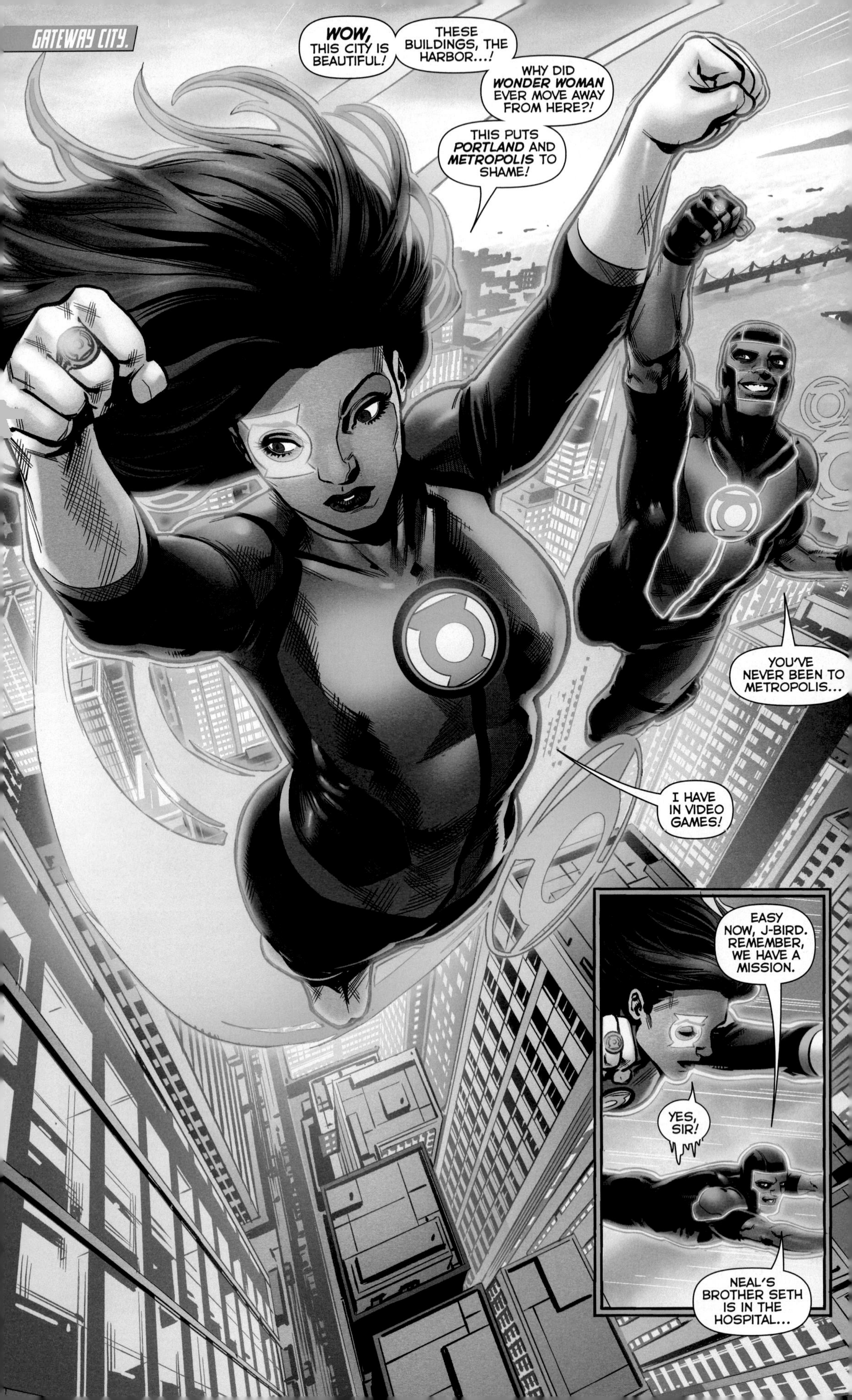
GATEWAY CITY.
WOW, THIS CITY IS BEAUTIFUL!
THESE BUILDINGS, THE HARBOR...!
WHY DID WONDER WOMAN EVER MOVE AWAY FROM HERE?!
THIS PUTS PORTLAND AND METROPOLIS TO SHAME!
YOU'VE NEVER BEEN TO METROPOLIS...
I HAVE IN VIDEO GAMES!
EASY NOW, J-BIRD. REMEMBER, WE HAVE A MISSION.
YES, SIR!
NEAL'S BROTHER SETH IS IN THE HOSPITAL...

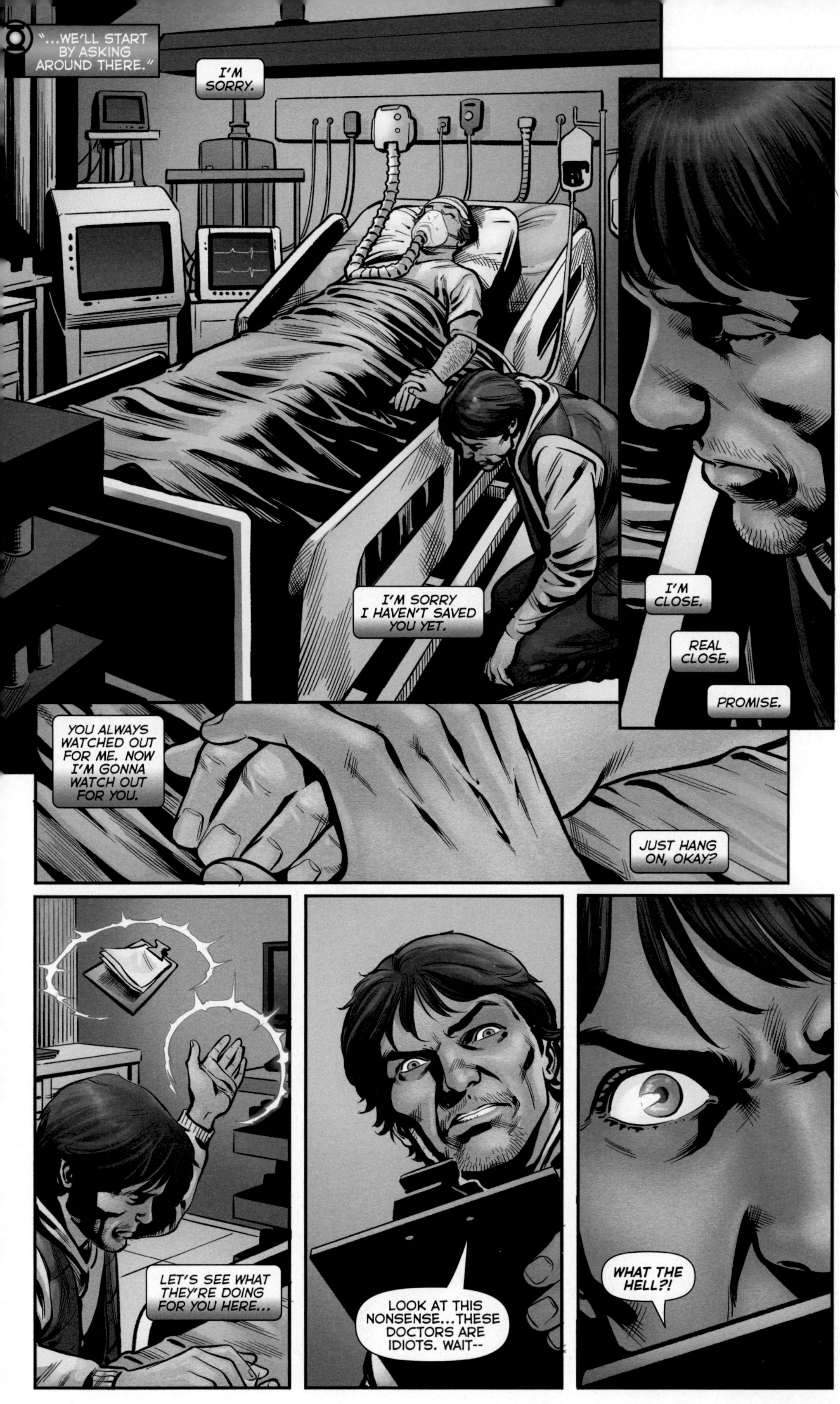
"...WE'LL START BY ASKING AROUND THERE."
I'M SORRY.
I'M SORRY I HAVEN'T SAVED YOU YET.
I'M CLOSE.
REAL CLOSE.
PROMISE.
YOU ALWAYS WATCHED OUT FOR ME. NOW I'M GONNA WATCH OUT FOR YOU.
JUST HANG ON, OKAY?
LET'S SEE WHAT THEY'RE DOING FOR YOU HERE...
LOOK AT THIS NONSENSE...THESE DOCTORS ARE IDIOTS. WAIT--
WHAT THE HELL?!

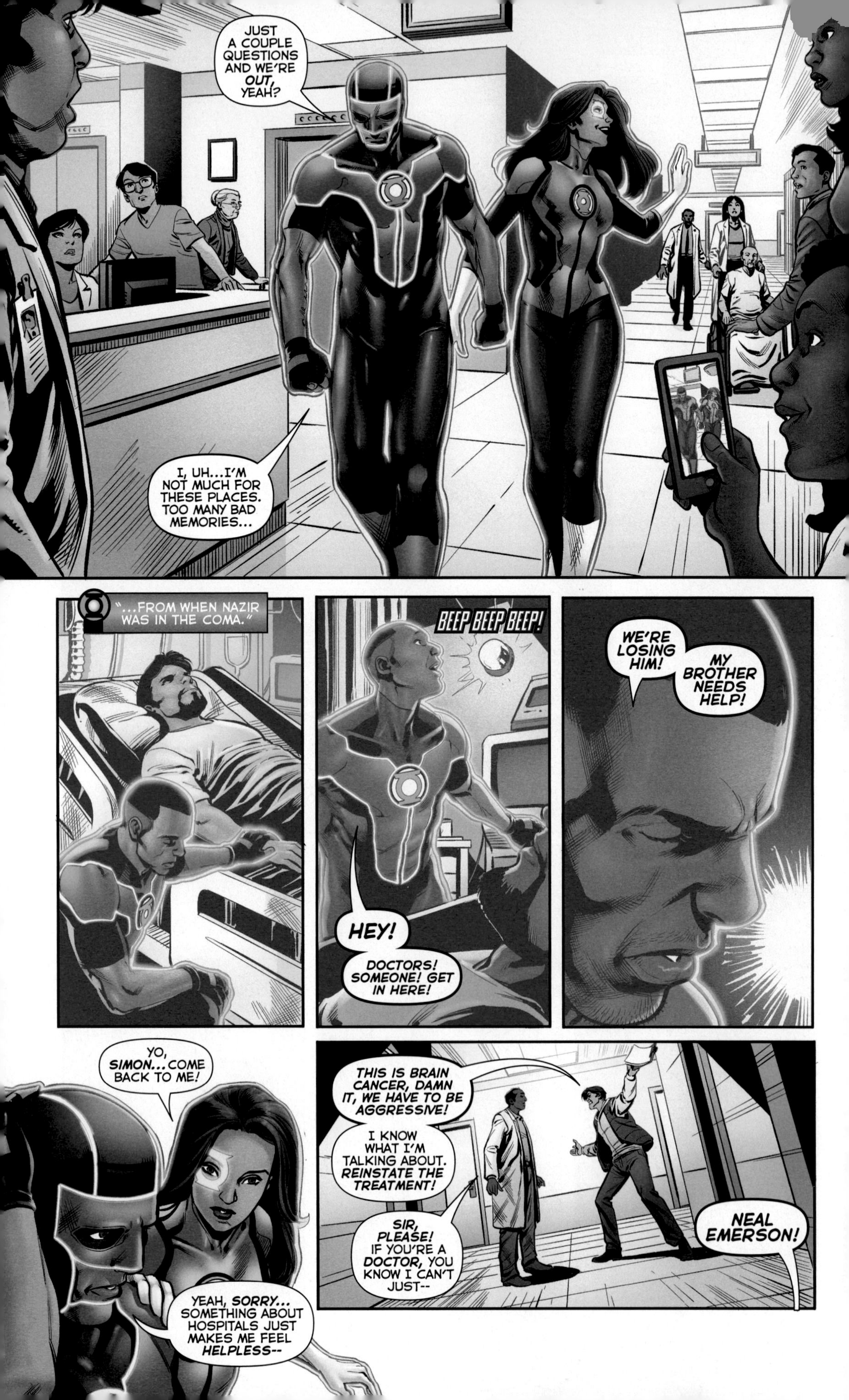

JUST A COUPLE QUESTIONS AND WE'RE OUT, YEAH?
I, UH...I'M NOT MUCH FOR THESE PLACES. TOO MANY BAD MEMORIES...
"...FROM WHEN NAZIR WAS IN THE COMA."
BEEP BEEP BEEP!
HEY!
DOCTORS! SOMEONE! GET IN HERE!
WE'RE LOSING HIM!
MY BROTHER NEEDS HELP!
YO, SIMON...COME BACK TO ME!
YEAH, SORRY... SOMETHING ABOUT HOSPITALS JUST MAKES ME FEEL HELPLESS--
THIS IS BRAIN CANCER, DAMN IT, WE HAVE TO BE AGGRESSIVE!
I KNOW WHAT I'M TALKING ABOUT. REINSTATE THE TREATMENT!
SIR, PLEASE! IF YOU'RE A DOCTOR, YOU KNOW I CAN'T JUST--
NEAL EMERSON!

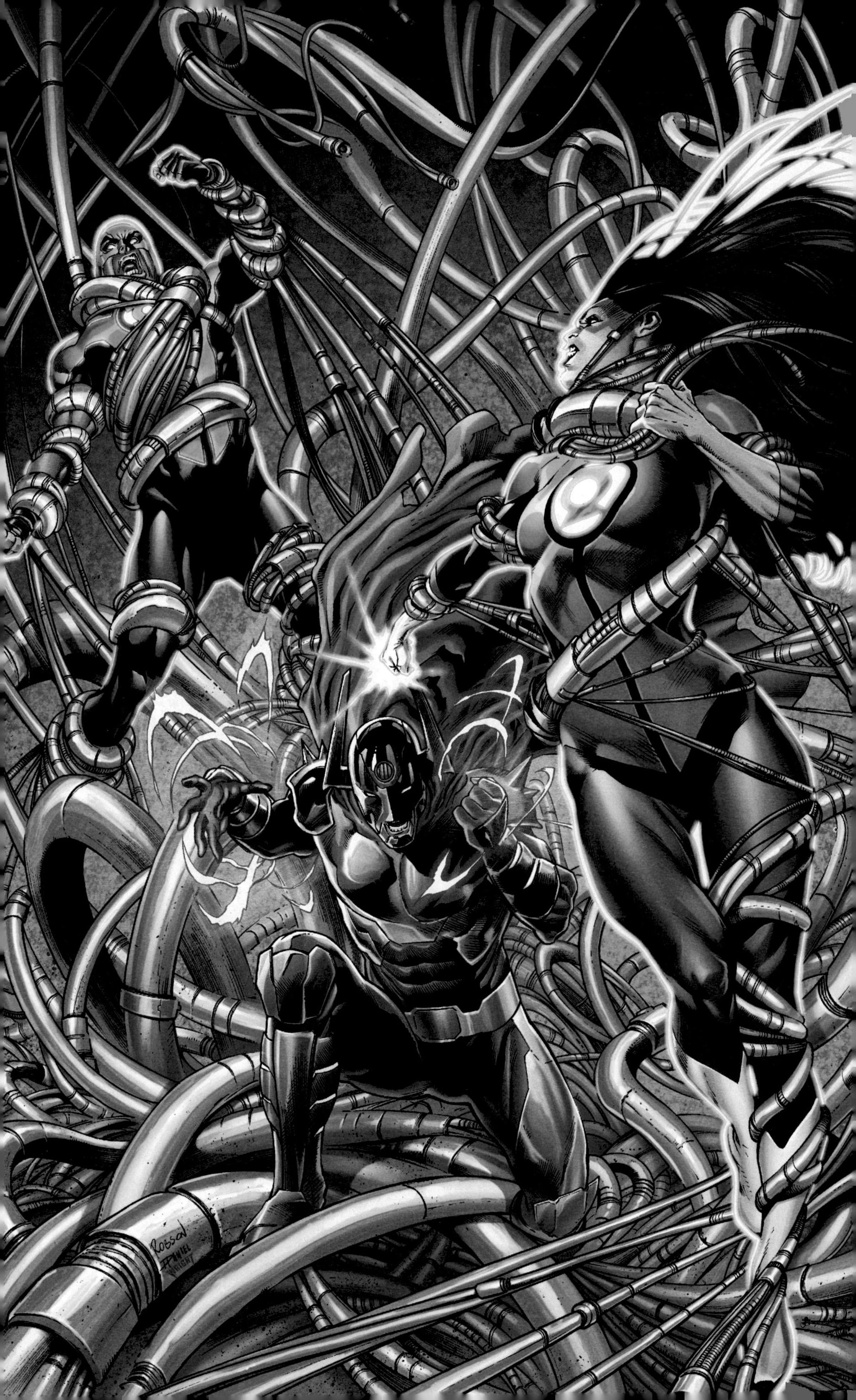
Robson
DANIEL

"POLARITY CHAPTER TWO: THE DROWNING"

EDUARDO PANSICA penciller ∗ JULIO FERREIRA inker

Cover by ROBSON ROCHA, DANIEL HENRIQUES and JASON WRIGHT

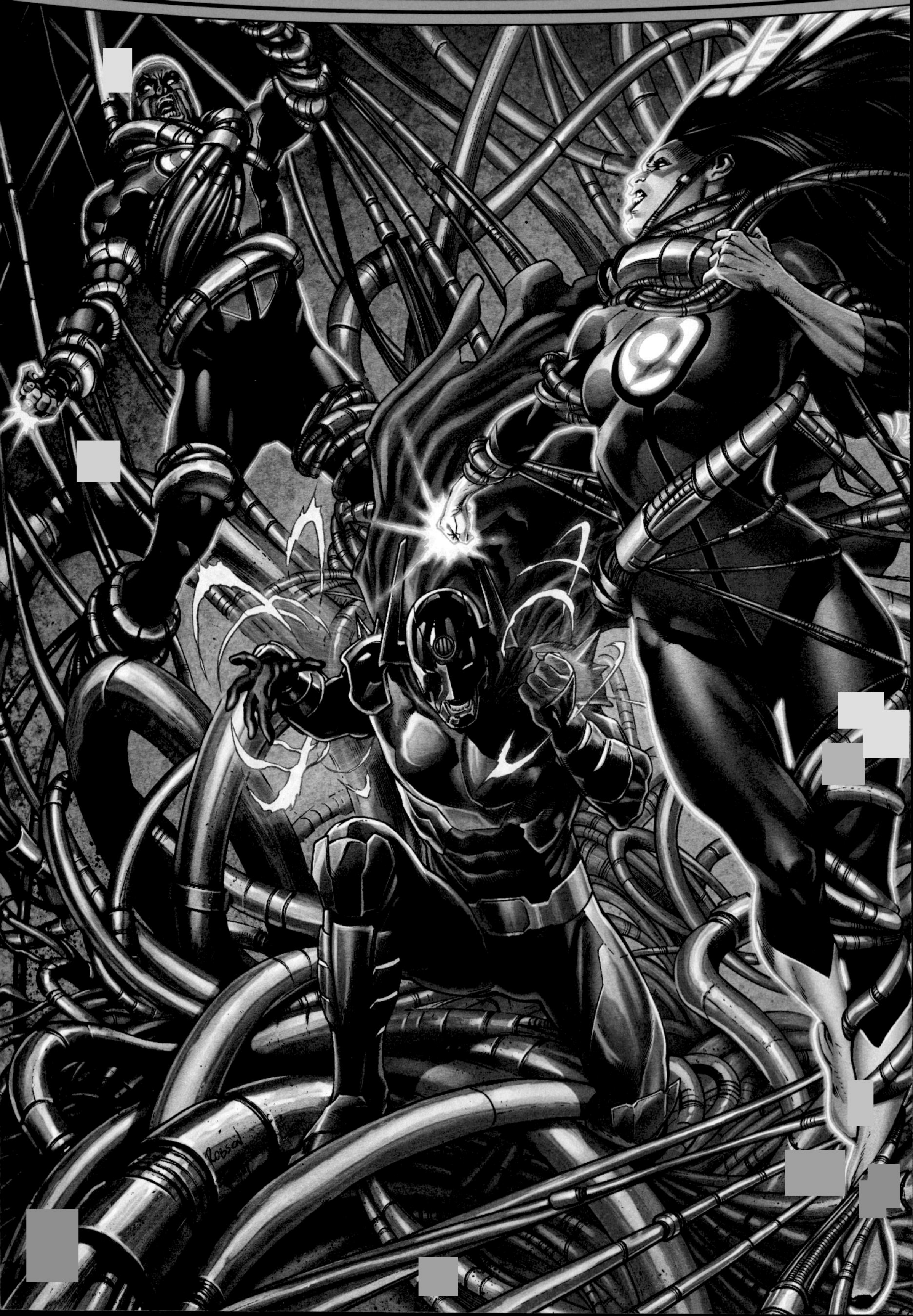

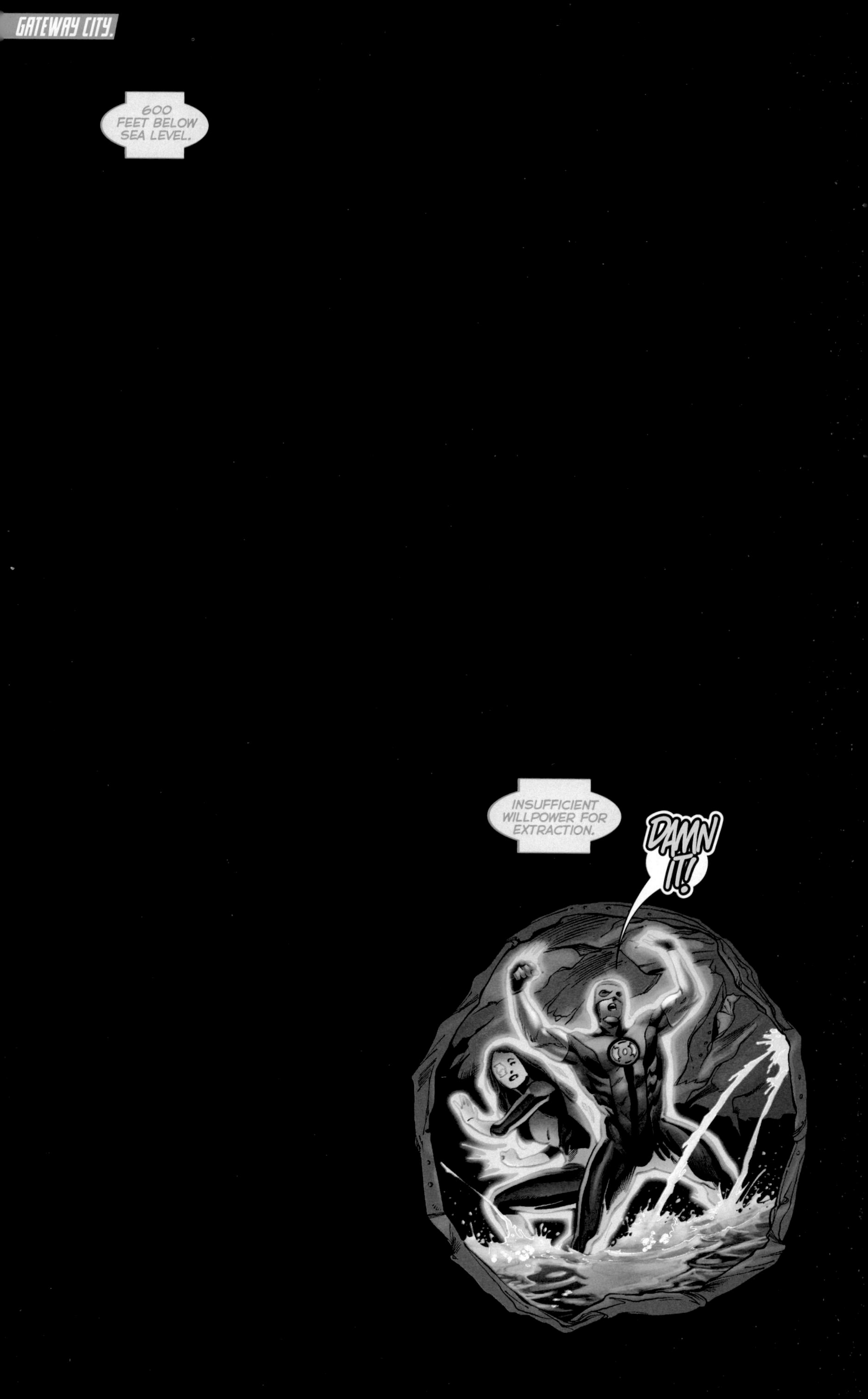
GATEWAY CITY.
600 FEET BELOW SEA LEVEL.
INSUFFICIENT WILLPOWER FOR EXTRACTION.
DAMN IT!

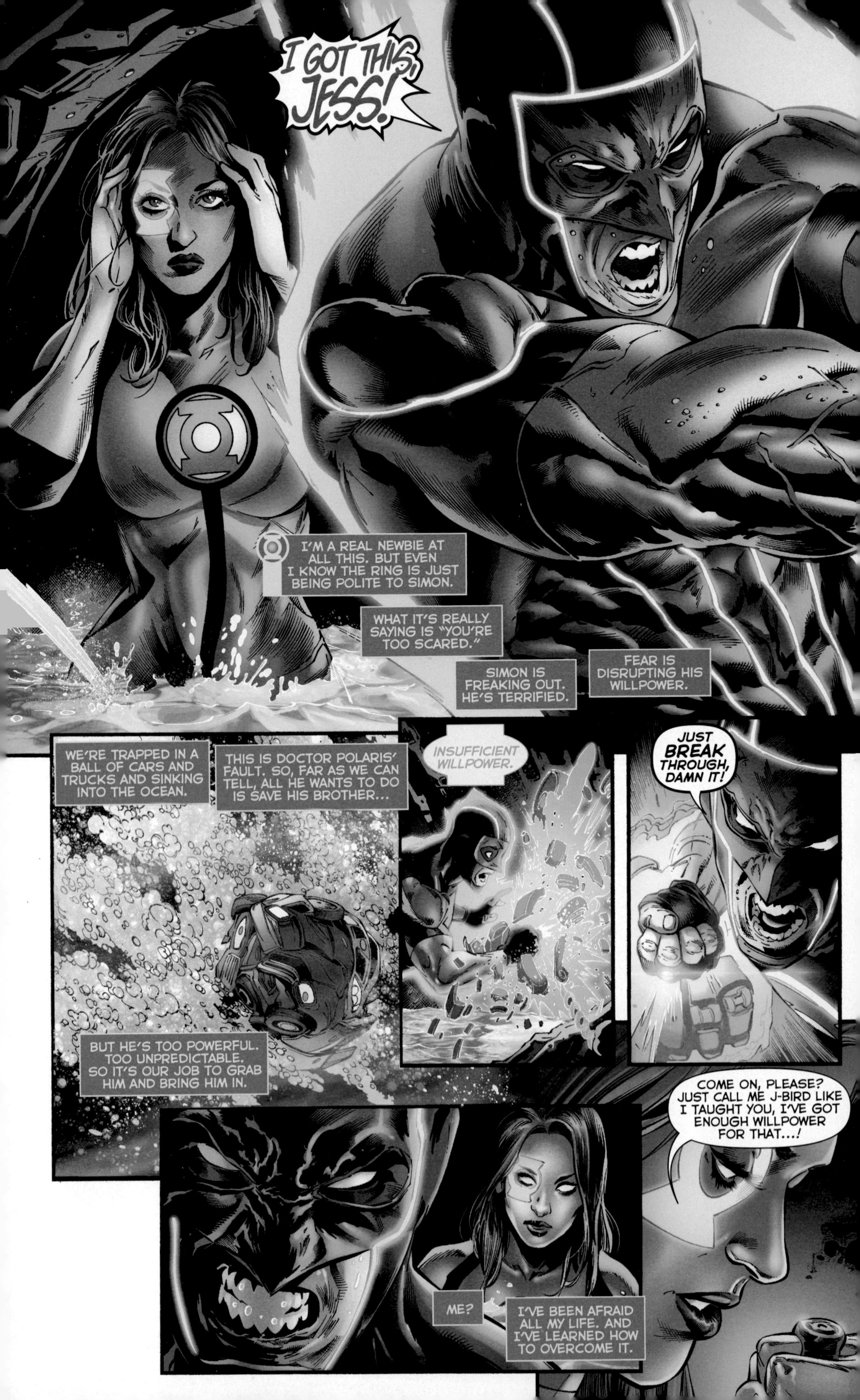
I GOT THIS, JESS!
I'M A REAL NEWBIE AT ALL THIS. BUT EVEN I KNOW THE RING IS JUST BEING POLITE TO SIMON.
WHAT IT'S REALLY SAYING IS "YOU'RE TOO SCARED."
SIMON IS FREAKING OUT. HE'S TERRIFIED.
FEAR IS DISRUPTING HIS WILLPOWER.
WE'RE TRAPPED IN A BALL OF CARS AND TRUCKS AND SINKING INTO THE OCEAN.
THIS IS DOCTOR POLARIS' FAULT. SO, FAR AS WE CAN TELL, ALL HE WANTS TO DO IS SAVE HIS BROTHER...
BUT HE'S TOO POWERFUL. TOO UNPREDICTABLE. SO IT'S OUR JOB TO GRAB HIM AND BRING HIM IN.
INSUFFICIENT WILLPOWER.
JUST BREAK THROUGH, DAMN IT!
COME ON, PLEASE? JUST CALL ME J-BIRD LIKE I TAUGHT YOU, I'VE GOT ENOUGH WILLPOWER FOR THAT...!
ME?
I'VE BEEN AFRAID ALL MY LIFE. AND I'VE LEARNED HOW TO OVERCOME IT.

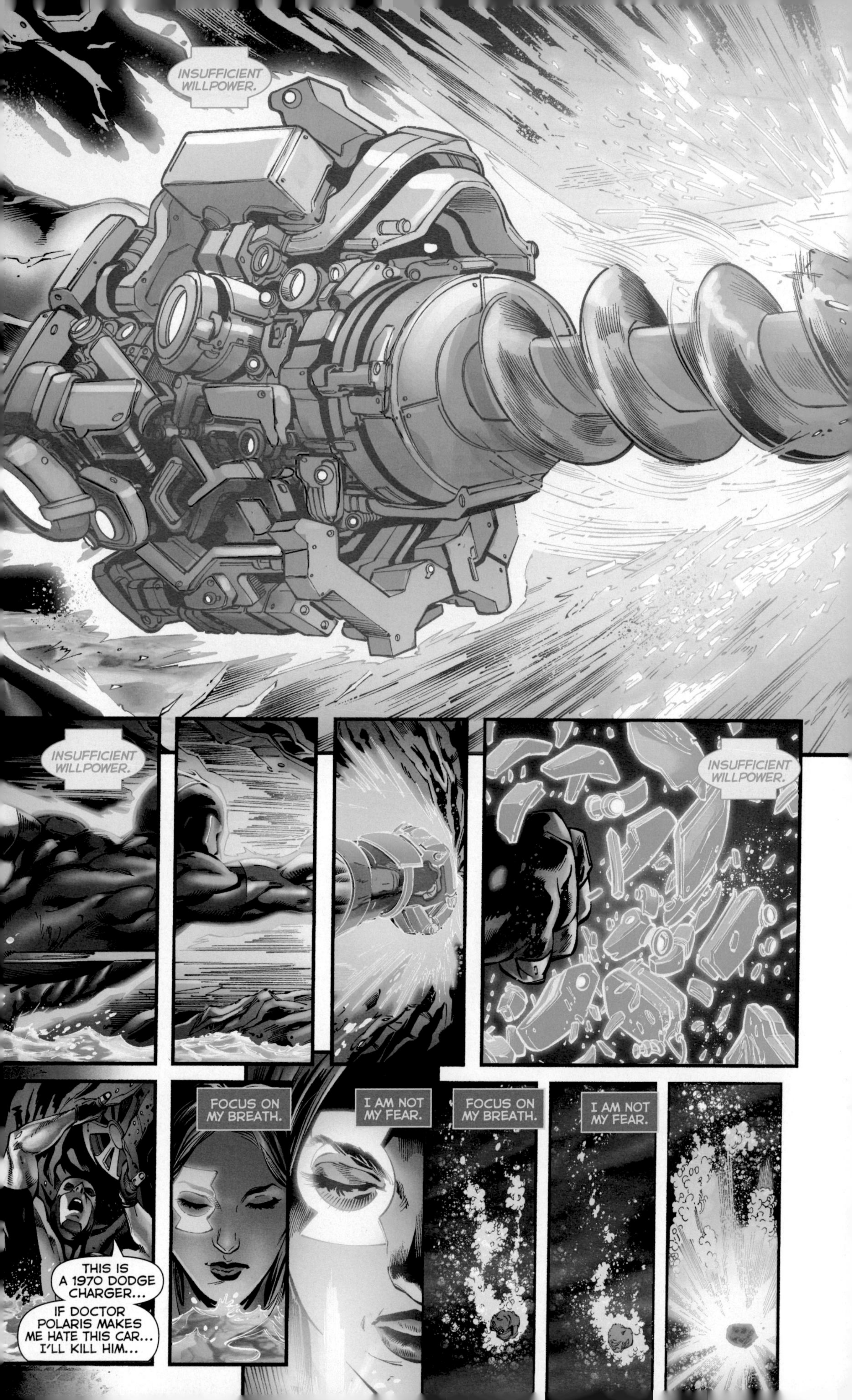
INSUFFICIENT WILLPOWER.
INSUFFICIENT WILLPOWER.
INSUFFICIENT WILLPOWER.
THIS IS A 1970 DODGE CHARGER... IF DOCTOR POLARIS MAKES ME HATE THIS CAR... I'LL KILL HIM...
FOCUS ON MY BREATH.
I AM NOT MY FEAR.
FOCUS ON MY BREATH.
I AM NOT MY FEAR.

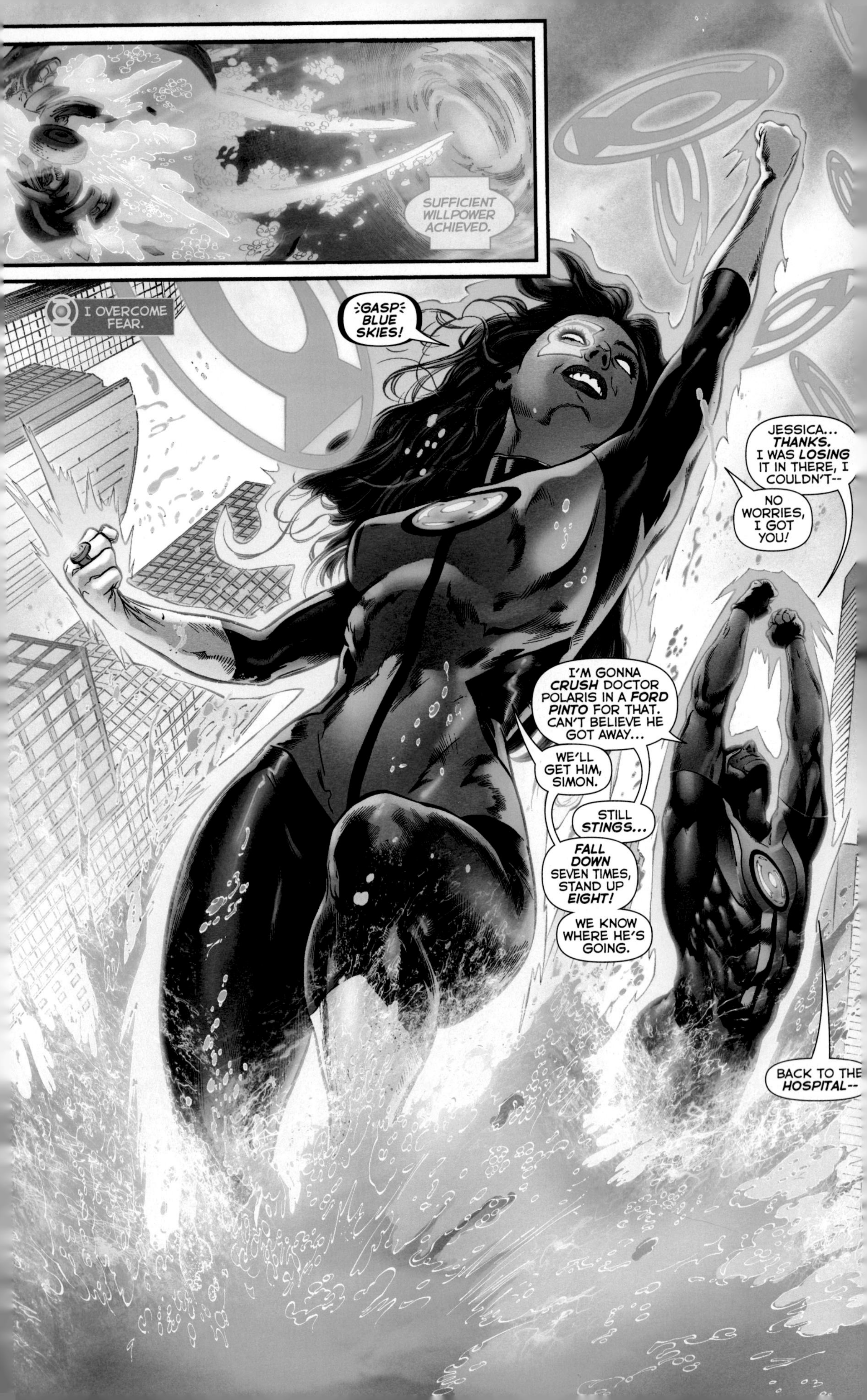
SUFFICIENT WILLPOWER ACHIEVED.
I OVERCOME FEAR.
GASP BLUE SKIES!
JESSICA... THANKS. I WAS LOSING IT IN THERE, I COULDN'T--
NO WORRIES, I GOT YOU!
I'M GONNA CRUSH DOCTOR POLARIS IN A FORD PINTO FOR THAT. CAN'T BELIEVE HE GOT AWAY...
WE'LL GET HIM, SIMON.
STILL STINGS...
FALL DOWN SEVEN TIMES, STAND UP EIGHT!
WE KNOW WHERE HE'S GOING.
BACK TO THE HOSPITAL--

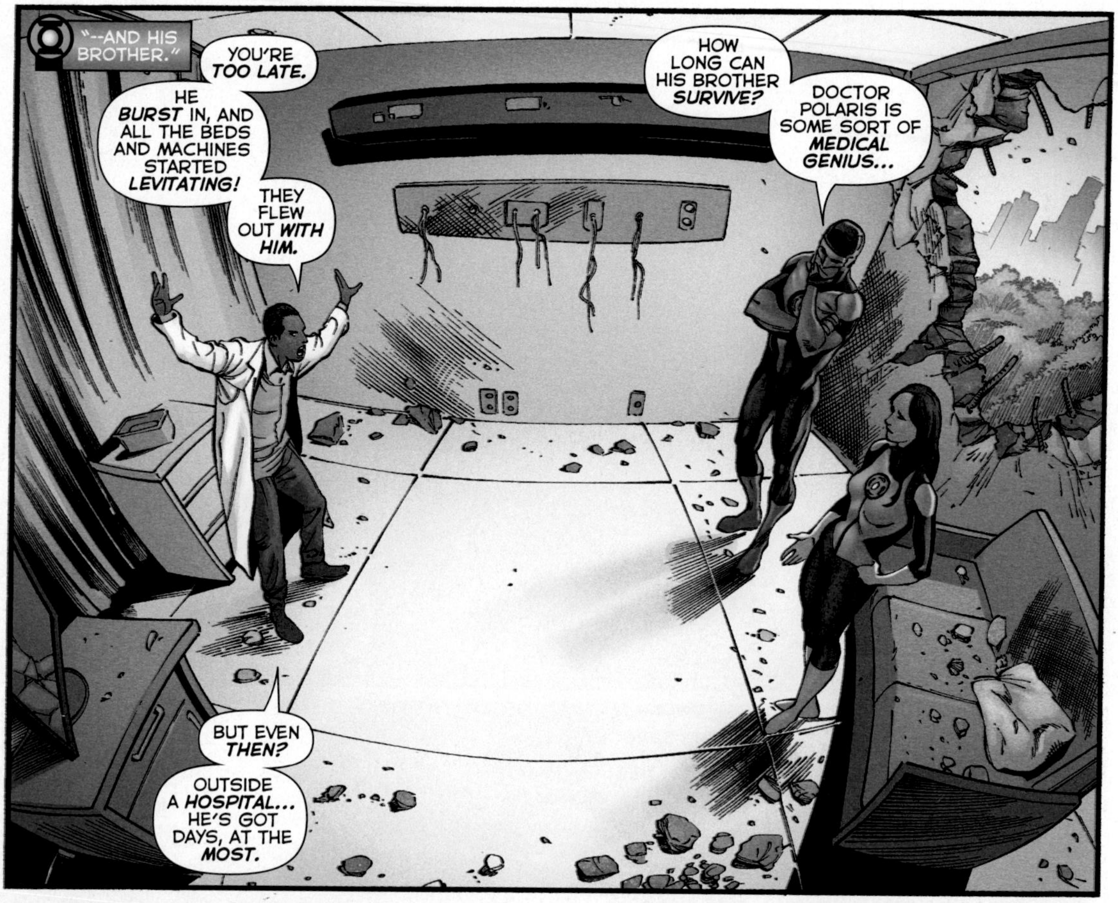
"--AND HIS BROTHER."
YOU'RE TOO LATE.
HE BURST IN, AND ALL THE BEDS AND MACHINES STARTED LEVITATING!
THEY FLEW OUT WITH HIM.
HOW LONG CAN HIS BROTHER SURVIVE?
DOCTOR POLARIS IS SOME SORT OF MEDICAL GENIUS...
BUT EVEN THEN?
OUTSIDE A HOSPITAL... HE'S GOT DAYS, AT THE MOST.

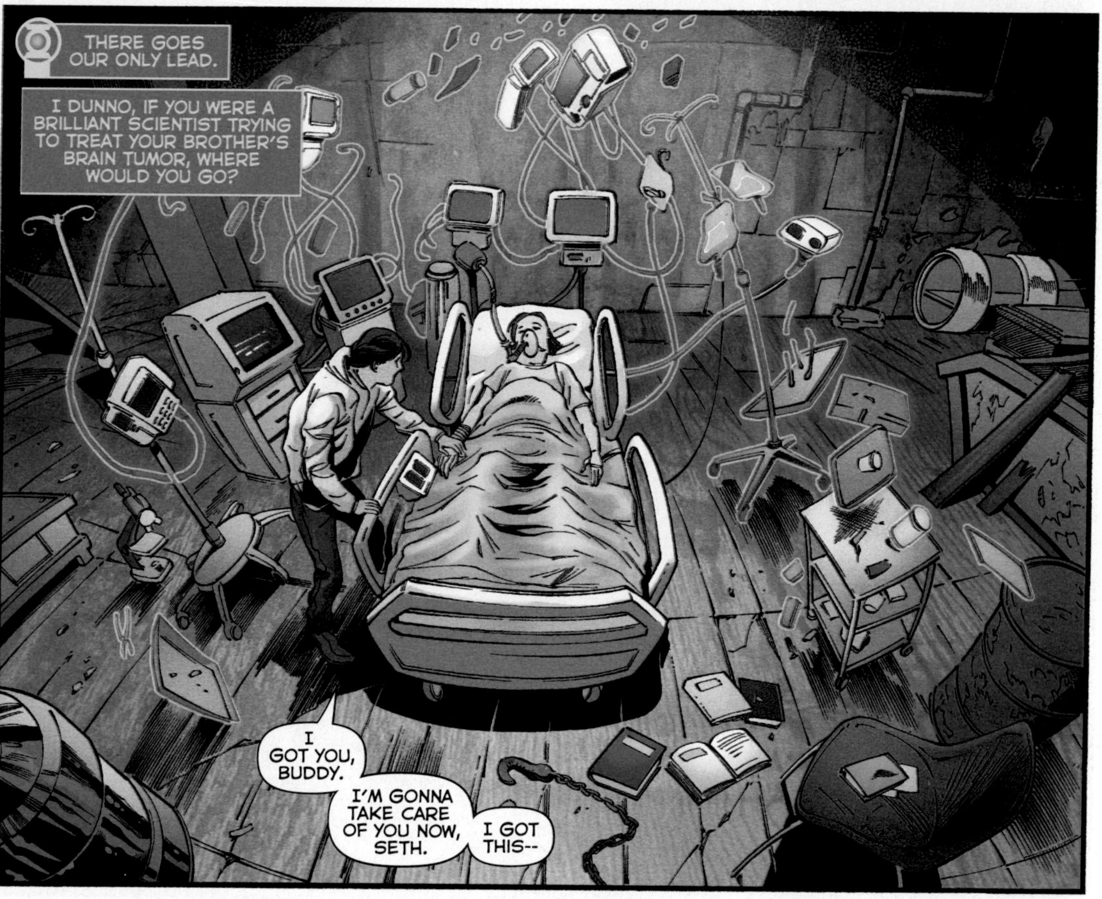
THERE GOES OUR ONLY LEAD.
I DUNNO, IF YOU WERE A BRILLIANT SCIENTIST TRYING TO TREAT YOUR BROTHER'S BRAIN TUMOR, WHERE WOULD YOU GO?
I GOT YOU, BUDDY.
I'M GONNA TAKE CARE OF YOU NOW, SETH.
I GOT THIS--

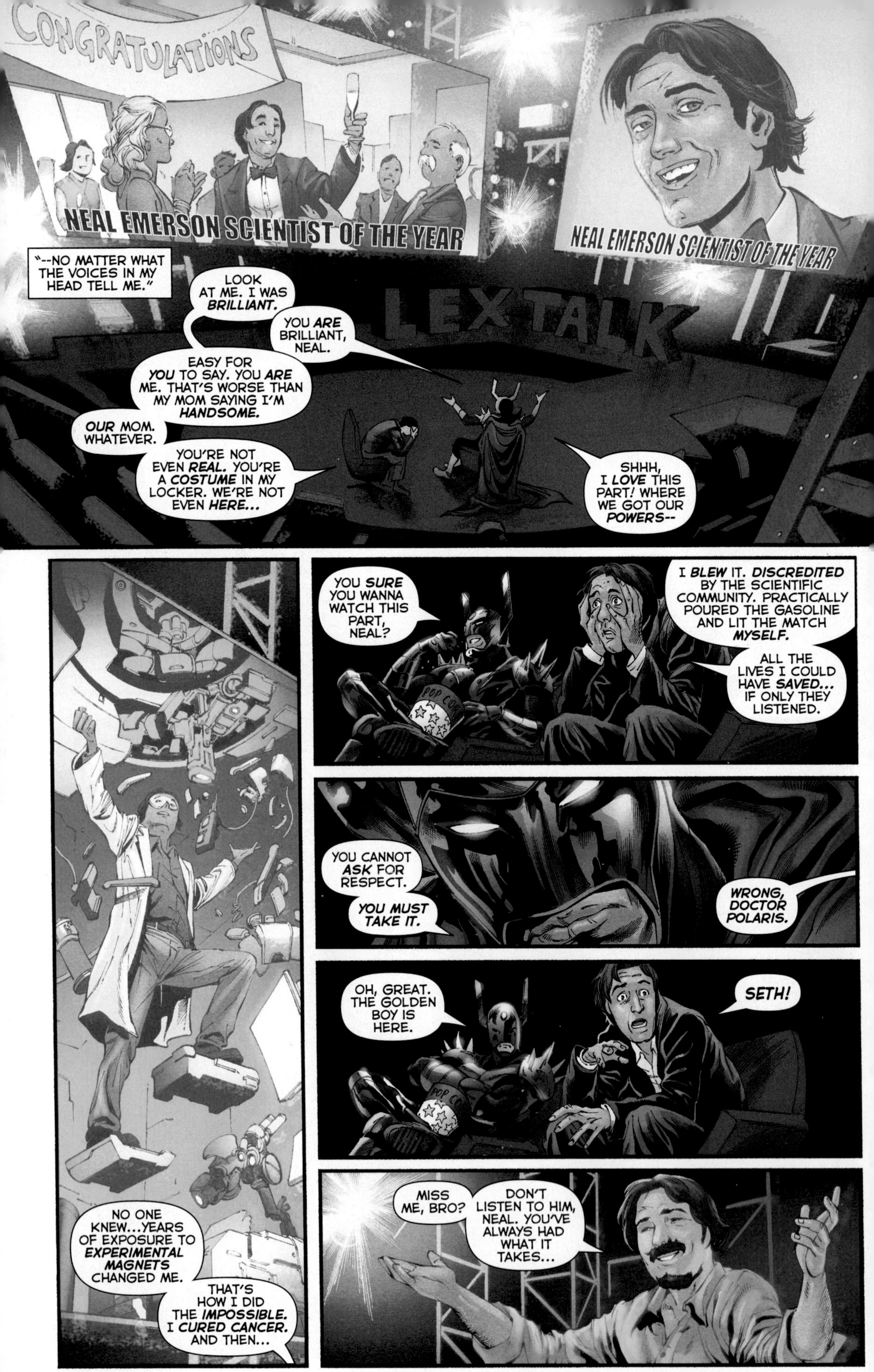
CONGRATULATIONS
NEAL EMERSON SCIENTIST OF THE YEAR
NEAL EMERSON SCIENTIST OF THE YEAR
"--NO MATTER WHAT THE VOICES IN MY HEAD TELL ME."
LEX TALK
LOOK AT ME. I WAS BRILLIANT.
YOU ARE BRILLIANT, NEAL.
EASY FOR YOU TO SAY. YOU ARE ME. THAT'S WORSE THAN MY MOM SAYING I'M HANDSOME.
OUR MOM. WHATEVER.
YOU'RE NOT EVEN REAL. YOU'RE A COSTUME IN MY LOCKER. WE'RE NOT EVEN HERE...
SHHH, I LOVE THIS PART! WHERE WE GOT OUR POWERS--
YOU SURE YOU WANNA WATCH THIS PART, NEAL?
I BLEW IT. DISCREDITED BY THE SCIENTIFIC COMMUNITY. PRACTICALLY POURED THE GASOLINE AND LIT THE MATCH MYSELF.
ALL THE LIVES I COULD HAVE SAVED... IF ONLY THEY LISTENED.
YOU CANNOT ASK FOR RESPECT.
YOU MUST TAKE IT.
WRONG, DOCTOR POLARIS.
OH, GREAT. THE GOLDEN BOY IS HERE.
SETH!
MISS ME, BRO?
DON'T LISTEN TO HIM, NEAL. YOU'VE ALWAYS HAD WHAT IT TAKES...
NO ONE KNEW...YEARS OF EXPOSURE TO EXPERIMENTAL MAGNETS CHANGED ME.
THAT'S HOW I DID THE IMPOSSIBLE. I CURED CANCER. AND THEN...

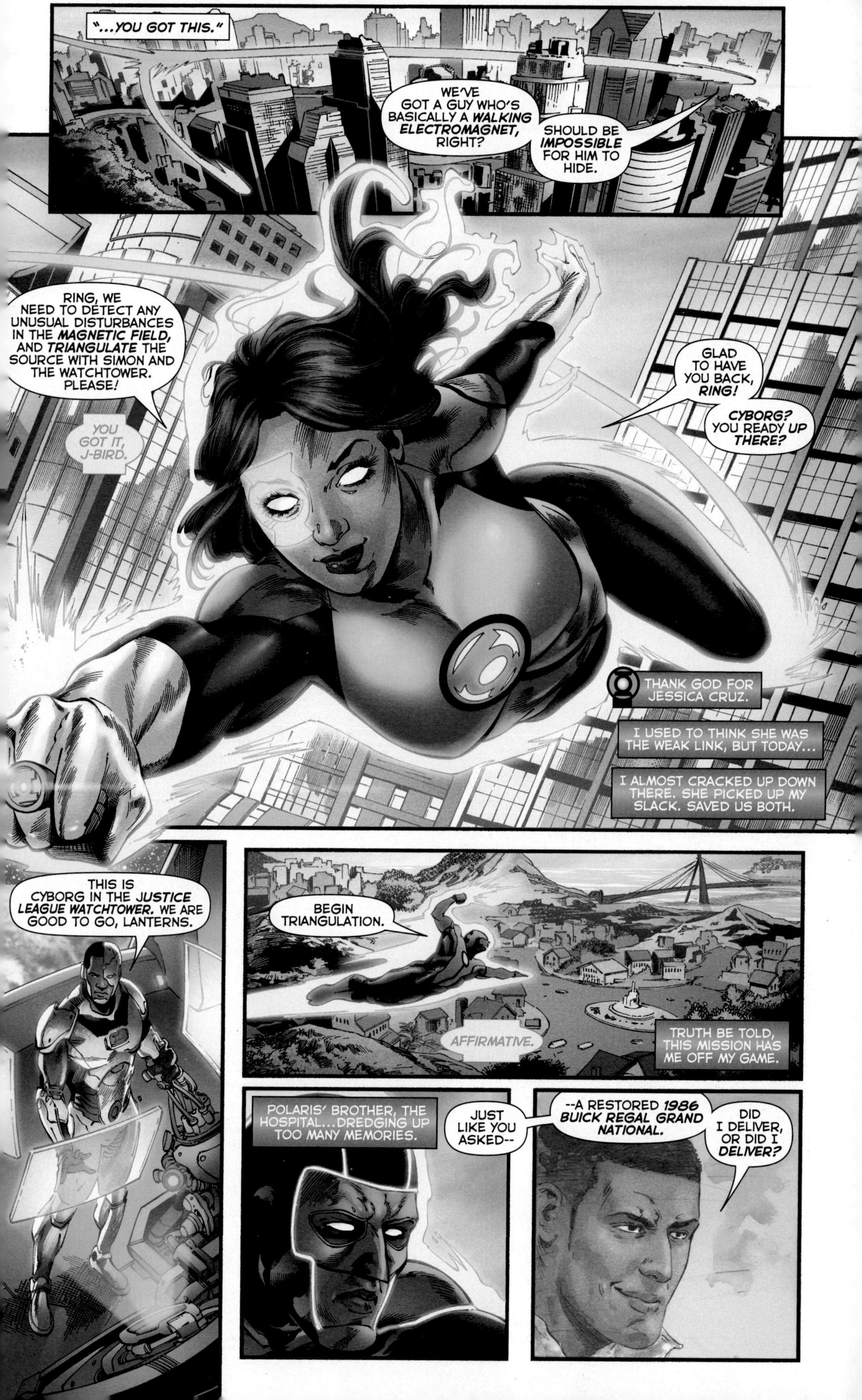
"...YOU GOT THIS."
WE'VE GOT A GUY WHO'S BASICALLY A WALKING ELECTROMAGNET, RIGHT?
SHOULD BE IMPOSSIBLE FOR HIM TO HIDE.
RING, WE NEED TO DETECT ANY UNUSUAL DISTURBANCES IN THE MAGNETIC FIELD, AND TRIANGULATE THE SOURCE WITH SIMON AND THE WATCHTOWER. PLEASE!
YOU GOT IT, J-BIRD.
GLAD TO HAVE YOU BACK, RING!
CYBORG? YOU READY UP THERE?
THANK GOD FOR JESSICA CRUZ.
I USED TO THINK SHE WAS THE WEAK LINK, BUT TODAY...
I ALMOST CRACKED UP DOWN THERE. SHE PICKED UP MY SLACK. SAVED US BOTH.
THIS IS CYBORG IN THE JUSTICE LEAGUE WATCHTOWER. WE ARE GOOD TO GO, LANTERNS.
BEGIN TRIANGULATION.
AFFIRMATIVE.
TRUTH BE TOLD, THIS MISSION HAS ME OFF MY GAME.
POLARIS' BROTHER, THE HOSPITAL...DREDGING UP TOO MANY MEMORIES.
JUST LIKE YOU ASKED--
--A RESTORED 1986 BUICK REGAL GRAND NATIONAL.
DID I DELIVER, OR DID I DELIVER?

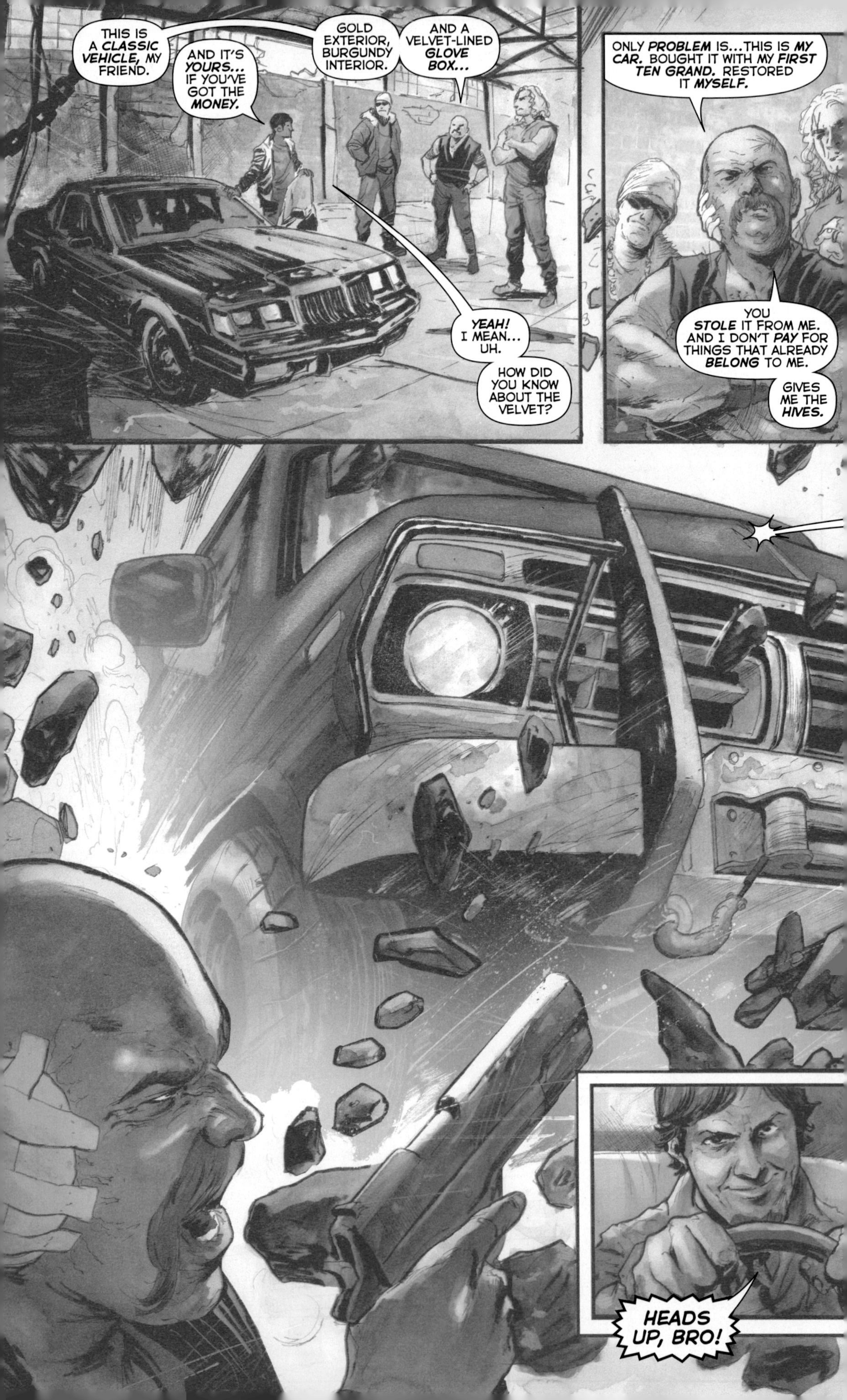
THIS IS A CLASSIC VEHICLE, MY FRIEND.
AND IT'S YOURS... IF YOU'VE GOT THE MONEY.
GOLD EXTERIOR, BURGUNDY INTERIOR.
AND A VELVET-LINED GLOVE BOX...
YEAH! I MEAN... UH.
HOW DID YOU KNOW ABOUT THE VELVET?
ONLY PROBLEM IS...THIS IS MY CAR. BOUGHT IT WITH MY FIRST TEN GRAND. RESTORED IT MYSELF.
YOU STOLE IT FROM ME. AND I DON'T PAY FOR THINGS THAT ALREADY BELONG TO ME.
GIVES ME THE HIVES.
HEADS UP, BRO!

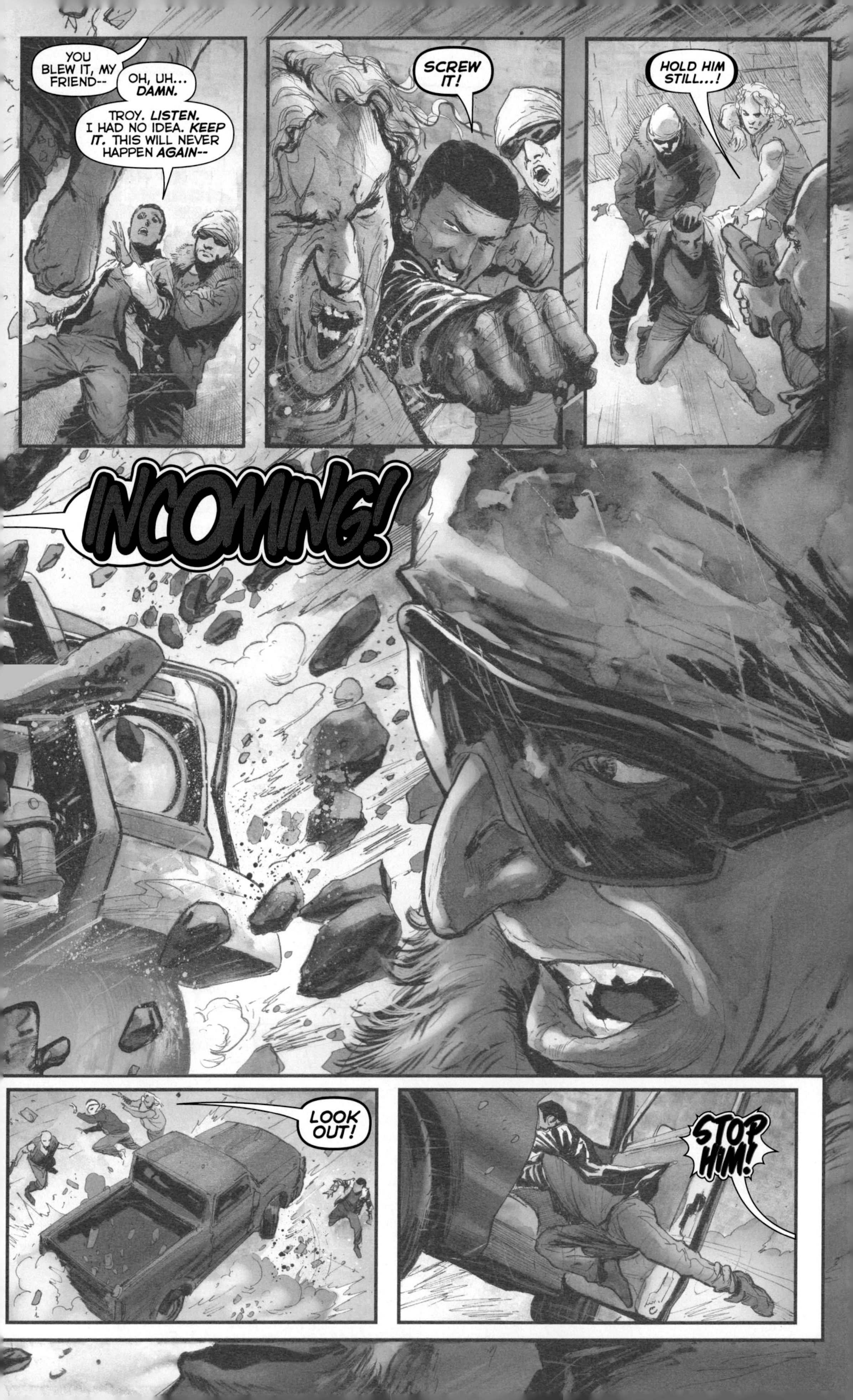
YOU BLEW IT, MY FRIEND--
OH, UH... DAMN.
TROY. LISTEN. I HAD NO IDEA. KEEP IT. THIS WILL NEVER HAPPEN AGAIN--
SCREW IT!
HOLD HIM STILL...!
INCOMING!
LOOK OUT!
STOP HIM!

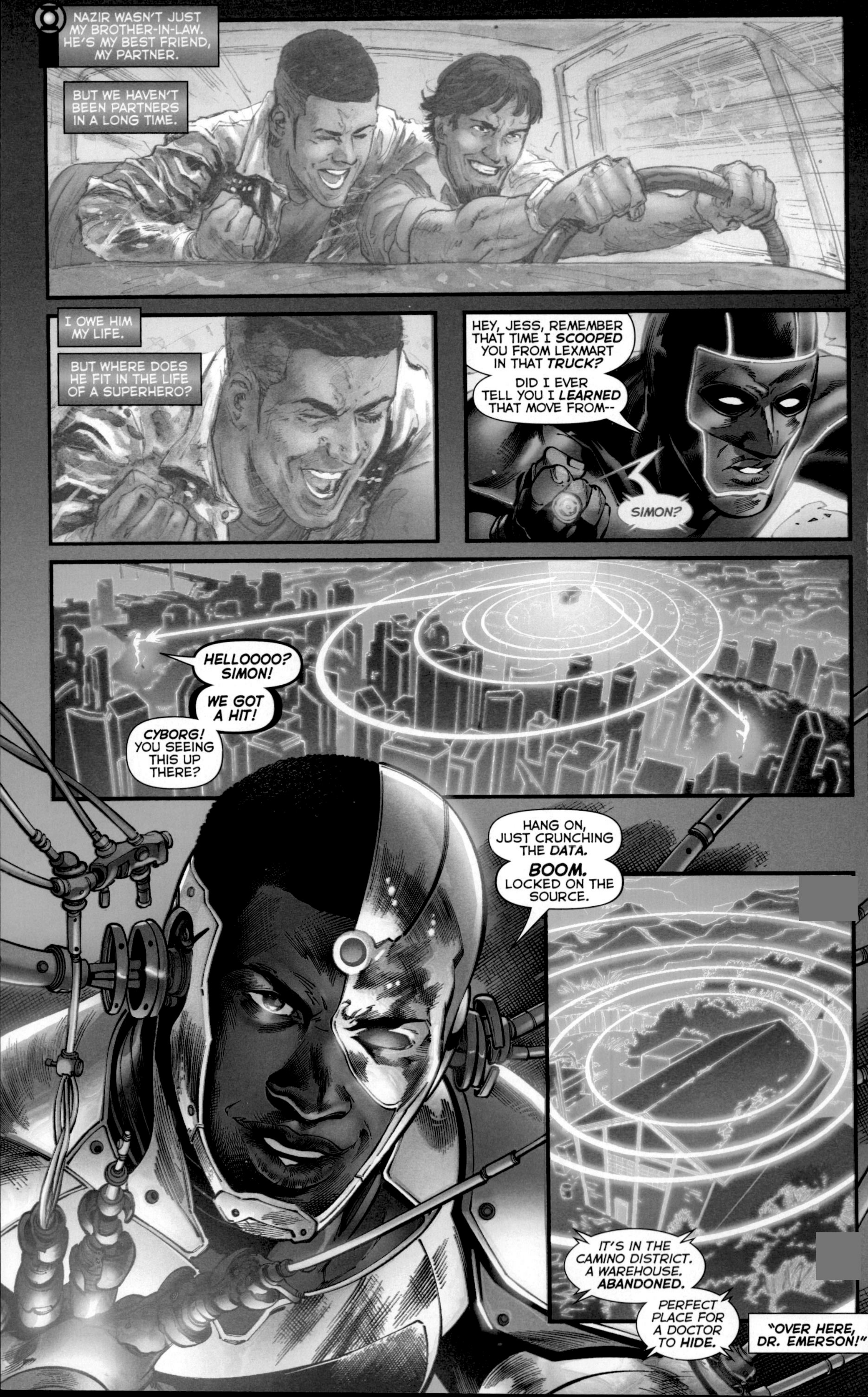
NAZIR WASN'T JUST MY BROTHER-IN-LAW. HE'S MY BEST FRIEND, MY PARTNER.
BUT WE HAVEN'T BEEN PARTNERS IN A LONG TIME.
I OWE HIM MY LIFE.
BUT WHERE DOES HE FIT IN THE LIFE OF A SUPERHERO?
HEY, JESS, REMEMBER THAT TIME I SCOOPED YOU FROM LEXMART IN THAT TRUCK?
DID I EVER TELL YOU I LEARNED THAT MOVE FROM--
SIMON?
HELLOOOO? SIMON!
WE GOT A HIT!
CYBORG! YOU SEEING THIS UP THERE?
HANG ON, JUST CRUNCHING THE DATA. BOOM. LOCKED ON THE SOURCE.
IT'S IN THE CAMINO DISTRICT. A WAREHOUSE. ABANDONED.
PERFECT PLACE FOR A DOCTOR TO HIDE.
"OVER HERE, DR. EMERSON!"

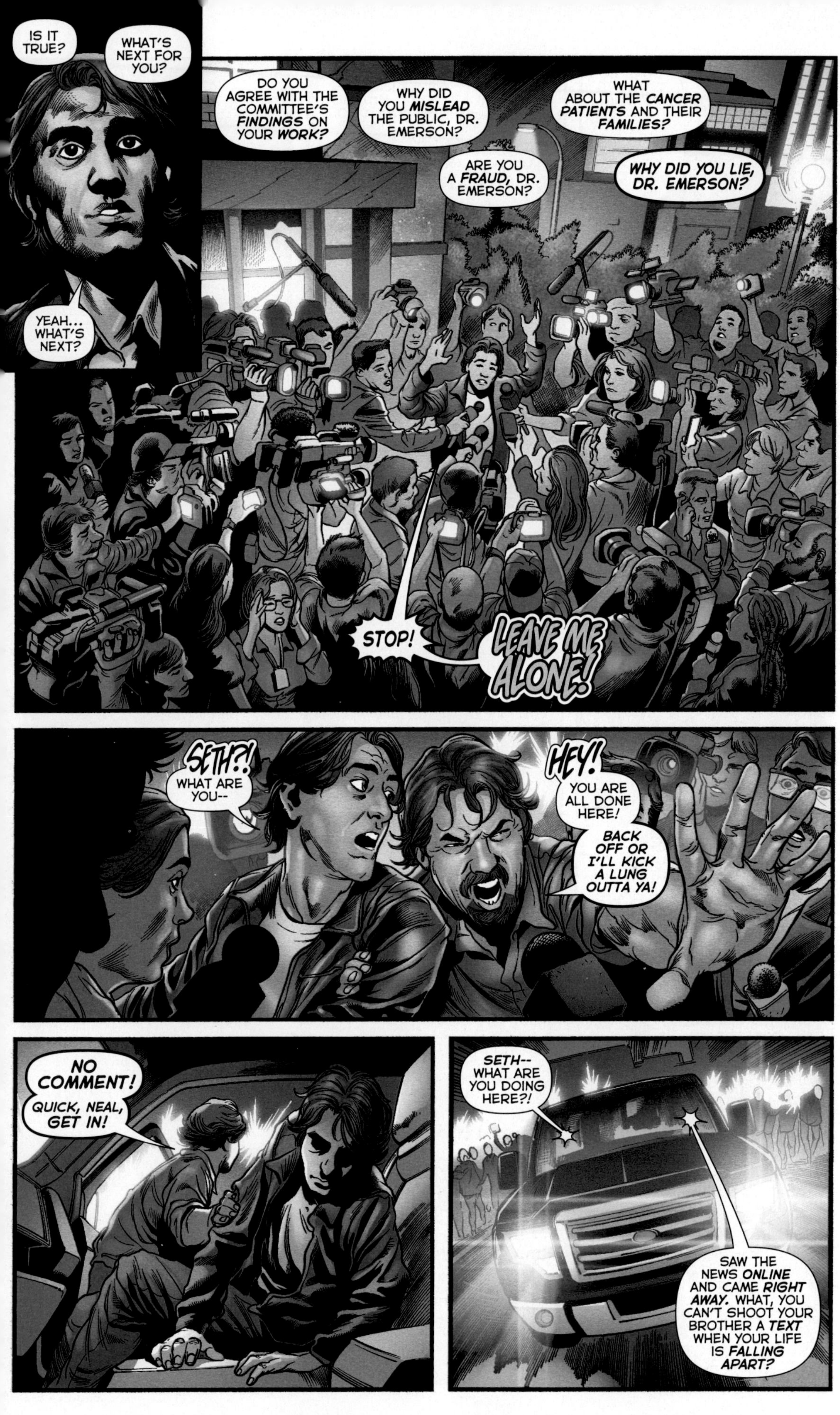
IS IT TRUE?
WHAT'S NEXT FOR YOU?
YEAH... WHAT'S NEXT?
DO YOU AGREE WITH THE COMMITTEE'S FINDINGS ON YOUR WORK?
WHY DID YOU MISLEAD THE PUBLIC, DR. EMERSON?
ARE YOU A FRAUD, DR. EMERSON?
WHAT ABOUT THE CANCER PATIENTS AND THEIR FAMILIES?
WHY DID YOU LIE, DR. EMERSON?
STOP!
LEAVE ME ALONE!
SETH?! WHAT ARE YOU--
HEY! YOU ARE ALL DONE HERE!
BACK OFF OR I'LL KICK A LUNG OUTTA YA!
NO COMMENT!
QUICK, NEAL, GET IN!
SETH-- WHAT ARE YOU DOING HERE?!
SAW THE NEWS ONLINE AND CAME RIGHT AWAY. WHAT, YOU CAN'T SHOOT YOUR BROTHER A TEXT WHEN YOUR LIFE IS FALLING APART?

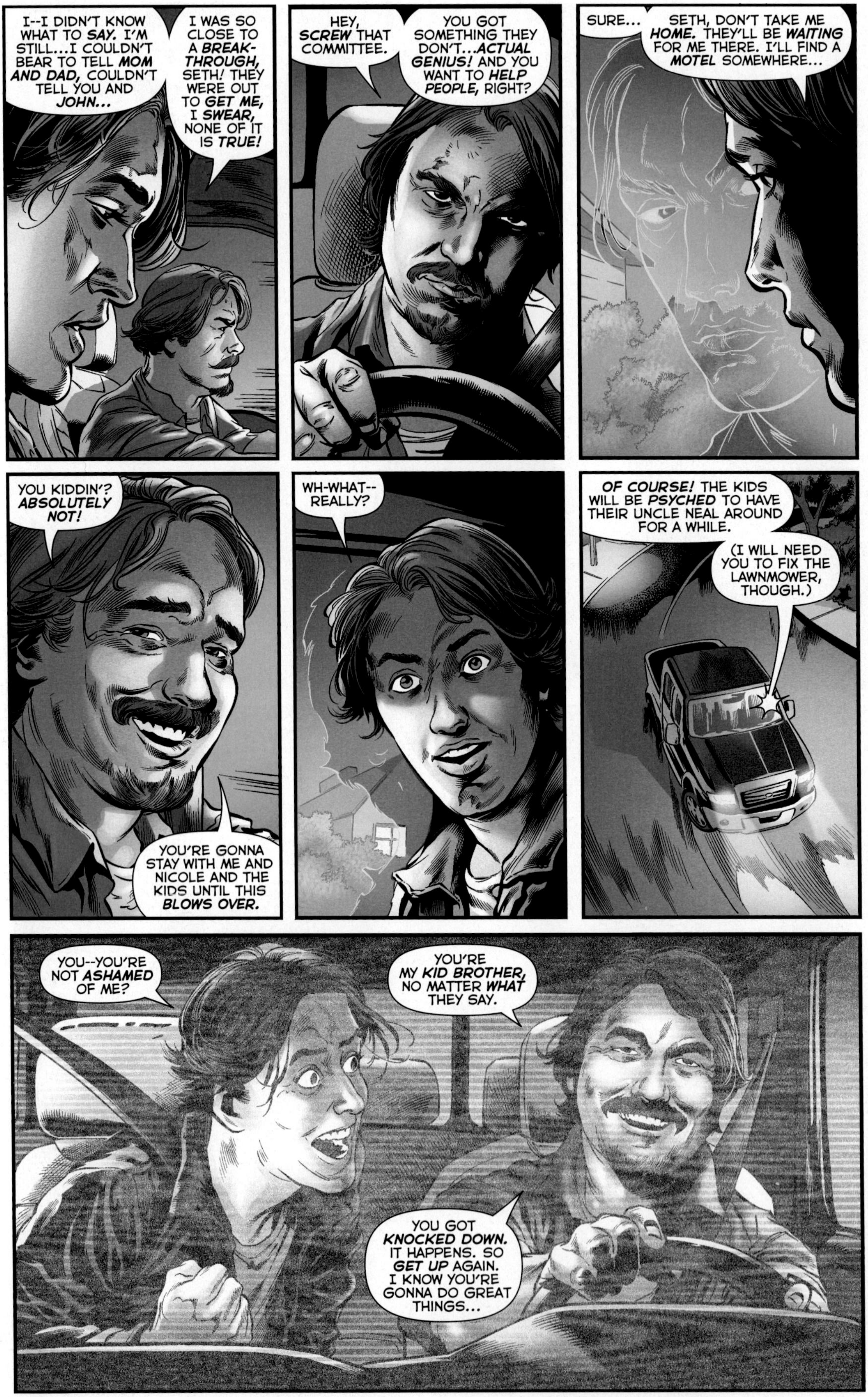
I--I DIDN'T KNOW WHAT TO SAY. I'M STILL...I COULDN'T BEAR TO TELL MOM AND DAD, COULDN'T TELL YOU AND JOHN...
I WAS SO CLOSE TO A BREAK-THROUGH, SETH! THEY WERE OUT TO GET ME, I SWEAR, NONE OF IT IS TRUE!
HEY, SCREW THAT COMMITTEE.
YOU GOT SOMETHING THEY DON'T...ACTUAL GENIUS! AND YOU WANT TO HELP PEOPLE, RIGHT?
SURE...
SETH, DON'T TAKE ME HOME. THEY'LL BE WAITING FOR ME THERE. I'LL FIND A MOTEL SOMEWHERE...
YOU KIDDIN'? ABSOLUTELY NOT!
YOU'RE GONNA STAY WITH ME AND NICOLE AND THE KIDS UNTIL THIS BLOWS OVER.
WH-WHAT-- REALLY?
OF COURSE! THE KIDS WILL BE PSYCHED TO HAVE THEIR UNCLE NEAL AROUND FOR A WHILE.
(I WILL NEED YOU TO FIX THE LAWNMOWER, THOUGH.)
YOU--YOU'RE NOT ASHAMED OF ME?
YOU'RE MY KID BROTHER, NO MATTER WHAT THEY SAY.
YOU GOT KNOCKED DOWN. IT HAPPENS. SO GET UP AGAIN. I KNOW YOU'RE GONNA DO GREAT THINGS...

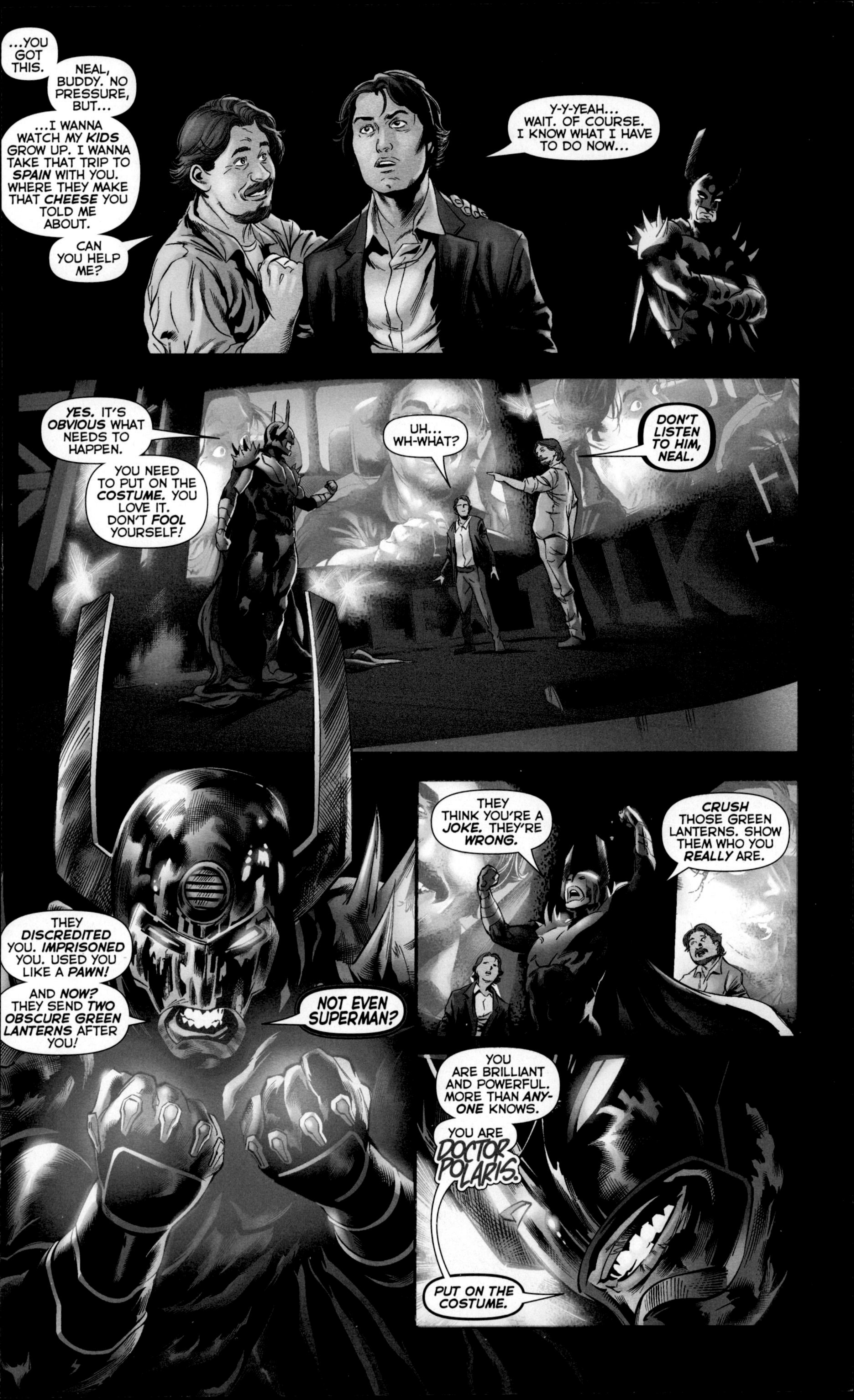
...YOU GOT THIS.
NEAL, BUDDY. NO PRESSURE, BUT...
...I WANNA WATCH MY *KIDS* GROW UP. I WANNA TAKE THAT TRIP TO *SPAIN* WITH YOU. WHERE THEY MAKE THAT *CHEESE* YOU TOLD ME ABOUT.
CAN YOU HELP ME?
Y-Y-YEAH... WAIT. OF COURSE. I KNOW WHAT I HAVE TO DO NOW...
YES. IT'S *OBVIOUS* WHAT NEEDS TO HAPPEN.
YOU NEED TO PUT ON THE *COSTUME.* YOU LOVE IT. DON'T *FOOL* YOURSELF!
UH... WH-WHAT?
DON'T LISTEN TO HIM, NEAL.
THEY THINK YOU'RE A *JOKE.* THEY'RE *WRONG.*
CRUSH THOSE GREEN LANTERNS. SHOW THEM WHO YOU *REALLY* ARE.
THEY *DISCREDITED* YOU. *IMPRISONED* YOU. USED YOU LIKE A *PAWN!*
AND *NOW?* THEY SEND *TWO OBSCURE GREEN LANTERNS* AFTER YOU!
NOT EVEN SUPERMAN?
YOU ARE BRILLIANT AND POWERFUL. MORE THAN *ANY-ONE* KNOWS.
YOU ARE *DOCTOR POLARIS.*
PUT ON THE COSTUME.

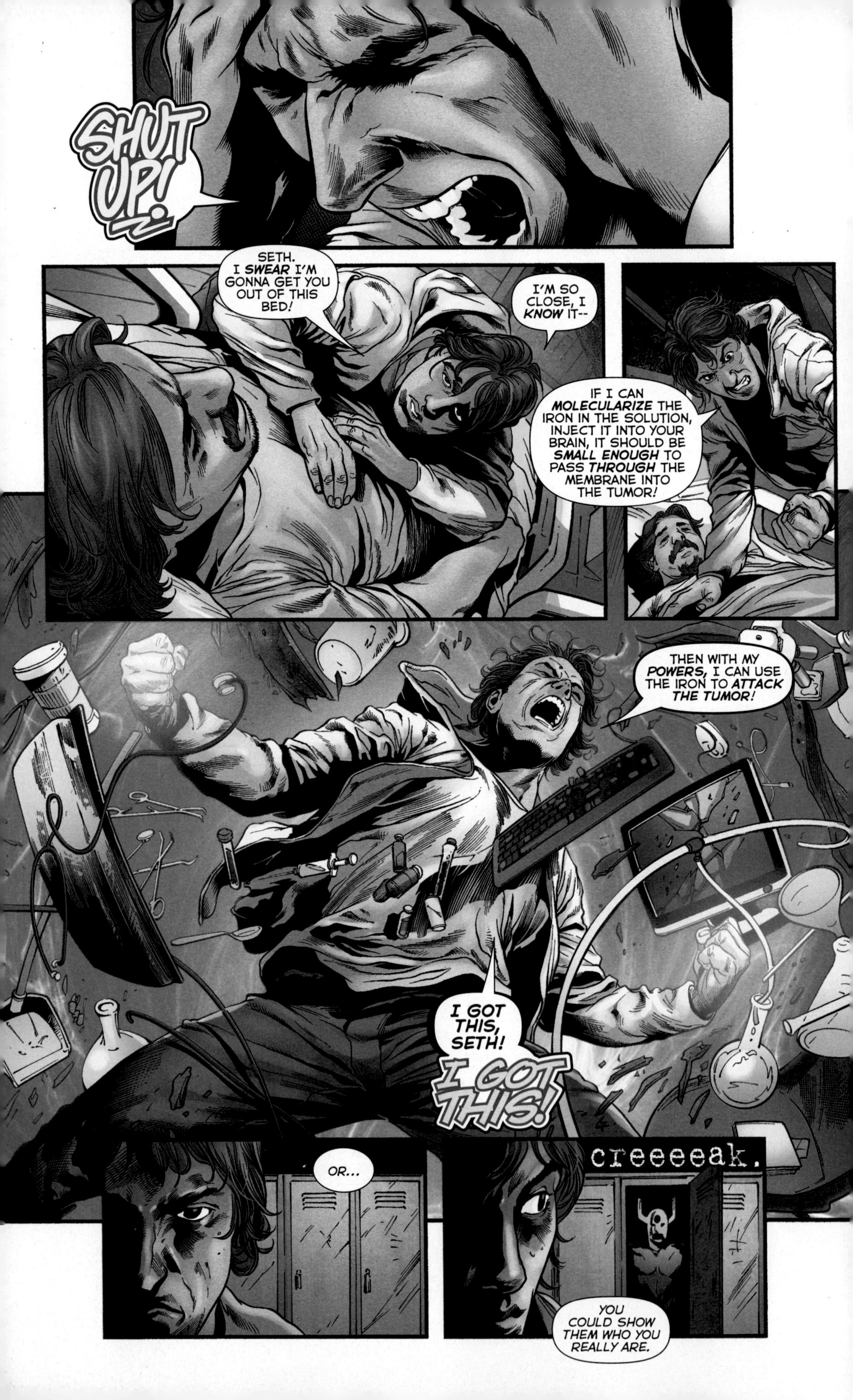
SHUT UP!
SETH. I SWEAR I'M GONNA GET YOU OUT OF THIS BED!
I'M SO CLOSE, I KNOW IT--
IF I CAN MOLECULARIZE THE IRON IN THE SOLUTION, INJECT IT INTO YOUR BRAIN, IT SHOULD BE SMALL ENOUGH TO PASS THROUGH THE MEMBRANE INTO THE TUMOR!
THEN WITH MY POWERS, I CAN USE THE IRON TO ATTACK THE TUMOR!
I GOT THIS, SETH!
I GOT THIS!
OR...
creeeeak.
YOU COULD SHOW THEM WHO YOU REALLY ARE.

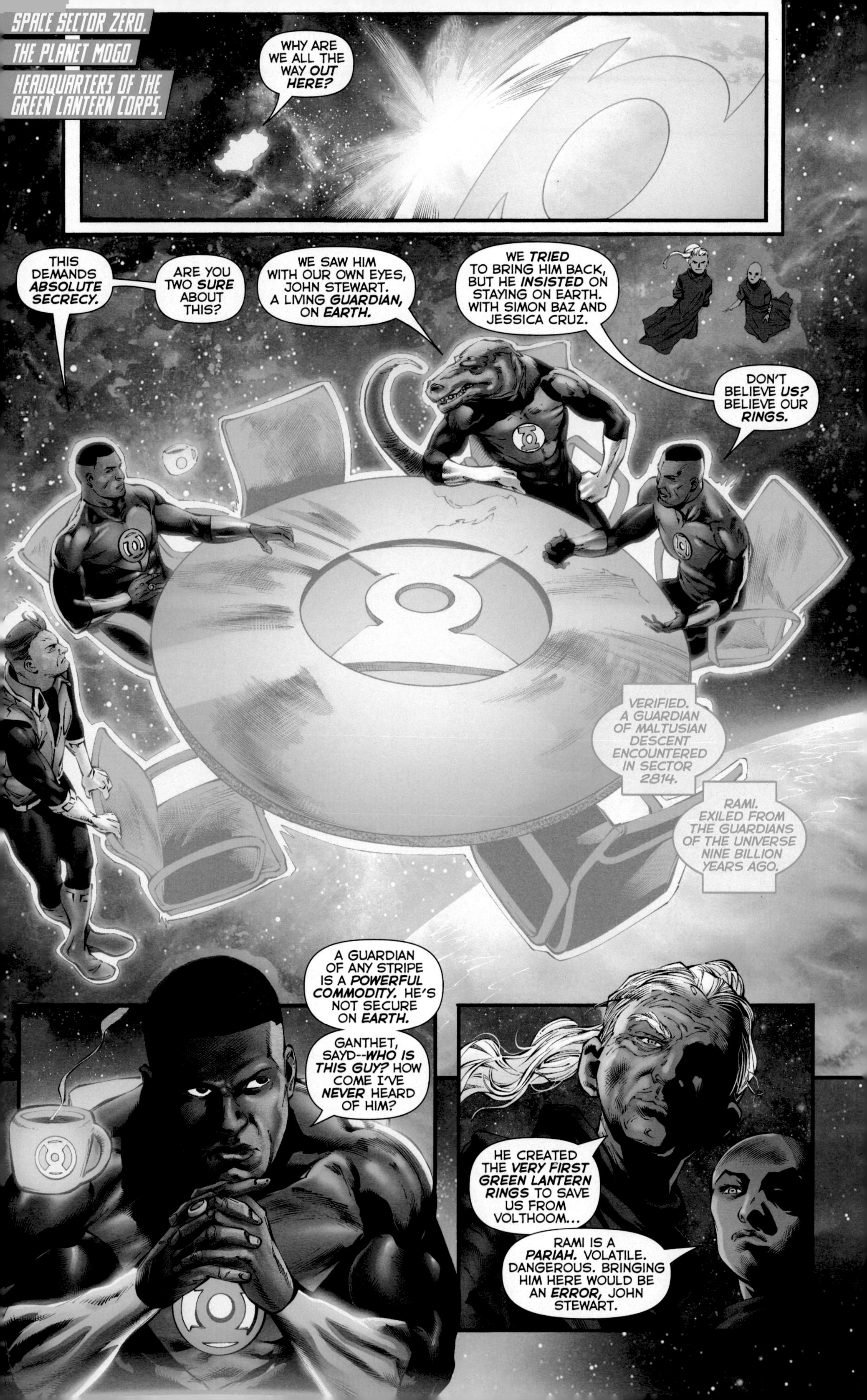
SPACE SECTOR ZERO.
THE PLANET MOGO.
HEADQUARTERS OF THE GREEN LANTERN CORPS.
WHY ARE WE ALL THE WAY OUT HERE?
THIS DEMANDS ABSOLUTE SECRECY.
ARE YOU TWO SURE ABOUT THIS?
WE SAW HIM WITH OUR OWN EYES, JOHN STEWART. A LIVING GUARDIAN, ON EARTH.
WE TRIED TO BRING HIM BACK, BUT HE INSISTED ON STAYING ON EARTH. WITH SIMON BAZ AND JESSICA CRUZ.
DON'T BELIEVE US? BELIEVE OUR RINGS.
VERIFIED. A GUARDIAN OF MALTUSIAN DESCENT ENCOUNTERED IN SECTOR 2814.
RAMI. EXILED FROM THE GUARDIANS OF THE UNIVERSE NINE BILLION YEARS AGO.
A GUARDIAN OF ANY STRIPE IS A POWERFUL COMMODITY. HE'S NOT SECURE ON EARTH.
GANTHET, SAYD--WHO IS THIS GUY? HOW COME I'VE NEVER HEARD OF HIM?
HE CREATED THE VERY FIRST GREEN LANTERN RINGS TO SAVE US FROM VOLTHOOM...
RAMI IS A PARIAH. VOLATILE. DANGEROUS. BRINGING HIM HERE WOULD BE AN ERROR, JOHN STEWART.

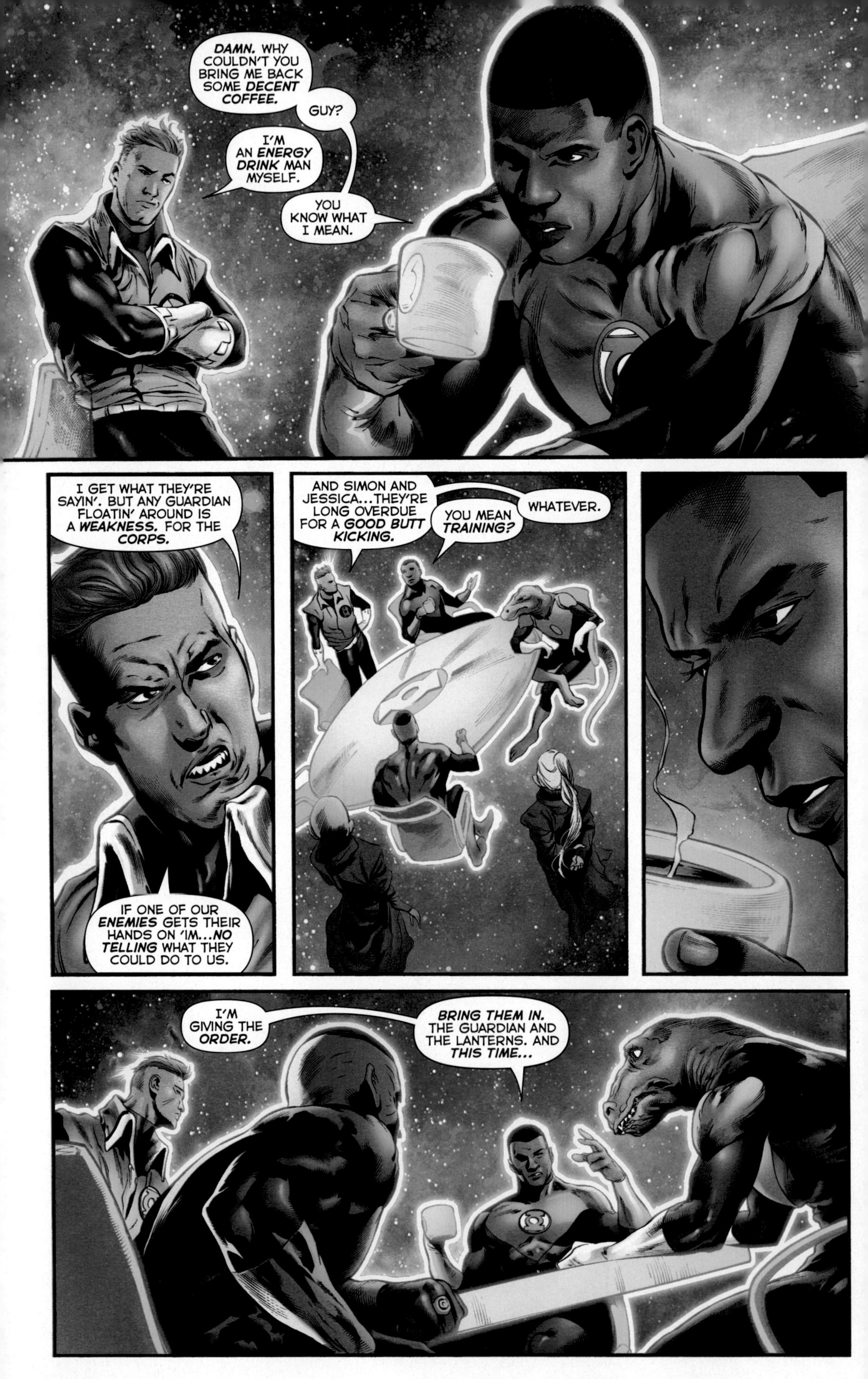
DAMN. WHY COULDN'T YOU BRING ME BACK SOME DECENT COFFEE.
GUY?
I'M AN ENERGY DRINK MAN MYSELF.
YOU KNOW WHAT I MEAN.
I GET WHAT THEY'RE SAYIN'. BUT ANY GUARDIAN FLOATIN' AROUND IS A WEAKNESS. FOR THE CORPS.
IF ONE OF OUR ENEMIES GETS THEIR HANDS ON 'IM...NO TELLING WHAT THEY COULD DO TO US.
AND SIMON AND JESSICA...THEY'RE LONG OVERDUE FOR A GOOD BUTT KICKING.
YOU MEAN TRAINING?
WHATEVER.
I'M GIVING THE ORDER.
BRING THEM IN. THE GUARDIAN AND THE LANTERNS. AND THIS TIME...

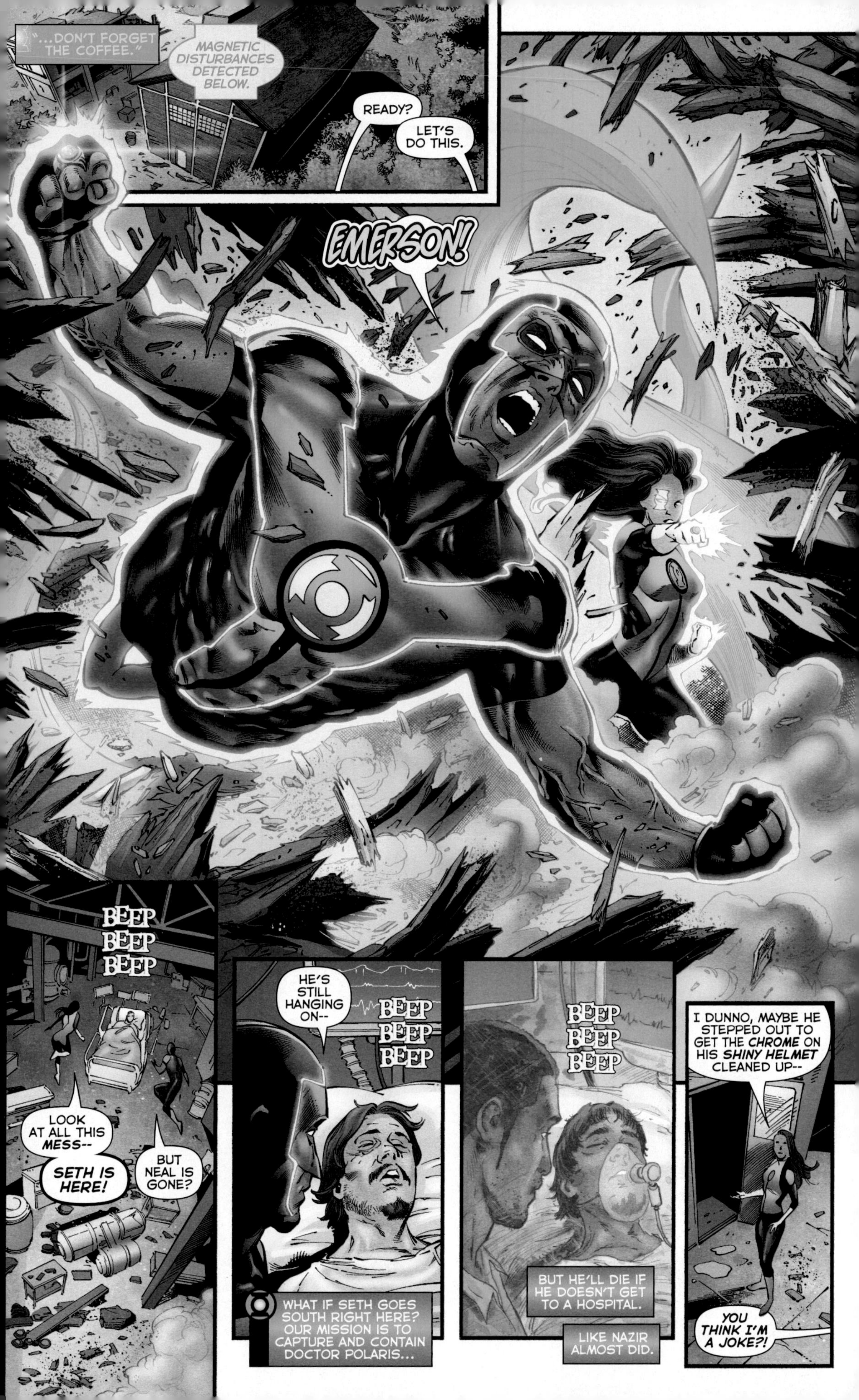
"...DON'T FORGET THE COFFEE."
MAGNETIC DISTURBANCES DETECTED BELOW.
READY?
LET'S DO THIS.
EMERSON!
BEEP BEEP BEEP
LOOK AT ALL THIS MESS--
SETH IS HERE!
BUT NEAL IS GONE?
HE'S STILL HANGING ON--
BEEP BEEP BEEP
WHAT IF SETH GOES SOUTH RIGHT HERE? OUR MISSION IS TO CAPTURE AND CONTAIN DOCTOR POLARIS...
BEEP BEEP BEEP
BUT HE'LL DIE IF HE DOESN'T GET TO A HOSPITAL.
LIKE NAZIR ALMOST DID.
I DUNNO, MAYBE HE STEPPED OUT TO GET THE CHROME ON HIS SHINY HELMET CLEANED UP--
YOU THINK I'M A JOKE?!

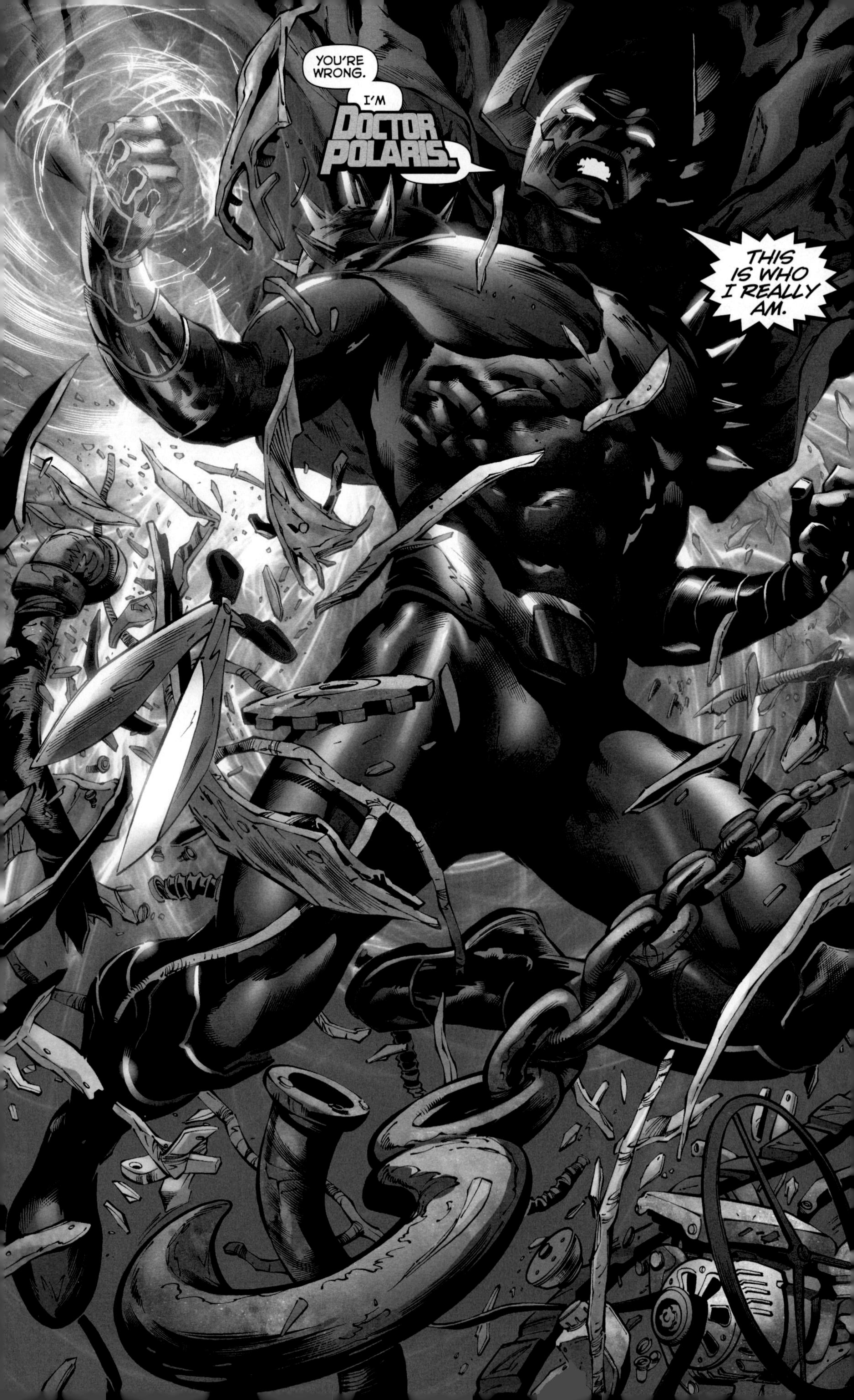
YOU'RE WRONG.
I'M
DOCTOR POLARIS.
THIS IS WHO I REALLY AM.

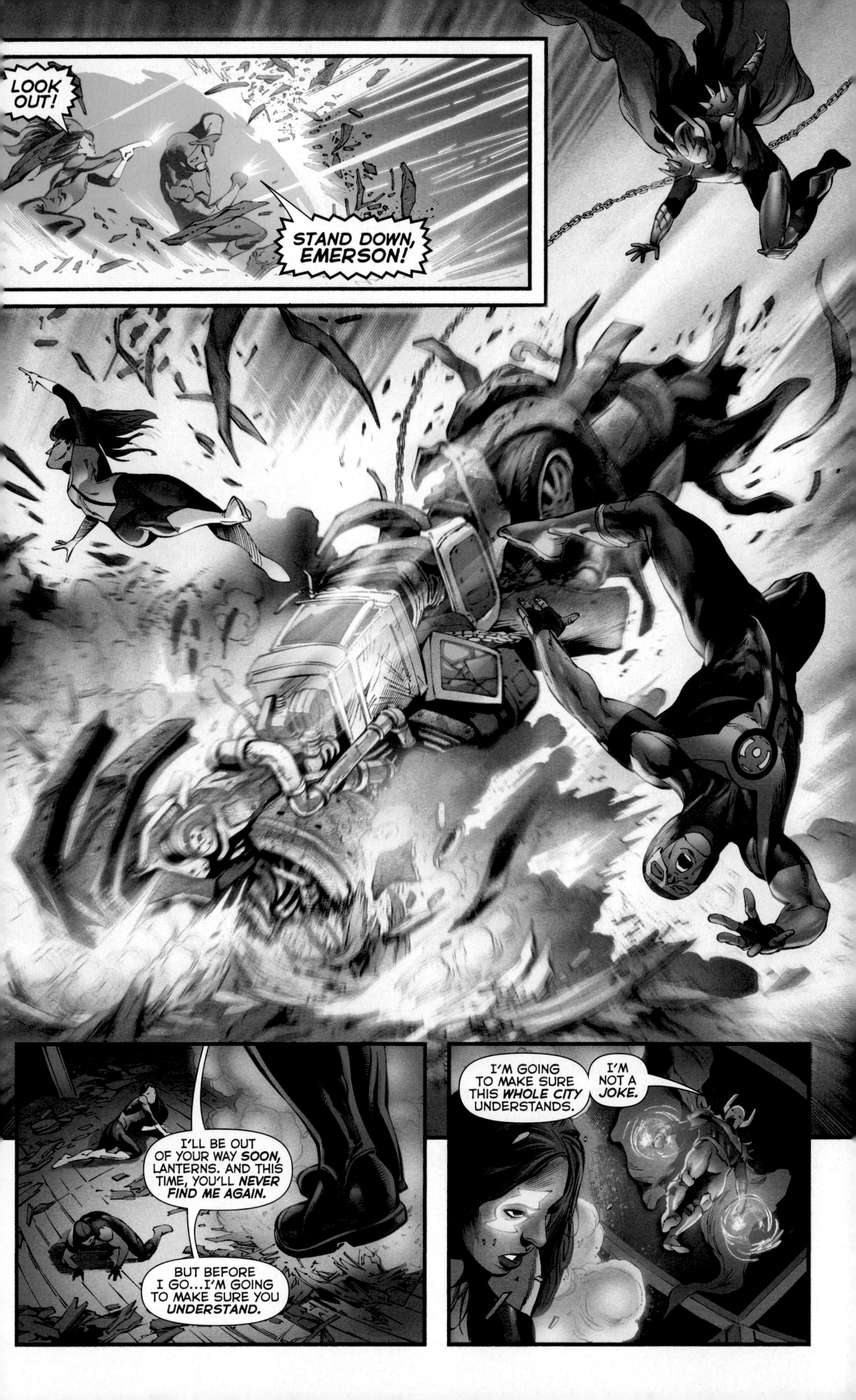
LOOK OUT!
STAND DOWN, EMERSON!
I'LL BE OUT OF YOUR WAY SOON, LANTERNS. AND THIS TIME, YOU'LL NEVER FIND ME AGAIN.
BUT BEFORE I GO...I'M GOING TO MAKE SURE YOU UNDERSTAND.
I'M NOT A JOKE.
I'M GOING TO MAKE SURE THIS WHOLE CITY UNDERSTANDS.

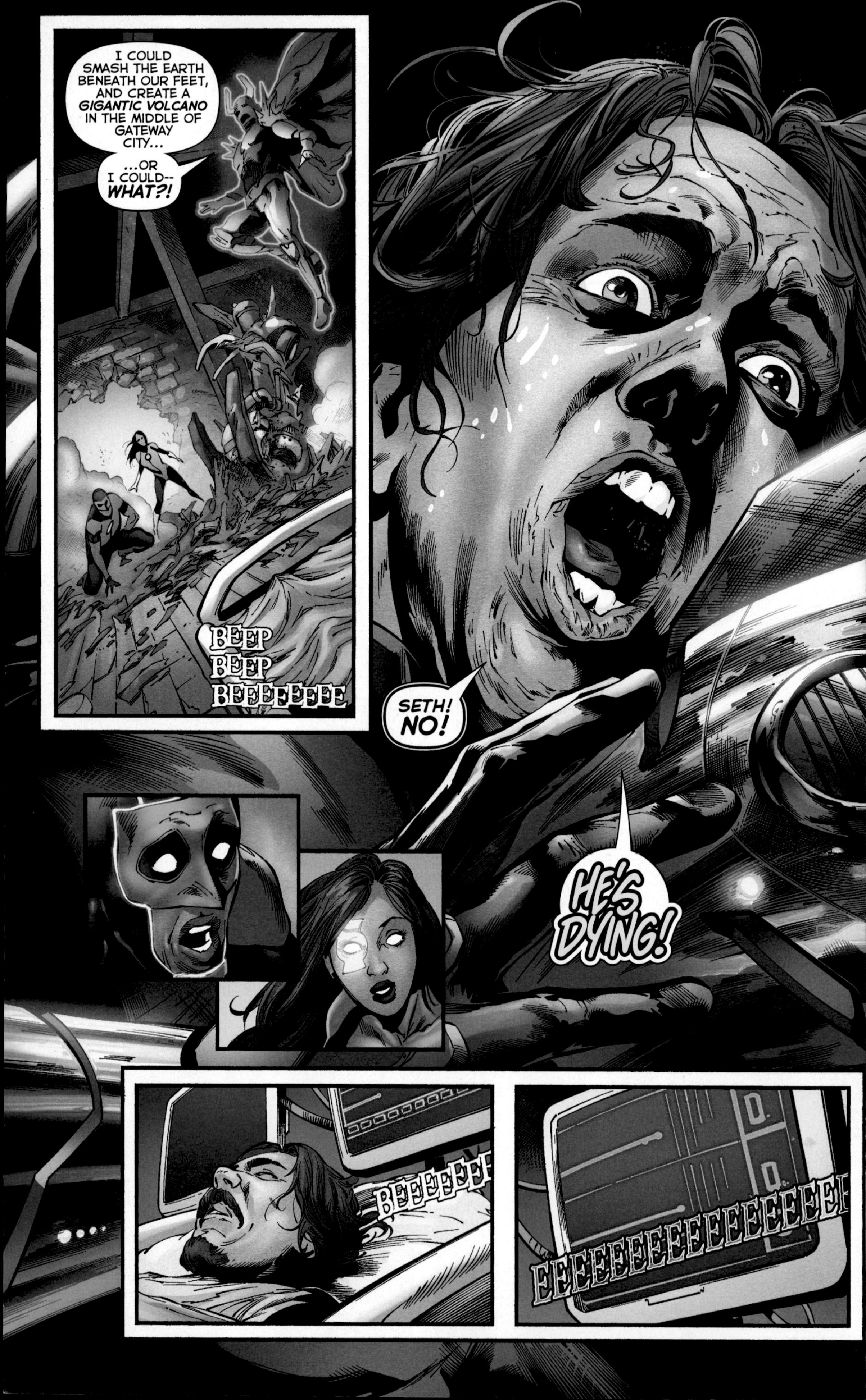
I COULD SMASH THE EARTH BENEATH OUR FEET, AND CREATE A GIGANTIC VOLCANO IN THE MIDDLE OF GATEWAY CITY...
...OR I COULD-- WHAT?!
BEEP BEEP BEEEEEEEE
SETH! NO!
HE'S DYING!
BEEEEEEE
EEEEEEEEEEEEEEEEEEE

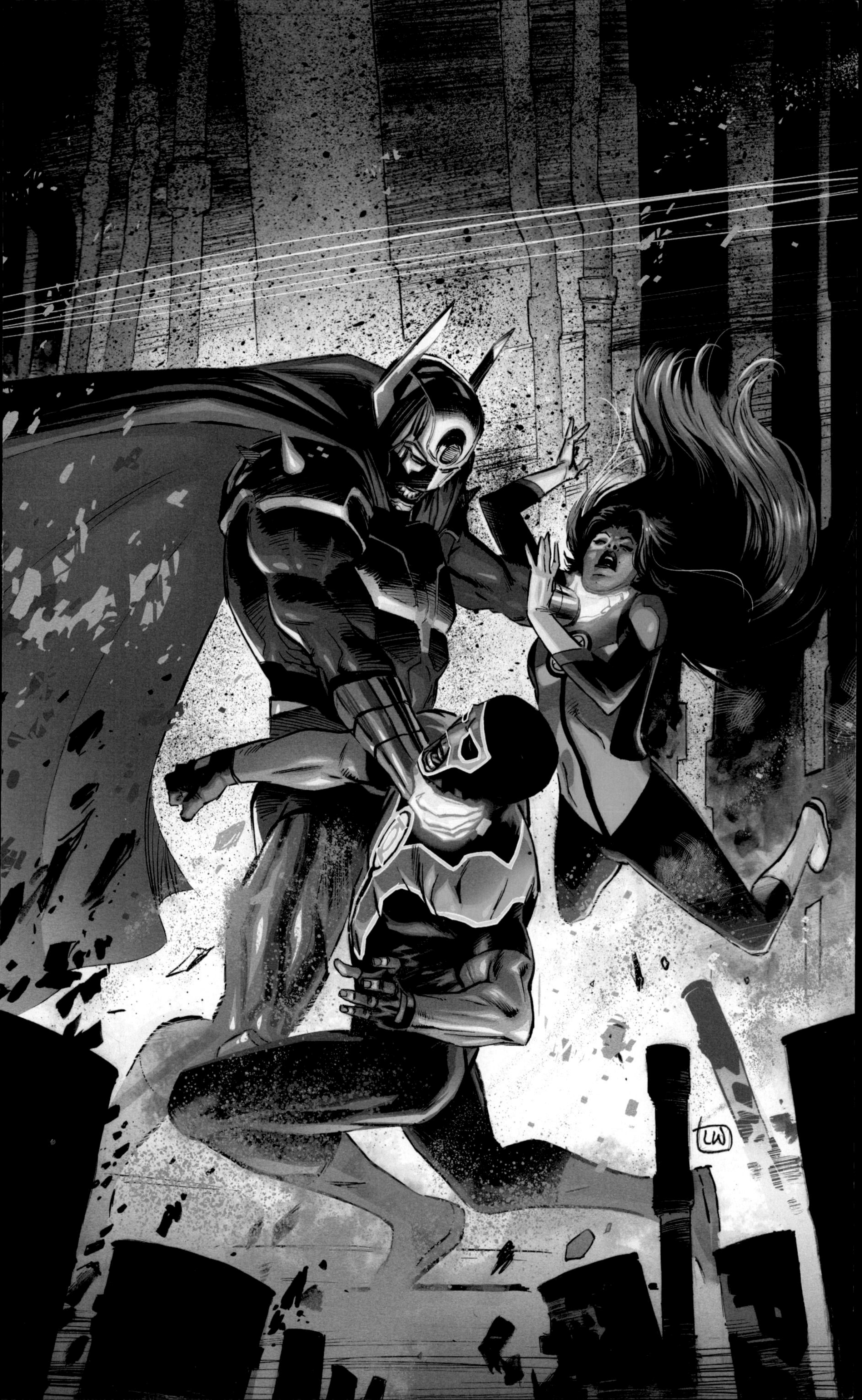

"POLARITY CHAPTER THREE: FLATLINE"

ROBSON ROCHA penciller ✶ DANIEL HENRIQUES JOE PRADO inkers

Cover by LEE WEEKS AND DAVE MCCAIG

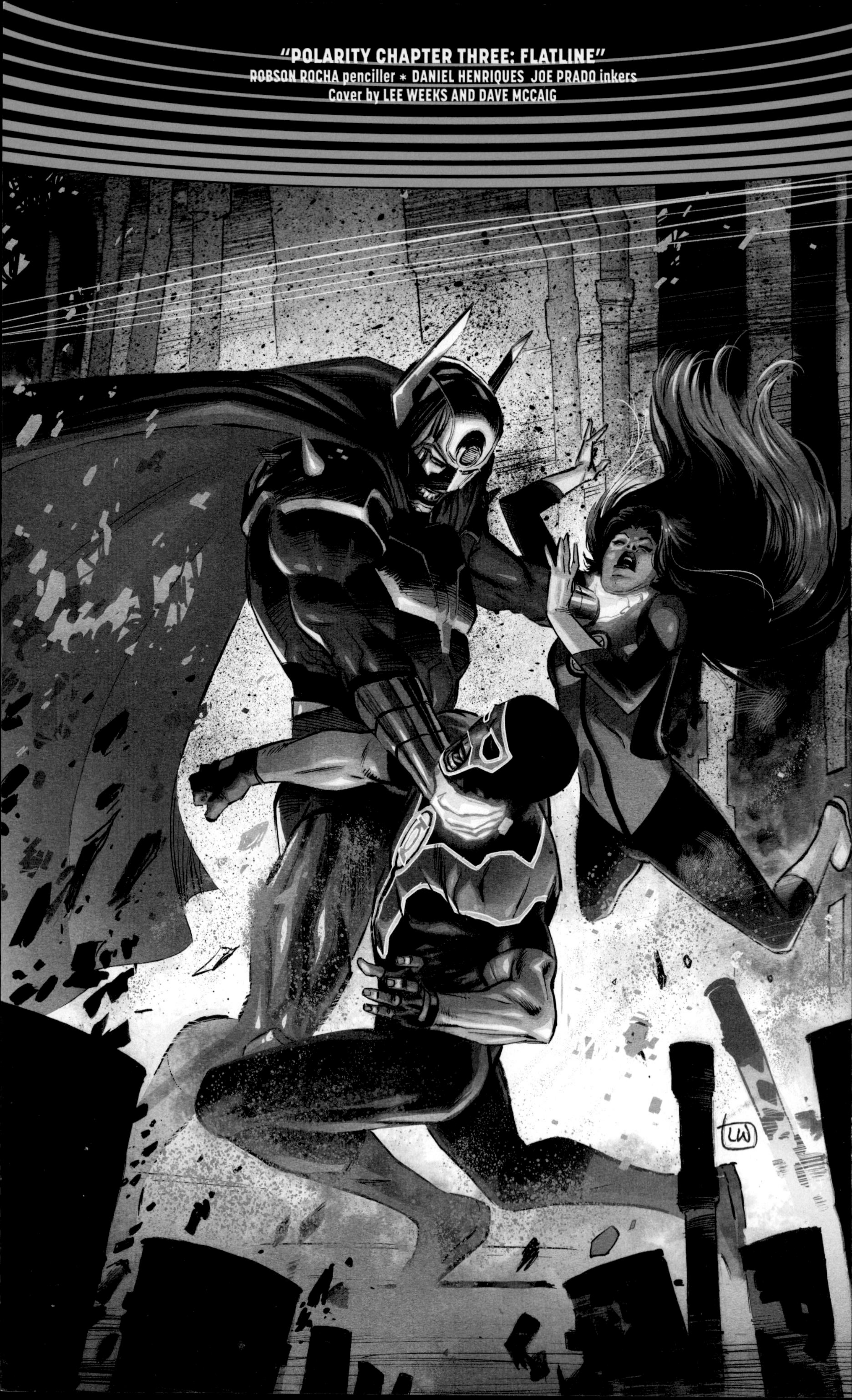
LW

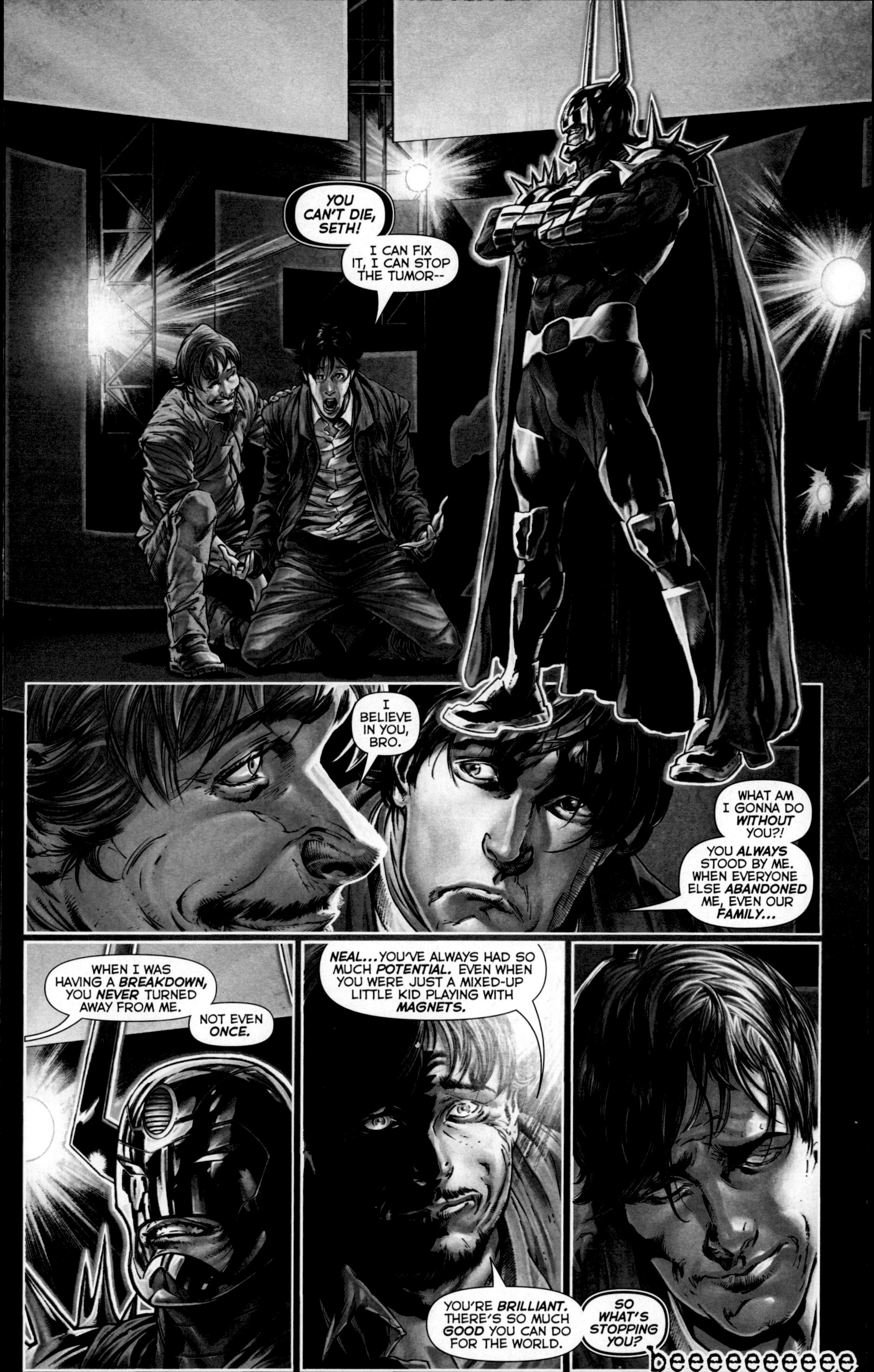
YOU CAN'T DIE, SETH!
I CAN FIX IT, I CAN STOP THE TUMOR--
I BELIEVE IN YOU, BRO.
WHAT AM I GONNA DO WITHOUT YOU?!
YOU ALWAYS STOOD BY ME. WHEN EVERYONE ELSE ABANDONED ME, EVEN OUR FAMILY...
WHEN I WAS HAVING A BREAKDOWN, YOU NEVER TURNED AWAY FROM ME.
NOT EVEN ONCE.
NEAL... YOU'VE ALWAYS HAD SO MUCH POTENTIAL. EVEN WHEN YOU WERE JUST A MIXED-UP LITTLE KID PLAYING WITH MAGNETS.
YOU'RE BRILLIANT. THERE'S SO MUCH GOOD YOU CAN DO FOR THE WORLD.
SO WHAT'S STOPPING YOU?
beeeeeeeeeee

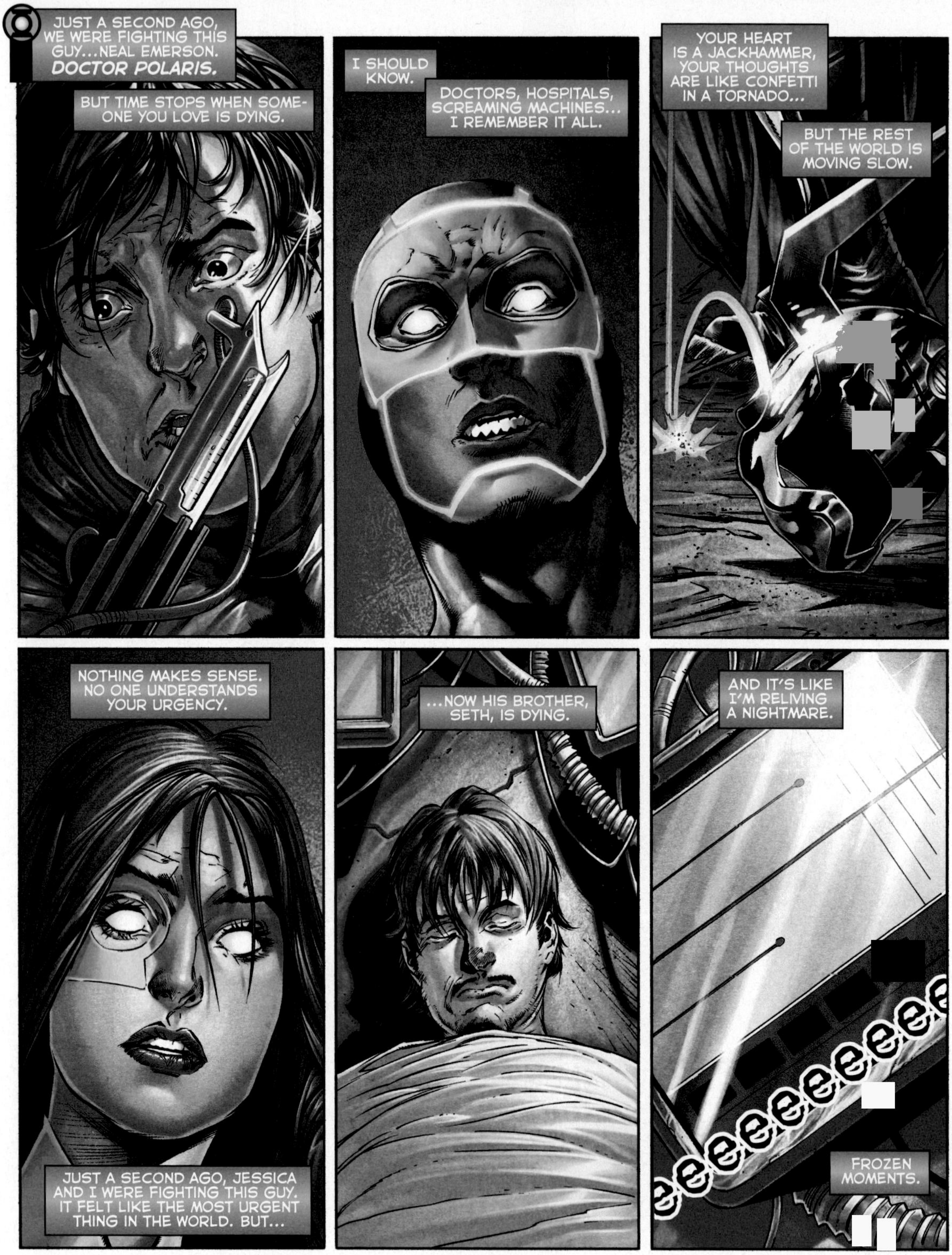
JUST A SECOND AGO, WE WERE FIGHTING THIS GUY...NEAL EMERSON. *DOCTOR POLARIS.*
BUT TIME STOPS WHEN SOMEONE YOU LOVE IS DYING.
I SHOULD KNOW.
DOCTORS, HOSPITALS, SCREAMING MACHINES... I REMEMBER IT ALL.
YOUR HEART IS A JACKHAMMER, YOUR THOUGHTS ARE LIKE CONFETTI IN A TORNADO...
BUT THE REST OF THE WORLD IS MOVING SLOW.
NOTHING MAKES SENSE. NO ONE UNDERSTANDS YOUR URGENCY.
JUST A SECOND AGO, JESSICA AND I WERE FIGHTING THIS GUY. IT FELT LIKE THE MOST URGENT THING IN THE WORLD. BUT...
...NOW HIS BROTHER, SETH, IS DYING.
AND IT'S LIKE I'M RELIVING A NIGHTMARE.
EEEEEEEEEEEE
FROZEN MOMENTS.

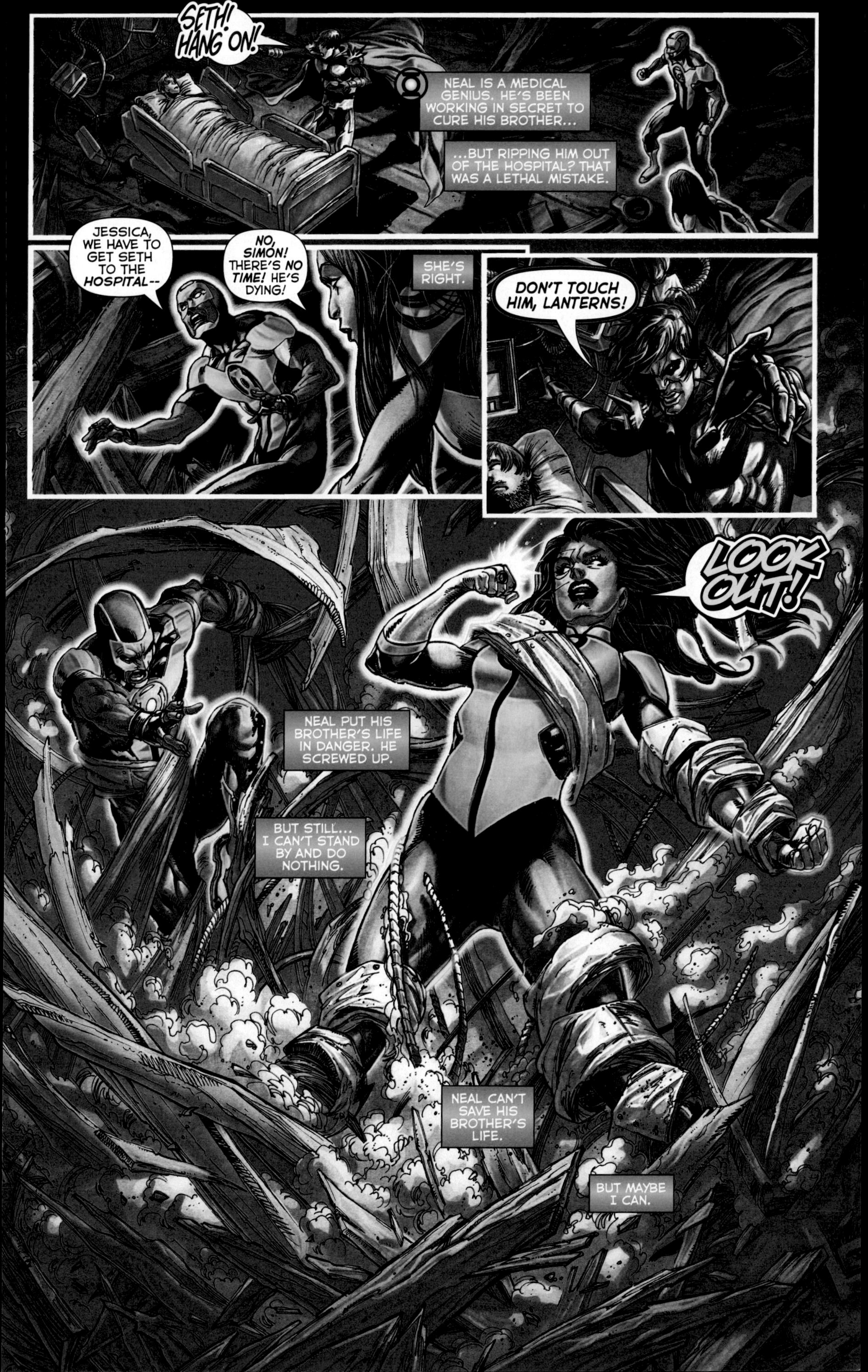
SETH! HANG ON!
NEAL IS A MEDICAL GENIUS. HE'S BEEN WORKING IN SECRET TO CURE HIS BROTHER...
...BUT RIPPING HIM OUT OF THE HOSPITAL? THAT WAS A LETHAL MISTAKE.
JESSICA, WE HAVE TO GET SETH TO THE HOSPITAL--
NO, SIMON! THERE'S NO TIME! HE'S DYING!
SHE'S RIGHT.
DON'T TOUCH HIM, LANTERNS!
LOOK OUT!
NEAL PUT HIS BROTHER'S LIFE IN DANGER. HE SCREWED UP.
BUT STILL... I CAN'T STAND BY AND DO NOTHING.
NEAL CAN'T SAVE HIS BROTHER'S LIFE.
BUT MAYBE I CAN.

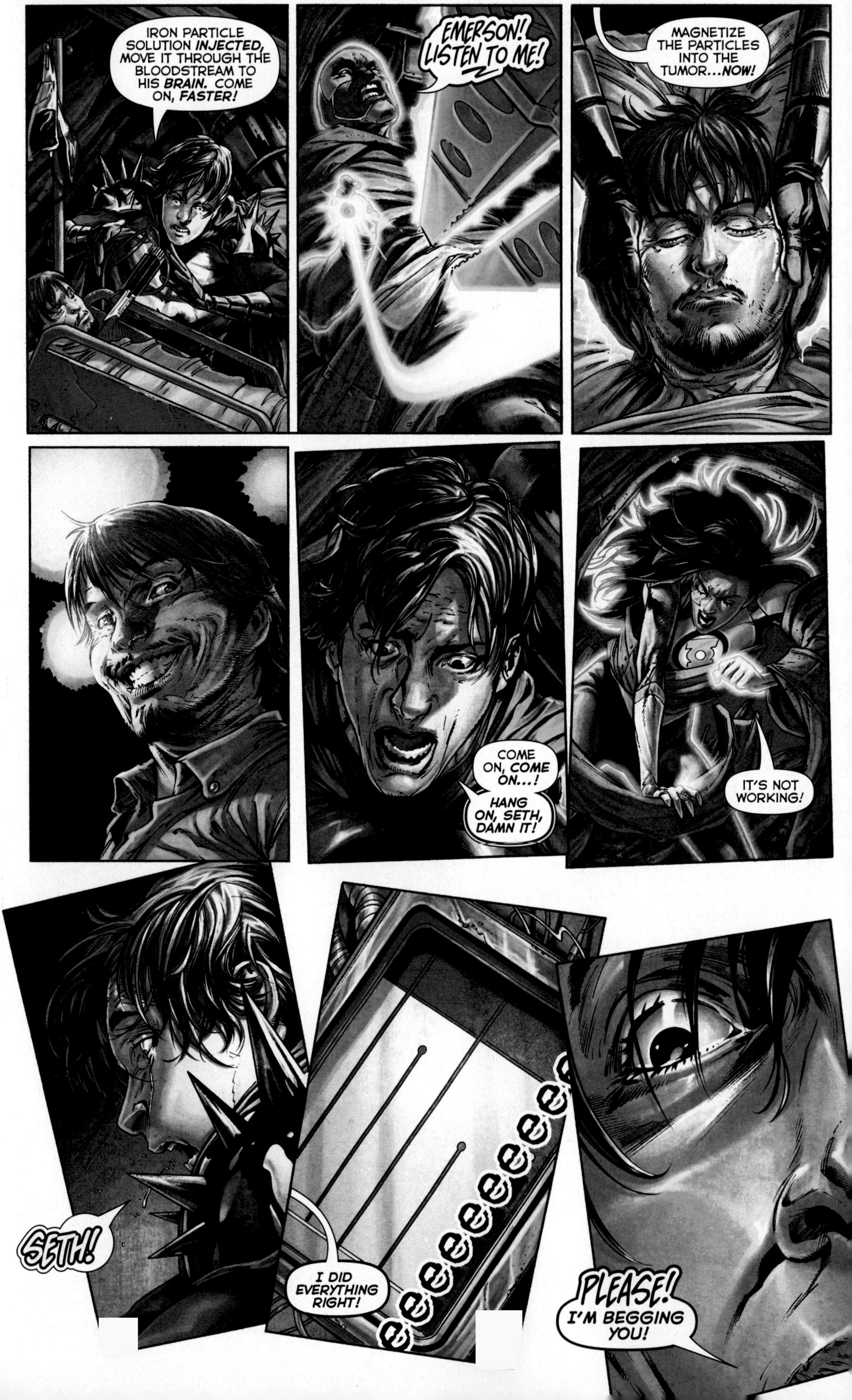
IRON PARTICLE SOLUTION INJECTED, MOVE IT THROUGH THE BLOODSTREAM TO HIS BRAIN. COME ON, FASTER!
EMERSON! LISTEN TO ME!
MAGNETIZE THE PARTICLES INTO THE TUMOR...NOW!
COME ON, COME ON...!
HANG ON, SETH, DAMN IT!
IT'S NOT WORKING!
SETH!
I DID EVERYTHING RIGHT!
EEEEEEEEEEE
PLEASE!
I'M BEGGING YOU!

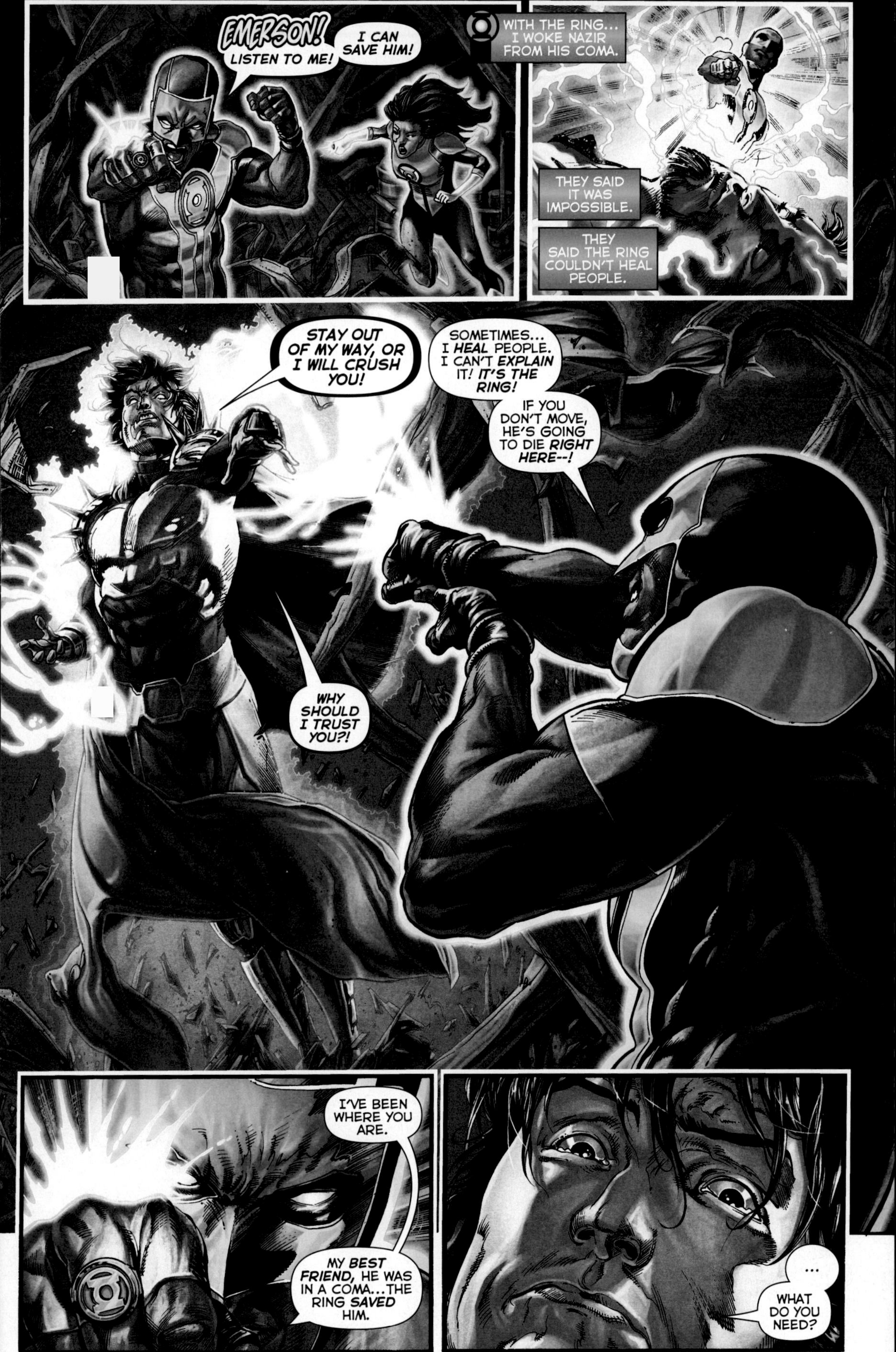
EMERSON!
LISTEN TO ME!
I CAN SAVE HIM!
WITH THE RING... I WOKE NAZIR FROM HIS COMA.
THEY SAID IT WAS IMPOSSIBLE.
THEY SAID THE RING COULDN'T HEAL PEOPLE.
STAY OUT OF MY WAY, OR I WILL CRUSH YOU!
SOMETIMES... I HEAL PEOPLE. I CAN'T EXPLAIN IT! IT'S THE RING!
IF YOU DON'T MOVE, HE'S GOING TO DIE RIGHT HERE--!
WHY SHOULD I TRUST YOU?!
I'VE BEEN WHERE YOU ARE.
MY BEST FRIEND, HE WAS IN A COMA...THE RING SAVED HIM.
...
WHAT DO YOU NEED?

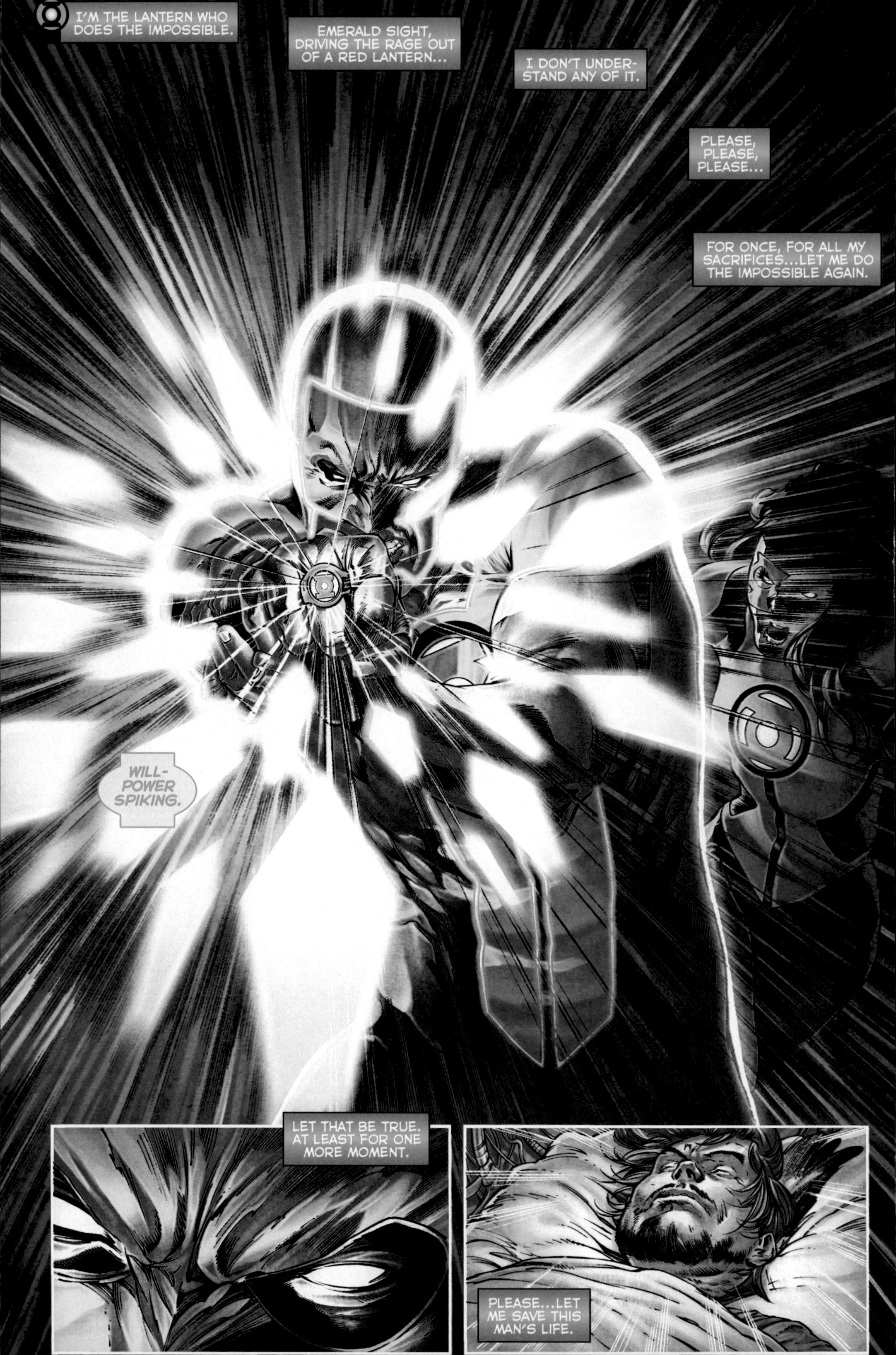
I'M THE LANTERN WHO DOES THE IMPOSSIBLE.
EMERALD SIGHT, DRIVING THE RAGE OUT OF A RED LANTERN...
I DON'T UNDERSTAND ANY OF IT.
PLEASE, PLEASE, PLEASE...
FOR ONCE, FOR ALL MY SACRIFICES...LET ME DO THE IMPOSSIBLE AGAIN.
WILL-POWER SPIKING.
LET THAT BE TRUE. AT LEAST FOR ONE MORE MOMENT.
PLEASE...LET ME SAVE THIS MAN'S LIFE.

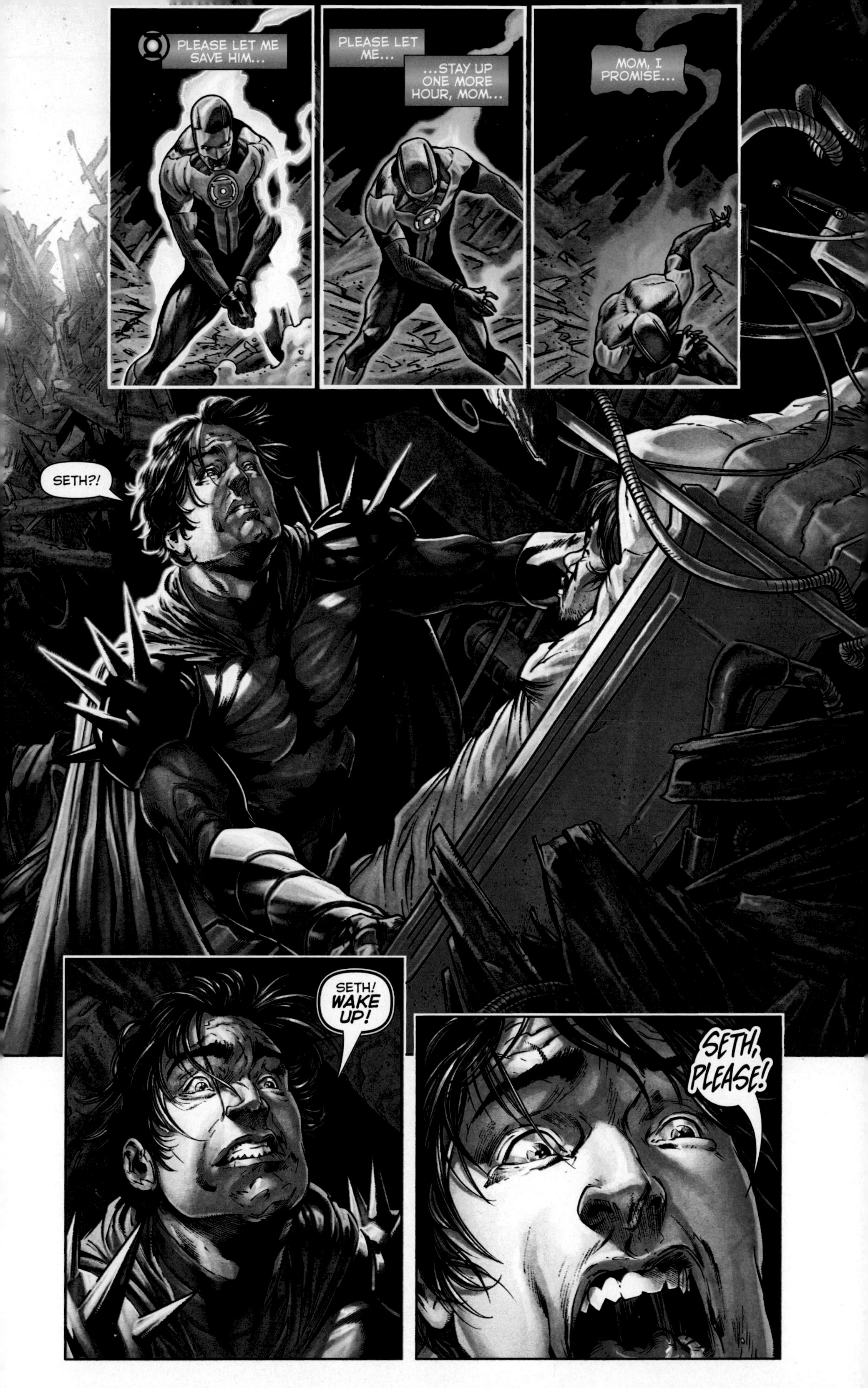
PLEASE LET ME SAVE HIM...
PLEASE LET ME...
...STAY UP ONE MORE HOUR, MOM...
MOM, I PROMISE...
SETH?!
SETH! WAKE UP!
SETH, PLEASE!

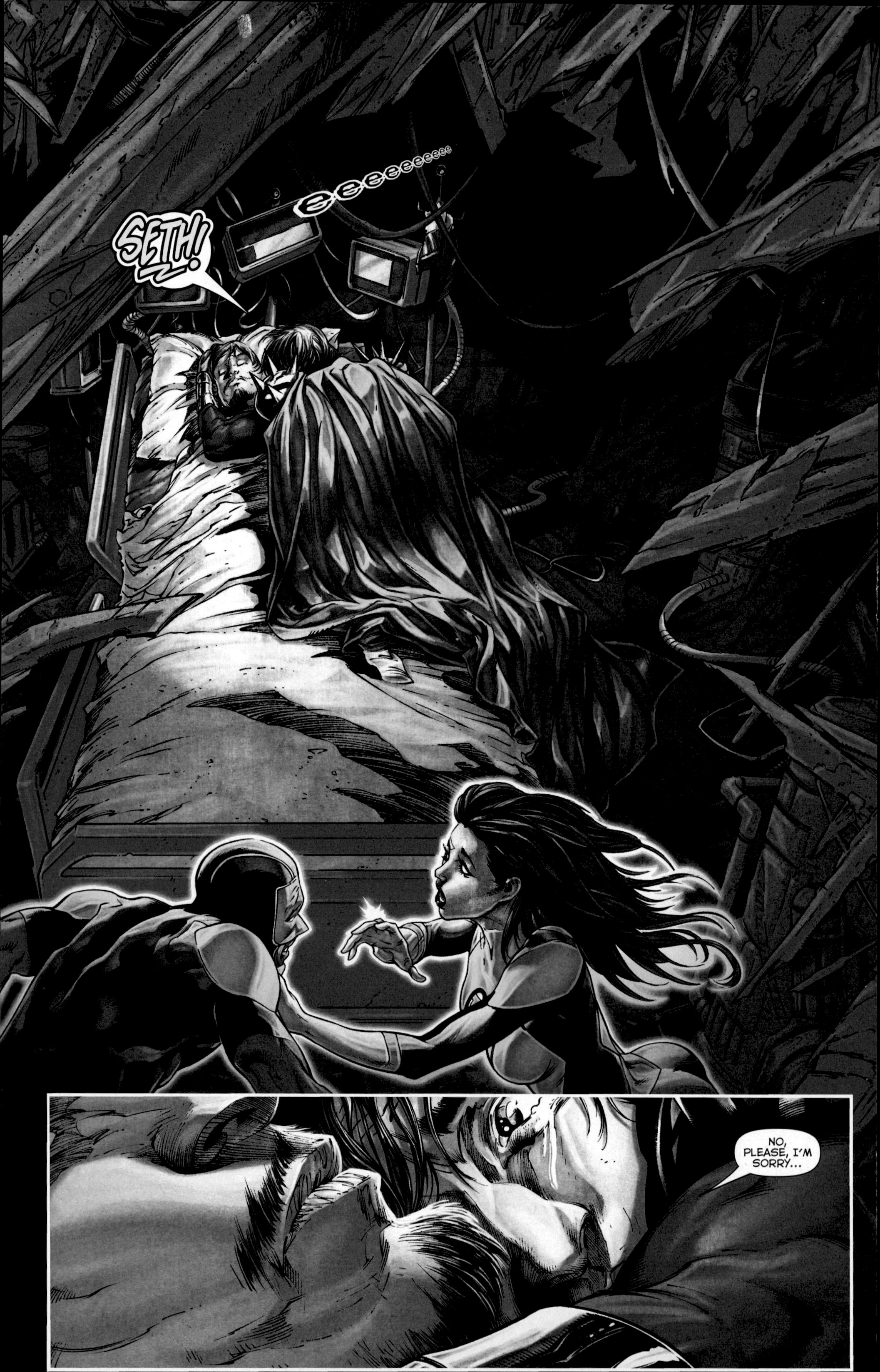
SETH!
NO, PLEASE, I'M SORRY...

HA! I FORGOT ALL ABOUT THAT DAY!

YEAH, I FELT BAD FOR YOU. MOM AND DAD WERE SO MAD. I KNOW YOU DIDN'T MEAN TO SMASH YOUR BIKE...

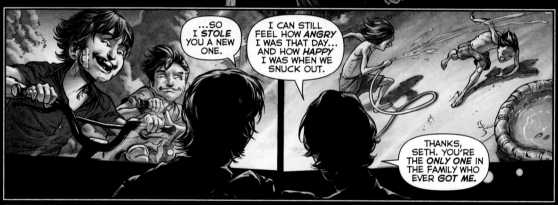

...SO I STOLE YOU A NEW ONE.

I CAN STILL FEEL HOW ANGRY I WAS THAT DAY... AND HOW HAPPY I WAS WHEN WE SNUCK OUT.

THANKS, SETH. YOU'RE THE ONLY ONE IN THE FAMILY WHO EVER GOT ME.

I TRIED SO HARD, SETH...

I KNOW YOU DID, PAL. BUT EVEN YOUR GENIUS CAN'T FIX EVERYTHING.

IT'S GONNA BE TOUGH ON YOU, BUT I JUST WANT YOU TO KNOW...

YOU GOT THIS. NO MATTER WHAT. OKAY?

SETH...?

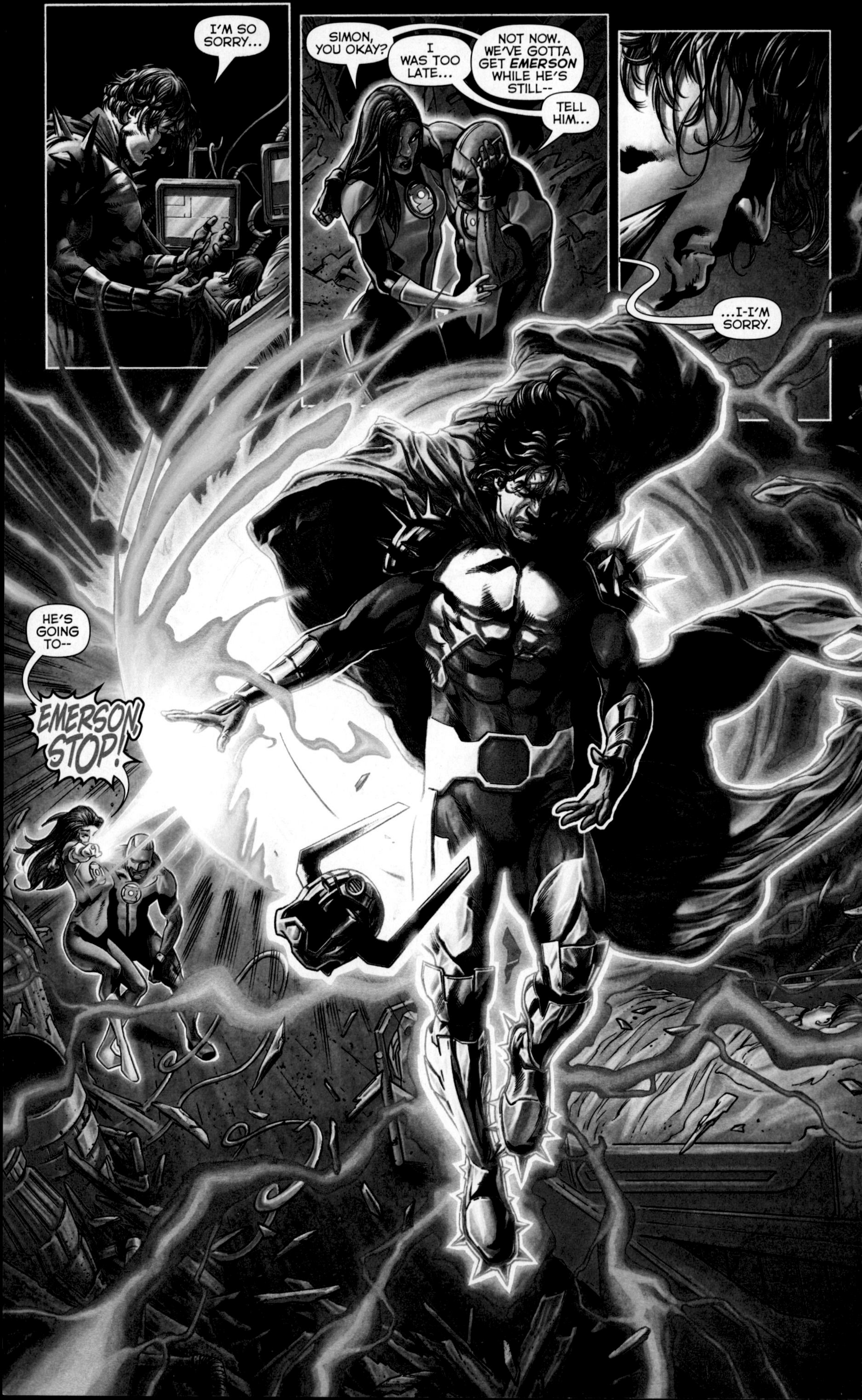
I'M SO SORRY...
SIMON, YOU OKAY?
I WAS TOO LATE...
NOT NOW. WE'VE GOTTA GET EMERSON WHILE HE'S STILL--
TELL HIM...
...I-I'M SORRY.
HE'S GOING TO--
EMERSON, STOP!

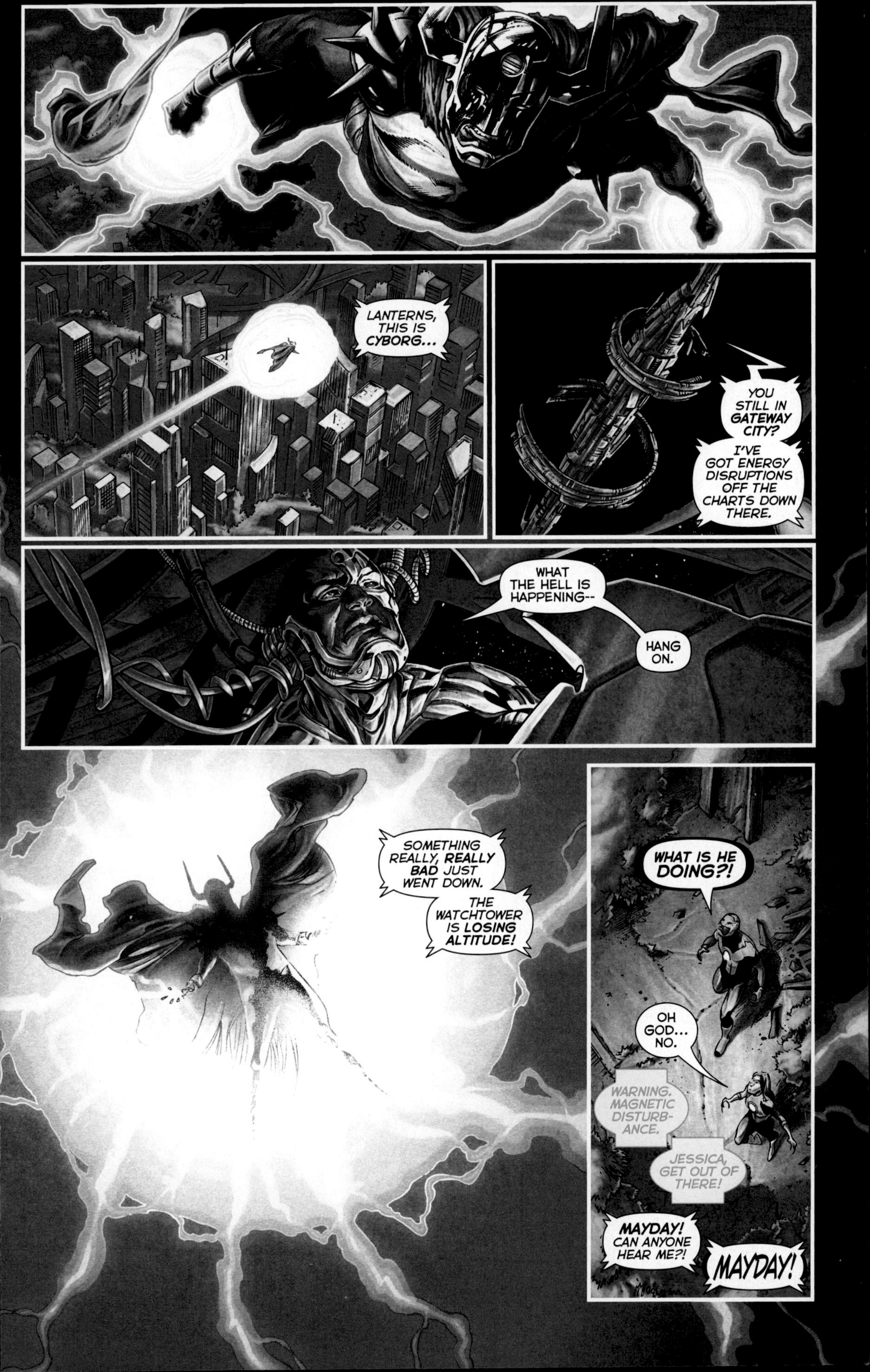
LANTERNS, THIS IS CYBORG...
YOU STILL IN GATEWAY CITY?
I'VE GOT ENERGY DISRUPTIONS OFF THE CHARTS DOWN THERE.
WHAT THE HELL IS HAPPENING--
HANG ON.
SOMETHING REALLY, REALLY BAD JUST WENT DOWN.
THE WATCHTOWER IS LOSING ALTITUDE!
WHAT IS HE DOING?!
OH GOD... NO.
WARNING. MAGNETIC DISTURB-ANCE.
JESSICA, GET OUT OF THERE!
MAYDAY! CAN ANYONE HEAR ME?!
MAYDAY!

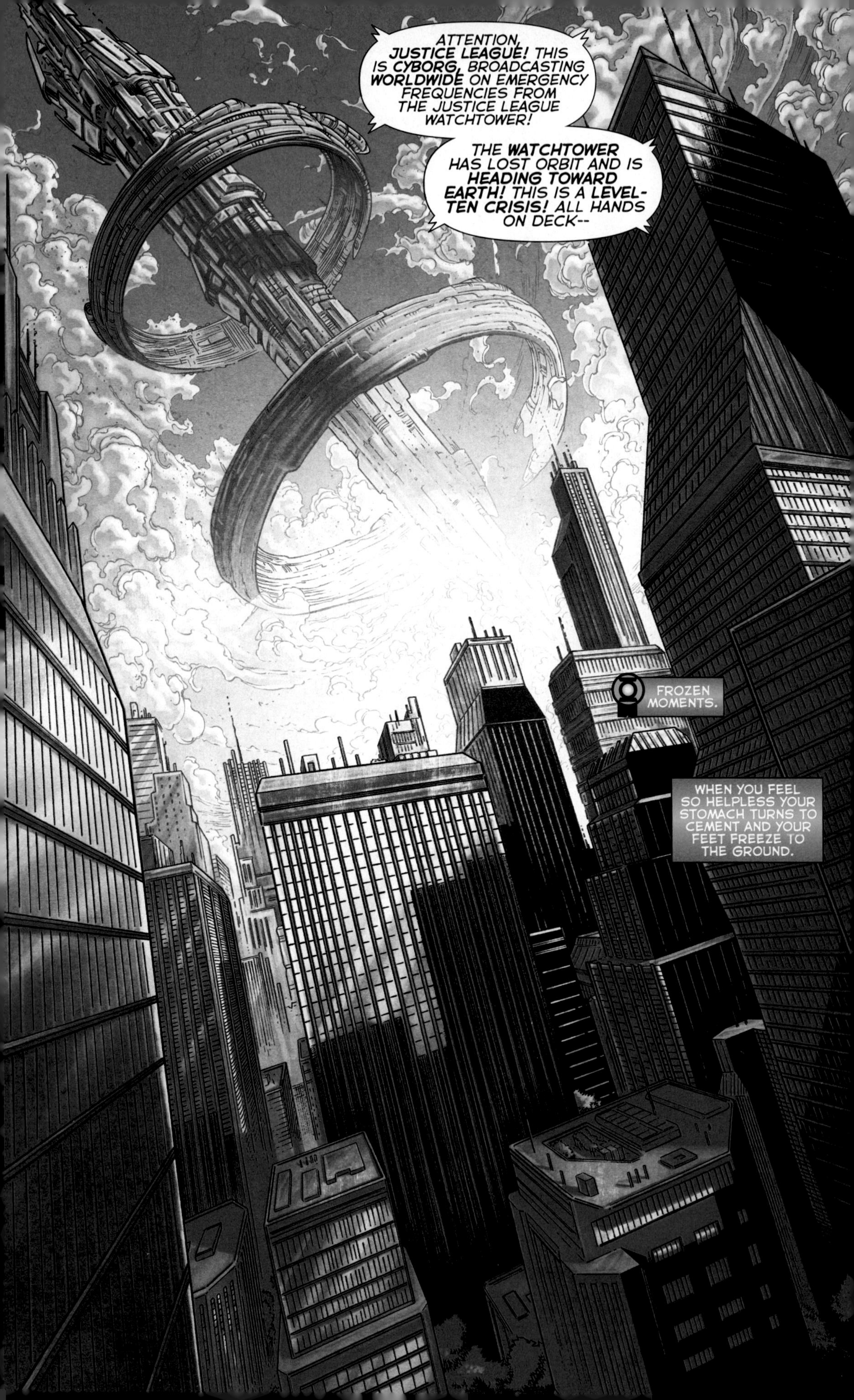
ATTENTION, JUSTICE LEAGUE! THIS IS CYBORG, BROADCASTING WORLDWIDE ON EMERGENCY FREQUENCIES FROM THE JUSTICE LEAGUE WATCHTOWER!
THE WATCHTOWER HAS LOST ORBIT AND IS HEADING TOWARD EARTH! THIS IS A LEVEL-TEN CRISIS! ALL HANDS ON DECK--
FROZEN MOMENTS.
WHEN YOU FEEL SO HELPLESS YOUR STOMACH TURNS TO CEMENT AND YOUR FEET FREEZE TO THE GROUND.

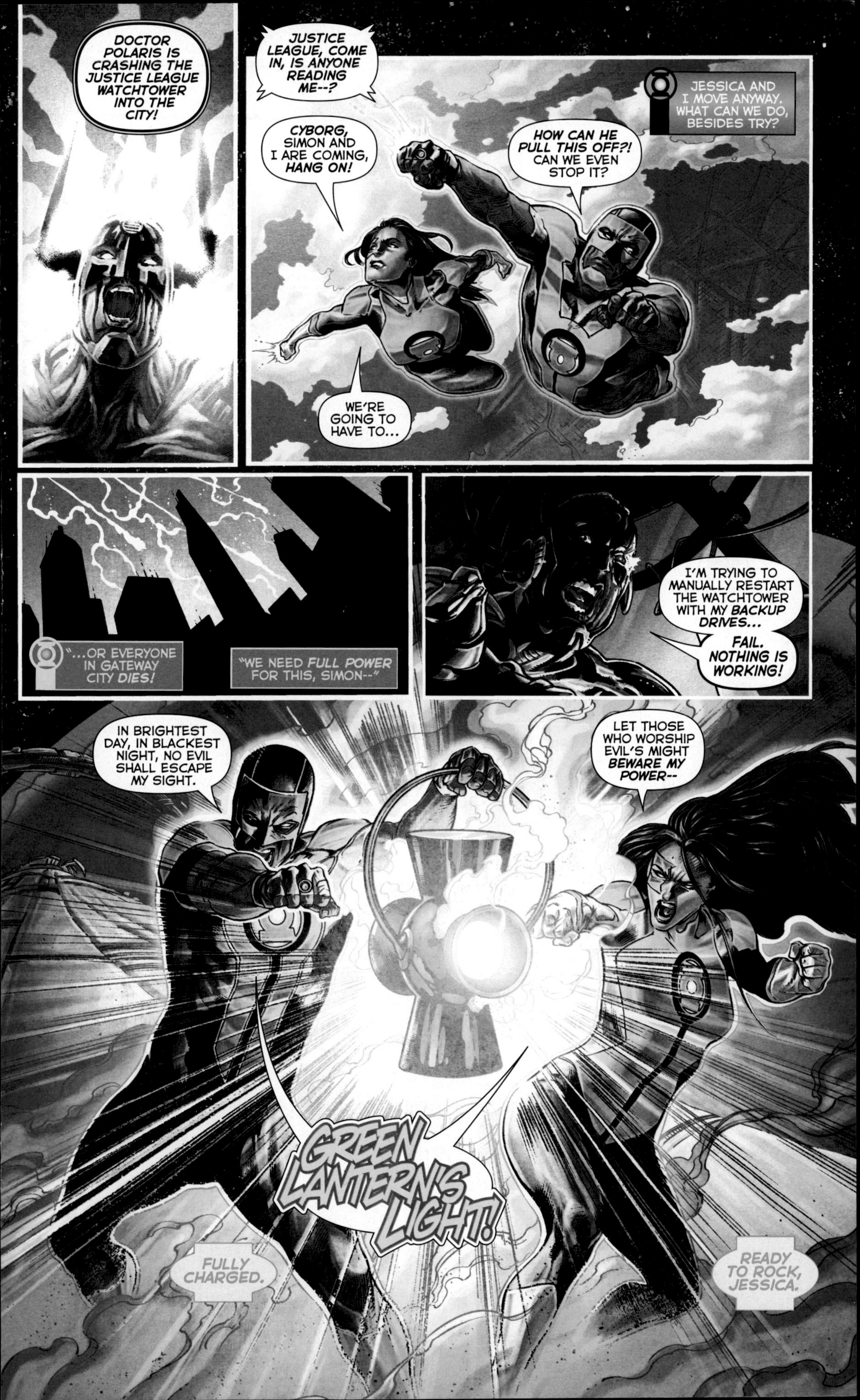
DOCTOR POLARIS IS CRASHING THE JUSTICE LEAGUE WATCHTOWER INTO THE CITY!
JUSTICE LEAGUE, COME IN, IS ANYONE READING ME--?
JESSICA AND I MOVE ANYWAY. WHAT CAN WE DO, BESIDES TRY?
CYBORG, SIMON AND I ARE COMING, HANG ON!
HOW CAN HE PULL THIS OFF?! CAN WE EVEN STOP IT?
WE'RE GOING TO HAVE TO...
"...OR EVERYONE IN GATEWAY CITY DIES!
"WE NEED FULL POWER FOR THIS, SIMON--"
I'M TRYING TO MANUALLY RESTART THE WATCHTOWER WITH MY BACKUP DRIVES...
FAIL. NOTHING IS WORKING!
IN BRIGHTEST DAY, IN BLACKEST NIGHT, NO EVIL SHALL ESCAPE MY SIGHT.
LET THOSE WHO WORSHIP EVIL'S MIGHT BEWARE MY POWER--
GREEN LANTERN'S LIGHT!
FULLY CHARGED.
READY TO ROCK, JESSICA.

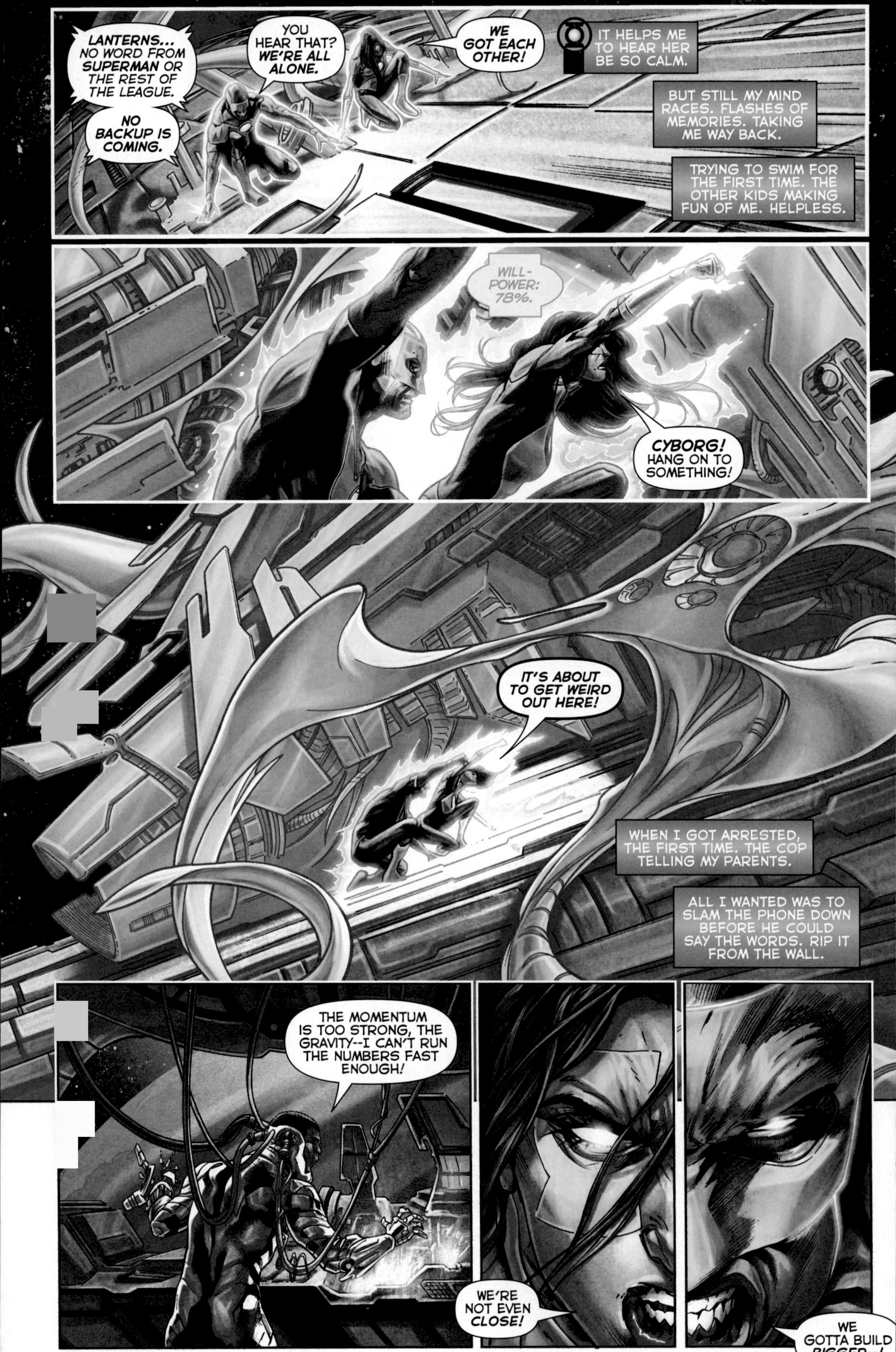
LANTERNS... NO WORD FROM SUPERMAN OR THE REST OF THE LEAGUE.
NO BACKUP IS COMING.
YOU HEAR THAT? WE'RE ALL ALONE.
WE GOT EACH OTHER!
IT HELPS ME TO HEAR HER BE SO CALM.
BUT STILL MY MIND RACES. FLASHES OF MEMORIES. TAKING ME WAY BACK.
TRYING TO SWIM FOR THE FIRST TIME. THE OTHER KIDS MAKING FUN OF ME. HELPLESS.
WILL-POWER: 78%.
CYBORG! HANG ON TO SOMETHING!
IT'S ABOUT TO GET WEIRD OUT HERE!
WHEN I GOT ARRESTED, THE FIRST TIME. THE COP TELLING MY PARENTS.
ALL I WANTED WAS TO SLAM THE PHONE DOWN BEFORE HE COULD SAY THE WORDS. RIP IT FROM THE WALL.
THE MOMENTUM IS TOO STRONG, THE GRAVITY--I CAN'T RUN THE NUMBERS FAST ENOUGH!
WE'RE NOT EVEN CLOSE!
WE GOTTA BUILD BIGGER--!

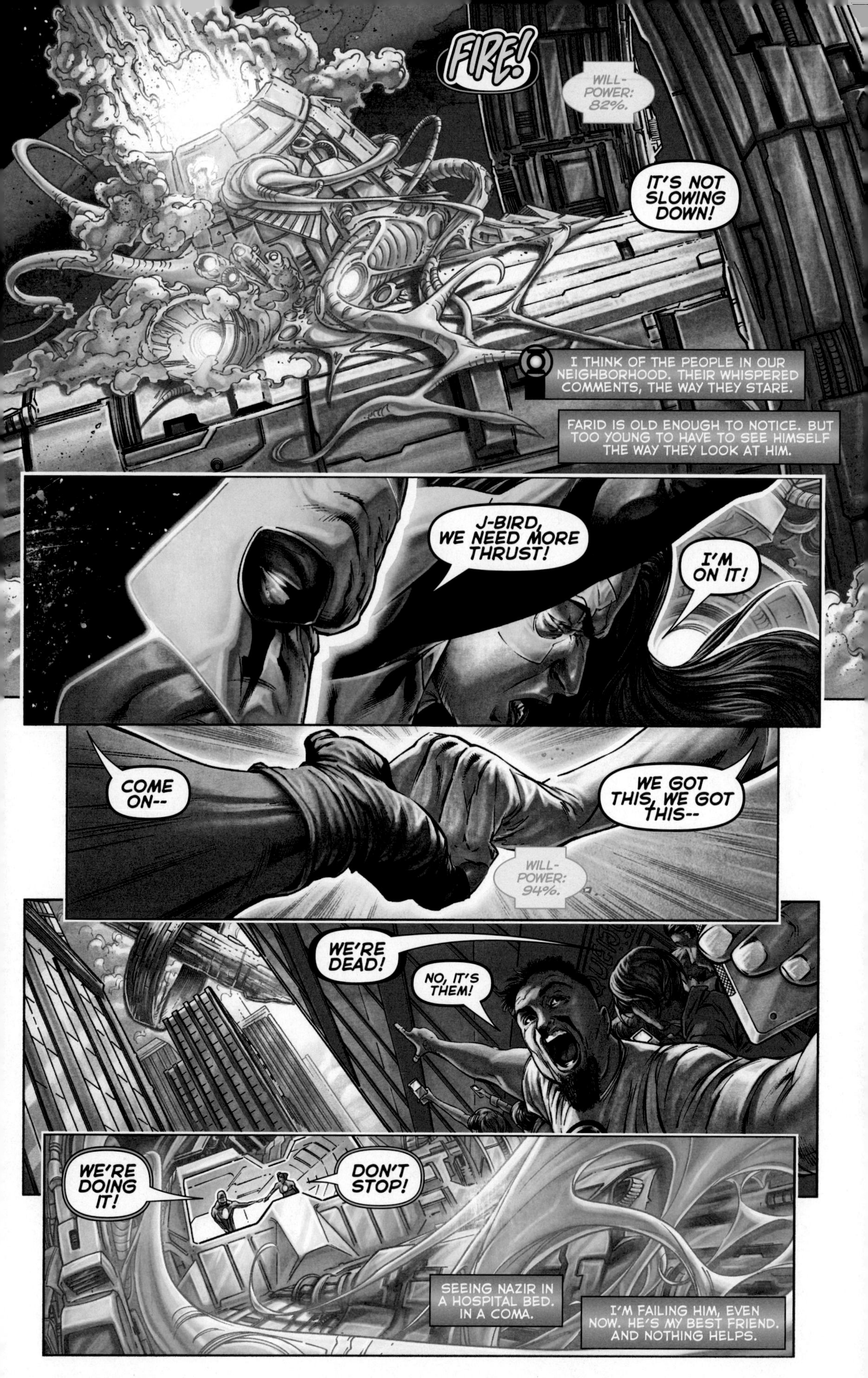
FIRE!
WILL-POWER: 82%.
IT'S NOT SLOWING DOWN!
I THINK OF THE PEOPLE IN OUR NEIGHBORHOOD. THEIR WHISPERED COMMENTS, THE WAY THEY STARE.
FARID IS OLD ENOUGH TO NOTICE. BUT TOO YOUNG TO HAVE TO SEE HIMSELF THE WAY THEY LOOK AT HIM.
J-BIRD, WE NEED MORE THRUST!
I'M ON IT!
COME ON--
WE GOT THIS, WE GOT THIS--
WILL-POWER: 94%.
WE'RE DEAD!
NO, IT'S THEM!
WE'RE DOING IT!
DON'T STOP!
SEEING NAZIR IN A HOSPITAL BED. IN A COMA.
I'M FAILING HIM, EVEN NOW. HE'S MY BEST FRIEND. AND NOTHING HELPS.

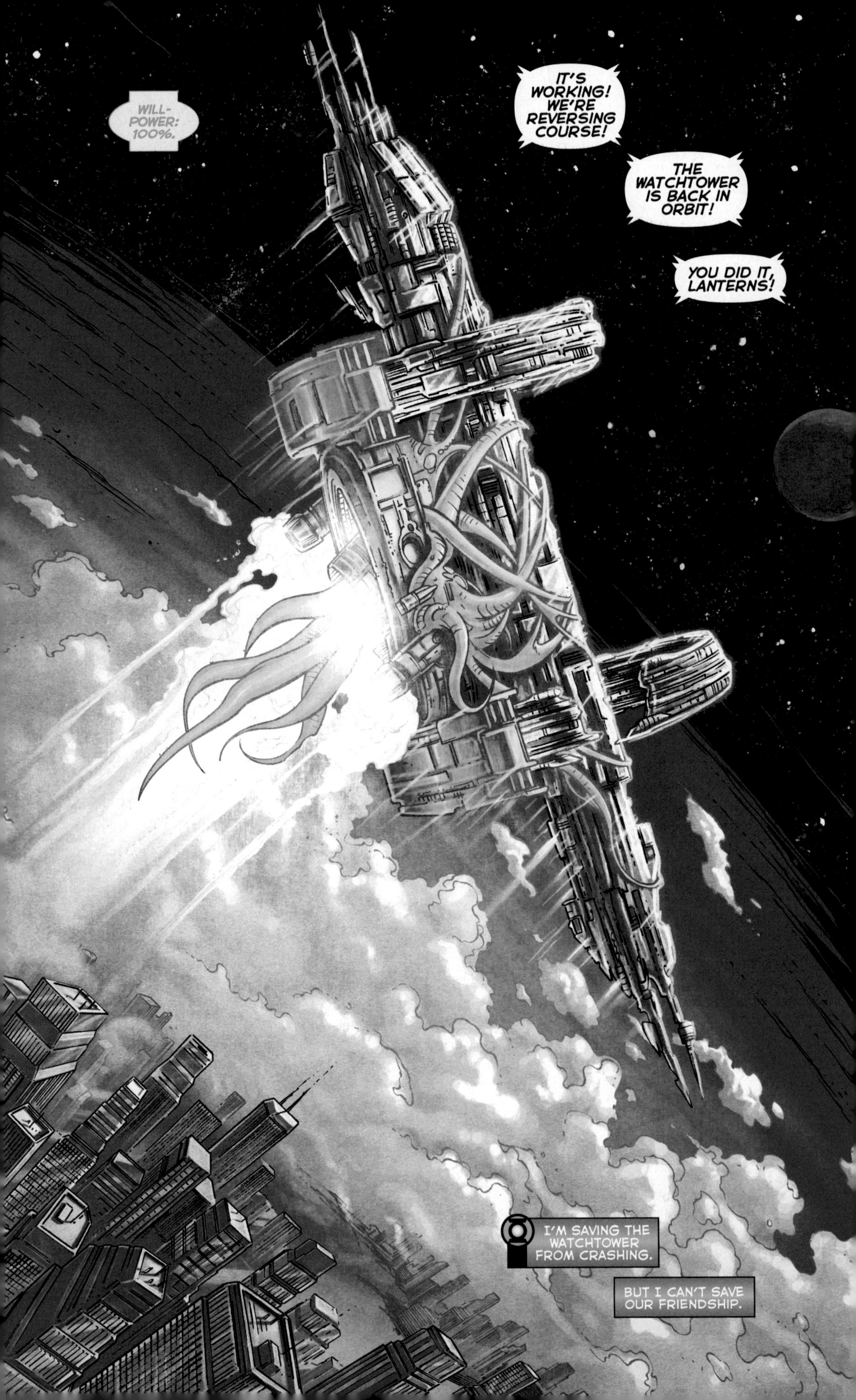
WILL-POWER: 100%.
IT'S WORKING! WE'RE REVERSING COURSE!
THE WATCHTOWER IS BACK IN ORBIT!
YOU DID IT, LANTERNS!
I'M SAVING THE WATCHTOWER FROM CRASHING.
BUT I CAN'T SAVE OUR FRIENDSHIP.

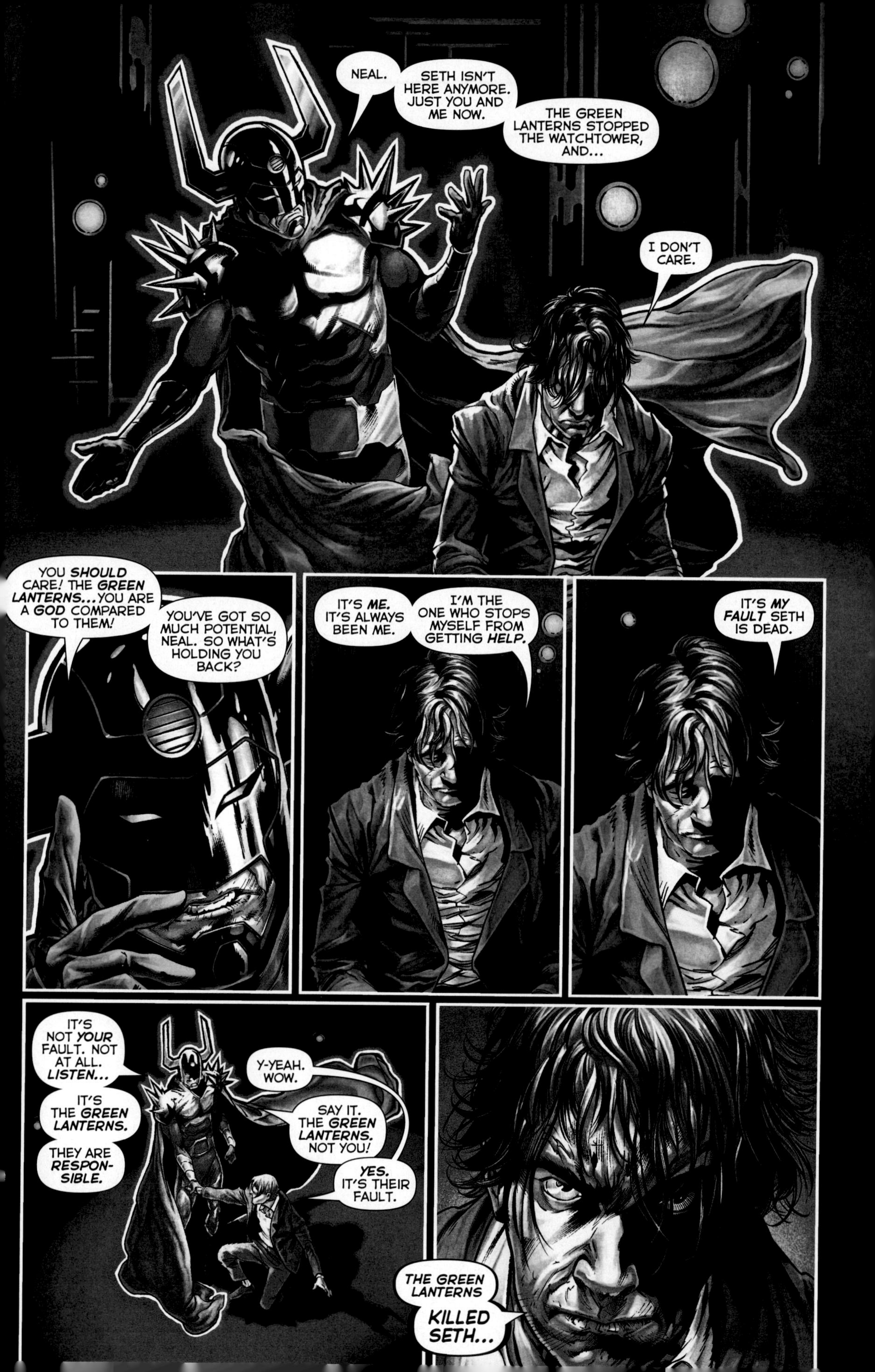
NEAL.
SETH ISN'T HERE ANYMORE. JUST YOU AND ME NOW.
THE GREEN LANTERNS STOPPED THE WATCHTOWER, AND...
I DON'T CARE.
YOU **SHOULD** CARE! THE ***GREEN LANTERNS...*** YOU ARE A **GOD** COMPARED TO THEM!
YOU'VE GOT SO MUCH POTENTIAL, NEAL. SO WHAT'S HOLDING YOU BACK?
IT'S ***ME.*** IT'S ALWAYS BEEN ME.
I'M THE ONE WHO STOPS MYSELF FROM GETTING ***HELP.***
IT'S ***MY FAULT*** SETH IS DEAD.
IT'S NOT ***YOUR*** FAULT. NOT AT ALL. ***LISTEN...***
IT'S THE ***GREEN LANTERNS.***
THEY ARE ***RESPONSIBLE.***
Y-YEAH. WOW.
SAY IT. THE ***GREEN LANTERNS.*** NOT YOU!
YES. IT'S THEIR FAULT.
THE GREEN LANTERNS
KILLED SETH...

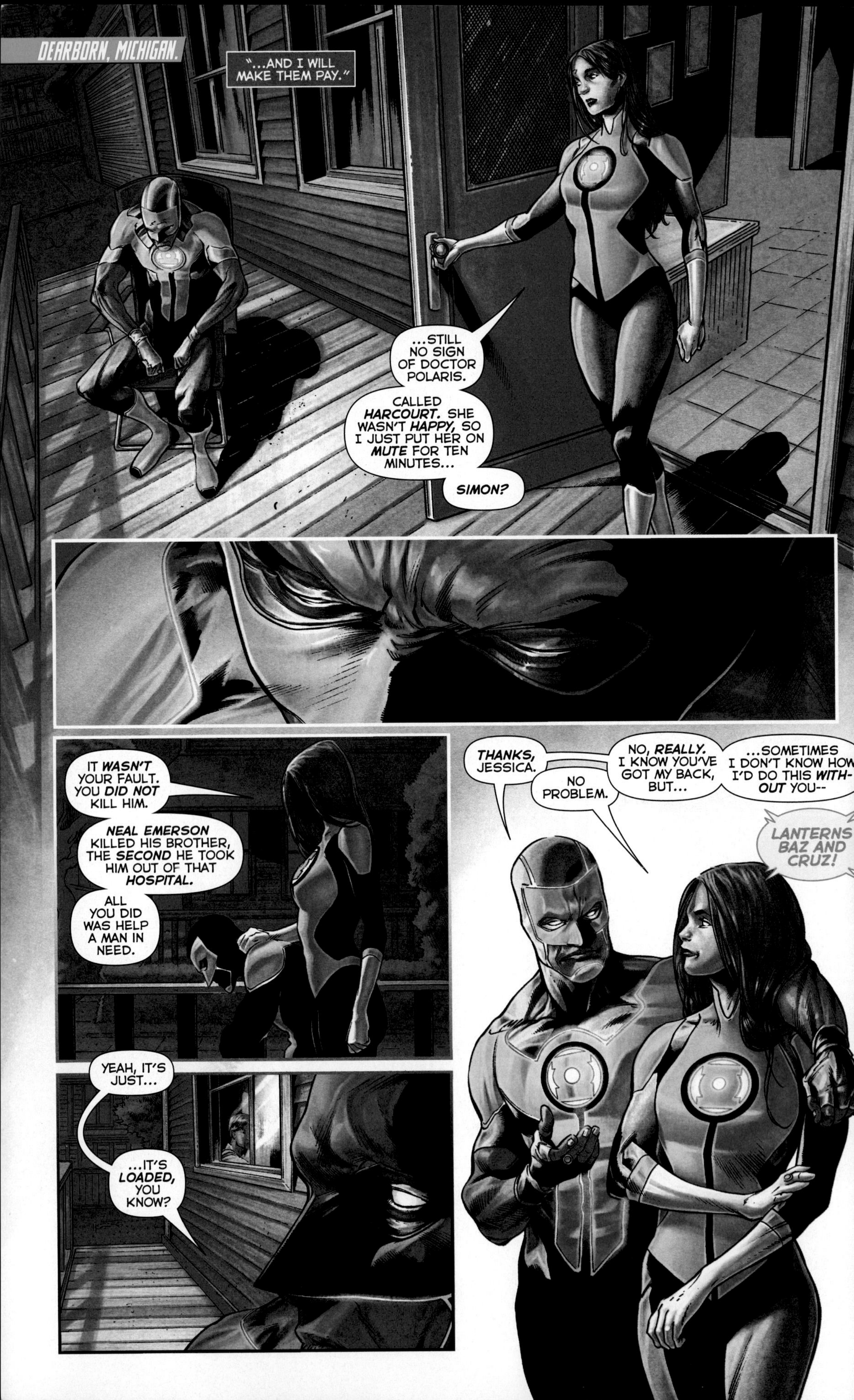
DEARBORN, MICHIGAN.
"...AND I WILL MAKE THEM PAY."
...STILL NO SIGN OF DOCTOR POLARIS.
CALLED HARCOURT. SHE WASN'T HAPPY, SO I JUST PUT HER ON MUTE FOR TEN MINUTES...
SIMON?
IT WASN'T YOUR FAULT. YOU DID NOT KILL HIM.
NEAL EMERSON KILLED HIS BROTHER, THE SECOND HE TOOK HIM OUT OF THAT HOSPITAL.
ALL YOU DID WAS HELP A MAN IN NEED.
YEAH, IT'S JUST...
...IT'S LOADED, YOU KNOW?
THANKS, JESSICA.
NO PROBLEM.
NO, REALLY. I KNOW YOU'VE GOT MY BACK, BUT...
...SOMETIMES I DON'T KNOW HOW I'D DO THIS WITH-OUT YOU--
LANTERNS BAZ AND CRUZ!

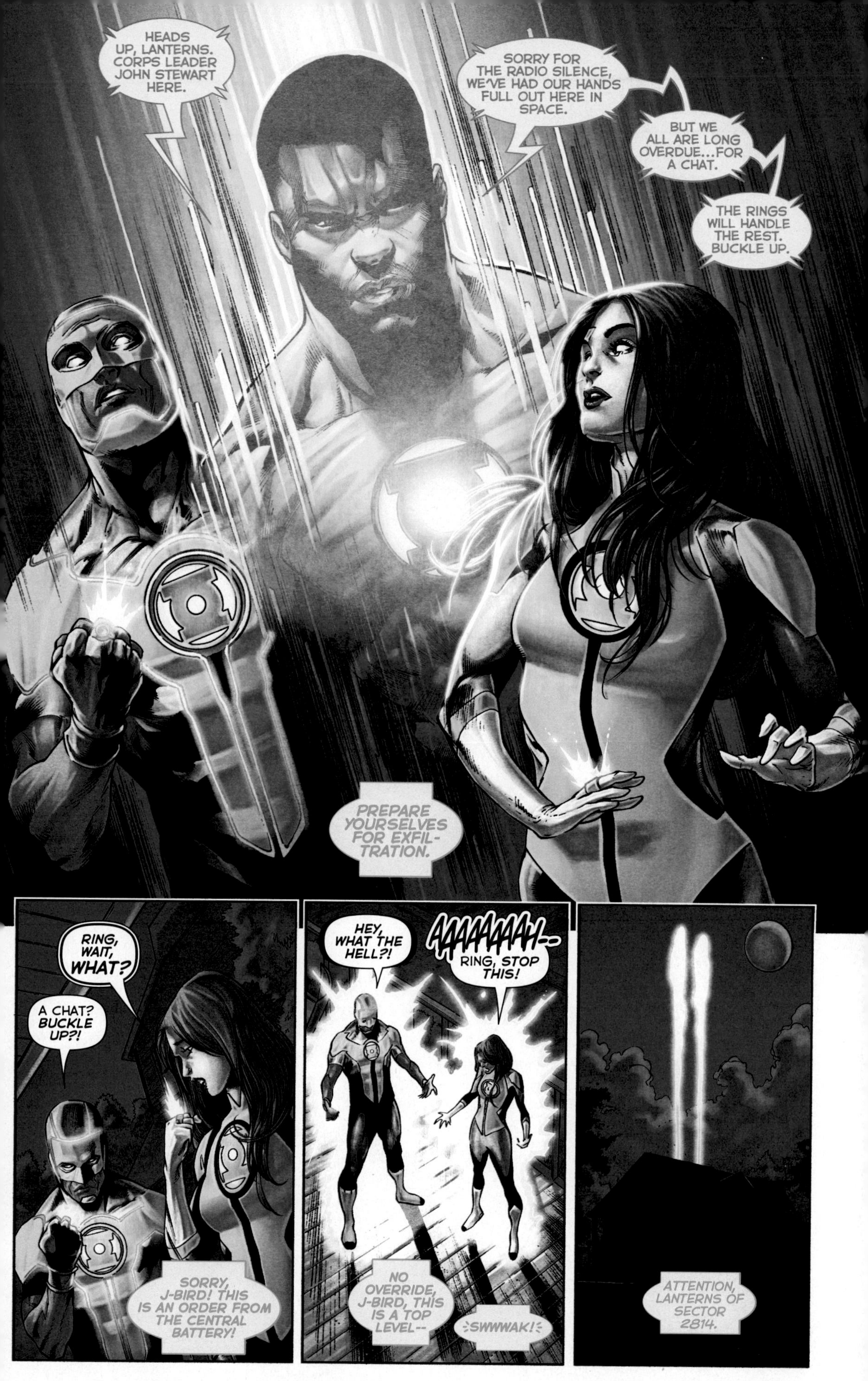
HEADS UP, LANTERNS. CORPS LEADER JOHN STEWART HERE.
SORRY FOR THE RADIO SILENCE, WE'VE HAD OUR HANDS FULL OUT HERE IN SPACE.
BUT WE ALL ARE LONG OVERDUE...FOR A CHAT.
THE RINGS WILL HANDLE THE REST. BUCKLE UP.
PREPARE YOURSELVES FOR EXFIL-TRATION.
RING, WAIT, WHAT?
A CHAT? BUCKLE UP?!
SORRY, J-BIRD! THIS IS AN ORDER FROM THE CENTRAL BATTERY!
HEY, WHAT THE HELL?!
AAAAAAAAH--
RING, STOP THIS!
NO OVERRIDE, J-BIRD, THIS IS A TOP LEVEL--
SWWWAK!
ATTENTION, LANTERNS OF SECTOR 2814.

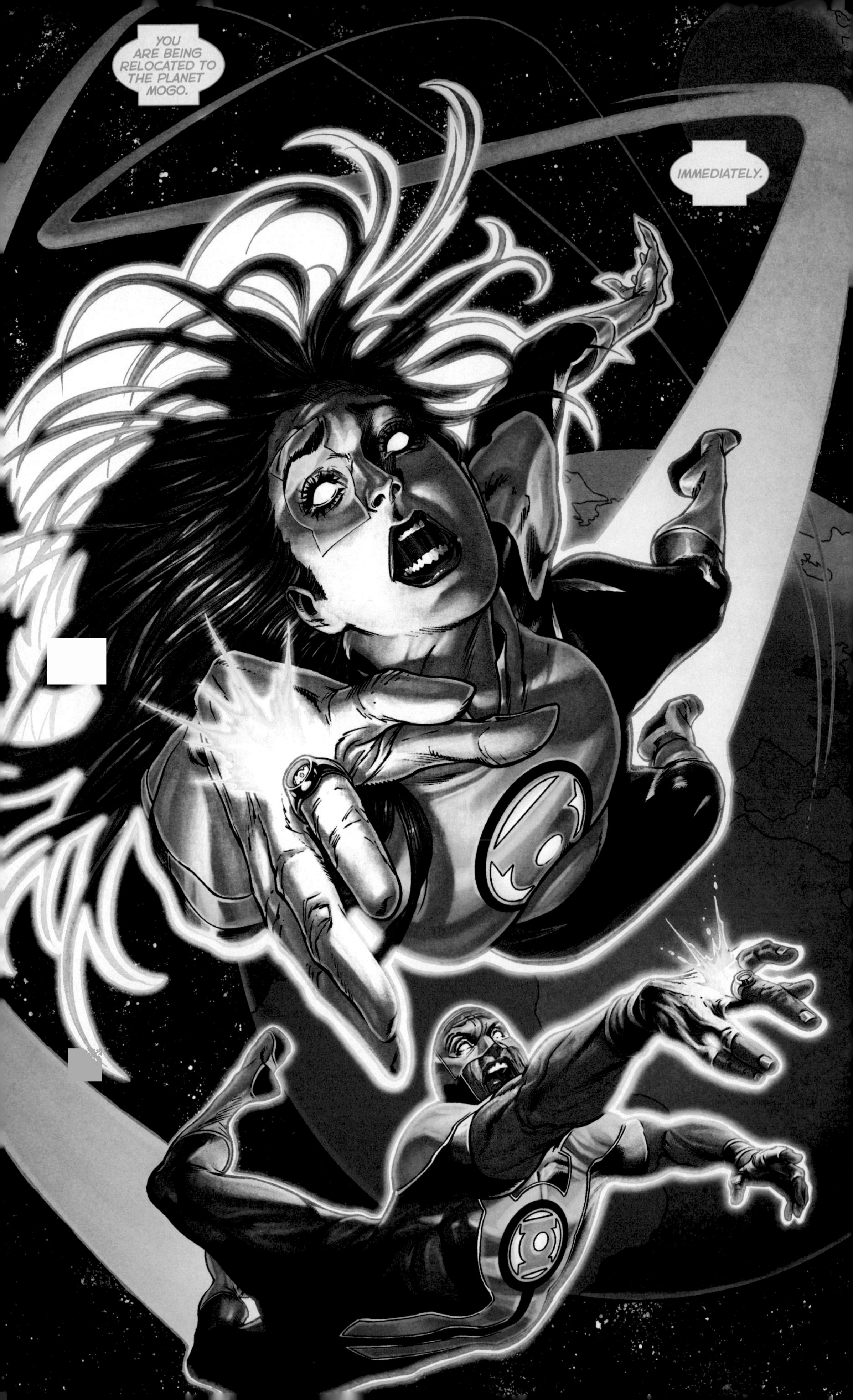
YOU ARE BEING RELOCATED TO THE PLANET MOGO.
IMMEDIATELY.

GREEN LANTERNS

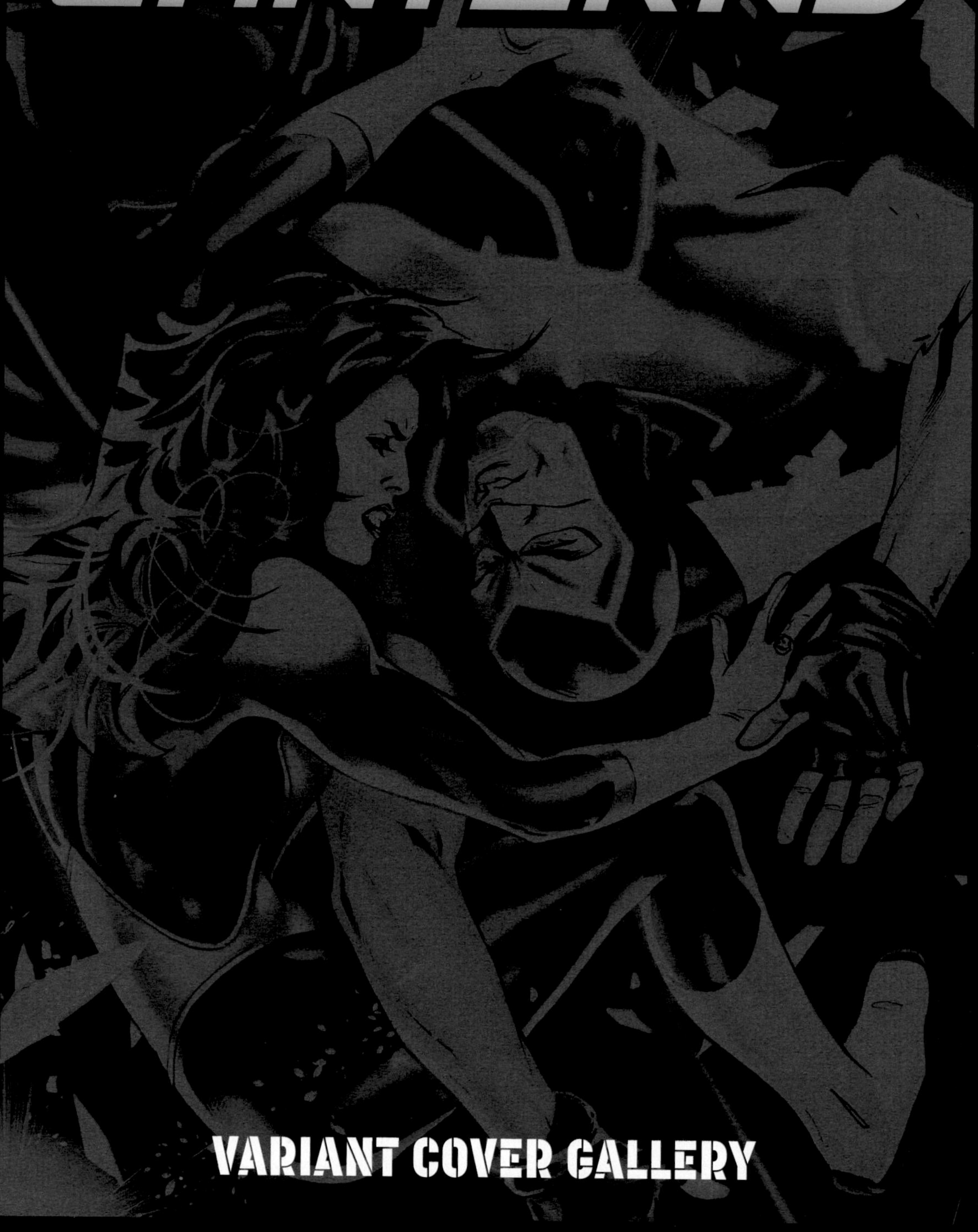

VARIANT COVER GALLERY

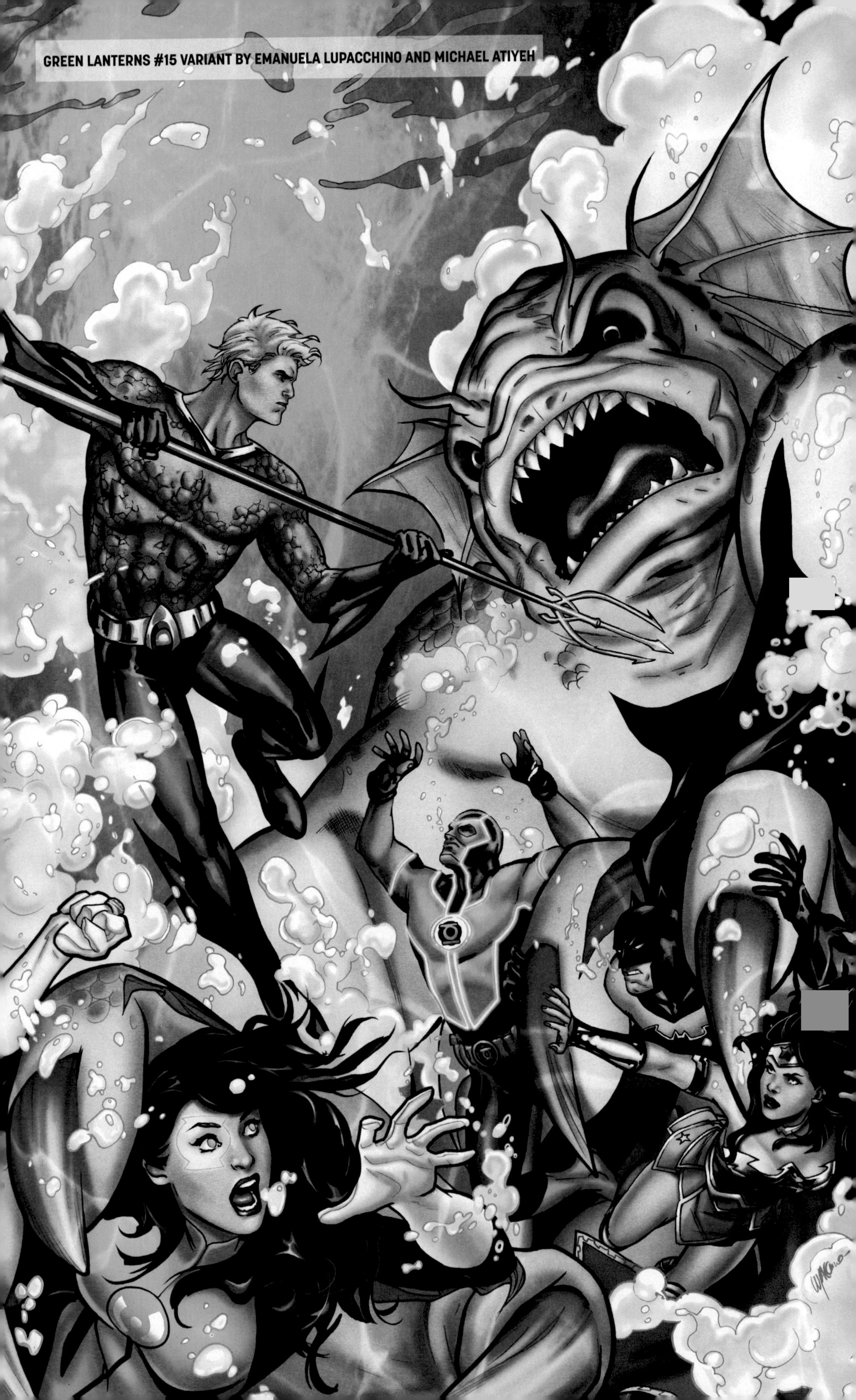

GREEN LANTERNS #15 VARIANT BY EMANUELA LUPACCHINO AND MICHAEL ATIYEH

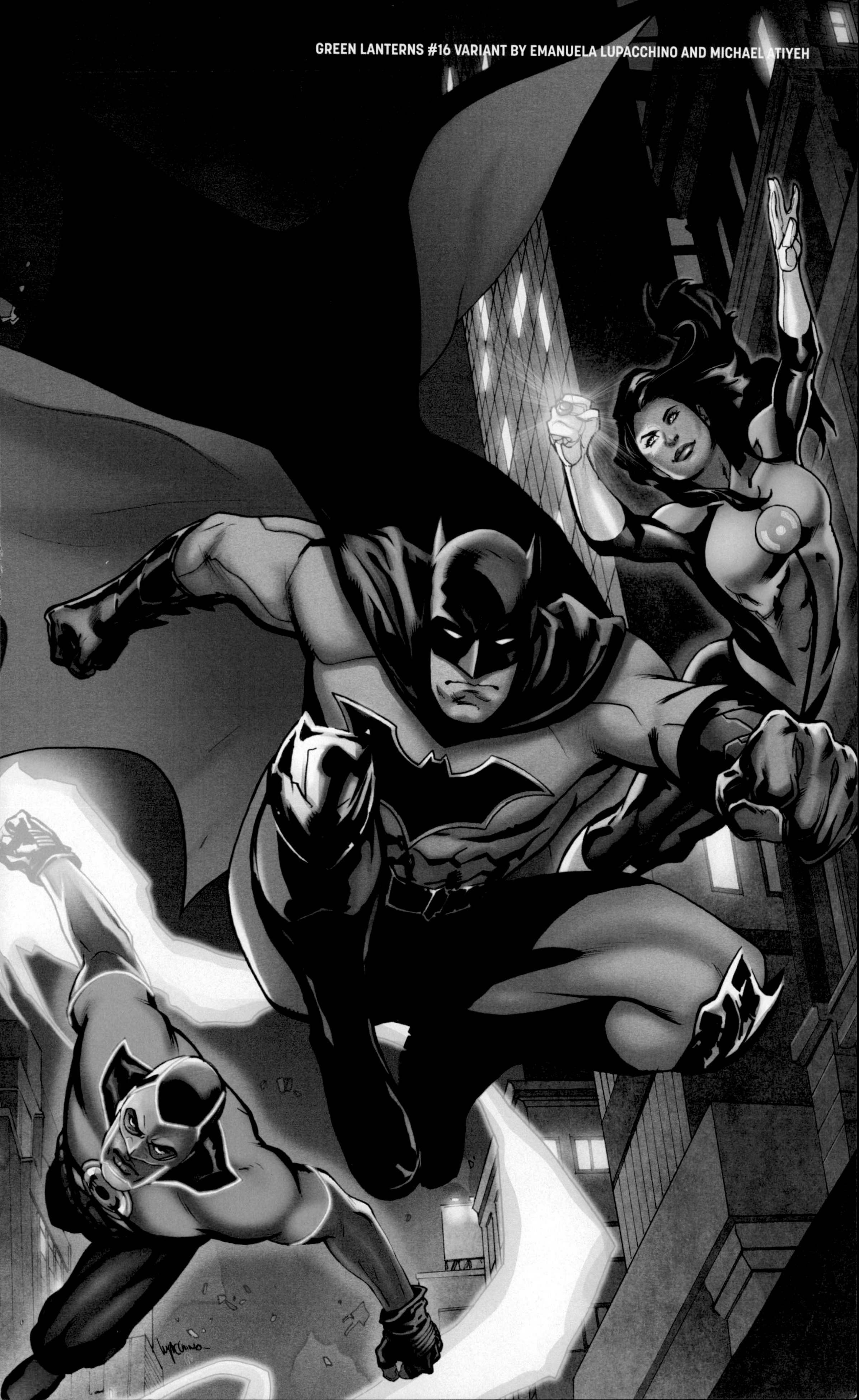

GREEN LANTERNS #16 VARIANT BY EMANUELA LUPACCHINO AND MICHAEL ATIYEH

GREEN LANTERNS #17 VARIANT BY EMANUELA LUPACCHINO AND MICHAEL ATIYEH

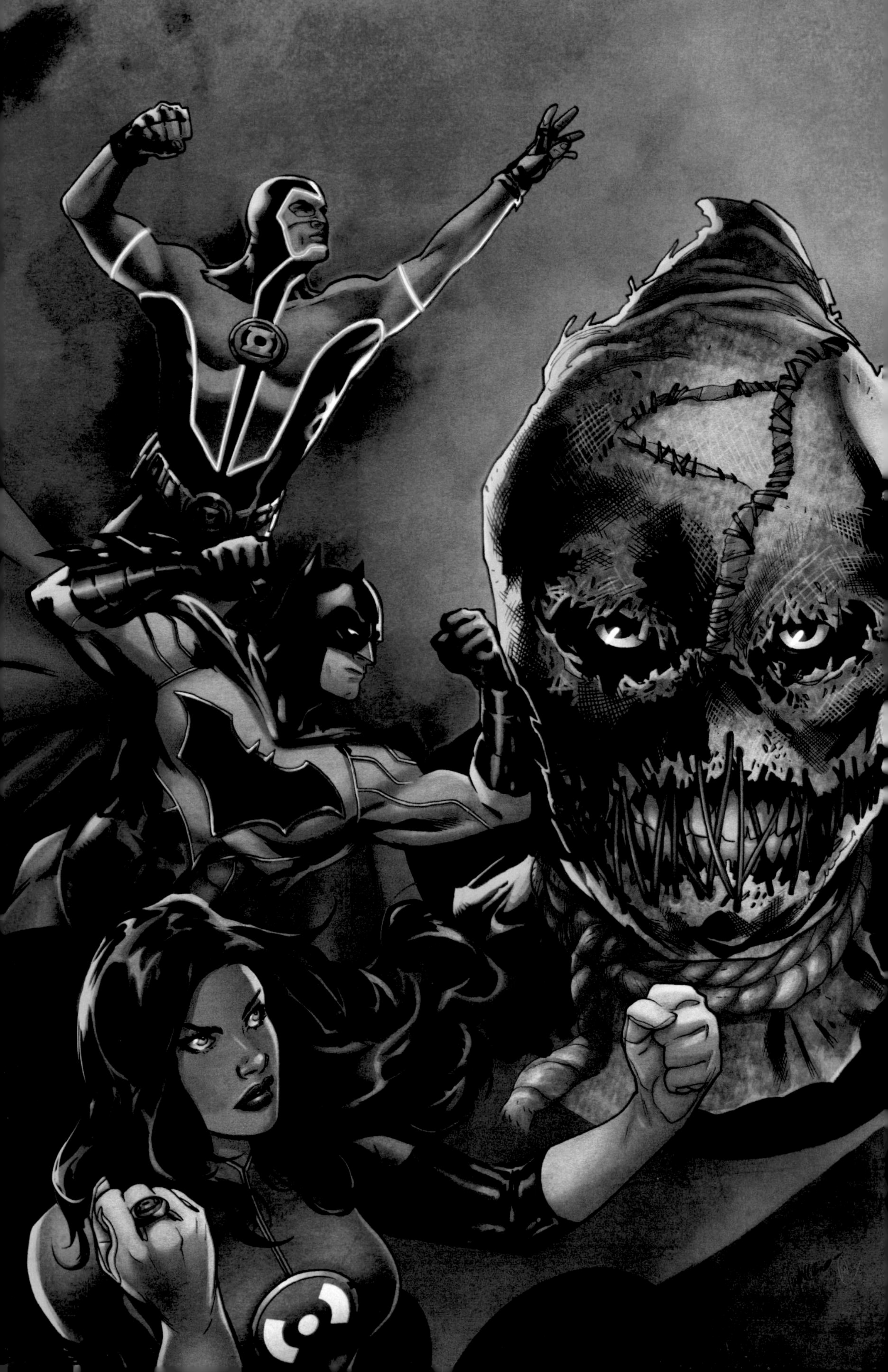

GREEN LANTERNS #18 VARIANT BY EMANUELA LUPACCHINO AND MICHAEL ATIYEH

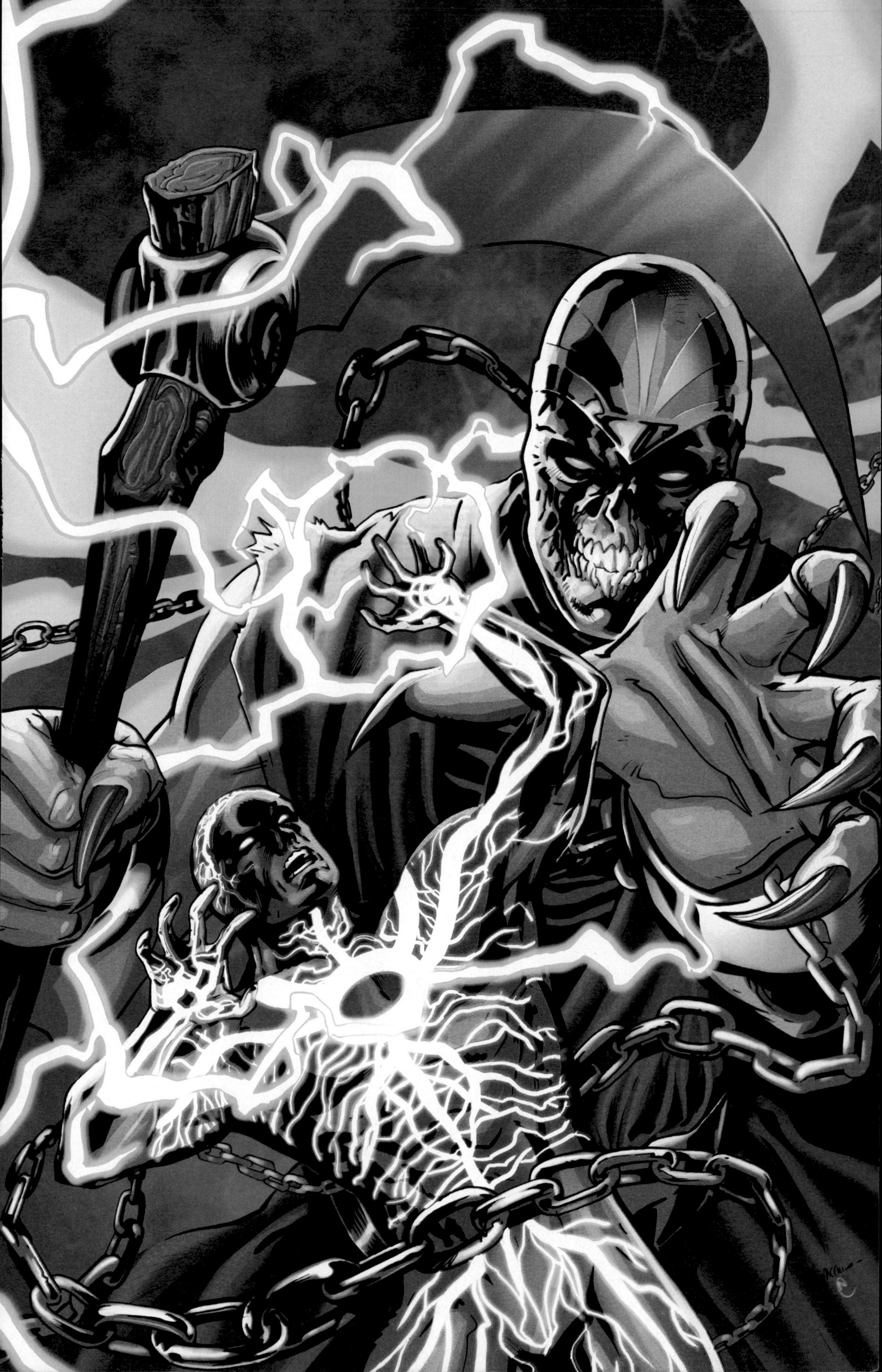

GREEN LANTERNS #19 VARIANT BY EMANUELA LUPACCHINO AND MICHAEL ATIYEH

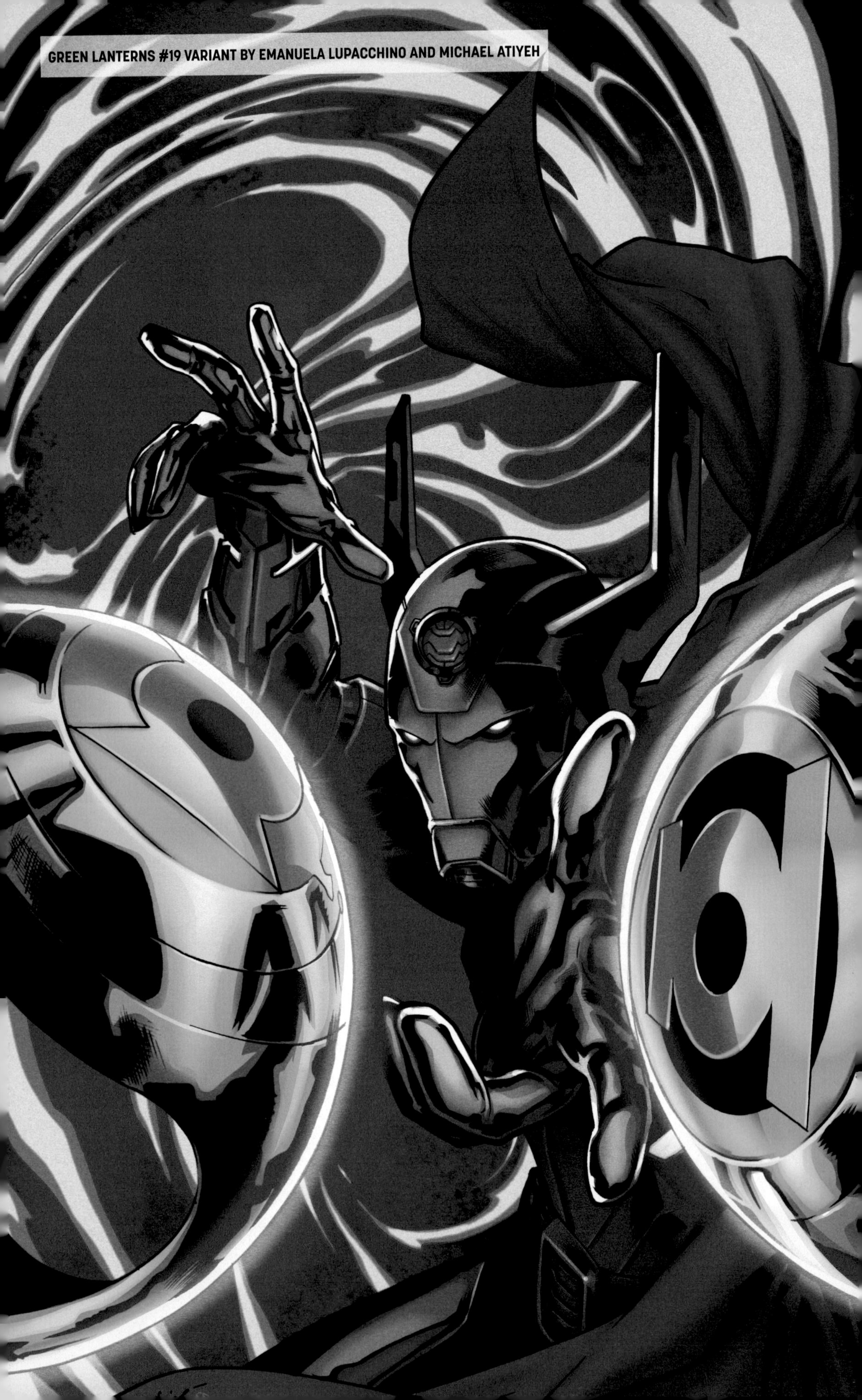

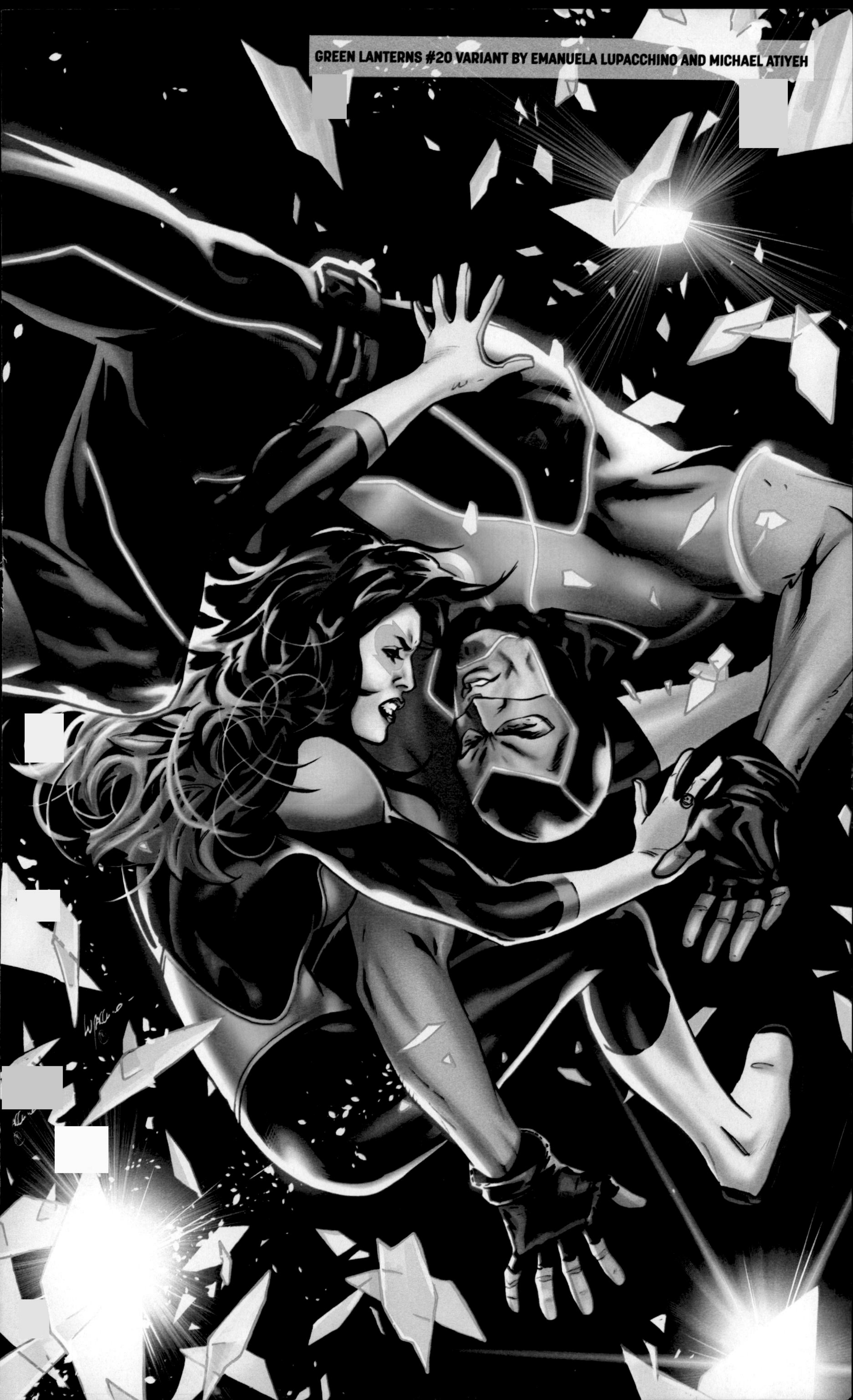

GREEN LANTERNS #20 VARIANT BY EMANUELA LUPACCHINO AND MICHAEL ATIYEH

GREEN LANTERNS #21 VARIANT BY EMANUELA LUPACCHINO AND MICHAEL ATIYEH

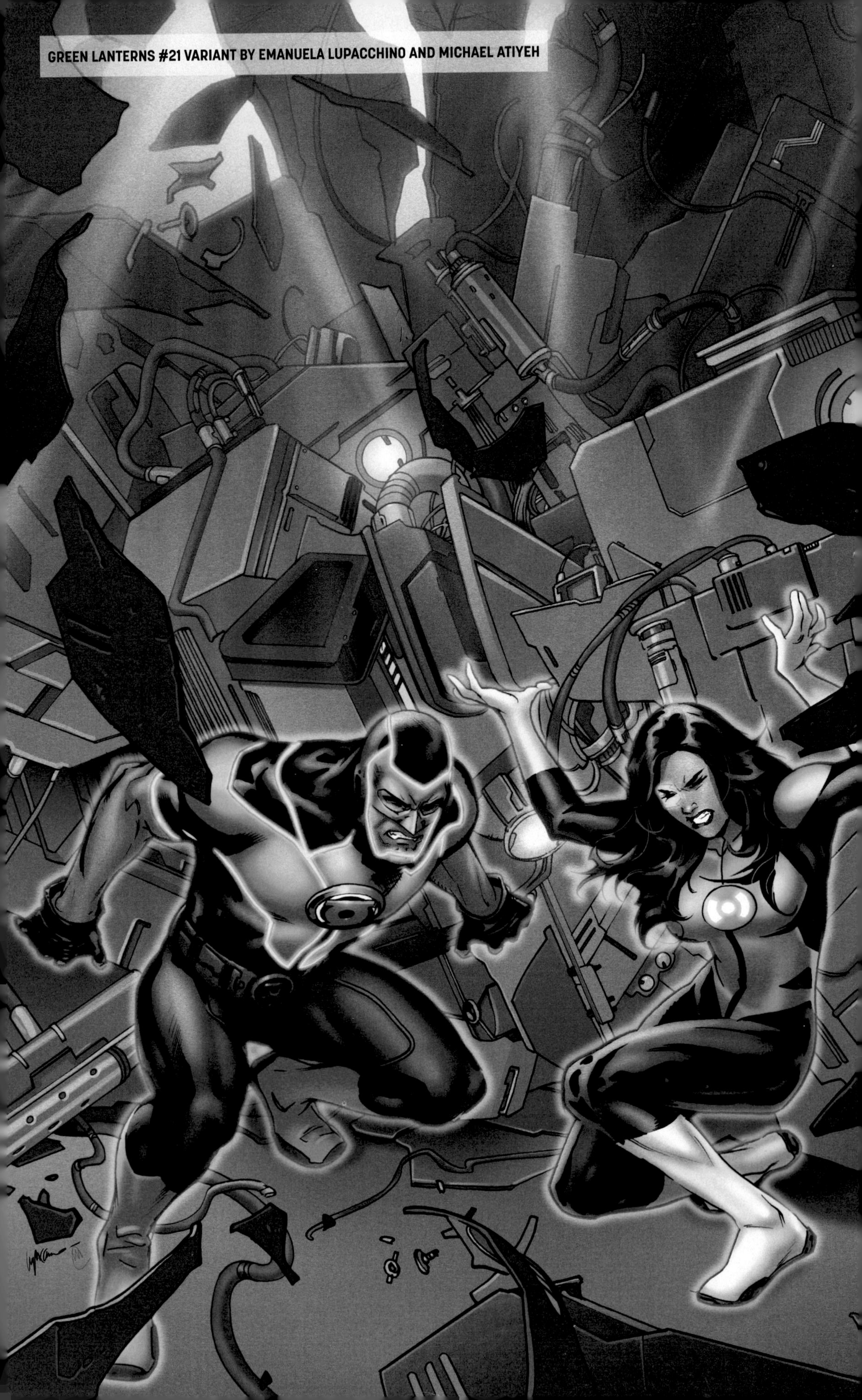

"This is comic book storytelling at its absolute finest."
–IGN

"If you've read a superhero comic book published by DC Comics within the last few years, and were completely blown away by it, there's a good chance that it was something written by Geoff Johns." **–WASHINGTON EXAMINER**

FROM THE WRITER OF
JUSTICE LEAGUE AND *THE FLASH*

GEOFF JOHNS

GREEN LANTERN: REBIRTH

GEOFF JOHNS
ETHAN VAN SCIVER
GREEN LANTERN
REBIRTH
Introduction by
BRAD MELTZER

GREEN LANTERN: BRIGHTEST DAY

BRIGHTEST DAY
GREEN LANTERN
GEOFF JOHNS DOUG MAHNKE

GREEN LANTERN: REBIRTH

GREEN LANTERN: NO FEAR

GREEN LANTERN: REVENGE OF THE GREEN LANTERNS

GREEN LANTERN: WANTED: HAL JORDAN

GREEN LANTERN: SINESTRO CORPS WAR

GREEN LANTERN: SECRET ORIGIN

GREEN LANTERN: RAGE OF THE RED LANTERNS

GREEN LANTERN: AGENT ORANGE

GREEN LANTERN: BLACKEST NIGHT

GREEN LANTERN: BRIGHTEST DAY

GREEN LANTERN: WAR OF THE GREEN LANTERNS

GREEN LANTERN VOL. 1: SINESTRO

GREEN LANTERN VOL. 2: THE REVENGE OF BLACK HAND

GREEN LANTERN VOL. 3: THE END

Get more DC graphic novels wherever comics and books are sold!

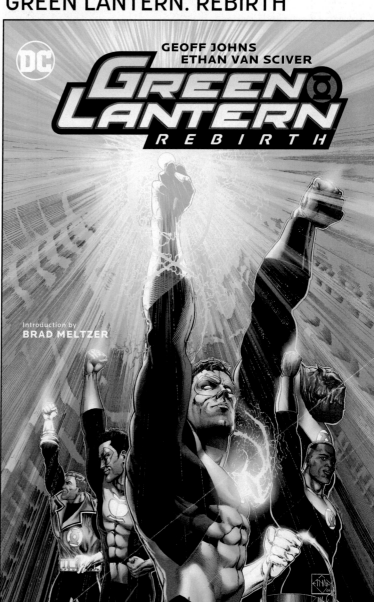

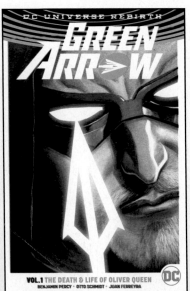